# APPLIED STATISTICS

# FOR PUBLIC

# ADMINISTRATION

# WADSWORTH SERIES IN PUBLIC ADMINISTRATION _____

**The Foundations of Policy Analysis** (1983)
Garry D. Brewer and Peter deLeon

**Public Administration: An Action Orientation** (1991)
Robert B. Denhardt

**Public Administration in Action: Readings, Profiles, and Cases** (1992)
Robert B. Denhardt and Barry R. Hammond

**Theories of Public Organization** (1984)
Robert B. Denhardt

**The Nonprofit Organization: Essential Readings** (1990)
David L. Gies, J. Steven Ott, and Jay M. Shafritz

**Organization Theory: A Public Perspective** (1987)
Harold F. Gortner, Julianne Mahler, and Jeanne Bell Nicholson

**Governmental Accounting and Control** (1984)
Leo Herbert, Larry N. Killough, Alan Walter Steiss

**Governing Public Organizations** (1990)
Karen M. Hult and Charles Walcott

**Government Budgeting: Theory, Process, and Politics**, Second Edition (1992)
Albert C. Hyde

**Democratic Politics and Policy Analysis** (1990)
Hank C. Jenkins-Smith

**Politics and the Bureaucracy: Policymaking in the Fourth Branch of Government**, Third Edition (1992)
Kenneth J. Meier

**Applied Statistics for Public Administration**, Third Edition (1992)
Kenneth J. Meier and Jeffrey L. Brudney

**Fiscal Administration: Analysis and Applications for the Public Sector**, Third Edition (1991)
John L. Mikesell

**Managing Urban America**, Third Edition (1989)
David R. Morgan

**Classic Readings in Organizational Behavior** (1989)
J. Steven Ott

**The Organizational Culture Perspective** (1989)
J. Steven Ott

**The Job of the Public Manager** (1989)
John Rehfuss

**Microcomputers and Government Management: Design and Use of Applications** (1991)
John F. Sacco and John W. Ostrowski

**Classics of Organization Theory**, Third Edition (1992)
Jay M. Shafritz and J. Steven Ott

**Classics of Public Administration**, Third Edition (1992)
Jay M. Shafritz and Albert C. Hyde

**Managing the Public Sector** (1986)
Grover Starling

**Strategies for Policy Making** (1988)
Grover Starling

**Financial Management in Public Organizations** (1989)
Alan Walter Steiss

**Critical Issues in Public Personnel Policy** (1989)
Ronald D. Sylvia

**Classics of Public Personnel Policy**, Second Edition, Revised and Expanded (1991)
Frank J. Thompson

**A Casebook of Public Ethics and Issues** (1990)
William M. Timmins

**Introduction to Budgeting** (1978)
John Wanat

**Quantitative Methods for Public Administration**, Second Edition (1988)
Susan Welch and John Comer

THIRD EDITION

# APPLIED STATISTICS

# FOR PUBLIC

# ADMINISTRATION

**Kenneth J. Meier**
University of Wisconsin, Milwaukee

**Jeffrey L. Brudney**
University of Georgia

**Wadsworth Publishing Company**
Belmont, California
A division of Wadsworth, Inc.

Public Administration Editor: *Kristine Clerkin*
Editorial Associate: *Cathleen S. Collins*
Production Coordinator: *Joan Marsh*
Production: *Cecile Joyner, The Cooper Company*
Designer: *John Edeen*
Copy Editor: *Barbara Kimmel*
Technical Illustrator: *Carl Brown*
Print Buyer: *Vena Dyer*
Cover Design: *Terri Wright*
Compositor: *Asco Trade Typesetting Ltd., Hong Kong*
Printer: *Malloy Lithographing, Inc.*

 *This book is printed on acid-free recycled paper*

1  2  3  4  5  6  7  8  9  10—97  96  95  94  93

**Library of Congress Cataloging-in-Publication Data**

Meier, Kenneth J., [date]
   Applied statistics for public administration / Kenneth J. Meier,
Jeffrey L. Brudney.—3rd ed.
     p.  cm.
   Includes bibliographical references and index.
   ISBN 0-534-19590-3
   1. Statistics.   2. Public administration—Statistical methods.
I. Brudney, Jeffrey L.   II. Title.
HA29.M46   1992
350′.0001′5195—dc20                92-17744

*To Diane and Nancy*

# ABOUT THE AUTHORS

**Kenneth J. Meier** is a professor of political science at the University of Wisconsin-Milwaukee. He has served as the chair of the Oklahoma State Ethics and Merit Commission, the Governor's Commission on Professional Licensing and Discipline (Wisconsin), and the Task Force on Property and Liability Insurance (Wisconsin). He has been the chair of the American Political Science Association's organized sections on Public Administration and on State Politics and Policy. Meier is the author or coauthor of many books and articles including: *Applied Statistics for Public Administration* (Wadsworth, 1993); *The Political Economy of Regulation: The Case of Insurance* (SUNY Press, 1988); *Race, Class and Education: The Politics of Second Generation Discrimination* (University of Wisconsin Press, 1989); and *The Politics of Hispanic Education* (SUNY Press, 1991).

**Jeffrey L. Brudney** is professor of public administration in the Department of Political Science at the University of Georgia. He received his B.A. degree in political science from the University of California at Berkeley and his M.A. and Ph.D. degrees, also in political science, from the University of Michigan at Ann Arbor. Dr. Brudney has published widely in political science and public administration journals. He is the author of *Fostering Volunteer Programs in the Public Sector: Planning, Initiating, and Managing Voluntary Activities* (San Francisco, CA: Jossey-Bass, 1990), recipient of the John Grenzebach Award for Outstanding Research in Philanthropy for Education for 1991. This award is given annually by the American Association of Fund-Raising Counsel (AAFRC) Trust for Philanthropy and the Council for Advancement and Support of Education (CASE). Dr. Brudney has served as chairperson of the American Society for Public Administration (ASPA) Section on Public Administration Education, as well as chairperson of the American Political Science Association (APSA) Section on Public Administration.

# CONTENTS

# Preface to the Third Edition

The first edition of this book was not the product of years of planning. It was written out of necessity. Assigned to teach a course entitled "Measurement and Analysis for Public Administrators," the authors could find no suitable text. So, we wrote one. Since we began work on the book in 1979 and its subsequent publication in 1981, a few other texts have appeared intended for the "methods" course(s) in Master's of Public Administration (MPA) programs. We believe, however, that ours still possesses unique advantages.

Because MPA students come from disparate backgrounds, their exposure to statistics and quantitative methods varies widely. For many MPA students, the last time they took a mathematics course was in high school. Given this audience, a rigorous presentation of statistics would have proved too difficult. Instead, we wanted a textbook that would presume little familiarity with the subject but one that would teach quantitative novices a great deal in very little time.

The second criterion for the methods text was that it address substantive problems that illustrate those faced by public administrators. Political science and sociology statistics texts rely predominantly on academic rather than practitioner-oriented examples. Although a number of excellent methods texts for business administration are available, as might be expected, they typically focus on a different set of issues and problems (for example, manufacturing production) than those that usually concern public administrators. We wanted a statistics text whose examples would appeal to this group.

In preparing this third edition, we have again followed these guidelines. In fact, the third edition is more faithful to them than is the original, for in the past eleven years we have had the opportunity to use the text—and receive valuable feedback from students and practitioners—at four major universities as well as at numerous off-campus sites. The new edition benefits from this experience.

## NASPAA STANDARDS FOR MASTER'S DEGREE PROGRAMS IN PUBLIC AFFAIRS AND ADMINISTRATION

The National Association of Schools of Public Affairs and Administration (NASPAA) has formulated standards for accreditation of master's-level programs in public affairs and administration. NASPAA requires that the curriculum common to all programs "provide each student with the ability to deal with techniques of analysis, including quantitative, economic, and statistical methods." More specifically, NASPAA criteria call for students to develop competencies "to define and diagnose decision situations, collect relevant data, perform logical analyses, develop alternatives, implement an effective and ethical course of action, and evaluate results." In addition, students should acquire the ability to organize and communicate information through various formats, such as oral presentations, written memoranda and technical reports, and statistical charts, graphs, and tables. The publication by NASPAA of "Curriculum Recommendations for Public Management Education in Computing" (see *Public Administration Review*, November 1986, Special Issue) has reinforced the emphasis on analytic methods in graduate programs in public affairs and administration.

We believe that this text can form the basis for courses that satisfy the NASPAA standards. The book elaborates statistical methods as a tool for assisting public managers in making decisions. By focusing on the assumptions underlying the various techniques, the careful interpretation of results, and the limitations as well as the strengths of the information conveyed, the text stresses the ethical and effective utilization of this tool.

With respect to the specific competencies designated by NASPAA, Part I of the text, Descriptive Statistics, is especially helpful for the presentation of statistical charts, graphs, and tables. Part II, Probability, assists students in defining and diagnosing decision situations and selecting and evaluating a course of action. Part III addresses Measurement and Research Design. These chapters, too, are strong in problem diagnosis and also treat issues of data collection, causal inference, and the logic of inquiry. The chapters in Part IV, Inferential Statistics, not only develop sophisticated analytic skills but also help in the definition of problems, formulation of alternatives, choice of decision, and evaluation of results.

Part V, Analysis of Nominal and Ordinal Data, introduces another set of quantitative skills useful for the public administrator. This type of analysis is employed very frequently in written memoranda and technical reports and in the evaluation of survey data. Regression analysis is both one of the most flexible and most utilized statistical techniques. The chapters on Regression in Part VI greatly enhance the decision-making, analytic, and evaluative capabilities of public managers. The final section discusses two Special Topics in Quantitative Management: linear programming and decision theory. These chapters expose students to different models of logical analysis, bases for decisions, and evaluation of alternatives.

## CHANGES IN THE THIRD EDITION

This edition maintains the tone, level of presentation, and basic chapter and organizational structure featured in the first two editions of the book. We have updated, corrected, amended, clarified, and elaborated the text as necessary. The third edition also incorporates several major changes.

First, we have added to Part VI, Regression Analysis, the chapter "Interrupted Time Series: Program and Policy Analysis." A table for the Durbin-Watson statistic appears in the Appendix of Statistical Tables. Time series techniques have become more widely used and accepted in public administration, and this book reflects this development.

Second, Part III, Measurement and Research Design, has been expanded to provide greater coverage of the issues involved. We have also added substantially to the discussion of measures of association in Chapter 14 and to the explanation of control table analysis in Chapter 15.

Third, the chapter "Additional Problems" that appeared in the previous edition of the book has been eliminated. Instead, these problems have been moved to the chapters where the relevant material is treated. In addition, we have greatly increased the number of problems and exercises that accompany each chapter.

Finally, the *Instructor's Manual* has been significantly upgraded. The *Manual* discusses chapter objectives, major points, and difficult points. It also includes solutions for all computational problems in the book and an enhanced test bank with problems for examinations, again with solutions. In addition, the *Instructor's Manual* includes a diskette with actual data sets from public administration. The last section of the *Manual* explains how to access and analyze these data on a personal computer, and presents sample problems for student use. We are grateful to students, colleagues, and reviewers for suggesting many of these changes.

## ACKNOWLEDGMENTS

A task of this magnitude could not have been accomplished without the assistance of others. We are grateful to colleagues who have kindly given us feedback that informs this third edition. A great many students at the University of Oklahoma, the University of Wisconsin, and the University of Georgia have provided us with a diverse teaching laboratory. They, too, have offered comments and suggestions that proved helpful. We appreciate their tolerance not only for errors that appeared in earlier printings of the text but also for a sense of humor that occasionally goes awry. (Otherwise reasonable people may disagree over the frequency of the latter occurrence.)

We owe a special debt of gratitude to Cindy Stormer, former Political Science/Public Administration Editor at Brooks/Cole for her commitment to the text. We also thank Joan Marsh, Cecile Joyner, Barbara Kimmel, and John Edeen for their contributions to the publication of this text.

Finally, thanks are due to the reviewers of the text for their valuable suggestions and comments: Jody Fitzpatrick, University of Colorado, Colorado Springs; Barry D. Friedman, Valdosta State College; John Piskulich, Oakland University; and Robert Wrinkle, University of Texas, Pan American. For helping us to improve this edition, we are also grateful to William C. Adams, George Washington University; Steve Percy, University of Wisconsin—Milwaukee; and Tom Holbrook, University of Wisconsin—Milwaukee.

We thank Sally Coleman Selden and Chilik Yu for their assistance in preparing the manuscript. We also thank Mary Maureen Brown and Teresa M. Kluesner for their assistance with the *Instructor's Manual*.

Although we appreciate the assistance rendered by all of these people, they share none of the blame for any errors of commission or omission. That responsibility rests solely with us.

*Kenneth J. Meier*
*Jeffrey L. Brudney*

# INTRODUCTION

Quantitative analysis has become a major element of public management. Agencies that only ten years ago made decisions based on seat-of-the-pants guesses now consult computer printouts, contingency tables, regression analyses, and decision trees to help make decisions. Personnel managers receive personnel projections to schedule recruitment efforts. Transportation planners rely on complex computer simulations to design urban transportation systems. Program evaluators are charged with making quantitative assessments of a program's effectiveness. Quantitative analyses have become so prevalent that no midlevel manager can avoid them.

The increasing sophistication of quantitative techniques affords public managers few options. At one extreme, a manager untutored in these methods can act as if they did not exist and refuse to read reports containing statistics. Unfortunately, this option is exercised all too often and at considerable cost: the manager loses valuable information presented in quantitative form. At the other extreme, the public manager may choose to accept uncritically the findings of the data analyst rather than reveal to others an ignorance of statistics. This option leads to an error as serious as the first. Although quantitative analysts will almost certainly possess a stronger background in statistics than does the manager (that's their job), the analysts lack the experience, management skills—and the responsibility—to make decisions in the public sector. This book is intended for students who consider *this* their current or future job.

The third option open to the manager—and the one favored by the authors—is to receive training in quantitative techniques. The training advocated and offered in this book, however, is *not* a standard course in statistics, which in recent years has become a required (and dreaded) element of most Master of Public Administration programs. Instead, we seek to develop appreciation for and intuitive understanding of basic elements of statistics and analysis for managers in the public sector.

Reading this book and working the problems at the end of the chapters will not transform public managers from quantitative novices into master statisticians. That is neither desired nor necessary. By and large, public managers do not set up research designs and select and calculate appropriate statistical measures. Far more often they receive information of this kind and are expected to make reasoned and responsible decisions based upon it. For this task, a course in mathematical statistics is not required. However, it is essential that managers become intelligent and critical consumers of quantitative information. Toward this end, this book stresses the application, interpretation, and evaluation of basic statistics.

This book is intended primarily for students who have no or only a very limited background in mathematics, statistics, or other quantitative methods. Material is presented in an applied, nonrigorous, easily readable format centered around practical problems of public management. The text is designed to involve readers in the discussion of these problems and to encourage students to seek and understand numerical answers to them. Statistical theory is discussed only rarely, and computational formulae that pepper most statistics books are reserved for those instances in which they enlighten rather than mystify.

We have elaborated some of the advantages of our approach, and we hope that they will become evident to you as you read the book. However, we would be remiss were we to overlook its shortcomings. The most obvious is that this is not a comprehensive text in formal statistics. As noted before, the book is not rigorous, and we have ignored and probably violated many elements of standard statistical theory. Whereas this approach may arouse the disapproval of some professional colleagues, we believe that it has its place—as an introduction to statistics for managers in the public sector. Too often, students are alienated by more formal courses that emphasize precision over application, and a first course in statistics becomes an eminently disliked and forgettable last one. We have endeavored to develop a text that will engage and hold the interest of public managers and at the same time present fundamental applied statistics—and, perhaps, whet the appetite for further training in this area. For those who seek a more mathematical and theoretical approach to managerial statistics, several good books are available (see the Annotated Bibliography at the end of this text).

Whenever possible, we have provided step-by-step instructions for performing statistical procedures and evaluating the results. We strongly recommend that you do these calculations and follow along. Statistics is unlike making love; if you don't practice using statistics, you forget how.

If you do not own a hand calculator, we suggest that you purchase an inexpensive one. A calculator not only will take much of the pain out of learning statistics but also will allow you to concentrate on understanding statistics instead of computing them. We strongly recommend a calculator with keys for square root, factorial, and exponentiation.

## A ROAD MAP FOR THE BOOK

This book is designed so that each of its parts is self-contained, yet each builds on the other parts. Part I discusses descriptive statistics. If you want to know how to take a large volume of data and visually summarize it with a table or a graph, see Chapter 1 on frequency distributions. To learn about the various ways to find the average for a large group of numbers, consult Chapter 2 on the mean, the median, and the mode. Techniques for these statistics are discussed for both data tables and raw data. If you want to find out how closely a set of data clusters about its average (how dispersed it is), Chapter 3 illustrates the way to calculate the variance and the standard deviation.

Part II on probability is the most difficult section in the text for students to understand. Do not become discouraged. To learn the basic rules of probability, see Chapter 4, which explains the basic law of probability and what is meant by a priori probabilities, posterior probabilities, joint probabilities, and conditional probabilities. If Chapter 4 is easy for you, the remainder of the text will likely present no problems.

Have you ever wanted to know the probability that an agency could hire three minorities for ten positions when 50% of the job applicants were minorities? For problems similar to this one, Chapter 5 introduces the binomial probability distribution. As part of this chapter, we explain the normal curve. Chapter 6 discusses some useful probability distributions for managers. The hypergeometric probability distribution is used when the manager wants to generalize to a finite population; the Poisson and exponential distributions are used whenever the manager needs to include time or distance in a probability statement: for example, 1.2 murders per day, 12 potholes per 100 meters.

Part III concerns methodological rather than statistical issues. Chapter 7 discusses how managers assign numbers to things—in other words, measurement. For answers to questions such as, What do I do about bad data, How do I know if data are bad, or What is the correct measure to use with these data, see Chapter 7. To learn how to set up a study so that the findings are valid, consult Chapter 8 on research design. This chapter discusses causality, operational definitions, hypotheses, and experimental and quasi-experimental designs of research.

Part IV begins the discussion of statistical inference—how one can generalize from a small sample to a much larger population. To see how a statistician can estimate the mean value for a population from a small sample, consult Chapter 9. This chapter also discusses the way to construct confidence limits around any mean estimate. Chapter 10 applies the techniques of Chapter 9 to test hypotheses. The chapter illustrates how a manager can generalize about the impact of a program from a small sample of cases. When you are concerned not about a mean but about the percentage of a group that does something (for example, drives faster than 55 miles per hour), the techniques in Chapter 11 can be used. When you want to compare two groups (for example, experimental and control groups, or before and after groups), Chapter 12 will tell you how to test for differences.

Part V discusses some analytical techniques for nominal and ordinal data (see Chapter 7 for definitions). Beginning with Part V, the remainder of the text deals with relationships between two or more variables. Is education related to income? Do police patrols reduce crime? If you want to know how to use percentages to analyze a table of data with two variables (we call them contingency tables), read Chapter 13. To learn about the more sophisticated statistics for table analysis, such as gamma, chi-square, and lambda, Chapter 14 is the one to consult. To learn how to look at the relationship between two variables while taking into account or controlling for a third, consult Chapter 15.

Part VI presents the same type of techniques as were discussed in Part V, but for interval-level data. Chapter 16 discusses how a line can summarize the relationship between two variables. This technique, called regression analysis, can be used for a variety of management situations. In Chapter 17, the limitations and assumptions of regression are noted. Predicting the value of some data trend in the future is the subject of Chapter 18 on time series. To forecast future population, service usage, sewage output, or various other managerially relevant information, consult this chapter. Chapter 19 on multiple regression is devoted to analyzing the relationships among three or more variables. For example, can the age of housing and the number of renters be used to predict fires? Chapter 20 on interrupted time series analysis explains how to estimate the impact of a policy or program over time. The manager can use this technique to evaluate whether a program, such as a senior citizen's center or a municipal volunteer office, has had a short-term, long-term, or short-term temporary impact (or perhaps no impact) on the health and welfare of city residents.

Part VII includes special techniques that are sometimes useful to public managers. If you want to know how to make decisions given various amounts of information, consult Chapter 21 on decision theory. This chapter discusses ways to analyze a decision. For decisions involving maximizing or minimizing some output under certain constraints, see Chapter 22 on linear programming.

For those motivated to learn more about statistics, we have included an annotated bibliography at the end of the book. The bibliography contains a wide range of texts that can be used for reference.

We have attempted, wherever possible, to include problems that are faced by administrators in the real world. Many of our midcareer students provided these examples. Although all the data and problems are hypothetical, they represent the types of situations that often confront public administrators.

# LIST OF SYMBOLS

| | |
|---|---|
| $\mu$ | population mean |
| $\sigma$ | population standard deviation |
| $\sum$ | summation of all listed numbers |
| $P$ | probability |
| $\cup$ | union of two events |
| $\cap$ | intersection of two events |
| $|$ | conditional probability (e.g., $P(A|B)$ means the probability of $A$ given $B$) |
| $!$ | factorial |
| $C_r^n$ | combination of $n$ things taken $r$ at a time |
| $p^r$ | probability $p$ raised to the $r$th power |
| EV | expected value |
| $\overline{X}$ | sample mean |
| $s$ | sample standard deviation |
| $n$ | size of the sample |
| N | size of the population |
| $\lambda$ | lambda for the Poisson distribution |
| $\alpha$ | population regression intercept |
| $\beta$ | population regression slope |
| $a$ | sample regression intercept |
| $b$ | sample regression slope |
| $\hat{Y}$ | predicted value of $Y$ |
| $e$ | error |
| s.e. | standard error of the mean |
| $S_{y|x}$ | standard error of the estimate |
| $r^2$ | coefficient of determination |
| $R^2$ | multiple coefficient of determination |
| s.e.$_\beta$ | standard error of the slope |

# Applied Statistics

# for Public

# Administration

# PART I

# DESCRIPTIVE

# STATISTICS

## CHAPTER 1

# FREQUENCY

# DISTRIBUTIONS

**Descriptive statistics** is nothing more than a fancy term for numbers that summarize a group of data. These data may be the number of arrests each police officer makes, the amount of garbage collected by city work crews, or the size of various government agencies. In their unsummarized form, data (affectionately known as raw data) are difficult to comprehend. For example, the list below gives the number of tons of trash collected by the Normal, Oklahoma, sanitary engineer teams for the week of June 8, 1992. Each entry is the number of tons of trash collected by a team during the week.

**descriptive statistics**

| 57 | 70 | 62 | 66 | 68 | 62 | 76 | 71 | 79 | 87 |
| 82 | 63 | 71 | 51 | 65 | 78 | 61 | 78 | 55 | 64 |
| 83 | 75 | 50 | 70 | 61 | 69 | 80 | 51 | 62 | 94 |
| 89 | 63 | 82 | 75 | 58 | 68 | 84 | 83 | 71 | 79 |
| 77 | 89 | 59 | 88 | 97 | 86 | 75 | 95 | 64 | 65 |
| 53 | 74 | 75 | 61 | 86 | 65 | 95 | 77 | 73 | 86 |
| 81 | 66 | 73 | 51 | 75 | 64 | 67 | 54 | 54 | 78 |
| 57 | 81 | 65 | 72 | 59 | 72 | 84 | 85 | 79 | 67 |
| 62 | 76 | 52 | 92 | 66 | 74 | 72 | 83 | 56 | 93 |
| 96 | 64 | 95 | 94 | 86 | 75 | 73 | 72 | 85 | 94 |

Presenting these data in their raw form clearly would tell the administrator little or nothing about trash collection in Normal.

The most basic restructuring of raw data to facilitate understanding is the **frequency distribution**. A frequency distribution is a table that shows the data grouped according to their numerical value. Table 1.1, for example, is a frequency distribution of the number of arrests each Morgan City police officer made in March 1992. Note that the entire table is labeled, as is each column.

**frequency distribution**

This procedure makes it easy to see that most Morgan City police officers made between 16 and 20 arrests in March 1992.

**TABLE 1.1**
Arrests per Police Officer: Morgan City, March 1992

| Number of Arrests | Number of Police Officers |
| --- | --- |
| 1–5 | 6 |
| 6–10 | 17 |
| 11–15 | 47 |
| 16–20 | 132 |
| 21–25 | 35 |
| 25+ | 7 |
| | 244 |

**variable**

**class**

**class boundary**

**class midpoint**

**class interval**

**class frequency**

**total frequency**

Some definitions are in order. A **variable** is the trait on which the classification is based; in the example above, the variable is the number of arrests per police officer. A **class** is one of the grouped categories of the variable. The first class, for example, is from 1 to 5 arrests. Classes have **class boundaries** (the lowest and highest values that fall within the class) and **class midpoints** (the point halfway between the upper and lower class boundaries). The class midpoint of the third class, for example, is 13; which is 11, the lower class boundary, plus 15, the upper class boundary, divided by 2, or $(11 + 15) \div 2$. The **class interval** is the distance between the upper limit of one class and the upper limit of the next higher class. In the preceding example, the class interval is 5. The **class frequency** is the number of observations or occurrences of the variable within a given class; for example, the class frequency of the fourth class (i.e., 16–20) is 132. The **total frequency** is the total number of observations in the table—in this case, 244. In the remainder of this chapter, we will discuss some important characteristics of frequency distributions and the procedures for constructing them.

## CONSTRUCTING A
## FREQUENCY DISTRIBUTION

Constructing a frequency distribution is a relatively simple task. To illustrate this process, we will use the Normal, Oklahoma, garbage collection data listed previously.

**STEP 1**    Scan the data to find the lowest and highest values. The lowest value in these data is 50 (column 3, the third value), and the highest value is 97 (column 5, the fifth value).

**STEP 2**     Make a list of the values from the lowest to the highest and then mark as follows: the number of times each value appears. This process is illustrated as follows:

| | | | | | | | | | |
|---|---|---|---|---|---|---|---|---|---|
| 50 | / | 60 | | 70 | // | 80 | / | 90 | |
| 51 | /// | 61 | /// | 71 | /// | 81 | // | 91 | |
| 52 | / | 62 | //// | 72 | //// | 82 | // | 92 | / |
| 53 | / | 63 | // | 73 | /// | 83 | /// | 93 | / |
| 54 | // | 64 | //// | 74 | // | 84 | // | 94 | /// |
| 55 | / | 65 | //// | 75 | ///// | 85 | // | 95 | /// |
| 56 | / | 66 | /// | 76 | // | 86 | //// | 96 | / |
| 57 | // | 67 | // | 77 | // | 87 | / | 97 | / |
| 58 | / | 68 | // | 78 | /// | 88 | / | 98 | |
| 59 | // | 69 | / | 79 | /// | 89 | // | | |

**STEP 3**     The tabulations in Step 2 could actually be called a frequency distribution, since the data are ordered by value. For a better visual presentation, however, the data should be compressed into classes. The rule of thumb is to collapse data into no fewer than 4 or no more than 20 classes. Fewer than 4 classes obscures the variation in the data; more than 20 presents too complex a picture to grasp quickly. The analyst chooses the actual number of classes in a table so that the table reflects the data as closely as possible. Other tips on constructing frequency distribution classes are:

1. Avoid classes so narrow that some intervals have zero observations.
2. Make all the class intervals equal unless the top or bottom class is open-ended. An open-ended class has only one boundary. In the Morgan City arrests table, for example, the last category (25+) is an open-ended category.
3. Use open-ended intervals only when closed intervals would result in class frequencies of zero. This usually happens when some values are extremely high or extremely low.
4. Try to construct the intervals so that the midpoints are whole numbers.

For the present example, let us collapse the data into five categories. Constructing the remainder of the table results in the frequency distribution shown in Table 1.2.

Note in the table that the upper limit of every class is also the lower limit of the next class; that is, the upper limit of the first class is 60, the same value as the lower limit of the second class. This is often done when the data are continuous; continuous data can take on values that are not whole numbers. In the situation given in Table 1.2, statisticians interpret the first interval as running from 50 tons up to but not including 60 tons (i.e., 59.999 tons). In this way, no value can fall in more than one class. When you see tables like this one, in which interval limits appear to overlap, remember that the upper limit means up to but not including the value, and that the lower limit begins with this value (for example, see Tables 1.3 and 1.4).

**TABLE 1.2**

Tons of Garbage Collected by Sanitary Engineer Teams in Normal, Oklaboma, Week of June 8, 1992

| Tons of Garbage | Number of Crews |
|---|---|
| 50–60 | 15 |
| 60–70 | 25 |
| 70–80 | 30 |
| 80–90 | 20 |
| 90–100 | 10 |
|  | 100 |

## THE PERCENTAGE DISTRIBUTION

Suppose the Normal city manager wants to know if Normal sanitary engineer crews are picking up more garbage than the city crews in Moore. The city manager may want to know this information because Moore crews only collect garbage that residents place in front of their houses, whereas Normal crews leave their trucks to collect trash that is located within a resident's yard. The city manager's goal is to collect more garbage, while holding down garbage collection costs.

**percentage distribution**

Table 1.3 shows the frequency distributions of garbage collection in both cities. But from the frequency distributions, the city manager cannot tell which method of trash collection is more efficient. Since Moore has a larger work force, it has a larger number of crews in all five of the classes. The data must be altered so that the two cities can be compared. The easiest way to do this is to convert both columns of data into percentage distributions. A **percentage distribution** shows the percentage of the total observations that fall into each class. To convert the data of Table 1.3 to percentage distributions, the frequency in each class should be divided by the total frequency for that city. In this instance, all Normal class frequencies should be divided by 100, and all Moore class frequencies should be divided by 165. (Chapter 13 presents a more detailed discussion of percentage distributions.) Table 1.4 shows the resulting percentage distribution. Is the Moore method of trash collection more efficient?

**TABLE 1.3**

Tons of Garbage Collected by Sanitary Engineer
Teams, Week of June 8, 1992

| Tons of Garbage | Numbers of Crews | |
|---|---|---|
| | *Normal* | *Moore* |
| 50–60 | 15 | 22 |
| 60–70 | 25 | 37 |
| 70–80 | 30 | 49 |
| 80–90 | 20 | 36 |
| 90–100 | 10 | 21 |
| | 100 | 165 |

**TABLE 1.4**

Tons of Garbage Collected by Sanitary Engineer
Teams, Week of June 8, 1992

| Tons of Garbage | Percentage of Work Crews | |
|---|---|---|
| | *Normal* | *Moore* |
| 50–60 | 15 | 13 |
| 60–70 | 25 | 22 |
| 70–80 | 30 | 30 |
| 80–90 | 20 | 22 |
| 90–100 | 10 | 13 |
| | 100 | 100 |
| | **N** = 100 | **N** = 165 |

Notice that some new items are included in the percentage table that were not included in the frequency table. At the bottom of each column, a number is found (**N** = 100 or **N** = 165). **N** stands for the total number of observations; it represents the total frequency (or number of observations) on which the percentages are based. Given this number, you can calculate the original class frequencies. Try it.

## CUMULATIVE FREQUENCY
## DISTRIBUTIONS

Frequency distributions and percentage distributions show the number or percentage of observations that fall in one or more classes. Sometimes the administrator needs to know how many observations (or what percentage of observations) fall below or above a certain standard. For example, the fire chief of Metro, Texas, is quite concerned about how long it takes his fire crews to arrive at the scene of a fire. The *Metro Morning News* has run several stories about fires in which it claimed the Metro fire department was slow in responding. Since the Metro fire department automatically records the time of fire calls on computer tape and also records the dispatched fire truck's report that it has arrived at the fire, the response times to all fires can be found. An analyst has made a frequency distribution of these response times (Table 1.5). The Metro fire chief considers 5 minutes to be an excellent response time, 10 minutes to be an acceptable response time, 15 minutes to be an unsatisfactory response time, and 20 minutes to be unacceptable. As a result, the fire chief wants to know the percentage of fire calls answered in under 5 minutes, under 10 minutes, under 15 minutes, and under 20 minutes. To provide the fire chief with the information he wants, the analyst must construct a cumulative percentage distribution.

**TABLE 1.5**

Response Times of the Metro Fire Department, 1991

| Response Time (Minutes) | Number of Calls | Running Total | Cumulative Percentage |
|---|---|---|---|
| 0–1 | 7 | | |
| 1–2 | 14 | | |
| 2–3 | 32 | | |
| 3–4 | 37 | | |
| 4–5 | 48 | | |
| 5–6 | 53 | | |
| 6–7 | 66 | | |
| 7–8 | 73 | | |
| 8–9 | 42 | | |
| 9–10 | 40 | | |
| 10–11 | 36 | | |
| 11–12 | 23 | | |
| 12–13 | 14 | | |
| 13–14 | 7 | | |
| 14–15 | 2 | | |
| 15–20 | 6 | | |
| | 500 | | |

**cumulative percentage distribution**     The first step in developing a **cumulative percentage distribution** is to prepare a running total of responses to fire calls. To the right of the "Number of Calls" column, you will find a blank column labeled "Running Total." In this column, we will calculate the total number of responses made that were less than each interval's upper limit. For example, how many fires were responded to in less than 1 minute? From the table, we can see seven fires had response times of under a minute. Enter the number 7 for the first class in the running total column. How many fire responses were under 2 minutes? There were 21: 7 under 1 minute, plus 14 between 1 and 2 minutes. Enter 21 as the value for the second class. Using this logic, fill in the rest of the values.

The second step is to construct a cumulative percentage column. This step is done by dividing each frequency in the "Running Total" column by the total frequency (in this case, 500). In the fourth column of the table, "Cumulative Percentage," enter the following numbers. The first entry should be 1.4 (7 ÷ 500); the second entry should be 4.2 (21 ÷ 500); the third entry should be 10.6 (53 ÷ 500). Fill in the remaining values for this column.

You now have a cumulative frequency distribution for the fire chief. The distribution is a bit awkward, however, because it has so many categories. The next step would be to collapse the cumulative percentage distribution into fewer categories. Since the fire chief is concerned with response times of 5, 10, 15, and 20 minutes, these times would be the best categories. Table 1.6 should result from your calculations. From this table, what can you tell the chief about fire department response times in Metro?

**TABLE 1.6**

Response Times of Metro Fire Department, 1991

| Response Time | Percentage (Cumulative) of Responses |
|---|---|
| Under 5 minutes | 27.6 |
| Under 10 minutes | 82.4 |
| Under 15 minutes | 98.8 |
| Under 20 minutes | 100.0 |
| N = 500 | |

## GRAPHIC PRESENTATIONS

Often an administrator wants to present information visually so that someone can get a general feel for a problem without reading a table. Two methods of visual presentation will be discribed here: the frequency polygon and the histogram.

Let us say that the Normal city manager, as part of her budget justification, wants to show the city council the number of complaints the city dog pound receives about barking dogs. An assistant has prepared the frequency distribution shown in Table 1.7.

**TABLE 1.7**

Complaints per Week About Barking Dogs, 1991

| Number of Complaints | Number of Weeks |
|---|---|
| 5–9 | 7 |
| 10–14 | 6 |
| 15–19 | 15 |
| 20–24 | 17 |
| 25–29 | 5 |
| 30–34 | 2 |
| | 52 |

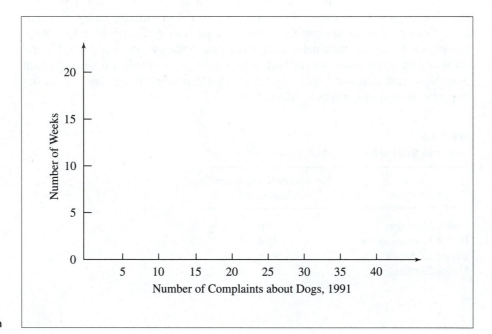

**FIGURE 1.1**

First Step in Constructing a Frequency Polygon

**frequency polygon**

To construct a **frequency polygon**, follow these steps.

**STEP 1** On a sheet of graph paper, write the name of the variable across the bottom and write the frequency along the side. Make sure that the scale for the variable encompasses all values in the distribution, so that the frequency of each value can be graphed. (See Figure 1.1.)

**STEP 2** Calculate the midpoints for each class interval. You should get the following values: 7, 12, 17, 22, 27, 32.

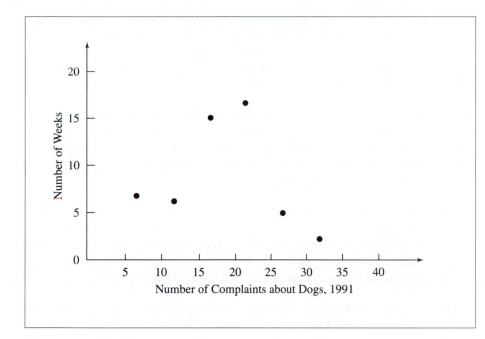

**FIGURE 1.2**
Third Step in Constructing a Frequency Polygon

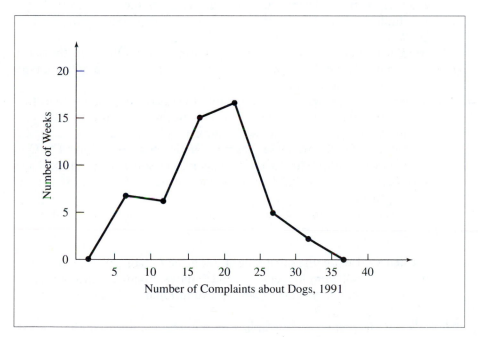

**FIGURE 1.3**
The Frequency Polygon

**STEP 3**    On the horizontal dimension of the graph, find the first class midpoint (7). From this point, use your pencil and move it straight up until you find the value equal to the class frequency (also 7). Make a dot. Repeat this process for the five other classes. At this point, your graph should look like the one in Figure 1.2.

**STEP 4**    Pretend that two more classes exist: one the class lower than the lowest class (this class would be 0–4 complaints), and one higher than the highest class (35–39). Calculate the midpoints for these make-believe classes and plot their midpoints with a frequency of 0 on your graph. This procedure makes the graph touch the horizontal line.

**STEP 5**    Starting from the leftmost point, draw a line connecting the points in sequence. You have now completed your first frequency polygon. If it looks like the one in Figure 1.3, congratulations. (Note that whereas the frequency polygon presents a useful visual representation of the data, the line segments do not correspond to actual data points.)

One nice aspect of frequency polygons is that the analyst can draw more than one on the same graph. For example, suppose that the Normal city manager wants to show how complaints about barking dogs have changed over time. The city manager gives you the data shown in Table 1.8. In the space provided on page 13, graph frequency polygons for both years on the same graph. What does the graph tell you about barking dog complaints in 1991 as opposed to those in 1990?

**Note:** Whenever two or more frequency polygons are drawn on the same graph, each polygon should be drawn in a different color or with a different type of line. Be sure to label each line.

**histogram**

**bar chart**

A **histogram** is a bar graph for a variable that takes on many values (for example, income). The term **bar chart** is sometimes used when a variable can take on only a very limited set of values (for example, a variable assessing an opinion that calls for the responses "agree," "undecided," or "disagree"). Our intention is not to multiply terms (or confusion), but some statistical package programs, such as the Statistical Package for the Social Sciences (SPSS), do make this distinction.

To construct a histogram of barking dog complaints in Normal for 1991, complete the following steps.

**STEPS 1, 2, and 3**    Follow the same procedures given for constructing frequency polygons in Steps 1, 2, and 3 above. Following this procedure should yield the graph shown in Figure 1.4.

**STEP 4**    From the points on the graph, draw a horizontal line to both the lower and upper class boundaries. Draw in the vertical lines along the class boundaries from these horizontal lines to the horizontal axis of the graph. Each class is now represented by a bar.

**TABLE 1.8**

Complaints per Week About Barking Dogs,
1990 and 1991

| Number of Complaints | Number of Weeks | |
|---|---|---|
| | *1990* | *1991* |
| 5–9 | 8 | 7 |
| 10–14 | 12 | 6 |
| 15–19 | 14 | 15 |
| 20–24 | 10 | 17 |
| 25–29 | 6 | 5 |
| 30–34 | 2 | 2 |
| | 52 | 52 |

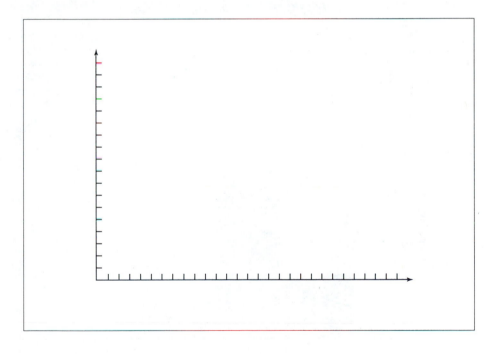

**STEP 5**   Shade in the bars you have drawn in Step 4. Your graph should appear
as shown in Figure 1.5.

Histograms, rather than frequency polygons, should be used whenever you
want to emphasize the distinctiveness of each class. The frequency polygon
tends to smooth out class differences. Frequency polygons should be used when-

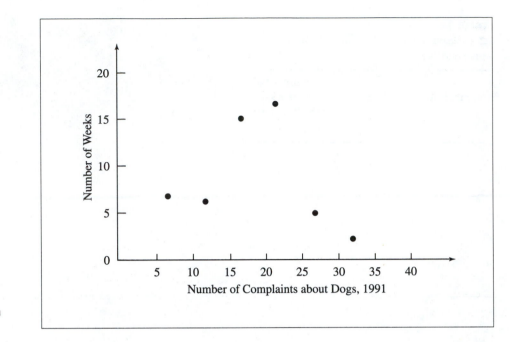

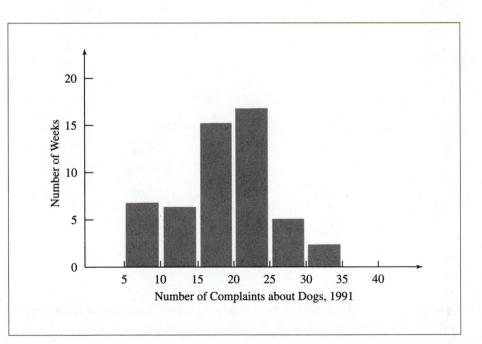

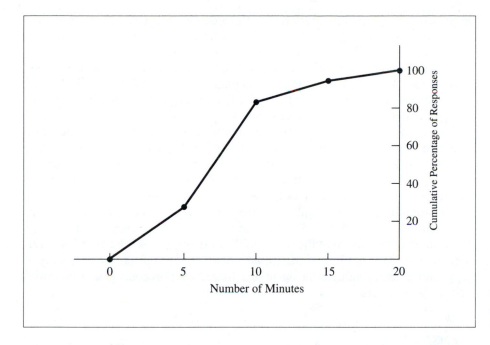

**FIGURE 1.6**
Cumulative
Frequency Polygon

ever you want to emphasize a smooth trend or when two or more graphs are placed on a single chart or table.

Cumulative frequency distributions can also be graphed. For example, the Metro fire response time distribution can be made into a frequency polygon. For convenience, we repeat Table 1.6 here as Table 1.9. Following the steps outlined previously should yield the frequency polygon shown in Figure 1.6. A frequency polygon for a cumulative frequency distribution is called an **ogive**.    **ogive**

**TABLE 1.9**

Response Times of Metro Fire Department, 1991

| Response Time | Percentage (Cumulative) of Responses |
|---|---|
| Under 5 minutes | 27.6 |
| Under 10 minutes | 82.4 |
| Under 15 minutes | 98.8 |
| Under 20 minutes | 100.0 |

$$N = 500$$

## Chapter Summary

Descriptive statistics summarize a body of raw data so that the data can be more easily understood. Frequency distributions, percentage distributions, and cumulative frequency distributions are three descriptive ways to combine raw data into a table. A frequency distribution is a table that displays data according to numerical values. Usually the table shows classes appropriate for the variable under study and the number of data points falling into each class. A percentage distribution shows the percentage of total data points that fall into each class. A cumulative frequency (or percentage) distribution displays the number (or percentage) of items that fall above or below a certain class.

To add visual appeal and to increase interpretability, graphic presentations of data are used. Graphic techniques discussed in this chapter include the frequency polygon, the histogram and bar chart, and the ogive. The frequency polygon shows a plot of the frequency distribution informaton (class versus frequency), with the plotted points connected (in sequence) by line segments. The histogram is a bar graph of a frequency distribution, with each class represented by the width of a bar, and with the frequency of that class represented by the height of the bar from the horizontal axis. The term *bar chart* is sometimes used in place of *histogram* when the variable can take on only a very limited set of values. An ogive is a frequency polygon for a cumulative frequency distribution.

## PROBLEMS

**1.1** You are the research assistant to the administrator of a small bureau in the federal government. Your boss has received some criticism that the bureau does not respond promptly to congressional requests. The only information you have is the day the agency received the request, and the day the agency mailed the response. From those figures, you have calculated the number of days the agency took to respond.

**Days Necessary to Respond to Congressional Requests**

| | | | | | | | | | |
|---|---|---|---|---|---|---|---|---|---|
| 9 | 1 | 6 | 10 | 8 | 12 | 9 | 14 | 15 | 7 |
| 19 | 8 | 21 | 10 | 50 | 37 | 9 | 4 | 28 | 44 |
| 9 | 18 | 8 | 39 | 7 | 1 | 4 | 15 | 7 | 28 |
| 47 | 9 | 6 | 7 | 24 | 10 | 41 | 7 | 9 | 29 |
| 6 | 4 | 12 | 7 | 9 | 15 | 39 | 24 | 9 | 2 |
| 20 | 31 | 18 | 9 | 33 | 8 | 6 | 3 | 7 | 16 |
| 20 | 26 | 9 | 9 | 16 | 5 | 3 | 12 | 36 | 11 |
| 8 | 6 | 28 | 35 | 8 | 10 | 11 | 20 | 3 | 10 |
| 16 | 8 | 12 | 4 | 6 | 9 | 10 | 10 | 9 | 16 |
| 4 | 14 | 11 | 8 | 5 | 8 | 11 | 9 | 7 | 6 |
| 11 | 9 | 7 | 8 | 10 | 9 | 11 | | | |

Do the following:
**(a)** Prepare a frequency distribution.
**(b)** Present the distribution graphically.

(c) Prepare a cumulative frequency distribution.

(d) Present the cumulative distribution graphically.

(e) Write a paragraph explaining what you have found.

**1.2** Allan Wiese, mayor of Orva, South Dakota, feels that the productivity of meter butlers has declined in the past year. Mayor Wiese's research assistant provides him with the accompanying data. Convert the frequency distributions to comparable distributions. What can you tell Mayor Wiese about the productivity of his meter butlers?

| Parking Tickets Issued per Meter Butler | Number of Butlers | |
|---|---|---|
| | *May 1991* | *May 1992* |
| 21–30 | 5 | 6 |
| 31–40 | 7 | 9 |
| 41–50 | 9 | 12 |
| 51–60 | 5 | 7 |
| 61–70 | 3 | 1 |
| | 29 | 35 |

**1.3** Scotty Allen, civil service director for Maxwell, New York, compiles the accompanying frequency distribution of scores on the Maxwell civil service exam. Construct a cumulative frequency distribution and a cumulative frequency polygon for Mr. Allen.

| Exam Score | Number of Applicants |
|---|---|
| 61–65 | 20 |
| 66–70 | 13 |
| 71–75 | 47 |
| 76–80 | 56 |
| 81–85 | 33 |
| 86–90 | 27 |
| 91–95 | 41 |
| 96–100 | 34 |

**1.4** The incumbent governor of a large state is campaigning on the platform that he eliminated a great many large, "do-nothing" bureaucracies. As the research assistant for the challenger, you are asked to present the accompanying data (numbers are the size of bureaus eliminated under the incumbent and under his predecessor) graphically in the most favorable manner for the challenger.

| Incumbent | | Predecessor |
|---|---|---|
| 6 | 16 | 15 |
| 14 | 5 | 28 |
| 7 | 3 | 48 |
| 3 | 7 | 104 |
| 24 | 19 | 37 |
| 6 | 21 | 56 |
| 3 | 12 | 15 |
| 1 | 4 | 6 |
| 2 | 3 | 3 |
| 21 | 6 | 27 |
| 41 | 1 | 39 |

**1.5**    Refer to Problem 1.4. Construct a frequency distribution, and present it to reflect favorably on the incumbent.

**1.6**    The city clerk has received numerous complaints over the past year that couples applying for a marriage license have to wait too long to receive one. Although the clerk is skeptical (couples applying for a license are usually young and impatient), she pulls a representative sample of marriage licenses issued in the past year. Because a machine stamps on each license application the times the application is received and issued, she can tell how long the young (and old) lovers had to wait for the marriage license. The clerk considers service received in less than 10 minutes good, and service received in less than 15 minutes acceptable. Her tabulation of the license data show:

| Minutes Waited for Marriage License | Number of Couples |
|---|---|
| Less than 5 | 28 |
| 5–9 | 36 |
| 10–14 | 60 |
| 15–19 | 82 |
| 20–24 | 44 |
| 25–29 | 39 |

Prepare the percentage distribution for the marriage license data and the appropriate graphical displays. Write a short memorandum explaining the results and addressing the issue of whether couples have to wait too long for marriage licenses.

**1.7**    The city clerk from Problem 1.6 is intrigued by the findings of her survey of marriage licenses issued in the past year (data analysis often has this effect). Accordingly, she decides to pull another representative sample of marriage licenses, this time from two years ago. She is interested in determining whether service to the public from her unit has improved or declined over the past two years. As before, the clerk considers service received in less than 10 minutes good, and service received in less than 15 minutes acceptable. Her tabulation of the sample of marriage licenses issued two years ago shows:

| Minutes Waited for Marriage License | Number of Couples |
|---|---|
| Less than 5 | 112 |
| 5–9 | 87 |
| 10–14 | 31 |
| 15–19 | 27 |
| 20–24 | 29 |
| 25–29 | 3 |

Prepare the percentage distribution for the marriage license data and the appropriate graphical displays. Write a short memorandum explaining the results and addressing the question whether service to the public from her unit has improved or declined over the past two years.

**1.8** Because of cutbacks in government funding, the state Bureau of Statistics has had to forego routine maintenance of its computer terminals for the past five years. (The equipment is made by the Indestructible Computer Company.) The head of the bureau is concerned that the bureau will face a major equipment crisis this year, since the recommended maintenance schedule for the terminals is once every three years. Over the past five years, the bureau has been able to purchase new terminals. In an effort to obtain more funding from the state legislature, the bureau chief compiles the following data. The data show the time since the last routine maintenance of the terminal or, if the terminal was purchased in the last two years, the time since the terminal was purchased.

| Time Since Last Maintenance | Number of Terminals |
|---|---|
| 1 year or less | 103 |
| 2 years | 187 |
| 3 years | 97 |
| 4 years | 56 |
| 5 years | 37 |
| 6 years | 12 |
| 7 years or more | 5 |

Prepare the percentage distribution for the terminal maintenance data and the appropriate graphical displays. Write a short memorandum both explaining the results and trying to convince the state legislature to provide funding for routine maintenance of computer terminals.

1.9 Assume that you are a staff analyst to a state legislator on the oversight committee of the Bureau of Statistics. Write a short memorandum both explaining the results of the data tabulation in Problem 1.8 and trying to convince the legislature that the equipment "crisis" at the bureau is overblown.

1.10 The Department of Animal Control is concerned about available space for impounded animals. The department keeps careful count of the number of animals it shelters each day. To determine the load on the department, the department head, Sheila Humane, selects a representative sample of days from the last two years and records the number of animals impounded on each day. Her data appear as follows:

| 65 | 49 | 84 | 72 | 43 | 91 |
|----|----|----|----|----|----|
| 57 | 46 | 77 | 69 | 90 | 64 |
| 85 | 67 | 52 | 44 | 95 | 79 |
| 48 | 63 | 55 | 96 | 75 | 48 |
| 88 | 81 | 93 | 67 | 58 | 72 |
| 51 | 49 | 96 | 79 | 73 | 80 |
| 65 | 54 | 86 | 98 | 42 | 63 |
| 92 | 71 | 79 | 84 | 59 | 45 |

Prepare the frequency and percentage distributions for the animal impoundment data and the appropriate graphical displays for Ms. Humane. Write a short memorandum explaining both the results and the demands on the Department of Animal Control to shelter animals.

1.11 The director of the state Department of Public Works wants to upgrade the department's automobile fleet; she claims that the fleet is too old. The governor appoints a staff analyst to investigate the issue. The analyst compiles data on both the age and the odometer readings (mileage) of the department's automobile fleet. Her data appear as follows:

| Age | Number of Automobiles |
|-----|-----------------------|
| Less than 2 years | 16 |
| 2–4 years | 24 |
| 4–6 years | 41 |
| 6–8 years | 57 |
| 8–10 years | 64 |
| 10 or more years | 39 |

| Mileage | Number of Automobiles |
|---|---|
| Less than 10,000 | 76 |
| 10,000–20,000 | 63 |
| 20,000–30,000 | 51 |
| 30,000–40,000 | 32 |
| 40,000–50,000 | 12 |
| 50,000 or more | 7 |

Prepare percentage distributions for the age and mileage data and the appropriate graphical displays. Write a short memorandum to the governor both explaining the results and making a recommendation regarding whether the department's automobile fleet should be upgraded.

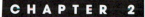

## CHAPTER 2

# MEASURES OF CENTRAL TENDENCY

The most commonly used descriptive statistics are the measures of central tendency. A **measure of central tendency** is one number that represents the average of a group of data. This chapter will discuss the mean, the median, and the mode and illustrate how they are calculated for both ungrouped and grouped data.

**measure of central tendency**

## THE MEAN

The **mean** is nothing more than the arithmetic average of a set of numbers. To calculate the mean, add all the numbers (or "observations"), and divide this new number (the "sum") by the total number of observations in the set, which we labeled **N** in Chapter 1.

**mean**

To illustrate, suppose that the head of the Bureau of Records wants to know the mean length of government service of the employees in the bureau's Office of Computer Support. Table 2.1 displays the number of years that each member of the office has been employed in government.

To calculate the mean length of government service of the employees in the bureau's Office of Computer Support, add together the years of service of each of the employees. You should come up with a total of 118 years. Divide this sum by the number of employees in the office (8). This procedure will give you the mean number of years of government service of the employees in the office (14.75).

**TABLE 2.1**

Years of Government Service

| Employee | Years | Employee | Years |
|----------|-------|----------|-------|
| Bush | 8 | Jackson | 9 |
| Clinton | 15 | Quayle | 11 |
| Reagan | 23 | Dukakis | 18 |
| Cuomo | 14 | Carter | 20 |

Many times this formula for the mean is presented:

$$\mu_X = \frac{\sum_{i=1}^{N} X_i}{N}$$

This formula is not as formidable as it seems. The Greek letter $\mu$ on the left side of the equal sign is the statistician's symbol for the mean; it is pronounced "mu." Mu of $X$ (the mean of $X$) is equal to the formula on the right side of the equal sign. $\Sigma$ is another statistician's symbol; it means add (or sum) all the values of $X$ (in our example, these were years of government service). The subscripts below and above the $\Sigma$ indicate to sum all the $X$'s from $X_1$, $X_2$ all the way to $X_N$, the last observation (here, the years of government service of the eighth employee). Finally, the formula says to divide the sum of all the $X$'s by $N$, the number of items being summed.

The mean has several important characteristics:

1. Every item in a group of data is used to calculate the mean.
2. Every group of data has one and only one mean; as mathematicians would say, the mean is rigidly determined.
3. The mean may take on a value that is not realistic. For example, the average U.S. family had exactly 1.7 children or 2.2 pets.

**outlier**

4. An extreme value, sometimes called an **outlier**, has a disproportionate influence on the mean and thus may affect how well the mean represents the data. For example, suppose that the head of the Bureau of Records decides to shake up the Office of Computer Support by creating a new position in the office with responsibility to expedite operations. To fill the position, the head appoints a newly graduated MPA with a fine background in computers but only one year of prior service in government. In the space provided, calculate the mean years of government service of the employees in the expanded Office of Computer Support.

If you performed the calculations correctly, you should get a mean length of government service of 13.2 years. This number tends to understate the years of government service of the employees in the Office of Computer Support. Why?

## THE MEDIAN

The **median** is nothing more than the middle item of a set of numbers when the items are ranked in order of magnitude. For example, the Stermerville City Council requires that all city agencies include an average salary in their budget requests. The Stermerville City Planning Office has seven employees. The director is paid $32,500; the assistant director makes $29,500. Three planning clerks are paid $12,600, $12,500, and $12,400. The secretary (who does all the work) is paid $7,500, and a receptionist is paid $6,300.     **median**

The planning director calculates the mean salary and finds that it is $16,186. This disturbs the director, because it makes the agency look fat and bloated. The secretary points out that the large salaries paid to the director and the assistant director are distorting the mean. The secretary then calculates the median, following these steps:

**STEP 1**   List the salaries in order of magnitude. You may start with the largest or the smallest; you will get the same answer. The secretary prepares the following list:

| | |
|---|---|
| Director | $32,500 |
| Assistant Director | 29,500 |
| Clerk 1 | 12,600 |
| Clerk 2 | 12,500 |
| Clerk 3 | 12,400 |
| Secretary | 7,500 |
| Receptionist | 6,300 |

**STEP 2**   Locate the middle item. With seven persons, the middle item is easy to find; it is the fourth item, or the salary paid to clerk 2 ($12,500). For larger data sets, the rule is to take the number of items (7, in this case) and add 1 to it ($7 + 1 = 8$). Divide this number by 2, and that number ($8 \div 2 = 4$) tells you that the median is the fourth item. Note that it makes no difference whether you use the fourth item from the top or the fourth from the bottom.

The Stermerville mayor tells the planning director that, because of the local tax revolt, the planning office must fire one person. The planning office responds as all bureaucracies do by firing the receptionist. After this action, what is the median salary of the planning office? Calculate in the space provided.

After arranging the salaries in order, you may have discovered that with six items, no middle item exists. The formula $(N + 1) \div 2$ is no help because $(6 + 1) \div 2 = 3\frac{1}{2}$. *But* the median is actually that, the $3\frac{1}{2}$th item from the top (or bottom). Since items cannot be split in half, we define $3\frac{1}{2}$ as halfway between the third and fourth items, in this case halfway between clerk 2 and clerk 1. Since clerk 2 makes $12,500 and clerk 1 makes $12,600, the median is $12,550 $[(12,600 + 12,500) \div 2]$. Whenever the number of items ($N$) is an even number, the median will be halfway between the two middle observations. This is easy to remember if you think of the median as the measure of central tendency that divides a set of numbers so that exactly half are smaller than the median and exactly half are larger than the median.

The median has several important characteristics:

1. The median is not affected by extreme values.
2. Although every item is used to determine the median, the actual value of every item is not used in the calculations. At most, only the two middle items are used to calculate the median.
3. If items do not cluster near the median, the median will not be a good measure of the group's central tendency.

4. The median usually does not take on an unrealistic value. The median number of children per family in the United States, for example, is 2.
5. The median is the 50th percentile in a distribution of data, since half the observations fall above it, and half fall below it.

## THE MODE

The **mode** is simply the most common value in any distribution. In the distribu-     **mode**
tion in Table 2.2, what is the mode number of tickets issued?

**TABLE 2.2**
Tickets Issued by Woodward Police,
Week of January 28, 1991

| Number of Tickets | Number of Police Officers |
|---|---|
| 0 | 2 |
| 1 | 7 |
| 2 | 9 |
| 3 | 14 |
| 4 | 3 |
| 5 | 2 |
| 6 | 1 |
| | 38 |

The most common value is 3 tickets issued, so 3 is the mode.

The distribution in Table 2.2 has only one mode; thus it is called unimodal. The distribution in Table 2.3 is bimodal; it has two modes. Since Kapaun had 9 arrests for 14 weeks and 11 arrests for 14 weeks, the modes are 9 and 11. Distributions also can be trimodal, tetramodal, and so on.

**TABLE 2.3**
Arrests per Week, Kapaun Air Station, 1991

| Number of Arrests | Number of Weeks |
|---|---|
| 7 | 2 |
| 8 | 4 |
| 9 | 14 |
| 10 | 8 |
| 11 | 14 |
| 12 | 10 |
| | 52 |

The mode has several important characteristics:

1. Since the most common value in a distribution of data can occur at any point, the mode need not be "central" or near the middle.
2. Unlike the mean and median, the mode can take on more than one value.
3. More often than not, when a variable is measured on a numerical scale (number of arrests, feet of snow plowed, etc.), the mode is of little interest. When a distribution has more than one distinct mode, however, it usually means something important. In addition, with variables measured at less precise levels, the mode is more useful (see Chapter 7).

## MEANS FOR GROUPED DATA

Commonly in public management you will encounter the problem of being asked to calculate some statistics using someone else's data. Often these data are in the form of a frequency distribution. Measures of central tendency can be calculated from frequency distributions (or grouped data). Raw ungrouped data should be collected and retained at every opportunity, but sometimes archival data and sensitive survey data require that grouped data be used. Since grouped data collapse frequencies and thus lose information, statistics calculated by using grouped data are less accurate than statistics calculated from ungrouped data. As a result, *never calculate statistics from grouped data if the ungrouped data are available.*

Sometimes, however, the analyst does not have a choice. Suppose the director of the Oklahoma Highway Department knows that the average (mean) speed on Oklahoma highways is 62.4 miles per hour. Federal Department of Transportation people are upset, charging Oklahoma with lax enforcement. The Oklahoma director feels that Oklahoma is no worse than any other state. But the only information the director has is the frequency distribution shown in Table 2.4. The director asks the analyst to calculate the mean speed on Texas highways.

**TABLE 2.4**
Frequency Distribution of Texas Motorists' Speeds

| Miles per Hour | Number of Drivers |
|---|---|
| 45–50 | 26 |
| 50–55 | 123 |
| 55–60 | 273 |
| 60–65 | 319 |
| 65–70 | 136 |
| 70–75 | 84 |
| 75–80 | 7 |
| | 968 |

By applying the logic of calculating means for ungrouped data, we find that the calculations for grouped data are straightforward. The mean is nothing more than the sum of all the values divided by the number of values. Examining the first class, we see that 26 drivers were clocked between 45 and 50 miles per hour, although we do not know their exact speeds. Whenever grouped data are used for calculations, statisticians assume that all values are spread evenly throughout the interval. Thus the mean of the first class, or any class, is equal to the midpoint of the class (in this case, $(45 + 50) \div 2 = 47.5$). For purposes of calculating the mean, we can then treat the first class as if it contained 26 items all equal to the class midpoint. With this assumption, the mean can be calculated by the following steps.

**STEP 1**   Make a new column in the frequency table for class midpoints and fill in the midpoints. (See Table 2.5.)

**TABLE 2.5**
Motorists' Speeds and Class Midpoints

| Class | Frequency | Midpoint |
|-------|-----------|----------|
| 45–50 | 26 | 47.5 |
| 50–55 | 123 | 52.5 |
| 55–60 | 273 | 57.5 |
| 60–65 | 319 | 62.5 |
| 65–70 | 136 | 67.5 |
| 70–75 | 84 | 72.5 |
| 75–80 | 7 | 77.5 |
|  | 968 |  |

**STEP 2**   Multiply the frequency in each class by the class **midpoint**, and place this value in a column labeled $F \times M$. This first value, for example, is $26 \times 47.5$, or 1235. In the space next to the midpoint column, calculate these values.                                    **midpoint**

**STEP 3**   Sum all the values in the $F \times M$ column. This sum is equivalent to the sum of the values in the calculations for ungrouped data. At this point, your table should look like Table 2.6.

**STEP 4**   Divide the sum of all values (the sum of the $F \times M$ column) by the number of values or **N**. This number is the mean ($59,140 \div 968 = 61.1$). How does the average speed in Texas compare with the average speed in Oklahoma? What should the Oklahoma highway director do with this information?

Following the steps just outlined, calculate the mean number of serious crimes per precinct for Metro, Texas. The data are given in Table 2.7.

**TABLE 2.6**
Motorists' Speeds

| Class | Frequency | Midpoints | $F \times M$ |
|---|---|---|---|
| 45–50 | 26 | 47.5 | 1,235 |
| 50–55 | 123 | 52.5 | 6,457.5 |
| 55–60 | 273 | 57.5 | 15,697.5 |
| 60–65 | 319 | 62.5 | 19,937.5 |
| 65–70 | 136 | 67.5 | 9,180 |
| 70–75 | 84 | 72.5 | 6,090 |
| 75–80 | 7 | 77.5 | 542.5 |
| | 968 | | $\Sigma F \times M = 59,140$ |

**TABLE 2.7**
Serious Crimes per Precinct, Metro, Texas, Week of March 7, 1991

| Number of Crimes | Number of Precincts | Class Midpoints | $F \times M$ |
|---|---|---|---|
| 1–5 | 6 | | |
| 6–10 | 9 | | |
| 11–15 | 14 | | |
| 16–20 | 5 | | |
| 21–25 | 1 | | |
| | 35 | | |

$\Sigma F \times M =$ _____
Mean number of serious crimes = _____

If you worked the example correctly, you should get a mean of 11.0. (**Hint:** Did you use midpoints of 3, 8, 13, 18, and 23?)

## MEDIANS FOR GROUPED DATA

Medians can also be calculated for grouped data. The logic is similar to that for ungrouped data; for grouped data, the median is the middle value. For the data listed in Table 2.7, the median can be calculated in a manner similar to that for ungrouped data. There are 35 precincts in Metro; the median precinct is the 18th one in order of magnitude ($35 + 1 = 36$; $36 \div 2 = 18$).

**STEP 1**  Find the 18th (the middle) item. There are 6 precincts with 5 or fewer crimes and 9 with 6 to 10 crimes. This means 15 precincts have 10 or fewer crimes, so the median is greater than 10. The 18th item is in the third class. In fact, it is the 3rd item in the third class.

**STEP 2**   Calculate how far into the class the median item is. Remember that for grouped data, we assume that the items are equally distributed throughout the class interval. Since there are 14 items in the third class and the median is the 3rd item, the median is $\frac{3}{14}$ths of the distance into the class. So in this case, the median is $11 + \frac{3}{14}$ of the third class.

**STEP 3**   Calculate how far $\frac{3}{14}$ths is into the third class. To do this, simply multiply this fraction by the class interval (in this case, 5). The resulting number ($\frac{3}{14} \times 5 = 1.07$) should be added to the lower limit of this class (in this case, 11) for a median of 12.07. The procedure you used to calculate how far into an interval a particular value (in this case, the median) lies is called **interpolation**.

**interpolation**

Some practice is in order. In the space provided, calculate the median score on the Morgan City civil service exam. The data are given in Table 2.8.

**TABLE 2.8**
Distribution of Morgan City Civil Service Scores, July Exam

| Civil Service Score | Number of Applicants |
|---|---|
| 50–60 | 14 |
| 60–70 | 11 |
| 70–80 | 12 |
| 80–90 | 33 |
| 90–100 | 20 |
| | 90 |

Calculate here.

Class median is in which class? _____

How far is the median into the class? _____

Multiply fraction by class interval = _____

Add to lower limit of this class to get the median = _____

_____

If you got a median civil service score of 82.6, congratulations. If not, check your calculations. Did you find the $45\frac{1}{2}$th item?

## MODES FOR GROUPED DATA

The crude mode (so named because it is a rough approximation) for grouped data is the midpoint of the class with the greatest frequency. For the Metro crimes example, the mode is 13. For the Morgan City example, the mode is 85.

## THE MEAN VERSUS THE MEDIAN

In most situations, data can be summarized well with the mean. However, situations can arise in which the mean gives a misleading indication of central tendency, and so the median is preferred. When extreme values or outliers occur on a variable, the mean is distorted or pulled toward them. By contrast, since the median is the value of the middle case—once the data points have been arranged in order—it will remain in the middle of the distribution even if the variable has an extreme value. In this situation, the median is the preferred measure of central tendency. (Chapter 3 returns to this issue.)

For example, suppose that a public administrator needed to estimate the average price of houses in a city in order to apply for a federal grant. She pulls a random sample of ten homes sold recently and discovers that nine of them sold for between $80,000 and $120,000, and one sold for well over $1 million. The mean housing price will be grossly inflated by the one outlying case and will yield a value unrepresentative of the price of houses in the city. The median will not be affected by the deviant case, however, and will have a value near the middle of housing prices, between $80,000 and $120,000.

## CHAPTER SUMMARY

Measures of central tendency are numbers used to summarize a body of data by indicating middle (or central) points in the data. Each measure of central tendency has a distinct meaning and method of calculation. The mean is the arithmetic average of all data points. The median is the number that is greater than 50% of all the data points and less than 50% of all the data points. The mode is the data value that occurs most often. This chapter illustrates the calculations for all three measures of central tendency, for both grouped (frequency distribution) and ungrouped data.

In the examples in this chapter and in the problems that follow, we use small numbers of cases to ease the burden of calculation of measures of central tendency, while still illustrating the crucial concepts and points. In actual situations in public administration, you will typically deal with much larger numbers of cases, and a computer will perform the necessary calculations. The concepts and points remain the same, however.

## PROBLEMS

**2.1** During a recent crackdown on speeding, the Luckenback, Texas, police department issued the following number of citations on seven consecutive days: 59, 61, 68, 57, 63, 50, and 55. Calculate the mean and median number of speeding citations.

**2.2** The dean of Southwestern State University is concerned that many faculty members at SSU are too old to be effective teachers. She asks each department to send her information on the average age of its faculty. The head of the sociology department does not wish to "lie" with statistics but, knowing the preference of the dean, he would like to make the department appear youthful. The names and ages of the sociology department's members are listed in the accompanying table. Calculate both the mean age and the median age. Should the department send the dean the mean age or the median age?

| Member | Age |
| --- | --- |
| Durkheim | 64 |
| Campbell | 31 |
| Weber | 65 |
| Likert | 27 |
| Stanley | 35 |
| Katz | 40 |
| Lazarsfeld | 33 |

**2.3** The average number of sick leave days used per employee per year in Normal, Oklahoma, is 6.7. The city manager feels the public works department is abusing its sick leave privileges. The only information available is the frequency distribution given in the accompanying table. Calculate the mean and median number of sick days used by the public works employees. Is the department abusing its sick leave?

| Number of Days of Sick Leave Taken | Number of Employees |
|:---:|:---:|
| 0–2 | 4 |
| 3–5 | 7 |
| 6–8 | 7 |
| 9–11 | 14 |
| 12–14 | 6 |

**2.4**   The U.S. Army is allowed only five test firings of the Lance missile. The following figures represent the number of feet the missles missed the target by: 26, 147, 35, 63, 51. Calculate the mean and the median. Which should the Army report?

**2.5**   The Department of Welfare wants to know the average outside income for all welfare recipients in the state. Calculate both the mean and the median from the data in the accompanying table.

| Income | Number of Families |
|:---:|:---:|
| 0–300 | 25 |
| 300–600 | 163 |
| 600–900 | 354 |
| 900–1200 | 278 |
| 1200–1500 | 421 |
| 1500–1800 | 603 |
| 1800–2100 | 211 |
| 2100–2400 | 84 |
| 2400–2700 | 32 |
| 2700–3000 | 5 |

**2.6**   When should the median be used in preference to the mean?

**2.7**   From the data in the accompanying table, calculate the mean and median age for the Quechan Indian Tribe. Which is the more appropriate measure?

| Age | Persons |
| --- | --- |
| 0–4 | 213 |
| 5–9 | 215 |
| 10–14 | 242 |
| 15–19 | 194 |
| 20–24 | 168 |
| 25–29 | 162 |
| 30–34 | 111 |
| 35–39 | 82 |
| 40–44 | 74 |
| 45–49 | 50 |
| 50–54 | 53 |
| 55–59 | 46 |
| 60–64 | 24 |
| 65–85 | 86 |

**2.8**  The legislature has limited the Bureau of the Audit to a monthly average of 34 employees. For the first nine months of the year, the employment figures were 31, 36, 34, 35, 37, 32, 36, 37, 34. Does it appear that the bureau will make the target? How many employees can the bureau have over the next three months and still meet the target?

**2.9**  The collective bargaining agreement between Carson County and the Federation of Social Workers specifies that the average case load for caseworkers cannot exceed 45. Using the accompanying data, the county claims compliance, yet the union argues that the county has violated the agreement. Who is correct?

| Caseworker | Case Load |
| --- | --- |
| A | 43 |
| B | 57 |
| C | 35 |
| D | 87 |
| E | 36 |
| F | 93 |
| G | 45 |
| H | 48 |
| I | 41 |
| J | 40 |

**2.10**  Refer to Problem 2.7. What is the mode age? Is this an appropriate measure of central tendency in this case?

**2.11**  Calculate the mean and median for the marriage license data in Problem 1.6 in Chapter 1.

**2.12**    Calculate the mean and median for the marriage license data in Problem 1.7 (Chapter 1). Compare these results with those obtained in Problem 2.11. Write a short memorandum addressing the question of whether service to the public in the issuance of marriage licenses has improved or declined over the past two years.

**2.13**    The director of the Doctor of Public Administration (DPA) program at Federal University is developing a report to the faculty on the entering class of DPA students. The director wants to present a statistical profile of the new students, including their grade point average (GPA) earned in master's degree programs. The GPAs for the eight entering students are 3.1, 3.7, 3.6, 3.2, 3.8, 3.5, 2.9, and 4.0. Calculate the mean and median GPA earned by these students in their master's degree studies.

**2.14**    Some faculty at Federal University have complained to the director of the Doctor of Public Administration program that DPA students typically have strong verbal skills but lack mathematical preparation. (Fortunately, a statistics book is available in public administration to meet the needs of these students.) In response to the complaint, the DPA director assembles the scores on the verbal and quantitative sections of the Graduate Record Examination (GRE) for the class of eight entering DPA students. Each section is scored on a scale of 200 to 800. The GRE scores of each student are listed below.

| GRE Verbal | GRE Quantitative |
| --- | --- |
| 590 | 620 |
| 680 | 510 |
| 630 | 550 |
| 700 | 600 |
| 610 | 540 |
| 650 | 570 |
| 620 | 590 |
| 670 | 580 |

Based on your analysis of these data, evaluate the complaint lodged by the faculty members at Federal University.

## CHAPTER 3

# MEASURES OF DISPERSION

A useful descriptive statistic complementary to the measures of central tendency is a measure of dispersion. A **measure of dispersion** tells how much the data do or do not cluster about the mean. For example, the data listed in Table 3.1 show the number of daily arrests in Wheezer, South Dakota, for 1989, 1990, and 1991. The mean number of daily arrests for all three years is the same (2.75). How much the daily arrests cluster about the mean, however, varies. In 1990, the numbers cluster less about the mean than they do in 1989. In 1991, the arrests cluster closer to the mean than do either the 1990 or the 1989 arrests. This clustering is illustrated by the frequency polygons in Figure 3.1. Clearly the dispersion of the data is a valuable descriptive statistic in analyzing a set of data.

**measure of dispersion**

Most statistics texts discuss a variety of dispersion measures, such as the range, the average deviation, the interquartile deviation, and the standard deviation. Of all these measures, only the standard deviation has any real value statistically, and hence this statistic is the only one we will discuss in this chapter. The only thing you need to remember about the other measures of dispersion is what they are. The **range** is the difference between the largest value and the smallest value. The **interquartile deviation** is the difference between two numbers. These two numbers are selected so that the middle 50% of all values fall between them. The **average deviation** is the average difference between the mean and all other values. If these measures of dispersion seem appropriate for any projects you are interested in, consult general statistics book to find out how to calculate them (for example, see the text by Neter, Wasserman, and Whitmore 1978; a list of other suitable texts is given in the bibliography at the end of the book).

**range**

**interquartile deviation**

**average deviation**

**TABLE 3.1**

Number of Daily Police Arrests in Wheezer, South Dakota

| Number of Arrests | Number of Days | | |
|---|---|---|---|
| | *1989* | *1990* | *1991* |
| 0 | 24 | 36 | 10 |
| 1 | 36 | 54 | 36 |
| 2 | 95 | 65 | 109 |
| 3 | 104 | 74 | 118 |
| 4 | 66 | 84 | 66 |
| 5 | 40 | 52 | 26 |
| | 365 | 365 | 365 |

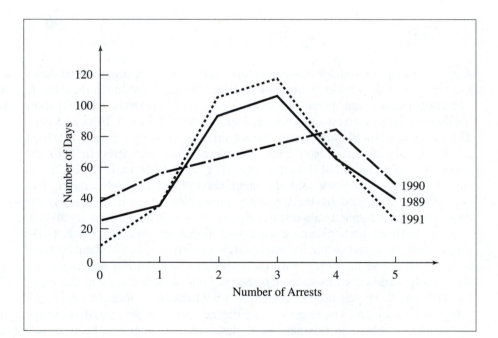

**FIGURE 3.1**

Frequency Polygons for the Data in Table 3.1

## THE STANDARD DEVIATION

**standard deviation**

The standard deviation is the most common measure of dispersion. The **standard deviation** is the square root of the average squared deviation of the data from the mean; that is, the standard deviation is based on the squared differences between every item in a data set and the mean of that set. An example can explain this process far better than words.

Normal, Oklahoma, has five street-cleaning crews. Listed in Table 3.2 are the

**TABLE 3.2**

Blocks of Streets Cleaned by Work Crews

| Work Crew | Number of Blocks |
|-----------|------------------|
| A | 126 |
| B | 140 |
| C | 153 |
| D | 110 |
| E | 136 |
|   | 665 |

numbers of blocks of city streets cleaned by the five crews. To determine the standard deviation for these data, follow these steps.

**STEP 1**  From the data, calculate the mean. Recall from Chapter 2 that to calculate the mean, you need to add the data values for all cases (here, 665) and divide that sum by the number of cases, or N (here, 5).

**STEP 2**  Subtract the mean from every item in the set. In this situation, subtract 133 from the number of streets cleaned by each crew. Often a table like Table 3.3 is helpful in performing these calculations. Note that the sum of the differences equals zero. In fact, in any distribution of data, the sum of the differences of the data values from the mean will always equal zero.

**TABLE 3.3**

Calculating the Differences

| Number of Blocks | Subtract the Mean | Difference |
|------------------|-------------------|------------|
| 126 | 133 | −7 |
| 140 | 133 | 7 |
| 153 | 133 | 20 |
| 110 | 133 | −23 |
| 136 | 133 | 3 |
|     |     | 0 |

**TABLE 3.4**

Calculating the Difference Squared

| Blocks | Mean | Difference | Difference Squared |
|--------|------|------------|--------------------|
| 126 | 133 | −7 | 49 |
| 140 | 133 | 7 | 49 |
| 153 | 133 | 20 | 400 |
| 110 | 133 | −23 | 529 |
| 136 | 133 | 3 | 9 |

**STEP 3**   Take the difference between each number and the mean (the third column), and square these values. As noted in Step 2, the differences sum to zero, regardless of how condensed or dispersed the data values are about the mean. Squaring the differences avoids this problem and is instrumental in measuring the actual amount of dispersion in the data (see Table 3.4).

**STEP 4**   Sum the squared differences. You should get a sum of 1036.

variance

**STEP 5**   Divide this sum by the number of items (N = 5). This number (207.2) is called the **variance**.

**STEP 6**   Take the square root of the variance to find the standard deviation (14.4). If you do not have a calculator to calculate the square root, look up the value in a square root table. Since we squared the differences between the mean and the data values in Step 3 (so that the differences would not sum to zero), it now makes sense to take the square root. In this manner, the standard deviation converts the variance from squared units to the original units of measurement.

After calculating this relatively simple statistic, you should not be surprised to learn that statisticians have a complex formula for the standard deviation. The formula for $\sigma$ (the Greek letter sigma, which statisticians call the standard deviation) is

$$\sigma = \sqrt{\frac{\sum_{i=1}^{N} (X_i - \mu)^2}{N}}$$

This formula is not as formidable as it seems. $(X_i - \mu)$ is nothing more than Step 2, subtracting the mean from each value. $(X_i - \mu)^2$ is Step 3, the squaring of the differences. $\sum_{i=1}^{N} (X_i - \mu)^2$ is Step 4, the summing of all the squared differences. The entire formula within the square root sign completes Step 5, the division by the number of items. Finally, the square root sign is Step 6.

The smaller the standard deviation in a set of data, the more closely the data cluster about the mean. For example, the standard deviations for the Wheezer, South Dakota, police arrests are 1.34 for 1989, 1.55 for 1990, and 1.16 for 1991. This calculation reinforces our perception that the 1990 data were the most dispersed and the 1991 data were the least dispersed.

## STANDARD DEVIATIONS FOR _____
## GROUPED DATA _____

The logic for calculating standard deviations from grouped data is the same as that for calculating a standard deviation from ungrouped data. *Again, never calculate a standard deviation from grouped data if the ungrouped data are available.* The data shown in Table 3.5 on Metro serious crimes per precinct will be used to illustrate this process.

**TABLE 3.5**

Serious Crimes per Precinct, Metro,
Week of March 7, 1992

| Number of Crimes | Number of Precincts |
|---|---|
| 1–5 | 6 |
| 6–10 | 9 |
| 11–15 | 14 |
| 16–20 | 5 |
| 21–25 | 1 |
| | 35 |

**STEP 1**    Calculate the mean. Using the steps outlined in Chapter 2 and illustrated in Table 3.6, you should find the mean to be 11.

**TABLE 3.6**

Calculating the Mean

| Class | Frequency | Midpoint | $F \times M$ |
|---|---|---|---|
| 1–5 | 6 | 3 | 18 |
| 6–10 | 9 | 8 | 72 |
| 11–15 | 14 | 13 | 182 |
| 16–20 | 5 | 18 | 90 |
| 21–25 | 1 | 23 | 23 |

Sum $F \times M = 385$
    Mean $= 385 \div 35 = 11$

**STEP 2**    Subtract the mean from the midpoint of each class. Note that the value of each item in the class is now considered to be the midpoint of the class (refer to Table 3.7).

**TABLE 3.7**

Calculating the Differences

| Frequency | Midpoint | Mean | Difference | Squared Difference |
|---|---|---|---|---|
| 6 | 3 | 11 | −8 | |
| 9 | 8 | 11 | −3 | |
| 14 | 13 | 11 | +2 | |
| 5 | 18 | 11 | +7 | |
| 1 | 23 | 11 | +12 | |

**STEP 3**    Square the differences between the mean and the class midpoints, and enter them in Table 3.7. You should get the following values: 64, 9, 4, 49, 144.

**STEP 3½**    This step is unique to grouped data. Step 4 is to sum the squared differences. But for the first class, there are six precincts with three crimes each (using the class midpoint). For these six precincts, the squared difference is 64. To get the correct sum of the squared differences, multiply the squared difference by the frequency for that class. You should get the results shown in Table 3.8.

**STEP 4**    Sum the squared differences. In this case, sum the numbers in the $F \times S$ column (frequency × squared differences). The answer is 910.

**STEP 5**    Divide this sum by $N$ (in this case, 35) to get the variance (26).

**TABLE 3.8**
Squared Difference Times Frequency

| Frequency | Squared Difference | $F \times S$ |
|---|---|---|
| 6 | 64 | 384 |
| 9 | 9 | 81 |
| 14 | 4 | 56 |
| 5 | 49 | 245 |
| 1 | 144 | 144 |

**STEP 6**    The square root of the variance is the standard deviation; in this case, the standard deviation is 5.1.

## SHAPE OF A FREQUENCY DISTRIBUTION

In addition to measuring the central tendency (Chapter 2) and dispersion of a variable, the public manager also needs to know something about the "shape" of the frequency distribution of data values. The shape arises from plotting the values of the variable horizontally against their corresponding frequency of occurrence, plotted vertically.

**symmetric**    Figure 3.2 shows a **symmetric** distribution. The data are evenly balanced on either side of the center or middle of the distribution. When a distribution is basically symmetrical, the mean and median will have very similar values.

**asymmetric**    The data may not be so evenly balanced, of course. In an **asymmetric** distribution, the data fall more on one side of the center or middle than on the other side. In that case, skewness exists in the data.

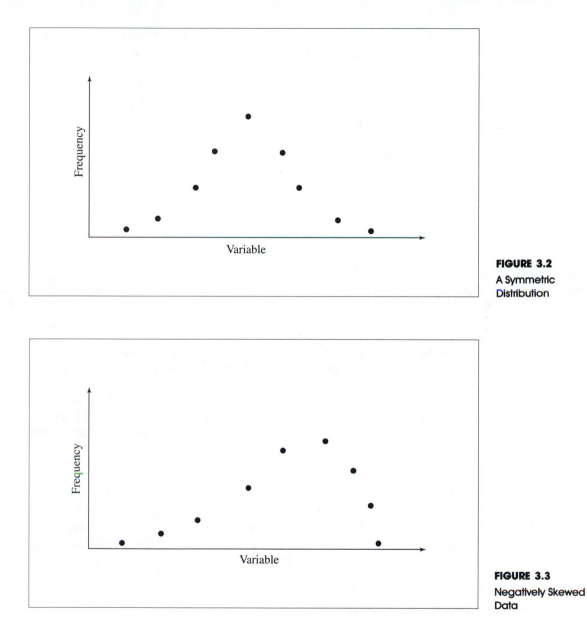

**FIGURE 3.2**
A Symmetric
Distribution

**FIGURE 3.3**
Negatively Skewed
Data

**Negatively skewed data** are data that have a few extremely low numbers that distort the mean. Negatively skewed data form a frequency distribution like the one in Figure 3.3.

**Positively skewed data** are data that have a few large numbers that distort the mean. The frequency distribution of positively skewed data resembles the one shown in Figure 3.4.

**negatively skewed data**

**positively skewed data**

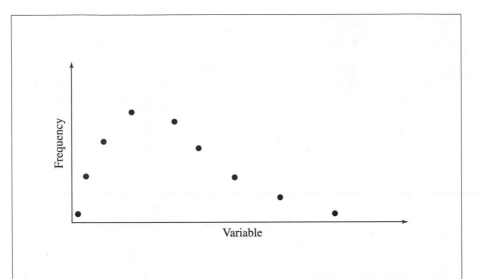

**FIGURE 3.4**
Positively Skewed
Data

If data are strongly skewed, the mean is not a good measure of central tendency. In that case, the median is a better measure, since it is basically unaffected by skewness.

Skewness is a difficult statistic to calculate by hand. If you want to learn how, consult Palumbo (1969). If you are sane, you will rely on a computer program to do it. Many programs of descriptive statistics will print out something similar to the following:

$$skewness = 1.34$$

This value indicates that the data are positively skewed and, therefore, the mean is artificially high. Skewness figures around zero indicate an unskewed (or symmetric) distribution. Negative numbers indicate negative skewness and, therefore, a mean that is artificially low.

## CHAPTER SUMMARY

Measures of dispersion indicate how closely a set of data clusters around the midpoint of the data. Measures of dispersion include the range, the interquartile deviation, the average deviation, the variance, and the standard deviation. The first three of these measures are not as useful statistically as the last two.

The standard deviation is the square root of the average squared deviation of the data from the mean, that is, the square root of the variance. This chapter illustrates the calculation of the standard deviation for both grouped and ungrouped data. A smaller standard deviation (and variance) indicates that the data cluster closely around the mean.

Another statistic that can be useful is the skewness of the data. Negatively skewed data are data that have a few very low numbers that will distort the mean. Positively skewed data are data that have a few large numbers that will distort the mean. For skewed data the median is the preferred measure of central tendency.

## PROBLEMS

**3.1**  Charles Jones, the local fire chief, wants to evaluate the efficiency of two different water pumps. Brand A pumps an average of 5000 gallons per minute with a standard deviation of 1000 gallons. Brand B pumps 5200 gallons per minute with a standard deviation of 1500 gallons. What can you say about the two types of pumps that would be valuable to Chief Jones?

**3.2**  Bobby Gene England, research analyst for the mayor of Chickasaw, is asked to provide information on the number of burglaries per day in Chickasaw for the past two weeks. For the accompanying data, calculate the mean, median, and standard deviation for Bobby Gene.

| 6 | 9 | 0 |
|----|----|----|
| 11 | 12 | 5 |
| 4 | 7 | 10 |
| 3 | 3 | 12 |
| 9 | 8 | |

median = _____

mean = _____

standard deviation = _____

**3.3**  Helen Curbside, chief custodial engineer for Placerville, has entered into the department computer the number of tons of garbage collected per day by all work crews in the city during a one-week period. One statistic on the computer puzzles her: "Skewness = $-2.46$." Interpret this result for Helen. What does it suggest about the performance of the city work crews?

**3.4**  Scotty Allen, whom you met in Chapter 1, now wants to know the mean, median, and standard deviation for Maxwell, New York, civil service exam scores. Using the accompanying data, perform the necessary calculations.

| Exam Score | Number of Applicants |
|------------|---------------------|
| 61–65 | 20 |
| 66–70 | 13 |
| 71–75 | 47 |
| 76–80 | 56 |
| 81–85 | 33 |
| 86–90 | 27 |
| 91–95 | 41 |
| 96–100 | 34 |

**3.5** Refer to Problem 2.4 on the Lance missile system (Chapter 2). Five shots missed the target by 26, 147, 35, 63, and 51 feet, respectively. What is the standard deviation of the data?

**3.6** The chief of supply for Winsor Hills, New Jersey, is concerned that certain orders are not filled within a uniform time period. She believes that requests for equipment should have a standard deviation no greater than 2.0 days. Calculate the standard deviation for the chief from the accompanying data. Also calculate all measures of central tendency. What can you tell the chief?

| Days to Fill Order | Number of Items |
|--------------------|-----------------|
| 0–1 | 10 |
| 2–3 | 14 |
| 4–5 | 17 |
| 6–7 | 12 |
| 8–9 | 4 |

**3.7** The head of research and development for the U.S. Army must select one of the antitank weapons from the accompanying listing for procurement. The listed results indicate the distance away from the intended target that 100 test rounds fell. Which system should the army select, and why?

| Weapon | Mean | Standard Deviation |
|--------|------|--------------------|
| A | 22.4 | 15.9 |
| B | 18.7 | 36.5 |
| C | 24.6 | 19.7 |

**3.8** The Whitehawk Indian Tribe believes the Bureau of Indian Affairs responds faster to grant applications from the Kinsa Tribe than it does to grants for the Whitehawk Tribe. From the accompanying data, what can you tell the Whitehawks?

Days to Respond to Grant
Applications

| Whitehawk | Kinsa |
|---|---|
| 64 | 50 |
| 58 | 72 |
| 66 | 74 |
| 54 | 46 |
| 70 | 75 |
| 66 | 81 |
| 51 | 43 |
| 56 | 46 |

**3.9**  An audit of the Utah Rehabilitation Agency reveals that the average 26 closure (rehabilitation talk for a successful effort) takes 193 days with a standard deviation of 49 days and a skewness of 3.15. What does this mean in English?

**3.10**  The U.S. Postal Service is concerned with the time it takes to deliver mail. It would like not only to deliver mail as quickly as possible but also to have as little variation as possible. Twenty letters are mailed from New York collection boxes to Cutbank, Montana. From the following number of days for delivery, what can you tell the Postal Service? Calculate all measures of central tendency and dispersion.

| 2 | 5 | 3 | 4 | 3 | 2 | 6 | 1 | 3 | 3 |
|---|---|---|---|---|---|---|---|---|---|
| 4 | 3 | 8 | 3 | 5 | 2 | 3 | 4 | 4 | 3 |

**3.11**  An employee at the Purchasing Department claims that he and a few other employees do almost all the work. In support of his claim, he collects the accompanying data on the number of purchase orders cleared and processed by each of the sixteen members of the department in a typical week. Calculate all measures of central tendency and dispersion for these data and evaluate this employee's claim. Do a few employees do almost all the work?

| 12 | 22 | 8 | 14 | 15 | 32 | 17 | 24 |
|---|---|---|---|---|---|---|---|
| 20 | 37 | 15 | 23 | 16 | 40 | 19 | 21 |

**3.12**  The director of the Department of Motor Vehicles (DMV) has become concerned about the health of the department's employees. She issues a directive to DMV offices advising all mangers to encourage employees to get a least 60 minutes of exercise per day. Following are the data on the number of minutes exercised per day (on the average) by the ten employees of the Hillsborough DMV office. Calculate all measures of central tendency and dispersion for these data. How well do these employees meet the standard for exercise recommended by the director of the Department of Motor Vehicles?

| 75 | 20 | 15 | 95 | 30 | 100 | 40 | 10 | 90 | 120 |

**3.13**  Complaints have reached the city manager of Normal that it is taking too long to pay bills submitted to the city. You are assigned to check how long it takes by looking at a few bills. Following are the lengths of time in days that it has taken the city to pay seven bills. Calculate the mean, median, and standard deviation. Would you report the mean or the median? Why?

| 34 | 27 | 64 | 31 | 30 | 26 | 35 |

**3.14**  The Texas State Penitentiary is concerned about the number of violent incidents in its prisons. After examining the ten prisons in the Texas system, a data analyst finds the following pattern of data for the number of violent incidents last month:

| 17 | 21 | 42 | 32 | 16 | 24 | 31 | 15 | 22 | 26 |

Calculate the mean, median, and standard deviation. Should the penitentiary use the mean or the median in its analysis? Why?

# PART II

# PROBABILITY

## CHAPTER 4

# INTRODUCTION TO

# PROBABILITY

Probability may be the most useful quantitiative technique available to a public manager. **Probability** tells a manager how likely it is that certain events will occur. Using the rules of probability as discussed in this and the following chapters, public managers can solve a variety of problems. For example, the head of maintenance in a city could use probability to determine how frequently major breakdowns will occur in the city's automobile and truck fleet and so could schedule maintenance personnel accordingly. A fire chief could use probability to allocate his work force to the areas of the city where most fires occur. An affirmative action officer could use probability to determine whether an agency discriminates.

    This chapter covers the basic rules and assumptions of probability. These rules and assumptions will permit us to cover some advanced probability techniques in the next two chapters.

**probability**

## BASIC CONCEPTS IN
## PROBABILITY

The basic **law of probability** (which you should commit to memory) is this: given that all possible outcomes of a given event are equally likely, the probability of any specified outcome is equal to the ratio of the number of ways that that outcome could be achieved to the total number of ways that all possible outcomes can be achieved. Now what does that mean? Equally likely events are events that all have an equal chance of occurring. If the events in question are equally likely, then the basic law of probability can be used, as follows.

**law of probability**

**STEP 1**    Determine the number of possible ways that the outcome you are interested in can occur.

**STEP 2**    Determine the number of possible ways that every possible outcome can occur.

**STEP 3**    Divide the first number by the second; the answer gives you the probability that the event in question will occur.

Let us look at some examples. Suppose you have an unbiased coin (an unbiased coin is one that has an equal probability of coming up heads or tails). What is the probability that the coin will land head side up if flipped? The number of possible ways a head can appear is one; there is only one head per coin. The number of total possible outcomes is two; a coin flip may come up either a head or a tail. Therefore, the probability of obtaining a head when flipping a coin is 1 divided by 2, or .5.

The probability of rolling a six on one roll of an unbiased die is .167. There are six sides to a die, all of which are equally likely to land that side up. Only one of those sides has a six on it, so the probability of rolling a six is 1 divided by 6, or .167. The probability of drawing a spade from a deck of 52 playing cards is the number of spades (13) divided by the total number of cards, or .25.

The same logic applies to events with more than one trial (that is, a flip, or a roll, or a draw). For example, what is the probability of obtaining two heads if an unbiased coin is flipped twice? This probability may be determined by a simple probability tree. On the first flip, a coin may land on either a head or a tail, as shown in Figure 4.1. If the result was a head on the first flip, the second flip could be either a head or a tail. If the coin was a tail on the first flip, then on the second flip it could be either a head or a tail. The probability tree in Figure 4.2 shows all possible results of two flips of a coin.

Examining the tree in Figure 4.2, you can see that the number of ways that two heads will appear is 1. The number of ways that all possible outcomes can occur is 4. Therefore, the probability of obtaining two heads on two flips of an unbiased coin is .25.

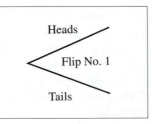

**FIGURE 4.1**

Probability Tree for
One Flip of a Coin

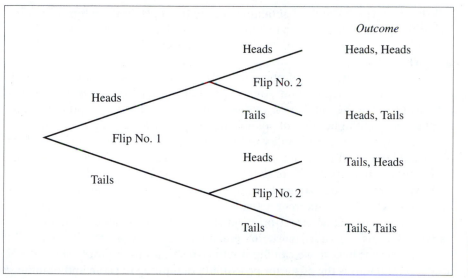

**FIGURE 4.2**
Probability Tree for
Two Flips of a Coin

The same logic can be applied to more than two trials in any event. For example, draw the probability tree in the space provided for all possible outcomes when a coin is flipped three times.

What is the probability that you will obtain three heads on three consecutive flips of a coin? If your answer was .125 (or $1 \div 8$), congratulations. If not, recheck your probability tree.

Using this same tree, determine the probability of obtaining two heads on three flips of a coin. Examining the tree reveals that the probability of two heads is .375 (three combinations: head-head-tail, head-tail-head, tail-head-head).

What is the probability of obtaining exactly two tails on three flips of a coin? Using the probability tree, you should find a probability of .375. What is the probability of obtaining three tails on three consecutive flips of an unbiased coin? The answer is .125.

What is the probability of obtaining *two or more* heads on three flips of an unbiased coin? In this situation, you would add the number of ways of achieving three heads (1) to the number of ways of achieving two heads (3) and divide this number by the total number of possible outcomes (8), for a probability of .5.

Finally, what is the probability of obtaining 0, 1, 2, or 3 heads on three flips of an unbiased coin? The answer is 1.0. This is one way to check that your probabilities are correct. The probability for all possible events should be 1.0.

**a priori probability**

**posterior probability**

Now let us consider some definitions. Any probability that can be determined logically before an event actually occurs is called an **a priori probability**. The examples just given are a priori probabilities. Probabilities generated by numerous trials are called **posterior probabilities**. For example, if we do not know if a coin is biased, we can flip it numerous times to find out. The ratio of heads to total flips is the posterior probability of flipping the coin and obtaining a head. An unbiased coin has a probability of .5 of coming up heads. Posterior probabilities may also be called *long-run probabilities*.

## AN APPLICATION TO
## GAME THEORY

Probability forms the basis of most games of chance as well as of decision theory (see Chapter 22). Since half of the states currently operate state lotteries, and some jurisdictions have a variety of other forms of legalized gambling, understanding how such games work is useful for the public manager. Let us construct a simple game in which people pay $1 to play. A coin is flipped; if heads comes up, the person wins $2.00; if tails, the player wins nothing.

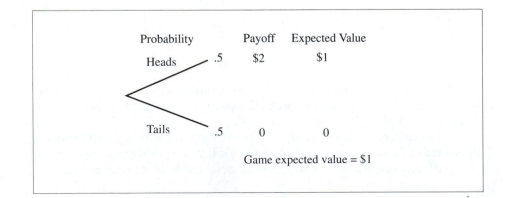

**FIGURE 4.3**

Simple Game of Chance

One thing a manager needs to do to assess whether or not a game will be profitable is to calculate the expected value of the game. The expected value of the game is nothing more than the average payoff per game played if the game were played *many times*. The expected value of any outcome is the probability that the outcome will occur multiplied by the payoff for that outcome. For the entire game, the expected value is the sum of all the expected values for the individual options. The expected value for the game in Figure 4.3 is [($2 × .5) + (0 × .5)], or $1. An expected value of $1 means that, on the average, the game will pay $1 to a player every time the game is played. Such a game would generate no profits that could be used for public programs. The game can be altered in two ways to generate income for the manager. First, the probabilities of each occurrence can be changed (by using a computer rather than flipping a coin), as shown in Figure 4.4.

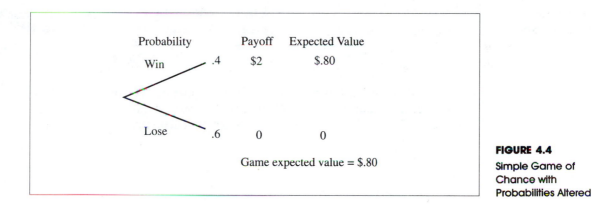

Probability      Payoff    Expected Value

Win        .4       $2          $.80

Lose       .6        0           0

Game expected value = $.80

**FIGURE 4.4**
Simple Game of Chance with Probabilities Altered

Second, the payoff for the options can be changed, as shown in Figure 4.5.

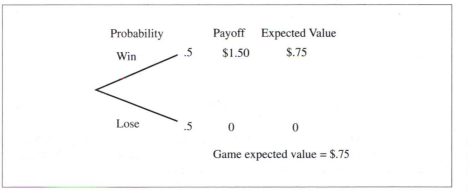

Probability      Payoff    Expected Value

Win        .5      $1.50         $.75

Lose       .5        0           0

Game expected value = $.75

**FIGURE 4.5**
Simple Game of Chance with Payoff Altered

The games in Figures 4.4 and 4.5 generate profits for the gamemaker; but the problem is in getting people to play such simple games, since they can easily see that they are better off by not playing. To get around this problem, we need to make a more complicated game, such as that in Figure 4.6.

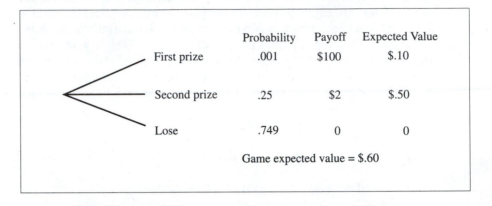

|  | Probability | Payoff | Expected Value |
|---|---|---|---|
| First prize | .001 | $100 | $.10 |
| Second prize | .25 | $2 | $.50 |
| Lose | .749 | 0 | 0 |

Game expected value = $.60

**FIGURE 4.6**
More Complex
Game of Chance

With a $100 first prize, this game should attract more players and yet produce revenue for the game manager. What would happen if the price of playing increased to $2 and all the prizes were doubled? Calculate the expected value of this game in the space provided.

Doubling the playing price and doubling the payoff has no impact on the profitability of the game.

State lotteries tend to make the games attractive to play by offering very large prizes. Calculate the expected value of the game in Figure 4.7, which has a $1 million first prize (assume that a playing chance cost $1).

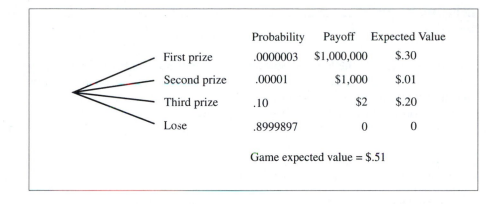

|  | Probability | Payoff | Expected Value |
|---|---|---|---|
| First prize | .0000003 | $1,000,000 | $.30 |
| Second prize | .00001 | $1,000 | $.01 |
| Third prize | .10 | $2 | $.20 |
| Lose | .8999897 | 0 | 0 |

Game expected value = $.51

**FIGURE 4.7**
Lottery-Style Game
of Chance

Such a game is probably much more attractive to players than is the game in Figure 4.6. Is it a more profitable game for players? What does this tell you about the design of public lotteries?

A word of caution about expected values is in order. For expected values to be meaningful, a game or a probability tree must be played/used many times. This is not a problem for a state government, since it can expect that millions of people might buy lottery tickets. It can be a problem for individuals, however. The game in Figure 4.8 illustrates this.

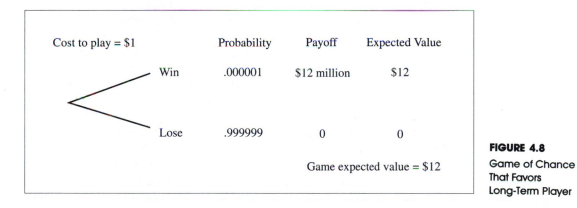

Cost to play = $1

|  | Probability | Payoff | Expected Value |
|---|---|---|---|
| Win | .000001 | $12 million | $12 |
| Lose | .999999 | 0 | 0 |

Game expected value = $12

**FIGURE 4.8**
Game of Chance
That Favors
Long-Term Player

Even though this game has an expected value of $12, an individual would be rational not to play this game. To acheive the expected value of $12 per play, an individual would have to play this game several million times. Few individuals would have the resources to convert this expected value into individual benefits.

# INTRODUCTION TO

# PROBABILITY LOGIC

To introduce you to the logic of probability, we will use Table 4.1, which lists data from the Flandreau income maintenance experiment. These data were collected to determine the impact of a guaranteed minimum income and other welfare options on the stability of welfare families.

**TABLE 4.1**

Preliminary Data, Flandreau Income Maintenance Experiment: Number of Families

| Treatment | Impact on the Family | | |
|---|---|---|---|
| | *Family Dissolved* | *Family Stayed Together* | *Total* |
| No welfare | 5 | 20 | 25 |
| Normal welfare | 15 | 65 | 80 |
| Guaranteed income | 20 | 75 | 95 |
| Income plus incentives | 10 | 50 | 60 |
| Workfare | 0 | 40 | 40 |
| | 50 | 250 | 300 |

For the data on the Flandreau income maintenance experiment, what is the probability that a family in the experiment received workfare? The probability that a family received workfare is the number of families that received workfare divided by the total number of families, or .133 (40 ÷ 300).

What is the probability that a family dissolved ("dissolved" is social science jargon for "the father abandoned the family")? Since 50 of the 300 families dissolved, the probability of a family dissolving is .167 (50 ÷ 300). If the situation that a family has dissolved is referred to as situation $F$, then the symbol for the probability of this event is $P(F)$.

What is the probability that a family dissolved or that it did not receive any welfare at all? In this situation, we are asking for the probability that either of two events might have occurred. Determining this probability is the same as determining the earlier probabilities. It is the ratio of the number of families that received no welfare plus the number of families that dissolved to the total number of families. The number of families that received no welfare is 25, and the number of families that dissolved is 50, for a total of 75. This total, however, counts the 5 families that received no welfare *and* dissolved twice. Subtracting this number (5) and dividing the difference (70) by the total number of families yields a probability of .233 (70 ÷ 300). Statisticians refer to the probability of one event or another as the **union** of two probabilities. Symbolically, this is denoted as $P(A \cup B)$ (read as "$P$ of $A$ union $B$," or "the probability of $A$ union $B$").

**union**

What is the probability that a family received a guaranteed income and that the family stayed together? In this situation, the logic is the same as used before. We divide the total number of families that received a guaranteed income and stayed together (75) by the total number of families. The probability that a family received a guaranteed income and stayed together is .25. The probability of two events occurring simultaneously is referred to as a **joint probability**. The symbolic representation of this is $P(A \cap B)$ (read as "$P$ of $A$ intersection $B$").

**joint probability**

What is the probability that a family dissolved, given that it received an income plus incentives? The number of families receiving an income plus incentives that also dissolved is 10. The total number of families in this situation, however, is not 300. We are interested only in those families that received an income plus incentives, a total of 60 families. The probability that a family dissolved, given that it received an income plus incentives, is $10 \div 60$, or .167. The probability of one event given that another event happened is called a **conditional probability**. The symbolic way of representing this is $P(A|B)$ (read as "the probability of $A$ given $B$," or "$P$ of $A$ given $B$").

**conditional probability**

## GENERAL RULES OF PROBABILITY

To this point, we have intuitively discussed probability and its relationships. Now it is necessary to provide some general rules for understanding probability.

### THE GENERAL RULE OF ADDITION

The **general rule of addition** applies whenever you want to know the probability that either of two events occurred. Statisticians express the general rule of addition symbolically as

**general rule of addition**

$$P(A \cup B) = P(A) + P(B) - P(A \cap B)$$

Although this rule may appear complex, it is actually fairly simple. In English, the rule states that the probability of either of two events occurring $[P(A \cup B)]$ is equal to the probability that one event will occur $[P(A)]$ plus the probability that the other event will occur $[P(B)]$ minus the probability that both events will occur simultaneously $[P(A \cap B)]$. Remember that the probability of both events occurring at once is subtracted, because this probability is contained in both the probability of the first event and the probability of the second event.

Perhaps the clearest way to illustrate the union of two probabilities is with a Venn diagram (see Figure 4.9). In this diagram, it is clear that adding the probability of $A$ to the probability of $B$ counts the shaded area twice. For that reason, the shaded area [or $P(A \cap B)$] needs to be subtracted from the total.

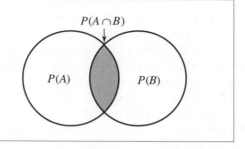

**FIGURE 4.9**

Venn Diagram for
$P(A \cup B)$

The probability of three events $[P(A \cup B \cup C)]$ is a simple extension of the logic used for two events. Statisticians use the following formula:

$$P(A \cup B \cup C) = P(A) + P(B) + P(C) - P(A \cap B) - P(A \cap C)$$
$$- P(B \cap C) + P(A \cap B \cap C)$$

In other words, the probability of any of three events occurring $[P(A \cup B \cup C)]$ is equal to the probability of the first event $[P(A)]$, plus the probability of the second event $[P(B)]$, plus the probability of the third event $[P(C)]$, minus the probability that the first and the second event both occur $[P(A \cap B)]$, minus the probability that the first and third event both occur $[P(A \cap C)]$, minus the probability that the second and the third event both occur $[P(B \cap C)]$, plus the probability that all three events occur at once $[P(A \cap B \cap C)]$.

Again, it is easier to visualize this using Venn diagrams (see Figure 4.10). Adding the probability of $A$, the probability of $B$, and the probability of $C$ together counts each of the lightly shaded areas twice, and counts the darkly shaded area three times. Subtracting the intersection of $A$ and $B$, the intersection of $A$ and $C$, and the intersection of $B$ and $C$ removes each of the lightly shaded sections once. However, it also removes all three counts of the darkly shaded section ($A \cap B \cap C$), so this must be added back in.

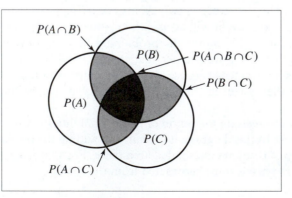

**FIGURE 4.10**

Venn Diagram for
$P(A \cup B \cup C)$

Clearly an example will help here. Individuals can be placed on the England County civil service list by either passing the civil service exam, having a college diploma, or being a member of Pi Alpha Alpha (a national public administration honorary society). Table 4.2 shows how the current list of eligibles qualified.

**TABLE 4.2**
Results for England County Civil Service List

| Exam Result | Pi Alpha Alpha Member | | | Not a Pi Alpha Alpha Member | | | |
|---|---|---|---|---|---|---|---|
| | College Degree | No Degree | Subtotal | College Degree | No Degree | Subtotal | Total |
| Passed exam | 26 | 14 | 40 | 64 | 16 | 80 | 120 |
| Failed exam | 4 | 16 | 20 | 36 | 74 | 110 | 130 |
| Subtotals | 30 | 30 | 60 | 100 | 90 | 190 | 250 |
| Totals | 60 | | | 190 | | | 250 |

What is the probability that one is on the England County eligibles list because he or she passed the exam, had a college degree, or was a member of Pi Alpha Alpha? The probability of passing the exam is .48 (120 ÷ 250). The probability of having a college degree is .52 (130 ÷ 250). The probability of being a member of Pi Alpha Alpha is .24 (60 ÷ 250). (If you do not understand how these probabilities were derived, review the beginning of this chapter.) The sum of these probabilities is 1.24. From this number, we subtract the probability that someone passed the exam and had a college degree (90 ÷ 250 = .36), the probability that someone was a member of Pi Alpha Alpha and passed the exam (40 ÷ 250 = .16), and the probability that someone was a college graduate and a member of Pi Alpha Alpha (30 ÷ 250 = .12). Subtracting these probabilities from 1.24, we get a difference of .6. To this number we add the probability that someone is a member of Pi Alpha Alpha, graduated from college, and passed the exam (26 ÷ 250 = .104), leaving us a probability of .704. Examining the table directly, we see that 176 persons were on the eligibles list (these three ways are the only ways to get on the list); the probability of being on the eligibles list, therefore, is .704 (176 ÷ 250).

You can calculate the probability that any of four or more events occurred by using the same logic that was used above. In practice, however, this calculation becomes fairly complex. If you are ever faced with such a problem, consult a statistics text or a statistician.

Whenever two events are mutually exclusive, a special rule of addition is used. Two events are **mutually exclusive** if the occurrence of $A$ means that $B$ will not occur. In other words, two events are mutually exclusive if only one of the events can occur at a time. As statisticians state it, if the probability of the intersection of $A$ and $B$ is zero, then $A$ and $B$ are mutually exclusive events.

**mutually exclusive events**

When two events are mutually exclusive, the probability of either $A$ or $B$ is equal to the probability of $A$ plus the probability of $B$.

**special rule of addition for mutually exclusive events**

The **special rule of addition for mutually exclusive events** is expressed symbolically as

$$P(A \cup B) = P(A) + P(B)$$

or as illustrated in the Venn diagram in Figure 4.11.

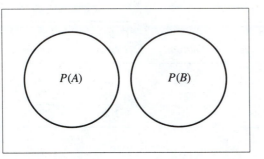

**FIGURE 4.11**
Venn Diagram for
$P(A \cup B) =$
$P(A) + P(B)$

### THE GENERAL RULE OF MULTIPLICATION

**general rule of multiplication**

The **general rule of multiplication** is applied when you want to know the joint probability of two events (i.e., the probability that both events will occur). The general rule of multiplication is denoted symbolically as follows:

$$P(A \cap B) = P(A) \times P(B|A)$$
$$= P(B) \times P(A|B)$$

In other words, the joint probability of two events is equal to the probability of one event multiplied by the conditional probability of the other event, given that the first event occurs.

The Venn diagram in Figure 4.12 shows the intersection of $A$ and $B$,

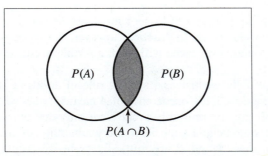

**FIGURE 4.12**

which is equivalent to the probability of *A* times the probability of *B* given *A*,

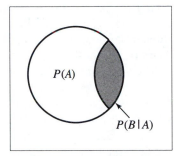

**FIGURE 4.13**

or the probability of *B* times the probability of *A* given *B*.

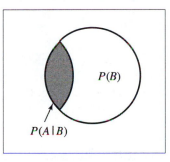

**FIGURE 4.14**

To illustrate the general rule of multiplication, let us use information supplied by the Bessmer, Michigan, City Hospital, which is shown in Table 4.3. The hospital officials collected these data because they perceived that their workload was much higher in the summer months (reflecting the fact that babies are conceived in the winter months when recreation activities in Bessmer are fairly limited).

**TABLE 4.3**

Case Data on Bessmer Hospital Births

|  | Time of Year | | Total |
|---|---|---|---|
|  | *October–March* | *April–September* | *Total* |
| Women pregnant 3 months or more | 216 | 53 | 269 |
| Women pregnant less than 3 months | 47 | 195 | 242 |
| Total | 263 | 248 | 511 |

What is the probability that a woman is at least three months pregnant and it is winter? From the table, we can see the probability is .42 (216 ÷ 511). The general rule of multiplication says we can also find this probability by multiplying the probability that a woman is at least three months pregnant (.53, or 269 ÷ 511) by the probability that it is winter, given that a woman is at least three months pregnant (.80, or 216 ÷ 269). (Not every example can make sense!) The product of these probabilities is .42.

From this information, should Bessmer set up a cable TV system?

When two events are independent, a special rule of multiplication applies. Two events are **independent** if the probability of one event is not affected by whether or not the other event occurs. For example, when flipping a coin twice, the probability of obtaining a head on the second flip is independent of the result of the first flip. The probability remains .5 regardless of what happened on the first flip. Statisticians say two events $A$ and $B$ are *independent* if $P(A|B) = P(A)$.

**independent
events**

When two events are independent, the probability of two events occurring is equal to the probability that one event will occur times the probability that the other event will occur. Or

$$P(A \cap B) = P(A) \times P(B)$$

This idea can be illustrated by the probability of obtaining two heads on conseccutive flips of an unbiased coin. The probability of obtaining two heads is equal to the probability of obtaining one head times the probability of obtaining one head (.5 × .5 = .25).

## CHAPTER SUMMARY _____

This chapter provides a basic introduction to the rules of probability. Probability tells you how likely it is that certain events will occur. Concepts introduced include the basic law of probability, a priori probability, posterior probability, the union of two probabilities, joint probability, conditional probability, and the rules of addition and multiplication.

The basic law of probability (for equally likely events) states that the probability of an outcome is equal to the ratio of the number of ways that that outcome could be attained to the total number of ways all possible outcomes could be attained. A probability that is determined before an event occurs is an a priori probability. Posterior probabilities are those generated by numerous trials.

The union of two probabilities is the probability of one event or the other. The probability of two events occurring simultaneously is a joint probablity. A conditional probability is the probability that one event will occur given that another event has already happened.

The general rule of addition for two events $A$ and $B$ is this: the probability of either $A$ or $B$ occurring is equal to the probability of $A$ plus the probability of $B$

minus the joint probability of A and B. This rule can be extended to more than two events. The general rule of multiplication for two events A and B is this: the joint probability of A and B is equal to the probability of one event times the conditional probability of the other event, given that the first event has occurred. This rule can also be extended to more than two events.

## PROBLEMS

**4.1** Answer the following questions by referring to the accompanying table, which lists the highway patrol's reasons for stopping cars and the number of tickets issued.

| Reason for Stopping Car | Issued Ticket | Did Not Issue Ticket | Total |
|---|---|---|---|
| Speeding | 40 | 170 | 210 |
| No taillights | 10 | 35 | 45 |
| Failure to use signals | 5 | 25 | 30 |
| Careless driving | 45 | 70 | 115 |
| Total | 100 | 300 | 400 |

Assume that a car was stopped.
**(a)** What is the probability that a ticket was issued? _____
**(b)** What is the probability that the car did not have taillights? _____

**(c)** What is the probability that a driver will get a ticket, given that he or she was stopped for careless driving? _____
**(d)** What is the probability that the person was stopped for speeding or for failure to use signals? _____
**(e)** Given that a ticket was not issued, what is the probability that the person was stopped for speeding? _____

**4.2** David Morgan, city manager of Yukon, Oklahoma, must negotiate new contracts with both the firefighters and the police officers. He plans to offer both groups a 7% wage increase and hold firm. Mr. Morgan feels that there is one chance in three that the firefighters will strike and one chance in seven that the police will strike. Assume that the events are independent.
**(a)** What is the probability that both will strike?
**(b)** What is the probability that neither the police nor the firefighters will strike?
**(c)** What is the probability that the police will strike and the firefighters will not?
**(d)** What is the probability that the firefighters will strike but the police will not?

**4.3**  What do we mean when we say that two events are independent?

**4.4**  In your own words, explain what mutually exclusive events are.

**4.5**  The probability that a smallpox case will be found in Metro City in any given week is .0034. In the week of July 17, four unrelated cases of smallpox are reported. If these are independent events, what is the probability that this would occur? Are these likely to be independent events?

**4.6**  The National Crop Reporting Service receives the accompanying information from the CIA on the Russian wheat harvest. Russian demand for wheat is approximately 210 million metric tons.
   **(a)** What is the probability that the harvest will be adequate?
   **(b)** If U.S. exports make up the difference, what is the probability that the United States will have to sell more than 20 million metric tons to the Russians?

| Millions of Metric Tons | Probability |
| --- | --- |
| Less than 170 | .05 |
| 170–180 | .15 |
| 180–190 | .23 |
| 190–200 | .31 |
| 200–210 | .15 |
| 210–220 | .07 |
| More than 220 | .04 |

**4.7**  The Department of Defense feels that the probability that the signal to fire an ICBM will reach a missile team is .96. For any given missile, the probability that the ignition mechanism will work is .89. For missiles with operative ignition systems, 15 of every 100 will explode in the silo or before reaching orbit. Given the command to fire, what is the probability of a successful launch for any given missile?

**4.8**  From a survey of the households in Grayson, Missouri, the crime figures shown in the accompanying table were estimated.

| Crime | Number Reported | Number Not Reported | Total |
| --- | --- | --- | --- |
| Murder | 12 | 12 | 24 |
| Robbery | 145 | 105 | 250 |
| Assault | 85 | 177 | 262 |
| Rape | 12 | 60 | 72 |
| Auto theft | 314 | 62 | 376 |
| Total | 568 | 416 | 984 |

   **(a)** What is the probability that a crime is reported?
   **(b)** What is the probability that a crime is reported, given that an assault occurs?

(c) What is the probability that a nonreported crime is either a robbery or an assault?

(d) What is the probability that a crime is a rape and that it is reported?

(e) What is the probability that a crime is reported or that the crime is a robbery?

**4.9** The city water department estimates that, for any day in January, the probability of a water main freezing and breaking is .2. For six consecutive days, no water mains break.

(a) What is the probability that this happens?

(b) Are the events independent?

**4.10** Jane Watson is running a youth recreation program to reduce the juvenile crime rate. If Jane can get a Law Enforcement Assistance Administration (LEAA) grant to expand the program, she feels that there is a .9 probability that the program will work. If she fails to get the grant, the probability of success falls to .3. If the probability of getting the LEAA grant is .6, what is the probability that Jane's program will be successful?

**4.11** Given $P(A) = .45$, $P(B) = .31$, and $P(A \cap B) = .26$, calculate:

(a) $P(A \cup B)$

(b) $P(A|B)$

(c) $P(B|A)$

**4.12** Given $P(A) = .21$, $P(B|A) = .75$, and $P(A|B) = .41$, calculate:

(a) $P(A \cap B)$

(b) $P(B)$

**4.13** Given $P(A) = .3$, $P(B) = .61$, and $P(A|B) = .3$, calculate:

(a) $P(A \cap B)$

(b) $P(A \cup B)$

**4.14** Sheriff Joe Bob Stewart thinks the odds that any law enforcement grant is funded is .25. He believes that the decision to fund one grant is independent of the decision to fund any other grant.

(a) Use a probability tree to tell Sheriff Stewart what the probability is that he can submit three grants and get none funded.

(b) What is the probability of getting exactly one funded?

(c) Exactly two?

(d) Two or more?

## CHAPTER 5

# THE BINOMIAL

# PROBABILITY

# DISTRIBUTION

The binomial probability distribution provides a method for estimating probability when events that you are concerned about take on certain characteristics. It permits you to determine the probability that an event will occur a specified number of times in a certain number of trials. In this chapter, we will discuss several characteristics of the binomial distribution.

## BINOMIAL PROBABILITIES

The binomial probability distribution can be used when the process under consideration is what is called a Bernoulli process. The first characteristic of a **Bernoulli process** is as follows: the outcome of any trial (a trial being one attempt, whether or not successful) can be classified into one of two mutually exclusive and jointly exhaustive categories. One of these two categories (the one you want to examine) is referred to as a success; the other category is referred to as a failure. Some examples are in order. Flipping an unbiased coin follows a Bernoulli process. Results of the flips can be classified as either a "head" or "not a head" (a tail). The solving of crimes by a police department can be described in a similar manner; a crime is either solved or not solved. Rolling a six on a die may be characterized as a six or not a six (any other number on the die).

    The second characteristic of a Bernoulli process is that the probability of success must remain constant from trial to trial and be totally unaffected by the outcomes of any preceding trial. In short, each trial is independent of the previous trials. Examples of independent events include, for example, the probability of obtaining a head on any flip of a coin. The probability on any given flip is not affected by the number of heads obtained on previous flips. The probability of a fire occurring in a community on a given night is not affected by whether or not

**Bernoulli process**

a fire occurred in the community the previous night (assuming that the city has no pyromaniacs).

Any process that meets these two characteristics is a Bernoulli process. When a Bernoulli process exists, the probability that any number of events will occur can be determined by using the binomial probability distribution. To determine a probability by using the binomial probability distribution, you must know three things. First, you must know the number of trials, that is, the number of times a certain event is tried. Second, you must know the number of successes, that is, the number of times you achieve or want to achieve a given event. Third, you must know the probability that the event in question will occur (either a priori or posterior probability).

With the knowledge of these three factors, the formula that follows can be used to calculate the probability of any one event for the binomial probability distribution.

$$C_r^n p^r q^{n-r}$$

where

$n$ = the number of trials
$r$ = the number of successes
$p$ = the probability that the event will be a success
$q = 1 - p$

**combination**

Although this formula looks complex, in actuality it is not. The $C_r^n$ is a symbol for something statisticians call a **combination** (read as "a combination of $n$ things taken $r$ at a time"). To illustrate a combination and its value, let us assume that we have four balls marked with the letters $a$, $b$, $c$, and $d$, respectively. We want to know how many different sets of three balls we could select from the four. In statistical language, we want to know the number of combinations of four balls taken three at a time. As the following illustration shows, a combination of four things taken three at a time equals 4.

|  | Balls Selected |
| --- | --- |
| Combination 1 | $a, b, c$ |
| Combination 2 | $a, b, d$ |
| Combination 3 | $a, c, d$ |
| Combination 4 | $b, c, d$ |

These four combinations of three balls represent all the possible ways that four items can be grouped into sets of three. In the space provided, use the same procedure to determine the value of a combination of four things taken two at a time.

If you found six combinations, congratulations ($ab, ac, ad, bc, bd, cd$).

Listing all possible combinations as a way to figure out the value of $C_r^n$ often gets burdensome. For example, the following combination would take a long time to calculate by the combination-listing method:

$$C_6^{15}$$

A shortcut method of determining combinations has been found using the formula

$$C_r^n = \frac{n!}{r!(n-r)!}$$

where $n!$ (called $n$ factorial) is equal to $n \times (n-1) \times (n-2) \times (n-3) \times \cdots \times 3 \times 2 \times 1$; $r!$ and $(n-r)!$ have the same interpretation. For example, $6! = 6 \times 5 \times 4 \times 3 \times 2 \times 1 = 720$.

In the preceding example, we find

$$C_6^{15} = \frac{15!}{6!9!}$$

$$= \frac{15 \times 14 \times 13 \times 12 \times 11 \times 10 \times 9 \times 8 \times 7 \times 6 \times 5 \times 4 \times 3 \times 2 \times 1}{6 \times 5 \times 4 \times 3 \times 2 \times 1 \times 9 \times 8 \times 7 \times 6 \times 5 \times 4 \times 3 \times 2 \times 1}$$

$$= 5005$$

The use of the binomial distribution can be best illustrated by working a problem. Assume that we are going to flip an unbiased coin three times, and we want to know the probability of getting exactly three heads. In this example, the number of trials ($n$) is equal to 3, the number of coin flips. The number of successes ($r$) is equal to 3, the number of heads. The probability of obtaining a head on one flip of a coin ($p$) is equal to .5; $q$, then, is equal to $1 - p$, or .5. Substituting these numbers into the binomial probability distribution formula, we get the following:

$$C_r^n p^r q^{n-r} = \left( \frac{3!}{3!0!} \right) .5^3 \times .5^0$$

Calculating the combination term first, we find that the numerator of the fraction is equal to 3! ($3 \times 2 \times 1$), or 6. This number is divided by 3!, or 6, times 0!. To keep the universe orderly, *statisticians define* 0! *as equal to* 1. The combination term, therefore, is 6 divided by 6, or 1. The probability terms are easily calculated: $.5^3$ is equal to $.5 \times .5 \times .5$, or .125, and $.5^0$ is equal to 1. Note again that *statisticians define any number to the* 0 *power as equal to* 1 to maintain an orderly universe. The probability of obtaining three heads in three flips of an unbiased coin, then, is $1 \times .125 \times 1$, or .125.

To test yourself, calculate the probability that in four flips of an unbiased coin exactly two heads will occur. Calculate in the space provided.

You should have found a probability of .375 that two heads would occur on four flips of an unbiased coin. The problem may be defined as one where $n = 4$, $r = 2$, and $p = .5$ (the number of trials, the number of successes, and the probability of success, respectively). The probability can be calculated as follows:

$$C_r^n p^r q^{n-r} = \left( \frac{4!}{2!2!} \right) \times .5^2 \times .5^2$$

Suppose you want to know the probability of obtaining *two or more* heads on four flips of an unbiased coin. In this situation, you would figure out the probability of obtaining four heads (.0625), the probability of obtaining three heads (.25), and the probability of obtaining two heads (.375). Since these three events are mutually exclusive, the probability of either two, three, or four heads is equal to the probability of two heads plus the probability of three heads plus the probability of four heads, or .6875.

An example of how the binomial probability distribution can be used in a public management setting is in order. Suppose that the Stermerville Public Works Department has been charged with racial discrimination in hiring practices. Last year, 40% of the persons who passed the department's civil service exam and were eligible to be hired were minorities. From this group, the public works department hired 10 individuals; 2 were minorities. What is the probability that, if the Stermerville Public Works Department did not discriminate, it would have hired 2 or fewer minorities? (Note that we assume, as a personnel analyst would have to in this situation, that anyone who passed the exam was capable of successful job performance. In other words, we assume that every individual had the same chance to be hired.)

The easiest way to figure out a problem of this nature is first to identify $n$, $r$, and $p$. In this case $p$, the probability that a minority is hired, is equal to the proportion of minorities in the job pool, or .4. And $q$, of course, is equal to .6. The number of trials ($n$) in this case is equal to the number of persons selected, or 10. The number of successes ($r$) is equal to the number of minorities selected, or 2. Since we are interested in the probability of 2 or fewer minorities selected, we must calculate the binomial probability distribution for 2 minorities, 1 minority, and 0 minorities.

The probability calculations for 2 minorities are as follows:

$$C_r^n p^r q^{n-r} = \left(\frac{10!}{2!8!}\right).4^2 \times .6^8 = 45 \times .4^2 \times .6^8 = 45 \times .16 \times .6^8$$

$$= 7.2 \times .6^8 = 7.2 \times .0168 = .120$$

The probability calculations for 1 minority are as follows:

$$C_1^{10}.4^1 \times .6^9 = \left(\frac{10!}{1!9!}\right) \times .4 \times .6^9 = 10 \times .4 \times .6^9 = 4 \times .6^9 = 4 \times .010 = .040$$

The probability calculations for 0 minorities are as follows:

$$C_0^{10}.4^0 \times .6^{10} = \left(\frac{10!}{0!10!}\right) \times .4^0 \times .6^{10} = 1 \times .4^0 \times .6^{10} = 1 \times 1 \times .6^{10} = .006$$

Statistically, a person can conclude that the probability that the Stermerville Public Works Department could hire two or fewer minorities from a pool of

40% minorities is .166 (.12 + .04 + .006 = .166) if the department shows no pref- erence in regard to hiring minorities. In other words, a pattern such as this could happen about one time in six.

This is a statistical statement. As a manager, you have to arrive at managerial conclusions. You need to know whether the department is engaged in discrimi- nation. The statistical finding is only one piece of evidence that a manager uses in arriving at a conclusion.

After receiving statistical information, the manager should always ask whether anything else could have produced a result similar to this, other than discrimination (or whatever other question is involved). For example, perhaps more minorities were offered jobs, but they turned them down for some reason. Sometimes it is helpful to examine past behavior. If last year the department hired 42% minorities, you might not be too concerned. If they only hired 20% minorities last year, you might be more concerned. The manager's task at this point is to examine all potential reasons that explain why the statistical pattern occurred and to eliminate them. Can you think of other causes for these statisti- cal results?

If no other reason (other than discrimination) can be found to account for the statistical pattern ($p = .166$), then the manager must decide how sure he or she wants to be. Since this pattern could have occurred by random chance 16.6% of the time, if the manager concludes that discrimination has occurred, there is a 1 in 6 chance that he or she is wrong. There is no magic number for how sure a manager should be. Social scientists often use a probability of less than 5% for making decisions. This is generally not a good idea for a manager. In some cases, a 5% risk is far too high. For example, would you authorize the launch of the space shuttle if there were a 5% chance of an explosion? Such a decision would mean that the manager would find it acceptable if one of every twenty launches resulted in an explosion. Alternatively, other decisions might not re- quire levels as low as .05. A probability of .25, or even .35, might be acceptable in deciding between two alternative methods of collecting trash. In short, the manager must take the responsibility for establishing a level of risk based on how important the decision is. The manager should never let his or her statisti- cal analyst set the probability level. This decision requires managerial judg- ment based on an individual's experience and willingness to take risks. Man- agers would do well to remember that statistical analysts are rarely fired when the manager they report to makes a bad decision.

Although the binomial probability distribution provides a good method for estimating the probability that a given number of events will occur, often the task of calculating the binomial probability distribution becomes fairly complex mathematically. For example, suppose that instead of hiring 2 minorities out of 10 persons, the Stermerville Public Works Department hired 43 minorities out of 150 persons. These figures would require the following probability to be estimated:

$$C_{43}^{150}.4^{43} \times .6^{107}$$

The estimation of this term for the probability of hiring exactly 43 minorities is complex. In addition, we would need to estimate the probability of hiring 42, 41, 40, and so on, minorities out of 150. Clearly the difficulty in estimating this probability exceeds the patience of most individuals. In situations like this, however, the binomial probability distribution can be estimated fairly well by using the normal distribution.

## THE NORMAL DISTRIBUTION

The normal distribution describes a great many phenomena in the real world. The **normal distribution** is a bell-shaped curve. The distribution of individuals' heights and weights, for example, fits the normal curve. Most individuals cluster about the mean, and fewer and fewer individuals are found the farther one moves away from the mean. **normal distribution**

The uniqueness of the normal distribution makes it useful in determining probabilities. Within one standard deviation from the mean in both directions fall approximately 68.26% of all values in a normal distribution. Within two standard deviations of the mean fall approximately 95.44% of all the values. Within three standard deviations of the mean in either direction fall approximately 99.72% of all the values. This phenomenon is illustrated in Figure 5.1.

Because the normal curve is regular, we can estimate the probability of an event if we know the mean and standard deviation of the distribution. For example, if a given event falls three standard deviations from the mean, we know that this event will occur with a probability of .0028 (1.0 − .9972 = .0028; the entire area under the curve is equal to 1.0). How is this regularity useful to the public manager?

The police department in Jefferson, California, gives an exam to all applicants for their police academy. Scores on the Jefferson police exam have a mean of 100 and a standard deviation of 10. (Any exam can be converted to one with a mean of 100 and a standard deviation of 10 by taking the raw scores, subtracting the mean from the score, and dividing by the standard deviation. This number is then multiplied by 10, and that number is added to 100. This process is called *standardization*.) Assume that the recruitment examiner gives the exam to an individual who scores 119.2. The next question is, how good is this score?

Another way of asking this question is to ask, what is the probability that a randomly selected individual would score 119.2 on the Jefferson police exam? To determine this probability, follow these steps.

**STEP 1**    Convert the score on the exam into a $z$ score. A $z$ **score** is calculated by subtracting the mean test score from the score in question and dividing the difference by the standard deviation. Symbolically, **$z$ score**

$$z = \frac{X - \mu}{\sigma}$$

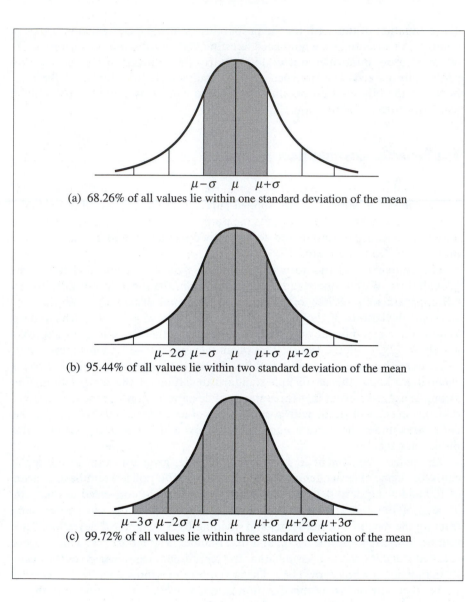

(a)  68.26% of all values lie within one standard deviation of the mean

(b)  95.44% of all values lie within two standard deviation of the mean

(c)  99.72% of all values lie within three standard deviation of the mean

**FIGURE 5.1**

The Normal
Distribution

In this case, subtract 100 from 119.2 to get 19.2; divide this number by
10 to get a $z$ score of 1.92. A $z$ score tells you how many standard
deviations (and in what direction) a score is from the mean (values
below the mean have negative $z$ scores).

**STEP 2**    Look up the value of a $z$ score of 1.92 in a normal distribution table.
Table 1 in the Appendix is a normal distribution table designed to
convert $z$ scores into probabilities. The numbers in the first column and
across the top of the table represent the values of the $z$ scores. The

values inside the table represent the area of the normal curve that falls between the $z$ score in question and the mean (the total area under the curve is 1.0). In this example, proceed down the first column until you find a $z$ score of 1.9. According to the numbers across the top of the table, the first number next to the 1.9 represents a $z$ score of 1.90; the second number is for a $z$ score of 1.91; the third number represents a $z$ score of 1.92 and is the one we are interested in. The value found here is .4726. This means that 47.26% of the police exam scores fall between the mean (100) and a $z$ score of 1.92 (119.2). Since 50% (or half) of the scores fall below the mean, a total of 97.26% of the scores fall below a score of 119.2. In probability tems, the probability that a randomly selected individual will score a 119.2 or better on the Jefferson police exam is .0274 (1.0 − .9726). Another way of stating this is that the individual in question scored at the 97th percentile.

Since the normal curve is extremely important to estimating probability, practice by finding the probability associated with the following $z$ scores:

1.34; probability = _____
 .62; probability = _____
2.40; probability = _____
−1.50; probability = _____ (**Hint:** this $z$ score is below the mean.)

One important aspect of the normal distribution is its flexibility. The following examples will illustrate the numerous uses of the normal distribution.

Suppose the police chief wants to know the percentage of job applicants that score between 100 and 106 on the Jefferson police exam. Since the mean score is 100, this question is equivalent to asking for the percentage of applicants who score between 106 and the mean. Following the logic outlined above, 106 is equivalent to a $z$ score of .6. Looking up a $z$ score of .6 in Table 1 reveals a value of .2257. So 22.6% of all applicants score between 100 and 106 on the exam.

What percentage of applicants score between 90 and 110 on the exam? This question is simple if you split it into two questions. First, what percentage of applicants fall between 100 and 110? Calculate this in the space provided.

Your answer should be 34.13%. Second, what percentage of applicants score between 90 and 100? Obviously, this is the same problem but in the opposite direction. Calculate in the space provided.

Again, your answer should be 34.13%. What percentage of applicants fall between 90 and 110? Adding the two percentages together gives the answer of 68.26%. How does this result compare to Figure 5.1(a)? Why?

What is the probability that a randomly selected person will score between 117 and 122 on the exam? Again, if we reduce this question to two questions, the answer is easy to find. The probability of scoring between 117 and 122 is equal to the probability of scoring between the mean and 122 minus the probability of scoring between the mean and 117. The probability of scoring between 100 and 122 is .4861 ($z$ score of 2.2). The probability of scoring between 100 and 117 ($z$ score of 1.7) is .4554. The probability of scoring between 117 and 122, therefore, is .0307 (.4861 − .4554).

What is the probability that a person will score 125 or more on the Jefferson police exam? Since we can calculate the probability that someone will score between the mean and 125, we can solve this problem. The probability of scoring between 100 and 125 ($z$ score = ?) is .4938. Since 50% of all persons score below the mean, the probability of scoring 125 or below is .9938 (.50 + .4938). This means the probability of scoring 125 or above is .0062.

Calculating a probability when given a score or a range of scores is only one way the normal distribution is used. Another common problem is to be given a probability or percentage and to be asked to find a raw score. For example, the Jefferson police force has a policy of accepting only those who score in the top 20% of the persons taking the police exam. What raw score should be used as the cutoff point? This question can be answered by following these steps.

**STEP 1**    The score associated with the top 20% is the same score that is associated with the bottom 80%. This problem is easier to solve for the bottom 80% than for the top 20%, so we will find the cutoff point for the bottom 80%. Of the bottom 80%, 50% by definition fall below the mean. Another 30% fall between the cutoff value and the mean. To find the $z$ score associated with the cutoff point, we look up the value of .3 on the inside of Table 1, and then find the $z$ score associated with a probability of .3. Scanning the inside of the table, we find that the closest value to .3, without going under .3, is .3023. This number is associated with a $z$ score of .85.

**STEP 2**     Convert the $z$ score to a raw score. To do this, multiply the $z$ score by the standard deviation (10 in this case), and add the mean to this number. This procedure yields a raw score of 108.5 $[(.85 \times 10) + 100 = 108.5]$. If the police academy class is limited to the top 20% of all applicants, only those who score 108.5 or above on the police exam should be admitted.

One more example is in order. The Lower Slobovian Army recruits its officer corps from the Slobovian universities. To be admitted to Officer Candidate School (OCS), the college graduate must score in the top 75% of all those taking the exam. Last year, the mean exam score was 80, with a standard deviation of 6. Exam scores were normally distributed. At what should the minimum passing score be set to admit only the top 75%?

Since we know 50% of the applicants will score above 80, we need to know the score below the mean that will contain 25% of the scores between it and the mean. Looking up a probability of .25 in the normal table, we find a value of .2486 associated with a $z$ score of .67. Since we are interested in scores below the mean, this $z$ score is $-.67$. Converting a $z$ score of $-.67$ to a raw score, we get a minimum passing grade of 76 $[(-.67 \times 6) + 80 = 76]$.

This chapter first introduced the normal distribution to simplify the calculations involved with the binomial distribution. Now we will return to this topic.

# The Normal Curve and
# the Binomial Distribution

As we stated before, the utility of the binomial distribution is somewhat limited when the number of trials or the number of successes becomes large. For example, Bill Povalla, the head of the Chicago Equal Employment Commission, believes that the Chicago Transit Authority (CTA) discriminates against Republicans. The civil service records show that 37.5% of the individuals listed as passing the CTA exam were Republicans; the remainder were Democrats (no one registers as an independent in Illinois). CTA hired 30 people last year, 25 Democrats and 5 Republicans. What is the probability that this situation could exist if CTA did not discriminate?

Clearly the binomial distribution could be used to determine this probability, with the following information:

$p = .375$, the probability of randomly hiring a Republican
$q = 1 - p = .625$
$n = 30$, the number of persons hired
$r = 5, 4, 3, 2, 1,$ or $0$, the number of Republicans hired (you need to know the probability of hiring 5 or fewer Republicans)

Determining this probability would take the normal human being several hours. Using the normal curve is much faster.

To use the normal curve to determine a probability, you need to know the mean and the standard deviation of the population, as well as the raw score in question.

The mean of a probability distribution is equal to its expected value. If numerous clusters of 30 CTA eligibles were selected randomly, what would be the average number of Republicans selected? Obviously, the average is the number of persons selected (30) times the probability of selecting a Republican (.375), or 11.25. This is the mean (and the expected value).

The standard deviation of a probability distribution is defined by statisticians as

$$\sigma = \sqrt{np(1 - p)}$$

In this case, we have

$$\sigma = \sqrt{30 \times .375(1 - .375)} = \sqrt{11.25 \times .625} = \sqrt{7.03} = 2.65$$

To determine the probability that 5 or fewer Republicans would be selected if the CTA hiring were nonpartisan, simply convert the number actually hired into a $z$ score.

$$z = \frac{X - \mu}{\sigma} = \frac{5 - 11.25}{2.65} = -2.36 \text{ or } 2.36$$

Looking up a $z$ score of 2.36 in the normal table, we find a value of .4909, indicating that over 49% of the values fall between a $z$ score of 2.36 and the mean. Converting this to a probability (.5000 − .4909), we find the probability that 5 or fewer Republicans would be hired by CTA if CTA were nonpartisan is .0091. In other words, CTA probably gives preference to Democrats for its vacancies. If you were Mr. Povalla, what would you do with this information?

## WHEN TO USE THE NORMAL CURVE

A word of caution is in order. The normal curve is a good approximation of the binomial distribution when $n \times p$ is greater than 10 and $n \times (1 - p)$ is greater than 10. If both these situations do not hold, the binomial distribution should be used. In addition, the normal curve tells you the probability only that $r$ or fewer events occurred (or $r$ or more). It does not tell you the probability of exactly $r$ events occurring. This probability can only be determined by using the binomial distribution.

## CHAPTER SUMMARY

The binomial probability distribution can be used whenever the outcome of any trial can be classified into one of two mutually exclusive and jointly exhaustive outcomes (one outcome termed a success) and whenever each trial is independent of the other trials. To determine a probability by using the binomial probability distribution, you must know the number of trials ($n$), the number of successes ($r$), and the probability of a success in any one trial ($p$). The probability of an event for the binomial probability distribution can be calculated by using the formula

$$C_r^n p^r q^{(n-r)}$$

where

$$C_r^n = \frac{n!}{r!(n-r)!}$$

In circumstances in which $n \times p > 10$ *and* $n \times (1 - p) > 10$, the normal curve can be used to approximate the binomial probability distribution. The normal distribution is a bell-shaped curve that describes a great many phenomena in the real world. A $z$ score, whose formula is

$$z = \frac{X - \mu}{\sigma}$$

is used to find probabilities when using the normal curve.

For the binomial probability distribution, the mean is equal to $n \times p$, and the standard deviation is equal to the square root of $n \times p \times (1 - p)$.

## PROBLEMS

**5.1**  The state legislative council has been charged with sex discrimination in hiring. Last year it hired only 3 women out of 12 new employees. The civil service lists show that women comprise 40% of the qualified applicants for these jobs. What is the probability of hiring 3 or fewer women if the legislative council does not discriminate? Show all calculations.

**5.2**   The Armenian Navy gives all persons who want to join the navy an intelligence test. Past tests had a mean of 90 and a standard deviation of 10.

    **(a)** What percentage of applicants scored between 82 and 104?

    **(b)** What percentage of applicants scored below 75?

    **(c)** What is the probability that a person taking the test will score 109 or more?

**5.3**   The foreign service exam gives a passing grade to only the top 10% of those taking the exam. The mean score is 84, with a standard deviation of 8. What should be the minimum passing grade?

**5.4**   In a grand jury case, a bookstore was indicted in Oklahoma County on several counts of selling an obscene book. The grand jury was composed of 22 Baptists and 8 other people. The defendant feels that Baptists are biased against free speech. What is the probability that 22 or more Baptists are selected on a jury if Oklahoma County is 40% Baptist?

**5.5**   Mary Doyle ran against Bernie Hobson for state senate. In one precinct, one of the two voting machines did not work, and 182 votes were cast on the broken machine. Mary needed to receive 177 of the 182 votes to win the election. On the other machine in the precinct, Mary received 51% of the votes. Since assignment of voters to ballot boxes is independent, what is the probability that Mary won the election?

**5.6**   Traditionally, one-half of all cities that apply get job training grants. Four southern cities apply for grants, but none receive them. Assume all the cities were equally qualified. What is the probability that no southern city gets a grant?

**5.7**   Seaman David Brady is one of 16 seamen in Petty Officer Rickels's unit. Every day 4 seamen are assigned to chip paint, and the others are assigned to screen movies to see if they are suitable for viewing. Seaman Brady believes that Rickels does not like him, because he has been assigned to the paint detail 16 times in the past 20 days. What can you tell Seaman Brady?

**5.8**   The Procurement Bureau runs tests on 30 brand X teletype machines. It finds that an average of 3 machines fail in any 1-day period. Against the bureau's advice, the Public Affairs Department purchases 140 of these machines for all state offices. On the first day, 26 machines fail. What is the probability that this would happen if the true failure rate were 10%?

**5.9**   This year, 620 persons are nominated to participate in the president's Management Internship Program. After screening, 212 are selected for the program. Maxwell George University nominates 5 persons, and all 5 receive awards. What is the probability that this event would occur if the events were independent and all nominees are equally qualified?

**5.10**   Refer to Problem 5.9. Of the 620 nominees, 211 are women; and of these, 91 are selected. Is there any preference with regard to sex?

**5.11**   Past experience has shown that 60% of all Captains are promoted to Major. The 819th Infantry Division has 48 Captains who are eligible for promotion. Nine of these Captains are West Point graduates. Eight of the nine West Pointers are promoted. Is there any reason to suspect that West Point graduates are given preferential treatment? Why? Show your work.

**5.12**   If one-third of the University of Wisconsin teaching assistants (TAs) sign a petition calling for a collective bargaining election, an election will be held. A survey of 50 TAs indicates that 40% will sign the petition. What is the probability that a sample such as this could have occurred if one-third or fewer of the TAs in the population will sign such a petition?

**5.13**   The area supervisor of the Occupational Safety and Health Administration has heard a story that a certain inspector is not enforcing safety regulations. Past statistics reveal that inspectors find safety violations in 91% of all inspections. The supervisor pulls the files for the eight most recent inspections for the inspector whose behavior is questioned. These files reveal that safety violations were cited in two of the eight cases. Analyze these data and present a statistical conclusion.

**5.14**   The BFOQ Job Training Corporation believes that it has a new program that will increase job placements. Essentially the corporation thinks that if it runs its trainees through a simulated interview before sending them out on a job interview, their likelihood of getting the job increases. BFOQ randomly selects 36 individuals of relatively equal skills on a matched pair basis. Eighteen of these individuals are run through the simulation. BFOQ then sends one pair, one person who went through the training and one person who did not, to interview for one of 18 different jobs. (These individuals are the only ones to interview for the jobs.) Thirteen of the 18 persons who went through the simulation get the jobs. What is the probability that 13 of the 18 would get jobs if there were no difference between the two sets of 18 persons? Show your work.

**5.15**   The Bureau of Paperwork wants to know whether agency personnel prefer to use HMOs for their health care benefits. If more than 25% favor using HMOs, then the bureau will begin to set up procedures for this type of health care. A sample of 100 of the bureau's personnel reveals that 29 favor the use of HMOs. What is the probability that less than 25% of the bureau's employees favor the use of HMOs?

**5.16**   The Bluefield Regional Employment Service needs to place five individuals in jobs this week to meet its yearly quota. During the past several years, the service's track record is that every person sent to interview for a job has a .6 probability of getting the job. The placements appear to be independent of each other. The service decides to send seven individuals for interviews this week. Based on what you know, what is the probability that the service will make its yearly quota this week?

5.17   The Department of Treasury is concerned because one member of Congress has charged that, by normal accounting standards, one-third of all savings and loans in the country are bankrupt. To refute this claim, chief economist Tom Holbrook takes a sample of six savings and loans and finds that only one is insolvent (his staff had intended to gather a larger sample, but they were too busy processing S&L failures). If the true proportion of insolvencies is one-third, what is the probability that the Treasury Department would get the results that it did?

## CHAPTER 6

# SOME SPECIAL
# PROBABILITY
# DISTRIBUTIONS

Although the binomial distribution and the normal curve cover a great many of the situations that a manager faces, in certain circumstances special probability distributions should be used. For example, assume that a finite number of persons apply for agency jobs and you want to know whether the agency discriminates. Or suppose that you need to determine the probability that an event will occur but have no idea about the number of trials. Or perhaps a fire department wants to know how long it can expect to wait between major fires. For situations similar to these, special probability distributions must be used. We will discuss three such distributions in this chapter.

## THE HYPERGEOMETRIC
## PROBABILITY DISTRIBUTION

The Andersonville City Fire Department contends that its civil service exam for firefighters is valid; that is, it feels that anyone who passes the exam is qualified to be a firefighter. Last year, 100 persons passed the firefighters exam, 66 men and 34 women. From this list of 100 persons, a fire academy class of 30 was chosen: 24 men and 6 women. One woman not selected filed a complaint with the federal Equal Employment Opportunity Commission (EEOC), alleging discrimination. Three years later, the EEOC decides it will hear the case. The question is, how probable is it that Andersonville does not discriminate against women and would by chance admit 6 or fewer women to the fire academy class in question?

Clearly, this question could be answered by using the normal curve to approximate the binomial distribution. The normal distribution, however, assumes that the population from which the trials are drawn is infinite. In the present situation, this is not the case. The population consists of those persons who passed the firefighters exam, and 100 is a long way from infinity. If the normal curve and the binomial probability distribution were used, the probability estimates would be conservative; that is, the test would be less likely to show discrimination.

**hypergeometric probability distribution**

With a finite population, the **hypergeometric probability distribution** should be used. To use the hypergeometric distribution, you need to know the same things that were needed for the normal curve plus the size of the population. The mean of the hypergeometric probability distribution is the distribution's expected value:

$$\mu = n \times p$$

In this case, $\mu$ equals 30 times .34 (the probability that a woman would be chosen at random), or 10.2. This mean is the same as the mean for the binomial distribution.

The standard deviation for the hypergeometric distribution is as follows:

$$\sigma = \sqrt{\left(\frac{N_p - n}{N_p - 1}\right)(np)(1 - p)}$$

where $N_p$ is the size of the population, $n$ is the number of trials, and $p$ is the probability of success. The only difference between this standard deviation and the one for the binomial distribution is the ratio $[(N_p - n)/(N_p - 1)]$.

Substituting the values of this problem into the formula for the standard deviation, we have

$$\sigma = \sqrt{\left(\frac{100 - 30}{100 - 1}\right) \times 30 \times .34 \times .66} = \sqrt{\frac{50}{99} \times 30 \times .34 \times .66}$$

$$= \sqrt{.71 \times 30 \times .34 \times .66} = \sqrt{4.78} = 2.19$$

Given a mean of 10.2 and a standard deviation of 2.19, is it probable that Andersonville could have randomly selected only 6 females for its firefighter class?

Converting 6 into a $z$ score, we find

$$z = \frac{x - \mu}{\sigma} = \frac{6 - 10.2}{2.19} = -1.92$$

Using the $z$ score of $-1.92$ and the normal distribution table, we find the probability (.0274) that Andersonville could select 6 or fewer women given that it had no preference in regard to sex.

Had we used the binomial distribution in this problem, the probability would have been higher. Calculate this probability in the space provided. Be sure to use the normal approximation to the binomial distribution with $n = 30$, $r = 6$ or less, and $p = .34$ (see Chapter 5).

If you found a probability of .0526, congratulations. If you found some other probability, reread Chapter 5. Since most social scientists require a probability of .05 or less to make a conclusion, why is it important to use the hypergeometric distribution in this situation?

## THE POISSON DISTRIBUTION

The **Poisson distribution** is a probability distribution that describes a pattern of behavior when some event occurs at varying, random intervals over a continuum of time, length, or space. Such a pattern of behavior is called a *Poisson process*. For example, if we graphed the number of muggings in Chickasaw, Oklahoma, on a time dimension, we might find the following (where the X's represent muggings):

**Poisson distribution**

$$\text{---}\!\!+\!\!\text{--- X --- X --------------- XXX ------- X --------- X ---}\!\!+\!\!\text{---}$$

12:00 P.M.                                                    12:00 A.M.

The number of potholes per foot on South Flood Street in Normal, Oklahoma, also follows a Poisson process, as shown in the following diagram.

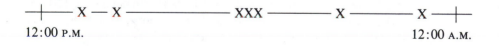

0 feet                                                        500 feet

In theory, each of these continuums can be divided into equal segments such that no more than one event (pothole, mugging) occurs in each segment. Every equal segment of Flood Street would either have a pothole or not have a pothole. In addition, for the process to be a Poisson process, the occurrence or nonoccurrence of any event must not affect the probability that other events will occur. That is, the fact that a pothole occurs at 621 South Flood does not affect whether or not a pothole occurs at 527 South Flood.

The process up to this point fits the description of a Bernoulli process: an event either occurs (success) or it does not (failure), and events are independent of each other. To determine the probability of any event when using the Bernoulli process, we need to know the probability of the event ($p$), the number of successes ($r$), and the number of trials ($n$). In the present situation, we could empirically determine the probability of a mugging occurring in Chickasaw during any time period ($p$). In this case, Chickasaw might experience .3 muggings per hour. Note that probabilities are based on time, length, or space. The number of successes ($r$) also could be determined. We can count the number of muggings in any period. *We do not, however, know, the number of trials.* How many potential muggings were there in Chickasaw? Clearly this information cannot be determined. The major difference between a Poisson process and a Bernoulli process, then, is that the number of trials is not known in a Poisson process.

The use of the Poisson distribution can best be illustrated with an example.

The Pelissero Rape Crisis Center wants to staff its crisis hot line so that a center member will always be present if a rape victim calls. The crisis center operates between the hours of 6:00 P.M. and 6:00 A.M. By examining the past records of the center, the director has determined that the mean number of rapes per hour is .05. This information can be found in police records.

The first question is, what is the probability that no rapes will occur on any given night? The steps in using the Poisson probability distribution are as follows.

**STEP 1**    Adjust the mean to reflect the number of hours (length or space) you want to consider. In the present example, the mean number of rapes in an hour is .05. You want to know the mean number of rapes in 12 hours. Since these events are independent, the mean for a 12-hour period is .6 (.05 × 12). This new mean is called $\lambda$, the Greek letter lambda (some texts refer to it as $\lambda t$, lambda $t$).

**STEP 2**    To determine the probability of zero rapes, you turn to the Poisson distribution tables (Table 2 in the Appendix). For those of you who feel that using a table is cheating, exact probabilities can be calculated with the following formula:

$$y = \frac{\lambda^x e^{-\lambda}}{x!}$$

where $\lambda$ is the probability of the event, $x$ is the number of occurrences, $e$ is a constant (2.71828), and $y$ is the probability of $x$ occurrences. If you are sane, turn to Table 2. Scanning across the top of the table, find $\lambda$ equal to .6. You should find the following information:

| X | $\lambda$ .06 |
|---|---|
| 0 | .5488 |
| 1 | .3293 |
| 2 | .0988 |
| 3 | .0198 |
| 4 | .0030 |
| 5 | .0004 |
| 6 | .0000 |

This table gives a Poisson probability distribution for $\lambda = .6$. It tells you that if $\lambda = .6$, the probability of no rapes in a single night is .5488. The probability of exactly one rape is .3293. The probability of exactly two rapes is .0988, and so on.

How might this information be used in a management setting? Suppose that the director believes that (based on past experience) assisting a rape victim takes about 4 hours. One crisis center staff member remains with the victim for this period to assist with the medical treatment and police procedures. If the center had one staff member and two rapes occurred in a 4-hour period, then no one would be at the center to assist the second victim. The director wants to avoid this situation. How many staff members should be at the center?

**STEP 1**  Adjust the mean to the time period. The mean is .05 for 1 hour and you want to know about 4-hour periods (the amount of time a staff member will be away from the center). Therefore, $\lambda$ is .2 (.05 × 4).

**STEP 2**  Find the probabilities in the Poisson distribution table for 0, 1, 2, 3, 4, and 5 rapes when $\lambda$ is .2.

| Number of Rapes | Probability |
|---|---|
| 0 | .8187 |
| 1 | .1637 |
| 2 | .0164 |
| 3 | .0011 |
| 4 | .0001 |
| 5 | .0000 |

To make the staffing decision, the director uses the preceding table. If 0 or 1 rape occurs in a 4-hour period, one staff member is sufficient. This will occur in 98% of the 4-hour periods (.8187 + .1637 = .9824). Since the director wants to minimize the time during which the crisis center cannot respond, the probability is interpreted as follows: if the crisis center staffs only one employee, this will be inadequate 1.8% of the time periods. Since the 12-hour day is equivalent to three 4-hour periods, a rape with no one present will occur on 5.4% (1.8% × 3) of the days (or once every three weeks). The director considers this risk unacceptable.

If two members are stationed at the crisis center, the probability of sufficient staff is .9988. Translating this into days when a rape will occur with no one at the crisis center (.0012 × 3 = .0036, or .36%) reveals that the staff will be inadequate .36% of the days, or once every 278 days (36 times in 10,000 days). The staff director feels that this risk is tolerable and decides to staff two persons.

(**Note:** Staffing three persons would increase the probability of sufficient staff to .9999. This means inadequate staff problems would occur once every 10,000 days.)

You may have noticed that the Poisson probability tables give values only for lambda less than or equal to 20. Poisson tables for larger lambda values are not presented because the normal distribution table provides fairly accurate probabilities when lambda is greater than 20. The normal distribution of this magnitude has a mean of lambda and a standard deviation equal to the square root of lambda. For a lambda value of 30, therefore, you would use the normal table with a mean of 30 and a standard deviation of 5.5 ($\sqrt{30} = 5.5$).

## THE EXPONENTIAL PROBABILITY DISTRIBUTION

**exponential probability distribution**

The **exponential probability distribution** is used when you want to know the most probable length of time between independent events. For example, in the Pelissero Rape Crisis Center case, the director might want to know the most probable length of time between rapes in order to plan center procedures. The exponential distribution is also used for scheduling. For example, it can be used to determine the time between arrivals at a municipal hospital or the time between fires in a city. Clearly this information can be useful to a manager in scheduling his or her work force.

The calculation procedures for the exponential distribution are fairly complex. As a result, we will not discuss them in this book. But you should be aware that the exponential distribution exists and that it can be used to schedule activities when events occur randomly. If the need for this distribution ever arises, we suggest that a statistician be hired to program the problem. For large problems, such as scheduling police calls in a large city, computer programs are available (see also Neter, Wasserman, and Whitmore 1978).

# CHAPTER SUMMARY

This chapter introduces three special probability distributions. The hypergeometric probability distribution is used, with finite populations, when one knows the number of trials (each trial is independent), the number of successes, and the probability of one success. Formulas for calculating the mean and the standard deviation are given for this distribution. The Poisson distribution is used whenever events are independent and events occur at varying, random intervals of time, length, or space. The exponential probability distribution is used to estimate the length of time between independently occurring events.

# PROBLEMS

6.1 One hundred cities (60 are northern cities) apply for CETA grants to train the unemployed. Fifty grants are awarded, 40 to northern cities. Is there any anti–Sun Belt bias?

6.2 The mean number of persons shot by the Metro City Police Department in an hour is .042. What is the probability that the MPD will shoot no one in a 24-hour period? What is the probability that the MPD will shoot one person? Two persons? More than two persons? Explain your work.

6.3 Police Chief Lenny Lawnorder has heard through a normally reliable source that 30% of his officers are not using regulation handguns. To see whether this is true, Lenny randomly inspects 35 of his 200 officers. Seventeen have nonregulation handguns. If the true proportion is .3, what is the probability that this event will occur?

6.4 The mean number of major fires in Flandreau, South Dakota, is .057 on any given day. What is the probability of no major fires occurring in any given week? What is the probability of one major fire? Two major fires? Three or more major fires?

6.5 In the First Army, 150 first lieutenants were up for promotion to captain (35 of these are West Point graduates). Of these, 120 were promoted, including 24 West Pointers. Does the Army discriminate in promotions?

6.6 The mean number of teletype machines in the Bureau of Communications that break down is .625 in any given hour. If repairs take 8 hours, how many people should the Bureau of Communications staff?

6.7 Congressman Lester Asperin has charged that 50% of all IRS agents would fail a simple test on tax law. IRS Commissioner John Tight believes no more than 15% would fail. Of the 1000 agents, 200 are randomly selected and given the test, and 60 fail. What is the probability that Asperin is correct? What is the probability that Tight is correct?

**6.8**    The mean number of murders reported in Metro City during the 8-hour graveyard shift is .5 for any hour. It takes two people 2 hours to investigate a homicide call. How many officers should be assigned to the homicide squad during these hours?

**6.9**    Refer to Problem 5.10, where 91 of the 211 women nominated for the president's Management Internship Program are selected and 212 of the 620 total nominees are accepted. Use what you have learned in this chapter to determine the probability of this happening if all persons are equally qualified. What can you say if you do not assume equal qualifications?

**6.10**    The mean number of contracts that consulting firms receive with the Department of Human Services is .4 for any given year. Ecosystems, Inc., a heavy contributor to political candidates, receives three contracts in one year. What is the probability that this event would occur by chance? What is the probability that Ecosystems will receive six contracts in two years?

**6.11**    The Madison Fire Department's files reveal that an average of six firefighters a year suffer heart attacks while on duty. The personnel office is concerned about this because it must budget funds to pay for disabilities. There are some concerns that the physical condition of firefighters is getting worse. This year, nine firefighters suffered heart attacks. What is the probability that an event this severe will occur? Given past history, what is the probability that no heart attacks will occur? Exactly one? Exactly two? Three or less?

**6.12**    The mean number of water main breaks is .4 per hour. In a ten-hour night shift, four mains break. What is the probability of exactly four mains breaking? Of four or more breaking? Which probability tells you the most about the chance of this situation happening?

**6.13**    The Nuclear Regulatory Commission estimates that the probability that a Westinghouse X-27 nuclear plant's warning system will fail in a year's time is .1. New York Power and Light operates six of the X-27 plants; last year one failed. What is the probability that one or more plants' warning systems will fail?

**6.14**    The mean number of fires per hour in Smallsville, Utah, is .1042. What is the probability that Smallsville will experience no fires on any given day? Five or more fires on any given day?

**6.15**    The Bureau of Paperwork has 1000 employees, and the personnel division wants to know whether agency personnel prefer to use HMOs for their health care benefits. If more than 25% favor using HMOs, then the bureau will begin to set up procedures for this type of health care. A sample of 100 of the bureau's personnel reveals that 29 favor the use of HMOs. What is the probability that less than 25% of the bureau's employees favor the use of HMOs?

**6.16**  The University of Wisconsin employs 200 teaching assistants (TAs). If one-third of the TAs sign a petition calling for a collective bargaining election, an election will be held. A survey of 50 TAs indicates that 40% will sign the petition. What is the probability that a sample such as this could have occurred if one-third or fewer of the TAs in the population will sign such a petition?

# PART III

# MEASUREMENT AND RESEARCH DESIGN

## CHAPTER 7

# MEASUREMENT

**Measurement** is the assignment of numbers to some phenomenon that we are interested in analyzing. For example, the effectiveness of army officers is measured by having senior officers rate junior officers on various traits. Educational attainment may be measured by how well a student scores on standardized achievement tests. Good performance from a city bus driver might be measured by the driver's accident record and by his or her record of running on time. **measurement**

Frequently, the phenomenon of interest cannot be measured so precisely, but only in terms of categories. For example, public administrators are often interested in characteristics and attitudes of the general populace and of various constituency groups. We can measure such things as the racial and gender composition of the individuals in these groups, their state of residence or their religious preferences, their attitudes toward a particular agency or government in general, their views on taxes and public spending, and so on. Although such variables do not have quantitative measurement scales, it is still quite possible to measure them in terms of categories—for instance, white versus nonwhite; female versus male; favor tax decrease, favor no change, favor tax increase; and so on. Although these phenomena cannot be measured directly with numerical scales, they are important variables nonetheless. The public administrator needs to know how to measure, describe, and analyze such variables statistically.

In many managerial situations the manager does not consciously think about measurement. Rather, the manager takes some data and subjects them to analysis. There are problems in this approach. In Chapter 10 we will discuss an example in which the Prudeville police crack down on prostitution in the city. The police chief increases daily arrests by the vice squad from 3.4 to 4.0. Based on these numbers, the police chief claims a successful program. This example illustrates a common measurement problem. The city council of Prudeville was concerned about the high level of prostitution activity, not the low level of prostitution arrests. Conceivably the number of prostitution arrests could be positively related to the level of prostitution activity. In this situation, the police chief's data may reveal increased prostitution, not decreased prostitution. In fact, the only thing an analyst can say, given the police chief's data, is that the number of prostitution arrests increased.

In this chapter, we will discuss some of the important aspects of measurement, both in theory and in application.

## THEORY OF MEASUREMENT

Measurement theory assumes that a concept representing some phenomenon that the analyst is concerned about cannot be directly measured. Army officer effectiveness, educational achievement, bus driver performance, level of prostitution activity, and program success are all concepts that cannot be measured directly. Such concepts are measured indirectly through indicators specified by operational definitions. An **operational definition** is a statement that tells the analyst how a concept will be measured. An **indicator** is a variable or set of observations that results from applying the operational definition. Examples of operational definitions include these:

**operational definition**

**indicator**

1. Educational attainment for Head Start participants is defined by the achievement scores on the Iowa Tests of Basic Skills.
2. Officer effectiveness is defined by subjective evaluations by senior officers using form AJK147/285-Z.
3. Program success for the Maxwell rehabilitation program is defined as a recidivism rate of less than 50%.
4. A convict is considered a recidivist if, within one year of release from jail, the convict is arrested and found guilty.
5. Clients' satisfaction with the service of the Department of Human Resources is measured according to the response categories clients check on a questionnaire item (high satisfaction, medium satisfaction, low satisfaction).

Operational definitions are often not stated explicitly but implied from the research report, the memo, or the briefing. A manager should always encourage research analysts to state explicitly their operational definitions. Then the manager can focus on these definitions and answer a variety of measurement questions, such as the ones we will discuss below.

Reading the preceding operational definitions, you may have been troubled by the lack of complete congruence between the concept and the indicator. For example, assume the city transit system evaluates the job performance of its bus drivers by examining each one's accident record and on-time rate. A driver may well have a good accident record and be on time in her bus runs, and yet be a bad bus driver. Perhaps the on-time record was achieved by not stopping to pick up passengers when the driver was running late. Or perhaps the driver's bus was continually in the shop because the driver did not maintain the bus properly.

This example suggests that indicators may not be a complete measure of a concept. Most students of measurement accept the following statement:

$$\text{indicator} = \text{concept} + \text{error}$$

A good indicator of a concept has very little error; a poor indicator is only remotely related to the underlying concept.

In many cases several indicators are used to measure a single concept. One reason for using **multiple indicators** is that a concept may have more than one dimension. For example, the effectiveness of a receptionist may be related to the receptionist's efficiency and the receptionist's courtesy to people. To measure effectiveness adequately in this instance, we would need at least one indicator of efficiency and one of courtesy. The term *triangulation* is sometimes used to describe how multiple indicators enclose or "home in" on a concept.

**multiple indicators**

Multiple indicators are also needed when the indicators are only poor representations of the underlying concept. The success of a neighborhood revitalization program would require several indicators. The increase in housing values might be one indicator. The decrease in crime, reduction in vandalism, willingness to walk outside at night, and general physical appearance might be other indicators. Each indicator reflects part of the concept of "neighborhood revitalization," but also reflects numerous other factors, such as economic growth in the entire city, pressure for housing, street lighting, and so on. The theory behind multiple indicators in this situation is that the errors in one indicator will cancel out the errors in another indicator. What remains will measure the concept far better than any single indicator would. For these reasons, a "multiple indicator strategy" to measure important concepts comes highly recommended.

## MEASUREMENT VALIDITY

An indicator is a **valid** measure of a concept if it accurately measures the concept it is intended to measure. In other words, if the indicator contains very little error, then the indicator is a valid measure of the concept. The validity of an indicator often becomes a managerial problem. For example, many governments give civil service exams that are supposed to be valid indicators of on-the-job performance. If minorities or women do not do as well as white males do on these exams, the manager is open to discrimination suits. The manager's only defense in such a situation is to prove that the civil service exam is a valid indicator of on-the-job performance (not an easy task).

**valid indicator**

**convergent validity**

**discriminant validity**

Validity can be either convegent or discriminant. In the preceding paragraph, we were discussing **convergent validity**—do the indicator and the concept converge? Does the indicator measure the concept in question? **Discriminant validity** asks whether the indicator allows the concept to be distinguished from other similar, but different, concepts. For example, using achievement scores on standardized tests may lack discriminant validity if the tests have some cultural bias. A good indicator of educational achievement will distinguish that concept from the concept of white, middle-class acculturation. A culture-biased test will indicate only educational achievement that corresponds with the dominant culture. As a result, such an indicator may not be valid.

**face validity**

**consensual validity**

**correlational validity**

**predictive validity**

Social scientists have long grappled with the idea of measurement validity. They have suggested several ways that validity may be established. An indicator has **face validity** if the manager using the indicator accepts it as a valid indicator of the concept in queston. An indicator has **consensual validity** if numerous persons in different situations accept the indicator as a valid indicator of the concept. The recidivism rate, for example, has consensual validity as a good measure of a prison's ability to reform a criminal. An indicator has **correlational validity** if it correlates strongly with other indicators that are accepted as valid. Finally, an indicator has **predictive validity** if it correctly predicts a specified outcome. For example, if scores on a civil service exam accurately predict on-the-job performance, the exam has predictive validity.

These four types of validity offer ways that a manager can argue that an indicator is valid. However, they do not guarantee that the indicator is a particularly effective measure of the concept in question. An indicator may have face validity, consensual validity, correlational validity, and predictive validity and still not be as effective as other measures. Consider the Law School Admissions Test (LSAT). The LSAT has face validity and consensual validity (numerous law schools use it to screen applicants). It also has correlational validity (it correlates with undergraduate grades) and predictive validity (it correlates with law school grades). Yet, the LSAT is not as strong a predictor of law school performance as is the socioeconomic status of the student's family.

With all the tests for validity and all the different ways an indicator can be validated, developing valid indicators of concepts is still an art. It requires all the skills that a manager has at his or her disposal. To be sure, in some cases, such as finding indicators of lawn mower efficiency, valid indicators are easy to derive. On the other hand, developing valid indicators of community police effectiveness is a Sisyphean task.

One way to ease this task is to review the published literature in a field. In general, if an indicator is used in the literature, it has at a minimum both face and consensual validity, and it may meet other validity criteria as well. Before (or while) you create your own indicators of an important concept, it is a good idea to consult the relevant literature. This approach carries additional benefits, such as making you aware of how other researchers have approached relevant problems and what they have found. Such information can make your analytical task easier.

## MEASUREMENT RELIABILITY

An indicator is **reliable** if it consistently assigns the same numbers to some **reliable indicator** phenomenon that has not, in fact, changed. For example, if a person measures the effectiveness of the police force in a neighborhood twice over a short period of time and arrives at the same value, then the indicator is termed *reliable*. If two different people use an indicator and arrive at the same value, then again, we say that the indicator is reliable. Another way of defining a reliable indicator is to state that an indicator is a reliable measure if the values obtained by using the indicator are not affected by who is doing the measuring, by where the measuring is being done, or by any other factors other than variation in the concept being measured.

The two major threats to measurement reliability are subjectivity and lack of precision. A **subjective measure** is a measure that relies on the judgment of the **subjective** measurer or of a respondent in a survey. A general measure that requires the **measure** analyst to assess the quality of a neighborhood is a subjective measure. Subjective measures have some inherent unreliability, because the final measures must incorporate judgment. Reliability can be improved by rigorous training of individuals who will do the measuring. The objective of this training is to develop consistency. Another method of increasing reliability is to have several persons assign a value and then select the consensus value as the measure of the phenomenon in question. Some studies report a measured inter-rater reliability based on the consistency of measurement performed by several raters.

Reliability can also be improved by eliminating the subjectivity of the analyst. Rather than providing a general assessment of the quality of the neighborhood, the analyst might have to answer a series of specific questions. Was there trash in the streets? Did houses have peeling paint? Were dogs running loose? Did the street have potholes? How many potholes?

Reliability problems often arise in survey research. For example, suppose that you were asked to respond to survey questions concerning the performance of one of your instructors—or a local political figure, or "bureaucrats"—on a day that had been especially frustrating for you. You might well evaluate these subjects more harshly than on a day when all had seemed right with the world. Although nothing about these subjects had changed, extraneous factors could introduce volatility into the ratings, an indication of unreliability. By contrast, if your views of these subjects actually did change and the survey instrument picked up the (true) changes, the measurement would be considered reliable.

Unfortunately, while removing the subjective element from a measure will increase reliability, it may decrease validity. Certain concepts important to the public manager—employee effectiveness, citizen satisfaction with services, the impact of a recreation program—are not amenable to a series of objective indicators. In such situations a combination of objective and subjective indicators may well be the preferred means of measurement.

**Lack of precision** is the second major threat to reliability. To illustrate this **lack of precision** problem, let us say that Barbara Kennedy, city manager of Barren, Montana, wants to identify the areas of Barren with high unemployment so that she can use her federal job funds in those areas. Kennedy takes an employment survey and measures the unemployment rate in the city. Because her sample is fairly small, neighborhood unemployment rates have a potential error of $\pm 5\%$. This lack of precision makes the unemployment measure fairly unreliable. For example, neighborhood A might have a real unemployment rate of 5%, but the survey measure indicates 10%. Neighborhood B's unemployment rate is 3.5%, but the survey measure indicates 10%. Clearly the manager has a problem.

The precision of these measures can be improved by taking larger samples. But in many cases, this task is not so easy. Let us say the city of Barren has a measure of housing quality that terms neighborhood housing as "good," "above average," "average," and "dilapidated." Assume that 50% of the city's housing falls into this last category, dilapidated. If the housing evaluation were undertaken to designate target areas for rehabilitation, the measure lacks precision. No city can afford to rehabilitate 50% of its housing. Barren needs a more precise measure that can distinguish among houses in the dilapidated category. This can be done by creating measures that are more sensitive to variations in dilapidated houses (the premise is that some dilapidated houses are more dilapidated than others). Improvement of precision in this instance is far more difficult than increasing the sample size.

### MEASURING RELIABILITY

Unlike validity, the reliability of a measure can be determined objectively. A common method for assessing measurement reliability is to measure the same phenomenon or set of variables twice over a reasonably short time period and to correlate the two sets of measures (see Chapter 16). This procedure is known as **test-retest reliability**.

**test-retest reliability**

Another approach to determining reliability is to prepare alternative forms that are designed to be equivalent to measure a given concept, and then to administer both of them at the same time. For example, near the beginning of a survey, a researcher may include a set of five questions to measure attitudes toward government spending, and toward the end of the survey may present five more questions on the same topic, all parallel in content. The correlation between the responses obtained on the two sets of items is a measure of **parallel forms reliability**. Closely related is **split-half reliability**, in which the researcher divides a set of items intended to measure a given concept into two parts or halves; a common practice is to divide the even-numbered questions and the odd-numbered questions. The correlation between the responses obtained on the two halves is a measure of split-half reliability. Cronbach's alpha, a common measure of reliability, is based on this method.

**parallel forms reliability**

**split-half reliability**

In all three types of reliability measurement—test-retest, parallel forms, and split-half—the higher the intercorrelations among the items, the higher the reliability of the indicators.

## TYPES OF MEASURES _____

We have already discussed two types of indicators—subjective and objective. The subjective indicator requires some judgment to assign a value, whereas the objective indicator seeks to minimize discretion. Assume that the city manager wants to know the amount of city services delivered to each neighborhood in the city. Objective measures of city services would be the acres of city parks, number of tons of trash collected, number of police patrols, and so on. Subjective measures of city services could be obtained by asking citizens whether the levels of various city services were adequate.

A third type of measure, the **unobtrusive measure**, is intended to circumvent the so-called Hawthorne effect, in which the act of measuring a phenomenon can alter the behavior being assessed. For example, asking city residents about the quality of police services may sensitize them to police actions. If an individual is asked his or her opinion again, the answer may be biased by the earlier sensitizing. A city employment counselor, for example, may know that his evaluation is based on the number of individuals who are placed in jobs. He may then focus his efforts on the easiest persons to place, to build up a favorable record. Any reactive measure (a measure that affects behavior when it is taken) has some inherent reliability and validity problems.

**unobtrusive measure**

One way to circumvent this problem is through the use of unobtrusive measures (see Webb et al. 1973). A library, for example, could determine its most useful reference books by asking patrons which reference books they use most frequently. In this situation, the problem is that many people who never use reference books might answer the question. An unobtrusive measure of reference book popularity (since they normally cannot be checked out) would be the amount of wear on each book.

Suppose the head of the Alcohol Beverage Control Board in Oklahoma wants to know how much liquor is consumed "by the drink." Since it is illegal to serve liquor by the drink in Oklahoma, sending a survey questionnaire to private clubs would yield little response. An unobtrusive measure would be to examine the trash of all private clubs and count the number of empty liquor bottles found in their trash.

Unobtrusive measures can be used in a variety of situations and can take on as many different forms as the creative manager can devise. They do have some limitations, however. Unless care is taken in selection, the measures may lack validity. For example, a manager may decide that she can determine the amount of time an office spends in nonproductive socializing by measuring the office's consumption of coffee and fountain water (this fountain uses bottled water). She assumes that more coffee and more water fountain meetings imply less productivity. In fact, one office might consume more coffee than another because it has older workers (thus more likely to drink coffee) or because the office puts in more overtime and needs coffee to make it through the night.

## LEVELS OF MEASUREMENT

In many cases, we have been discussing data that are actual numbers—tons of garbage collected in a given town, number of arrests made by the police per week, response times in minutes of a local fire department. Since this information consists of real numbers, it is possible to perform all types of arithmetic calculations with them—addition, subtraction, multiplication, and division—just as we have been doing all along. Thus we have been able to compute the mean or average number of tons of garbage collected per week as well as the average response time of the fire department.

Unfortunately for the public administrator, available data are often not measured in nearly as precise a fashion as are these variables. There are several reasons for the lack of precision. In some cases, it is a reflection of the state of the art of measurement. For instance, although it may be possible to say that a citizen is very satisfied, satisfied, neutral, dissatisfied, or very dissatisfied with a new state-financed welfare program, it usually is *not* possible to state that his or her level of satisfaction is exactly 2.3—or 5 or 9.856 or 1.003. Most measures of attitudes and opinions do not allow this level of exactitude. In other instances, loss of precision results from errors in measurement or, perhaps, from lack of foresight. For example, you may be interested in the number of traffic fatalities in the town of Berrysville over the past few years. As a consequence of incomplete records or spotty reporting in the past, you may not be able to arrive at the exact number of fatalities in each of these years, but you may be quite confident in determining that there have been *fewer* fatalities this year than *last* year.

Finally, some variables inherently lack numerical precision: one could classify the citizens of a community according to race (white, black, Hispanic, other), sex (male, female), religion (Protestant, Catholic, Jewish, Buddhist, other), or any of a number of other attributes. However, it would be futile to attempt to calculate the arithmetic average of sex or religion, and it would be meaningless to say that a citizen is more black than white: a person is either one or the other.

In discussing these different types of variables, social scientists usually refer to
**levels of measurement** the concept of **levels of measurement**. Social scientists conventionally speak of three levels of measurement. The first or highest (most precise) level is known as
**interval level** the **interval level** of measurement. The name derives from the fact that the measurement is based on a unit or interval that is accepted as a common standard and that yields identical results in repeated applications. Weight is measured in pounds or grams, height in feet and inches, distance in miles. The variables discussed at the beginning of this section are all measured at the interval level: *tons* of garbage, *number* of arrests, response times in *minutes*. As a consequence of these standard units, it is possible to state not only that there were more arrests last week than this week, but also that there were exactly *18* more arrests. (Some texts discuss a fourth level of measurement—*ratio*—but it is effectively the same as interval measurement.)

**ordinal level** The second level of measurement is called **ordinal**. At this level of measurement, it is possible to say that one object (or event or phenomenon) has *more* or *less* of a given characteristic than another, but it is not possible to say *how much* more or less. Generally, we lack an agreed-upon standard or unit at this level of measurement. Almost all assessments of attitudes and opinions are at the ordinal level.

Consider the previous example which focused on citizen satisfaction with a new welfare program. At this time, no one is quite sure how to measure satisfaction or how a unit of satisfaction may be defined. Nevertheless, an interviewer could be dispatched to the field to ask a representative sample of citizens: "How satisfied are you with the new welfare program recently instituted in this community? Very satisfied, satisfied, neutral, dissatisfied, or very dissatisfied?" Of course, it would not be possible to ascertain from a citizen his or her exact numeric level of satisfaction (e.g., 4.37, 16.23). However, if one citizen answers that he is "very satisfied" with the program, it is safe to conclude that he is *more* satisfied than if he had stated that he was "satisfied" (or "neutral," "dissatisfied," or "very dissatisfied"); similarly, a response of "very dissatisfied" indicates *less* satisfaction than one of "dissatisfied" (or "neutral," "satisfied," or "very satisfied"). How *much* more or less remains a mystery. The interviewer might also ask citizens how good a job the mayor is doing in running the city (very good, good, average, poor, very poor), and to what extent they are interested in community affairs (very interested, interested, neutral, uninterested, very uninterested). These also are ordinal level variables and are subject to the same limitations as is the satisfaction measure.

The name *ordinal measurement* derives from the ordinal numbers: first, second, third, and so on. These allow the *ranking* of a set of objects (or events or phenomena) with respect to some characteristic, but they do not indicate the exact distances or differences between the objects. For example, in an election, the order of finish of the candidates does not say anything about the number of votes each one received. The order of finish indicates only that the winner received more votes than did the runner-up, who in turn received more votes than the third-place finisher. By contrast, the exact vote totals of the candidates are interval information.

At the third level of measurement, one loses not only the ability to state exactly how much of a trait or characteristic an object or event possesses (interval measurement) but also the ability to state that it has more or less of the characteristic than has another object or event (ordinal measurement). In short, the **nominal level** of measurement totally lacks any sense of relative size or magnitude: it allows one to say only that things are the same or different. Some of the most important variables in the social sciences are nominal. These were mentioned before: race, sex, and religion. It is easy to expand this list to management: occupation, type of housing, job classification, sector of the economy, employment status.

Now that you have some idea of the three levels of measurement, write several examples of interval, ordinal, and nominal variables in the space provided on page 106. After you have finished, fill in the level of measurement for each of the variables listed in Table 7.1.

**nominal level**

**TABLE 7.1**
Some Variables: What Is the Level of Measurement?

| Variable | Level of Measurement |
|---|---|
| 1. Number of children | |
| 2. Opinion of the way the president is handling economy (strongly approve; approve; neutral; disapprove; strongly disapprove) | |
| 3. Age | |
| 4. State of residence | |
| 5. Mode of transportation to work | |
| 6. Perceived income (very low; below average; average; above average; very high) | |
| 7. Income in dollars | |
| 8. Interest in statistics (low; medium; high) | |
| 9. High school attended | |
| 10. Hours of overtime per week | |
| 11. Your comprehension of this book (great; adequate; forget it) | |

# LEVELS OF MEASUREMENT AND MEASURES OF CENTRAL TENDENCY

It is time to address the "so what?" question about levels of measurement: What difference does it make that the types of variables with which public administrators must deal are measured at the three levels?

The answer is both simple and important: *the statistics that may be calculated to summarize the distribution of single variables and to describe the relationship between variables differ from level to level.* For these statistics, it is also easy to see the source of the differences. Each of the levels expresses a different amount of information about a variable, and this idea is reflected directly in the kind of statistics that may be calculated and used.

For example, if a variable is measured at the interval level, we usually know everything about it that we may wish to know. It is possible to locate precisely all the observations along a scale: $17,529 yearly income, 4.57 prostitution arrests per week, 38 years of age, 247 cubic feet of sewage. Because for these variables an equal distance separates each whole number on the measurement scale (dollars, arrests, years, cubic feet), all mathematical operations can be performed. Thus, as we saw in Chapter 2, the scores of a group of individuals can be added and the sum divided by the number of observations to obtain the mean income, number of arrests, age, and cubic feet of sewage. It is also possible to find the *median* or the middle score of the group for each of these variables. And, of course, the *mode*—the value occurring most frequently in a distribution—presents no problem.

Table 7.2 displays the number of pilots at selected air bases. At what level of measurement are these data? Be sure that you can calculate the mean ($11886 \div 7 = 1968$), median (896), and mode (0) for this distribution. If you have any problems, refer back to Chapter 2. As shown there (and here), with *interval* level data the manager can calculate and use all three measures of central tendency.

Now consider *ordinal* data. At this level of measurement we are able to rank objects or observations, but it is not possible to locate them precisely along a scale. A citizen may "strongly disapprove" of the Normal mass transit system's performance, but no number is available that expresses her exact level of disapproval or how much less she approves than if she had said "disapprove." Because there are no numerical scores or numbers attached to the responses—which, in the case of interval variables, are added and divided to compute the mean—*it is not possible to calculate the mean for a variable measured at the ordinal level.*

**TABLE 7.2**

Pilots at Selected Air Bases

| Air Base | Number of Pilots |
| --- | --- |
| Minot | 0 |
| Torrejon | 2974 |
| Kapaun | 896 |
| Osan | 0 |
| Andrews | 6531 |
| Yokota | 57 |
| Guam | 1428 |

How about the median? Can it be calculated for ordinal data? Suppose an interviewer obtains from 11 citizens their responses to the question, "Do you approve or disapprove of the Normal mass transit system's performance?

Strongly approve, approve, neutral, disapprove, strongly disapprove?" (See Table 7.3, names withheld for purposes of confidentiality.) To find the median, follow these steps.

**TABLE 7.3**

Citizens' Responses to Question
About Normal's Mass Transit System

| Citizen | Response |
| --- | --- |
| 1 | Strongly disapprove |
| 2 | Approve |
| 3 | Neutral |
| 4 | Strongly disapprove |
| 5 | Disapprove |
| 6 | Strongly disapprove |
| 7 | Strongly approve |
| 8 | Strongly disapprove |
| 9 | Neutral |
| 10 | Approve |
| 11 | Disapprove |

**STEP 1**  Arrange the responses in rank order. This ordering is possible because ordinal data preserve the ranking of cases (see earlier discussion). That is, you can rank the responses in order of expressing strongest approval of the mass transit system's performance to expressing least approval. Alternatively, you can order them from least approval to strongest. If you did it the first way, your data will look like those shown in Table 7.4.

**TABLE 7.4**

Rank Ordering of Citizens' Responses

| Citizen | Response |
| --- | --- |
| 7 | Strongly approve |
| 2 | Approve |
| 10 | Approve |
| 3 | Neutral |
| 9 | Neutral |
| 5 | Disapprove |
| 11 | Disapprove |
| 1 | Strongly disapprove |
| 4 | Strongly disapprove |
| 6 | Strongly disapprove |
| 8 | Strongly disapprove |

If you ranked the citizens in the other direction, read the list from the bottom up.

**STEP 2**   Now that the cases have been arranged in order with respect to the variable (opinion of the Normal mass transit system's performance), it is a simple matter to find the median. The median is the middle score, or the score of the case that falls in the middle. Since there are 11 cases, the sixth score falls in the middle. (The rule is to add 1 to the number of cases and divide this result by 2. So $11 + 1 = 12$, and $12 \div 2 = 6$. See Chapter 2.) Counting from either the top or the bottom of the list (it makes no difference), the middle score belongs to citizen 5: *disapprove* is the median response of the group.

Be sure to note that the median is *not* citizen 5. She is just one of the respondents, not a score on the variable of interest (opinion about the Normal transit system's performance). Also, make sure that you understand that the median is *not* the score of citizen 6. He just happened to be the sixth person interviewed. After the scores have been arranged in order, his score falls tenth in the list (or second, if you count up from the bottom). Clearly his is not the middle response.

**STEP 3**   Convert the data into a frequency distribution; that is, show how many citizens gave each of the responses. See Table 7.5. If you have any difficulties, refer to Chapter 1.

A frequency distribution is the form in which ordinal data are most often displayed. The median still corresponds to the middle or the sixth case. Just as before, counting either up or down the list shows that the sixth case gave the response "disapprove," so it is the median.

It is important to note that the median is *not* "neutral." Although "neutral" is the middle response category, it does not tell us anything about the middle response given by the 11 citizens. "Neutral" falls in the middle of the scale but not in the middle of the 11 citizens. Note also that the median is the middle score of the 11 citizens, or the response "disapprove."

**TABLE 7.5**

Frequency Distribution for Citizens' Responses

| Response | Number of Citizens |
|---|---|
| Strongly approve | 1 |
| Approve | 2 |
| Neutral | 2 |
| Disapprove | 2 |
| Strongly disapprove | 4 |

We have now shown that the median can be calculated for ordinal variables. So can the mode. In Table 7.5, the most frequently mentioned response is "strongly disapprove," given by four citizens. Therefore, it is the mode or modal response.

Finally, at the *nominal* level of measurement, it is not possible to assign numerical scores to cases (interval level). A score of 1.7 on religion or 458 on nationality would be arbitrary and would make no sense. *Thus it is not possible to calculate the mean for nominal data.*

Furthermore, the values of a group of cases on a nominal variable cannot be ranked in any kind of meaningful ordering of least to most, or vice versa (ordinal level). There is no meaningful or correct way to order the categories of race, religion, sex, or any other nominal variable. Because the median is predicated on the ability to rank cases or observations of a variable so that the middle or median value may be found, *it is not possible to calculate the median for nominal data.*

However, the mode can be found for nominal data. For the data in Table 7.6, which is the modal occupation of the employees of the Civil Service Commission?

**TABLE 7.6**
Civil Service Commission Employees by Occupation

| Occupation | Number of People | Percentage |
|---|---|---|
| Lawyer | 192 | 61% |
| Butcher | 53 | 17% |
| Doctor | 41 | 13% |
| Baker | 20 | 6% |
| Candlestick maker | 7 | 2% |
| Indian chief | 3 | 1% |
| | N = 316 | 100 |

The mode is "lawyer," since it is the occupation of the largest number of people (192) in the distribution. Usually, the percentage of observations in the modal category is given, here 61%. Make sure that you can calculate the percentage distribution. If you have any difficulty, see Chapter 1.

## HIERARCHY OF MEASUREMENT

We can summarize this discussion of levels of measurement and measures of central tendency in a convenient table. In Table 7.7, place an X in the column of a row if the designated measure of central tendency (mode, median, mean) can be calculated for a given level of measurement (interval, ordinal, nominal).

If you have completed the table correctly, X's will appear in the upper left triangle of the table above the diagonal that slopes upward from left to right. If you did not find this pattern, you should review earlier parts of the chapter.

**TABLE 7.7**

Hierarchy of Measurement

| Level of Measurement | Measure of Central Tendency | | |
| --- | --- | --- | --- |
| | *Mode* | *Median* | *Mean* |
| Interval | | | |
| Ordinal | | | |
| Nominal | | | |

What Table 7.7 indicates is that any statistic that can be calculated for a variable at a lower (less precise) level of measurement can also be calculated at all higher (more precise) levels of measurement. Thus the mode is available at all three levels, the median at the ordinal and the interval levels, and the mean only at the interval level. This rule is usually stated as the "hierarchy of measurement," to indicate the ascending power of the higher levels of measurement. To the degree possible, then, it is always to your advantage to construct and use variables measured at higher levels.

With this knowledge, you are now in a position to describe phenomena of interest in quantitative terms. For example, consider your work organization. The mean age of employees may be 37.1 years, the median 35, and the mode 39. The median opinion of employees with respect to the in-house information system's performance may be "disapprove"; perhaps the modal opinion is "strongly disapprove." Most of the employees are probably white and male; and so on.

## SOME CAUTIONS

Two cautions regarding this discussion of levels of measurement should be kept in mind. First, most of the time you will not calculate statistics yourself; instead, a computer program will compute them for you. In order to store information compactly in a computer, the *substantive category names for ordinal variables*—such as strongly agree, agree, neutral, disagree, strongly disagree—*as well as for nominal variables*—such as white, black, Hispanic—*are entered and stored in the machine as numbers.* These numbers are usually called *codes.* For example, the coding schemes in Table 7.8 may apply.

The researcher keeps track of the correspondence between the substantive categories and the numeric codes for each variable through the use of a *code-book.* The codebook shows how each variable is coded—or stored—in the computer. The important point to remember is that *the computer contains only the numeric codes, and it calculates all statistics on the basis of them.* (For interval level variables, the codes are the actual data values—7.123, 5.6, 10075.9, and so

**TABLE 7.8**

Examples of Two Coding Schemes

| Coding Scheme 1 | | Coding Scheme 2 | |
| --- | --- | --- | --- |
| *Code* | *Response* | *Code* | *Response* |
| 1 | Strongly agree | 1 | White |
| 2 | Agree | 2 | Black |
| 3 | Neutral | 3 | Hispanic |
| 4 | Disagree | | |
| 5 | Strongly disagree | | |

on.) As a result, if instructed to do so, the computer can and will calculate a mean or a median for nominal variables or a mean for ordinal variables based on the codes—even though these statistics have no meaning at these levels of measurement. It is up to you as the analyst to recognize such statistics as a mean attitude of 2.7 or a median race of 1 for what they are: garbage.

The second caution is in part a consequence of the first. Because ordinal variables frequently are coded for computer utilization in the manner shown above—1 = strongly agree, 2 = agree, 3 = neutral, and so on—some students have jumped to the incorrect conclusion that these codes are actually meaningful numbers on a scale that expresses the precise level of an individual's agreement or disagreement with an interviewer's question. In other words, they have assumed that the coding categories are actual numbers and can be treated as such for statistical calculations—just as if they were interval data. This practice, which is rather common in the social sciences, has led to the ordinal-interval debate. (Don't feel bad if you have missed it; it is not exactly a household term.) As the title suggests, the debate has focused on the justification for—or lack of it—and the advantages of treating ordinal data as interval. Both sides have produced some persuasive evidence, and the debate has yet to be resolved definitively.

Our recommendation for students just starting out in quantitative work in public management is that you adopt the stance of the statistical purist—that you calculate and use for ordinal data only those statistics that are clearly appropriate for that level of measurement. For now, when you need to summarize or describe the distribution of an ordinal variable, rely on the median and mode. In the future, if you decide to continue your work in statistics, you can read some of the literature in the ordinal-interval debate and come to your own conclusions.

You may be wondering why we are placing such emphasis on the ordinal-interval debate. When you see the steps involved in examining and interpreting *relationships* among ordinal variables—as compared to those involved in the analysis of interval data (see the chapters on regression)—the significance of this debate will grow. But that is the purpose of Chapters 13 through 15.

# SOME MEASUREMENT
# TECHNIQUES BASED ON
# STANDARDIZED SCORES

Although most of measurement is an art, in certain areas techniques are available to assist the manager. For example, John Pelissero, data analyst for the mayor, feels that excellent performance by city garbage collection crews can be summarized by two measures—tons of trash collected and number of complaints phoned in by citizens. This information for all five city work crews is listed in Table 7.9.

**TABLE 7.9**
Performance of Garbage Collection Crews

| Crew | Tons Collected | Complaints Against |
|------|----------------|--------------------|
| A | 127 | 6 |
| B | 132 | 8 |
| C | 118 | 4 |
| D | 170 | 9 |
| E | 123 | 3 |

Since John wants to transform these two indicators into a single measure, he follows these steps.

**STEP 1**  Calculate the mean ($\mu$) and standard deviation ($\sigma$) for each indicator. They are shown in Table 7.10.

**TABLE 7.10**
Mean and Standard Deviation for Each Indicator

|  | Tons | Complaints |
|------|------|------------|
| $\mu$ | 134 | 6 |
| $\sigma$ | 18.6 | 2.3 |

**STEP 2**  Convert each of the raw scores of trash and complaints into $z$ scores by taking the raw score, subtracting the mean, and dividing that difference by the standard deviation. These calculations are shown in Tables 7.11 and 7.12. Since complaints indicate poor performance, all the complaints' $z$ scores were multiplied by $-1$ to reverse the scale.

**TABLE 7.11**

z Scores for Tons of Trash Collected

| Tons $- \mu$ | $(X - \mu) \div \sigma = z$ |
|---|---|
| $127 - 134 = -7$ | $\div 18.6 = -.38$ |
| $132 - 134 = -2$ | $\div 18.6 = -.11$ |
| $118 - 134 = -16$ | $\div 18.6 = -.86$ |
| $170 - 134 = \phantom{-}36$ | $\div 18.6 = \phantom{-}1.94$ |
| $123 - 134 = -11$ | $\div 18.6 = -.59$ |

**TABLE 7.12**

z Scores for Complaints

| Complaints $-\mu = (X - \mu) \div \sigma = z$ | | | $-z$ |
|---|---|---|---|
| $6 - 6 =$ | $0 \div 2.3$ | $= \phantom{-}0$ | $0$ |
| $8 - 6 =$ | $2 \div 2.3$ | $= \phantom{-}.87$ | $-.87$ |
| $4 - 6 =$ | $-2 \div 2.3$ | $= -.87$ | $.87$ |
| $9 - 6 =$ | $3 \div 2.3$ | $= \phantom{-}1.30$ | $-1.30$ |
| $3 - 6 =$ | $-3 \div 2.3$ | $= -1.30$ | $1.30$ |

**STEP 3**    For each crew, add the z scores together, as shown in Table 7.13, to obtain performance scores. The performance scores can then be used to compare the trash collection crews with each other on a single measure. The z-score procedure simply converts each indicator to a common base (standard deviations from the mean) so that the indicators can be added. Note that the highest-performing trash crew was fourth in total tons of trash collected.

**TABLE 7.13**

Performance Scores for Garbage Collection Crews

| Crew | Tons | Complaints | Performance |
|---|---|---|---|
| A | $-.38$ | $0$ | $-.38$ |
| B | $-.11$ | $-.87$ | $-.98$ |
| C | $-.86$ | $.87$ | $.01$ |
| D | $1.94$ | $-1.30$ | $.64$ |
| E | $-.59$ | $1.30$ | $.71$ |

This procedure weights both tons of grabage collected and complaints equally. If John felt that tons of trash was twice as important as complaints, he would multiply the tons' z scores by 2 before adding them to the complaints' z scores, as shown in Table 7.14. Note that some of the trash crews change ranking when tons of trash collected is given a higher weighting.

**TABLE 7.14**

Performance Scores When Tons Weighted Twice as Heavily as Complaints

| Crew | Tons × 2 | Complaints | Performance |
|------|----------|------------|-------------|
| A | $-.38 \times 2 = -.76$ | 0 | $-.76$ |
| B | $-.11 \times 2 = -.22$ | $-.87$ | $-1.09$ |
| C | $-.86 \times 2 = -1.92$ | .87 | $-1.05$ |
| D | $1.94 \times 2 = 3.88$ | $-1.30$ | 2.58 |
| E | $-.60 \times 2 = -1.20$ | 1.30 | .10 |

Another useful equal-weighting scheme is to weight the tons' $z$ scores and the complaints' $z$ scores by one-half. This procedure is equivalent to calculating the mean performance score for each garbage collection crew. The resulting performance scores retain the value of a $z$ score in indicating how many units (standard deviations) a score is above or below the mean. Positive scores indicate performance above the mean, and negative scores indicate performance below the mean. Performance scores calculated in this manner, as displayed in Table 7.15, show that crews A and B are below the mean in performance, crew C is at the mean, and crews D and E are above the mean.

**TABLE 7.15**

Performance Scores When Tons and Complaints Are Weighted by One-Half

| Crew | Tons × .5 | Complaints × .5 | Performance |
|------|-----------|-----------------|-------------|
| A | $-.38 \times .5 = -.19$ | $0 \times .5 = 0$ | $-.19$ |
| B | $-.11 \times .5 = -.055$ | $-.87 \times .5 = -.435$ | $-.49$ |
| C | $-.86 \times .5 = -.43$ | $.87 \times .5 = .435$ | .005 |
| D | $1.94 \times .5 = .97$ | $-1.30 \times .5 = -.65$ | .32 |
| E | $-.59 \times .5 = -.295$ | $1.30 \times .5 = .65$ | .355 |

The manager can assign any weights desired as long as the weights can be justified. In addition, the number of indicators that can be combined when using this procedure has no limit. A manager can use 2, 4, 6, or 50 indicators and combine them by adding $z$ scores.

A note of caution is in order. The $z$ score technique should only be used when the manager believes that the concept being measured has only one dimension. If the concept has two or more dimensions (as the effectiveness of a receptionist is a function of efficiency and courtesy), then a more sophisticated statistical technique called *factor analysis* should be used to combine several indicators. When you have multiple indicators of a multidimensional concept and want to combine some of the indicators, consult a statistician.

# CHAPTER SUMMARY _____

Measurement is the assignment of numbers to some phenomenon. Some variables cannot be measured so precisely but only in terms of categories. An operational definition tells the analyst how a concept will be measured. An indicator is a variable linked to a concept through an operational definition. The two key issues in measurement are reliability or consistency of measurement and validity or meaningfulness (Are we measuring what we think we are measuring?). Several kinds of validity and three types of measures (subjective, objective, and unobtrusive) are discussed in the chapter.

In management, we use three levels of measurement: interval, ordinal, and nominal. Interval measurements are based on a standard unit or interval. Ordinal measurements lack such an agreed-upon standard or unit. Nominal measurements lack any sense of relative size or magnitude; they only allow one to say that things are the same or different.

The level of measurement determines the statistics that can be calculated. More specifically, the hierarchy of measurement shows that the more precise the measurement, the more numerous the statistics that can be calculated and used. Thus the mean, the median, and the mode can be calculated for interval level data. The median and the mode can be calculated for ordinal level data. Only the mode can be calculated for nominal level data.

# PROBLEMS _____

**7.1** A prominent social scientist believes that she can measure the effectiveness of police departments by asking citizens how effective they feel their police department is. What are the advantages and disadvantages of this measure?

**7.2** Compile a list of indicators that could be used to evaluate the quality of a city's sanitary landfill (garbage dump).

**7.3** A major city's police force requires all police applicants to be 5 feet 8 inches tall and to be able to chin themselves on an 8-foot bar. What concept does the police force want to measure? Evaluate these indicators.

**7.4** Compile a list of indicators that could be used to evaluate a building maintenance crew.

**7.5** What are the relative advantages of subjective and objective indicators of a concept?

**7.6** The civic center of Kulture City is badly in need of refurbishment. However, before the city council allocates funds for this purpose, its members want to get a better idea of how frequently the residents of Kulture City actually use the center. To find out, they hire a public opinion polling firm to survey citizens. The pollsters ask a random sample of residents the following question: "In the last year, how many times have you attended performances or activities at the Kulture City civic center?" The responses of the sample are listed in the accompanying table.

| Number of Performances or Activities Attended | Number of Citizens |
|:---:|:---:|
| 0 | 587 |
| 1 | 494 |
| 2 | 260 |
| 3 | 135 |
| 4 | 97 |

(a) At what level of measurement are these data?
(b) Calculate the appropriate measures of central tendency and the percentage distribution.
(c) Should the city council allocate money to refurbish the civic center?
(d) Write a short memorandum in which you use these results to make a recommendation to the city council.

**7.7** The head of the data processing department in Normal wants to estimate the amount of waste and inefficiency in her department. She conducts a survey of employees in the department. One question asks, "To what extent does this department have waste and inefficiency in its operations?" The responses to the item are given in the accompanying table.

| Response | Number of Employees |
|:---|:---:|
| To a very great extent | 42 |
| To a great extent | 31 |
| To a moderate extent | 19 |
| To some extent | 12 |
| Not at all | 7 |

(a) At what level of measurement are these data?
(b) Calculate the percentage distribution and the appropriate measures of central tendency.
(c) According to these data, does the department appear to have a problem with waste and inefficiency? Explain your answer.

**7.8** Refer to Problem 7.7. Evaluate the validity and reliability of the survey question as a measure of the waste and inefficiency in the department. Suggest other measures that the department could use to measure waste and inefficiency, and explain why they would be an improvement over the survey question.

**7.9**  The head of a city's recreation department feels that the employees of the department are the best in the city. Each year, all city employees receive a standardized performance evaluation that rates them on a scale of performance: "far above expectations," "above expectations," "meets expectations," "below expectations," and "far below expectations." (Each rating has an operational definition.) The department head feels that his assessment of employees will be justified if at least 90% of them fall into the top two categories. The ratings received by department employees are shown in the accompanying table.

| Rating | Number of Employees |
|---|---|
| Far above expectations | 15 |
| Above expectations | 22 |
| Meets expectations | 77 |
| Below expectations | 9 |
| Far below expectations | 8 |

(a) At what level of measurement are these data?

(b) Calculate the percentage distribution and the appropriate measures of central tendency.

(c) What can you tell the head of the recreation department?

**7.10**  The head of the recreation department from Problem 7.9 has decided that he is not satisfied with the city's standardized performance evaluation form for employees. The form consists largely of the summary evaluation and operational definitions of the five ratings of employee performance (see Problem 7.9). He wants to develop improved measures of employee performance. Help him by suggesting improved measures and by evaluating their validity and reliability. Consider objective as well as subjective measures, and obtrusive as well as unobtrusive measures of employee performance.

**7.11**  The director of a city's personnel office is concerned that the city have a diverse work force. One variable she uses to measure diversity is race. According to records kept by the personnel office, the city employs 59 blacks, 73 whites, 41 Hispanics, 38 Asians, and 17 from other ethnic groups.

(a) At what level of measurement are these data?

(b) Prepare the percentage distribution for these data, and calculate appropriate measures of central tendency.

(c) What can you tell the director of the personnel office?

**7.12**  Identify a crucial concept in public administration, such as bureaucracy, professionalism, or responsiveness, and explain how this concept has been measured in the literature.

**(a)** What are some of the ways that researchers have measured the concept?

**(b)** To what degree have they established valid and reliable measures of the concept?

**(c)** Suggest new indicators that might improve upon the measurement of the concept.

## CHAPTER 8

# RESEARCH DESIGN

Winston Lewis, mayor of the city of Bison, Kansas, is upset. The showcase of his community pride program, "Stand Up for Bison," is a failure. The program was intended to upgrade the quality of life of senior citizens in Bison by relocating those living below the poverty line to new federally subsidized public housing. Because termination of the program means a loss not only of federal funds but also of local jobs to Bison, Mayor Lewis is especially perturbed.

To add to the mayor's problems, in a blistering front-page editorial, the local newspaper *The Bison News* blamed the failure on the incompetence of Lewis and his staff. The editorial claimed that the mayor did not take a personal interest in running the program, instead leaving its administration largely to cronies, none of whom had education or training in the needs and problems of senior citizens. As a result, the editorial contends, the senior citizens were treated shabbily—"as a product"—by the program, and insufficient attention was paid to their rights, convenience, and welfare. The editorial also made vague allegations that some of the federal funds tied to the program were skimmed by the mayor and his staff.

Lewis' initial reaction was to counterattack in the public media. He and his staff assembled information intended to refute the charges made in the editorial, and a press conference was tentatively scheduled.

Before the press conference took place, however, the mayor's chief strategist, Dick Murray, informed Lewis of his misgivings about this type of response to the editorial. In the first place, argued Murray, it would be certain to occasion a rejoinder from the newspaper, further publicity, and perhaps an official investigation of the program. Understandably, the mayor would prefer to avoid all of these. Second, even if the mayor were able to refute the newspaper charges, the nagging question would remain: What *did* cause the program to fail? Murray maintained that if he could demonstrate that *factors other* than those pertaining to the mayor and his staff were responsible for the failure of the program, then he could limit the adverse publicity and take the heat off Lewis—a nice solution to the mayor's problems. Suitably impressed, Lewis canceled the press conference and told Murray to proceed.

Murray first undertook his research. A telephone call to Washington, D.C., yielded the information that the federal government had funded the same program for senior citizens in Virtuous, Montana, a city similar to Bison in area, population, and other crucial characteristics (economic base, form of government, and so forth). In contrast to the experience in Bison, however, the federal government was quite pleased with the program in Virtuous; the Washington bureaucrat quipped that the program has enjoyed a success "as big as the sky." Murray reasoned that if Lewis and his staff have a level of interest and a level of competence in running the program comparable to their counterparts in Virtuous, then these factors *cannot* be the cause of the failure of the program in Bison, for the program has succeeded in Virtuous with the *same* level of official involvement. Murray checked with the Virtuous authorities and found that, in both cities, the levels of interest and of competence of the mayor and staff were very similar. Thus Murray concluded that some other factor must be responsible for the failure of the program in Bison.

What might this factor be? Murray had been around long enough to feel that in administering a program, the bottom line is always money: the more money, the greater is the likelihood of success. He checked again with the Virtuous authorities and learned that Bison was awarded far less in federal funds to run the senior citizen program than was Virtuous. This information provided support for Murray's hunch. He concluded that the program in Bison failed *not* because of a lack of official involvement—recall that the program in Virtuous succeeded with the same level of involvement—but because of a lack of federal funding. He reasoned that had the program in Bison received the same level of funding as had that in Virtuous, it would have been a success. After all, look at the experience in Virtuous, where more money was made available.

Murray delivered his findings to Mayor Lewis, who naturally was pleased. At a newly scheduled press conference, the mayor presented Murray's evidence to refute the allegations of *The Bison News* editorial and to establish a new possible cause of the failure of the program in Bison. The press conference had the desired impact. Murray was given a raise.

The process in which Murray was engaged—attempting to determine the cause of a relationship or event—is at the core of all social research. Social scientists seek to discover the causes of phenomena and to rule out possible rival causes. The nature of this enterprise provides the focus for this chapter.

The first section of the chapter introduces the process and terminology commonly used by social scientists in constructing causal explanations. The second portion of the chapter discusses the formal criteria necessary to establish a relationship as causal. In other words, what evidence must the researcher present in order to demonstrate that A causes B? The final chapter segment is devoted to research design. A research design is a systematic program intended to evaluate proposed causal explanations on the basis of data. The two major types of design—experimental and quasi-experimental—are distinguished and elaborated.

## CONSTRUCTING CAUSAL _____
## EXPLANATIONS _____

In contrast to Mayor Lewis' strategist Dick Murray—who sought the causes of a single event (the failure of the senior citizens program in Bison)—social scientists typically are interested in accounting for *entire classes* of events or relationships. For example, what are the causes of success or failure of social programs? Does congressional oversight lead to a more responsive bureaucracy? Does federal regulation of interstate commerce result in lower prices? These broad questions go far beyond isolated outcomes. Do more open and fluid structures in public organizations lead to more effective agencies?

The basic building block in answering these questions and, more generally, in constructing causal explanations is the **concept**. From the mass of detail, and often confusion, surrounding the particular events in a class, the concept pinpoints an idea or element thought to be essential in accounting for the entire class. Concepts abstract or summarize the critical aspects in a class of events. For example, in his research, Murray isolated official involvement and level of funding as important elements in the senior citizens program in Bison. These are concepts on the basis of which he might have attempted to explain the success or failure of *all* social programs. The concept points out a common trait or characteristic shared by the members of a class: in this case, social programs have varying levels of official involvement and funding.

**concept**

To provide a more complete explanation of program success, Murray could have highlighted more abstract concepts. These might include power, social class (of clientele groups), and organizational goals. Because broader concepts potentially allow the researcher to account for a greater number of events, the more abstract the concept, and the more applicable to a wide range of phenomena, the more useful it is. Thus a relatively small array of concepts tends to appear repeatedly in social science research, such as power, role, motivation, environment, system, exchange.

Concepts act as a perceptual screen that sensitizes researchers to certain aspects of objects or events and leaves them oblivious to others. For this reason, the process of abstraction to arrive at concepts is perhaps the most critical element in the research process. In one sense, it is a process similar to those used in everyday life: inevitably we tune in to some characteristics and tune out to others. For example, after you meet a person for the first time, you are almost certain to remember his or her sex; you are less likely to recall elements of personal appearance, and less likely still to recall specific attitudes, opinions, and preferences. However, in another sense it is quite different, because in scientific research, conceptualization is a much more self-conscious, painstaking endeavor.

To construct explanations of events or relationships, concepts must be defined. Two types of definitions are necessary for empirical or data-based research. The first is called a **nominal** or **conceptual definition**. It is the standard dictionary definition that defines the concept in terms of other concepts. For example, *patriotism* may be defined as love for one's country; *intelligence* may be defined as mental capacity; *occupation* may be defined as the type of work that an individual primarily performs.

In social research, nominal definitions must satisfy a set of conditions. Concepts should be defined as clearly and precisely as possible. A concept must not be defined in terms of itself. For example, to define "happiness" as the state of being happy is meaningless. Also, the definition should say what the concept is, rather than what it is not. For example, to define "duress" as the absence of freedom does not distinguish it from several other concepts (coercion, imprisonment, compulsion, and so on). Inevitably many other concepts will fit the description of what the concept is not. Furthermore, unless there is good reason, the definition should not constitute a marked departure from what has generally been accepted in the past. A good reason might be that you feel that previous definitions have misled research in the area. Whereas nominal definitions are arbitrary—they are neither right nor wrong—in order to advance knowledge, researchers attempt to make definitions as realistic and sensible as possible. Although it could not be proven incorrect to define a cat as a dog, it would be counterproductive.

The second type of definition is called **operational** or **working**. The operational definition translates the nominal definition into a form in which the concept can be measured empirically. The process of operationalizing a concept results in indicators, or variables designed to measure the concept (see Chapter 7).

By converting abstract ideas (concepts) into a form in which the presence or absence, or the degree of presence or absence, of a concept can be measured for every individual or case in a sample of data, operational definitions play a vital role in research. They allow researchers to assess the extent of empirical support for their theoretical ideas.

For example, Dick Murray felt that the degree of success attained by federal programs is determined by the level of funding rather than by local involvement. He operationalized these concepts as the size of the federal allotment to each city in the program, and the level of interest and training of the local mayor and staff in the program, respectively. Program success is a difficult concept to operationalize, but Murray might have used a variety of indicators: the perceived satisfaction with the program (assessed in a survey) felt by public housing residents and by the larger community, the number of new housing units constructed, the cost per square foot, the degree to which the housing met federal standards, and so forth. He would have needed to combine these indicators into an overall measure, as explained in Chapter 7. By comparing the cities of Bison

**nominal definition**

**operational definition**

and Virtuous, he was then able to demonstrate that although local involvement seemed to make no difference in the success of the senior citizens program (since the cities rated about the same on this dimension), the level of funding (here the cities differed) did make a difference.

Once concepts have been operationalized and measured in a sample of data, they are called **variables**. A variable assigns numerical scores or categories to each case in the sample on a given characteristic. For example, in a study examining the job-related behavior of bureaucrats, a researcher may obtain data for five bureaucrats on the variables "race," "sex," "time wasted on the job per day" (minutes), and "attitude toward the job" (like, neutral, dislike). These data are displayed in Table 8.1, with each column representing a variable.

**variable**

**TABLE 8.1**

Data for Five Bureaucrats

| Case | Variable | | | |
| --- | --- | --- | --- | --- |
| | *Race* | *Sex* | *Time Wasted on Job (minutes)* | *Attitude Toward Job* |
| *Bureaucrat 1* | *White* | *Female* | 62 | Dislike |
| Bureaucrat 2 | White | Male | 43 | Neutral |
| Bureaucrat 3 | Black | Male | 91 | Like |
| Bureaucrat 4 | Hispanic | Male | 107 | Like |
| Bureaucrat 5 | White | Female | 20 | Dislike |

Variables can be classified into two major types. It is the goal of most research to explain or account for changes or variation in the **dependent variable**. For example, Dick Murray sought to explain the failure of the senior citizens program in Bison (and implicitly, to understand how the program might be made a success). What factors could account for the different outcomes of the programs in Bison and Virtuous? A variable thought to lead to or produce changes in the dependent variable is called independent. **Independent variables** are thought to affect or have an impact on the dependent variable. Murray examined the effects on program success of two independent variables: interest and training of mayor and staff and federal funding. For terminological convenience, independent variables are sometimes referred to as *explanatory*, *predictor*, or *causal* variables, and the dependent variable as the *criterion*.

**dependent variable**

**independent variables**

To account for changes in the dependent variable, researchers link the criterion explicitly to independent variables in statements called **hypotheses**. A hypothesis formally proposes an expected relationship between an independent variable and a dependent variable.

**hypotheses**

The primary value of hypotheses is that they allow theoretical ideas and explanations to be tested against actual data. To facilitate this goal, hypotheses must meet two requirements. First, the concepts and the variables that they relate must be measurable. Although propositions connecting unmeasurable concepts (or those for which data are unavailable) are important in research, they cannot be evaluated empirically and must be treated as assumptions. Second, hypotheses must state in precise language the relationship expected between the independent and dependent variables. For example, two hypotheses guided the research of Dick Murray:

1. The greater the local involvement in a program, the greater is the chance of program success.
2. The greater the level of federal funding for a program, the greater is the chance of program success.

In both hypotheses, the expected relationship is called *positive*, because increases (decreases) in the independent variable are thought to lead to increases (decreases) in the dependent variable. In contrast, a *negative* or *inverse* relationship proposes that increases in the independent variable will result in decreases in the dependent variable, or vice versa. An example of a negative relationship is this hypothesis:

3. The higher the degree of federal restrictions on administering a program, the less is the chance of program success.

Once the concepts specified by these hypotheses have been operationalized, data can be brought to bear on them to evaluate the degree of empirical support for the anticipated relationships.

Hypotheses intended to provide an explanation for a phenomenon of interest (for example, success or failure of federal programs) most often propose a positive or a negative relationship between an independent and a dependent variable. One merit of this procedure is that because the direction of the relationship (positive or negative) is made explicit, it is relatively easy to determine the degree of confirmation for (or refutation of) the hypothesis. However, researchers are not always this circumspect in stating hypotheses, and it is not unusual to find in the literature examples in which the independent variable is said to "affect," "influence," or "impact on" the dependent variable, without regard for direction. This practice not only condones imprecision in thinking and hypothesis formulation, but also creates difficulties in assessing empirical support for a hypothesis. For these reasons, this practice should be avoided.

**theory**
An integrated set of propositions intended to explain or account for a given phenomenon is called a **theory**. The propositions link the important concepts together in anticipated relationships so that the causal mechanisms underlying the phenomenon are elucidated. In some of these propositions, it will be possible to operationalize the concepts and to collect the data necessary to evaluate the hypothesized relationships empirically. However, as a consequence of difficulties in measuring some concepts or lack of available data, it may not be possible to test all propositions. Untested propositions constitute **assumptions**.

**assumptions**
Although assumptions lie outside the boundaries of empirical testing, they should not be accepted uncritically. Evidence from past research, as well as logical reasoning, can be used to assess their validity.

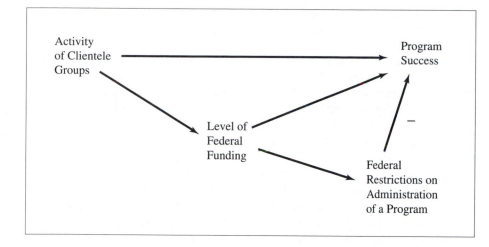

**FIGURE 8.1**
Arrow Diagram and Model

A full-blown theory to explain an important phenomenon, such as representativeness in public bureaucracy or relationships between political appointees and career civil servants, can be highly abstract and comprehensive. It may contain numerous assumptions not only about how concepts are related but also about how they are measured. Because of difficulties in specifying and operationalizing all relevant elements and collecting all necessary data, theories are rarely, if ever, tested directly against actual data or observations. Instead, a simplified version of the theory called a **model** is developed and put to an empirical test. Usually the relationships proposed by the theory are depicted as a set of equations or, equivalently, as an arrow diagram (see Figure 8.1). Regardless of the form, the model is a compact version of the theory intended for an empirical test. It identifies the essential concepts and the interrelationships among them that are proposed by the theory, and it presumes the existence of adequate measurement and relevant data (see Chapter 7). Ultimately, it is the model that is tested statistically, but the results will be brought to bear indirectly on the validity and utility of the theory.

**model**

As an example of a model, consider again the question of the determinants of success of social programs. Perhaps the activity of clientele groups leads to high levels of federal funding, which in turn increase the likelihood of program success. In addition, the activity of clientele groups may help to achieve program success directly through support at the local level. Federal funding, however, may be a mixed blessing. Although high levels of funding may enhance the prospects of success, they may also bring increased federal restrictions on administration of the program. These restrictions may reduce the chance of program success. This heuristic theory is by no means complete. To yield a more satisfactory explanation, we might want to add several components, such as the interest of elected officials in the program, the organizational structure of the program, and the degree to which the means of achieving program success are well understood (for example, issuing checks for unemployment compensation versus improving mental health). The relationships with program success that have been proposed formally here can be displayed schematically in an arrow diagram, in which each arrow represents an expected causal linkage between a pair of concepts. A negative sign above an arrow indicates an inverse relationship, and an unmarked arrow corresponds to a positive relationship. Figure 8.1 presents the resulting heuristic model of the success of social programs.

To the extent that data provide confirmation for the relationships proposed by a theory and tested in the model, support is obtained for the theory, and its validity is enhanced. Analogously, the failure to find empirical support for a theory detracts from its validity and suggests the need for revisions. However, researchers usually are more willing to subscribe to the first of these principles than to the second. Whereas they rarely question data that offer support for their theoretical ideas, in the face of apparent empirical disconfirmation, revision of the theory is seldom their immediate response. Instead, operational definitions are critically evaluated; possible problems in the selection, collection, and recording of the sample of data are considered; numerical calculations are checked; and so on. As a result of the state of the art of social science research, these are reasonable steps to take prior to revising the theory. However, if these measures fail to lead to alternative explanations for the lack of empirical support obtained (such as a biased sample of data) or possible procedures to amend this situation (for instance, by devising new operational definitions for some concepts), the researcher has no choice but to reconsider and revise the theory.

The revision usually leads to new concepts, definitions, operationalizations, and empirical testing, so that the process begins all over again. Generally, it is through a series of repeated, careful studies, each building on the results of earlier ones, that researchers come to understand important subject areas.

## CAUSAL RELATIONSHIPS

In the preceding discussion of theory, repeated reference was made to the concept of causality, the idea that one phenomenon is the cause of another. A theory may be considered a system of interrelated causal statements intended to account for or explain a given phenomenon. However, these are tentative statements of relationship whose validity cannot be taken for granted. The purpose of this section is to discuss the four formal criteria identified by most social scientists as necessary to establish a relationship as causal.

**time order**     Probably the most intuitive of these criteria is the notion of **time order**. If A is the cause of B, then A must precede B in time; that is, changes in A must occur before changes in B. This stipulation is just another way of saying that cause must precede effect.

In many hypothesized relationships, the question of time order between variables is obvious. For example, if the researcher is interested in the effect of sex, race, country of birth, or other ascribed characteristics on certain attitudes and behaviors, it is clear that the former set of variables precedes the latter. Unfortunately this issue cannot always be resolved so easily. Consider the relationship between tenure on the job and job satisfaction: does tenure lead to satisfaction, or does satisfaction lead to tenure? Both viewpoints seem reasonable. Or consider the relationship between attitude toward bureaucrats and attitude toward a particular government agency. Which variable comes first? Again the question of temporal priority is problematic. In most relationships between attitudes and behaviors, it is difficult to establish time order with certainty. For this reason, causal statements linking these types of variables should be considered carefully.

The second criterion that must be satisfied for the relationship between two variables to be considered causal is **covariation** or statistical **association** between the variables. Covariation means that the two variables move or vary together. That is, if A changes and B also changes, this covariation provides some evidence that A is the cause of B. Analogously, if changes in A are never accompanied by changes in B (no covariation), then A cannot be the cause of B. One way to understand this idea is to consider that, if as A changes, B always remains constant, then A can have no impact on B. In that case, changes in A do not matter with respect to B.

**covariation**

For example, suppose a researcher hypothesized that higher salaries lead to more productive workers. If in a sample of data she found that salary and productivity covaried—that is, those paid higher salaries were more productive than those paid less—then she would have evidence for a causal relationship. However, if she found that as salaries increased, productivity showed no concomitant change, then the hypothesized causal relationship would be in jeopardy.

Of the four criteria of causality, perhaps the most difficult to comprehend is **nonspuriousness**. A nonspurious relationship is a covariation or association between two variables or phenomena that cannot be explained by a third factor. A nonspurious relationship implies that there is an *inherent* link between the two variables in the sense that changes in one produce changes in the other, and that their observed covariation is not the result of an accidental connection with some associated (third) variable.

**nonspuriousness**

For example, just about everyone knows someone who claims to predict the weather—usually rain—based on "a feeling in their bones." Interestingly enough, these predictions may turn out to be correct more often than not. Thus, one would observe a covariation between the prediction and the weather. However, a moment's reflection will show that there is no inherent link between these two phenomena. Instead, changes in pressure and moisture in the atmosphere cause both changes in the state of the human body (such as a feeling in the bones) and changes in the weather (such as rain). The original covariation between feeling in the bones and rain is observed not because the variables are causally related, but because both of them are associated with a third factor, changes in the atmosphere. Hence, the original relationship is **spurious**: it can be explained by the effects of a third variable.

**spurious relationship**

Although it may be relatively easy to think of examples of likely nonspurious relationships (fertilizer use and crop yield, exposure to sunlight and tan skin), it is far more difficult to *demonstrate* that an observed covariation is nonspurious. Establishing a relationship as nonspurious is an inductive process that requires that the researcher take into account *all* possible sources of an observed covariation between two variables. If, after the effects of all third factors are eliminated, the original covariation remains, then the relationship is nonspurious.

Because the stipulation requiring the elimination of all possible third variables is based on logical grounds (one would be incorrect in claiming a causal relationship between two variables if it could be explained by the effects of *any* other factor), nonspuriousness cannot be proved by data analysis alone. However, to the extent that a researcher explicitly takes into account possible sources of an observed covariation between two variables and is able to eliminate them as alternative explanations for the covariation, the vaidity of the causal inference is enhanced. In other words, the greater the number of relevant third variables considered and eliminated, the greater is the confidence that the original relationship is causal. For example, a researcher who finds that a covariation between interest in public affairs and performance in a Master of Public Administration program persists after the effects of education, occupation, amount of time available for study, and so on have been taken into account would have more confidence in the causal inference than if only one of these third factors had been considered.

theory
The final criterion for establishing a relationship as causal is **theory**. Not only must the conditions of time order, covariation, and nonspuriousness be satisfied, but also a theoretical or substantive justification or explanation for the relationship must be provided. Theory interprets the observed covariation; it addresses the issue of how and why the relationship occurs. In one sense, theory serves as an additional check on nonspuriousness. It lends further support to the argument that the link between two phenomena is inherent rather than the artifact of an associated third factor.

As this discussion has illustrated, the criteria necessary for proof of a causal relationship are demanding. It is essential to balance this view with the idea that the determination of causation is not a yes-no question but is a matter of degree. Satisfaction of each criterion lends further support to the causal inference. Additionally, for each criterion, there are varying levels of substantiation. Confidence in the time order of phenomena is variable; observed covariations can assume a range of magnitude from small to large; demonstrating nonspuriousness is nearly always problematic; and the validity of a given theory is usually the subject of debate. Evidence for a causal relationship is based upon the extent to which these criteria are satisfied.

multiple causation
In this context, two final points merit consideration. First, social scientists accept the concept of **multiple causation**. It is widely acknowledged that an event or phenomenon may have several causes. Consequently, social researchers rarely speak of *the* cause; instead they seek the causes or determinants of a phenomenon. Thus it can and does happen that an observed covariation between an

independent variable and a dependent variable turns out to be neither totally nonspurious nor totally spurious, but partially spurious. Data analysis frequently suggests that both the independent variable and a third variable are potential causes of the dependent variable. The chapters on multivariate statistical techniques explain how to assess such effects.

Second, in developing and evaluating causal explanations, it can be extremely useful to construct an arrow diagram like the one in Figure 8.1. Depicting graphically a system of proposed causal relationships helps to uncover possible interrelationships among suspected causes, sources of spuriousness, and omitted variables whose effects should not be ignored. It is also a quick and easy procedure. For all these reasons, the arrow diagram is a highly recommended technique, no matter how simple or complicated the model may be.

# RESEARCH DESIGN

A **research design** is a systematic program for evaluating empirically proposed **research design** causal relationships. The design specifies a model of proof for testing the validity of these relationships. The research design guides the collection, analysis, and interpretation of the relevant data. There are many types of research design, and they differ in their ability to generate reliable inferences concerning causality.

The concept of causality has long been a source of controversy among social scientists. Partly for this reason, several different conceptions of the validity or viability of a causal relationship have been proposed and utilized. The two most important of these are internal validity and external validity. **Internal validity** **internal validity** addresses the question of whether, *in a given study or research project*, the independent variable did indeed cause or lead to changes in the dependent variable. The criteria for assessing internal validity are those considered in the previous section: time order, covariation, nonspuriousness, and theory.

**External validity** captures a different idea: it is concerned with the issue of **external validity** whether and to what extent results obtained in a given study can be *inferred* or generalized to hold true in settings, time periods, and populations different than the ones used in the study. For instance, are the findings of a study of college sophomores generalizable to the population of all U.S. citizens? Are the results of a study conducted twenty years ago still applicable today? To what extent might findings from a program evaluation in one state be generalizable to the same type of program in a different state? The names of the two key types of validity can be remembered easily because they refer to contexts that are internal and external to a study, respectively.

A major distinction can be made between *experimental* research designs and *quasi-experimental* designs. Nearly everyone has some familiarity with the setup of an experiment. A researcher assembles two groups of subjects; to ensure a valid comparison, the groups should be as similar as possible. The *experimental* group receives some treatment or stimulus, whereas the second or *control* group does not; instead it serves as a baseline or reference point for evaluating the behavior of the first group. Before and after administration of the experimental stimulus, both groups are measured on relevant variables. By comparing the scores of the experimental group with those of the control group, the researcher is able to determine whether the treatment led to a difference in areas of interest (attitude, behavior, performance). This procedure is called the classical **experimental design**.

For example, suppose that a researcher wanted to examine whether inspection of automobiles reduced the rate of traffic accidents. One way to do so would be to select two random samples of drivers in a given state. The first group would be required to have their automobiles inspected within six months (experimental group); the second group would be left alone (control group). Data would be collected regarding the past driving records of the drivers in both groups and, after two years, data would be collected again to encompass the period of the study. If in this period the rate of accidents decreased in the experimental (inspection) group relative to the rate in the control group, then the researcher would have some evidence for inferring that automobile inspections reduce traffic accidents. Conversely, if the data failed to show this pattern, the proposed causal relationship would be rejected.

**Quasi-experimental designs** of research have been given this appellation because they fail to incorporate some or all of the features of experimental designs. In particular, in many research designs it is difficult to control exposure to the experimental stimulus or independent variable. Consider a television information program funded by the government and intended to promote energy conservation. To examine the effectiveness of this program, the researcher would ideally want to study the behavior of two random samples of people: one that viewed the program and another that did not. In this situation, it would be relatively easy to determine whether the program led to energy conservation. In actuality, however, people interested in conservation will tend to watch the program, and those not interested in conservation will tend to seek other diversion—and there is little reason to assume that these two groups are random or matched in any sense. (For one thing, the groups differ dramatically in interest in energy conservation.) Thus, although the researcher may find that those who viewed the program were subsequently more likely to conserve energy than those who did not, it is not clear whether the program—or initial attitude—was responsible for the impact.

A second aspect of the classical experimental research design that is often lacking in quasi-experimental designs is repeated measurement. To evaluate whether the independent variable produces changes in the dependent variable, it is very helpful to know respondents' scores on the variables prior to a change in the independent variable. Then one can determine whether this change is accompanied by a change in the dependent variable. In the experiment, this function is served by measurement before and after the experimental treatment, which is intended to affect or change the level of the independent variable in the experimental group (for example, auto inspections are intended to increase the safety of automobiles).

Unfortunately, repeated measurements are not always available or feasible. For example, a researcher may be interested in the determinants of the effectiveness of an agency, but data on effectiveness may not have been collected until very recently, or relevant data from the past may not be comparable to current information. Or a researcher may be interested in the determinants of public opinion toward an agency, but funding may limit the study to a single survey of respondents, so that repeated measurement is not possible. In both these situations, the researcher is likely to obtain only one set of data for one point in time. Although it may be possible with such data to observe covariations between variables (such as between the funding of agency divisions and their performance), establishing time order between variables is necessarily problematic.

In the following sections, we discuss experimental and quasi-experimental designs of research in greater detail. Our primary objective is to assess the internal and external validity of these two major families of design. Within the category of the quasi-experiment, some texts further distinguish designs, such as "descriptive" and "pre-experimental" designs. If that distinction is important in your work, consult an advanced text in research methods.

# EXPERIMENTAL DESIGNS
# OF RESEARCH

## INTERNAL VALIDITY

Experimental research designs offer the strongest model of proof of causality. The basic components of the classical experimental design can be summarized briefly.

**STEP 1**    Assign subjects to two or more groups, with at least one "experimental" and one "control," so that the groups are as comparable as possible. The best way to assemble comparable groups is through random assignment of subjects to groups.

**STEP 2**    Measure all subjects on relevant variables. Although a pre-experiment measurement or pretest is usually administered, some experimental designs do not require a pretest.

**STEP 3**    Expose the experimental group(s) to a treatment or stimulus, the independent variable. Ensure that the other control group(s) is not exposed. Exposure to the treatment should constitute the only difference between the groups.

**STEP 4**    Measure the groups again on the requisite variables in a post-experiment measurement, or posttest.

**STEP 5**    Compare the measurements of the groups. If the independent variable does lead to changes in the dependent variable, this result should be evident in pretest-posttest comparisons between the experimental and control groups. Or, if the groups are large and known to be equivalent through random assignment, the analyst can simply compare posttest scores between the two groups. If the causal inference is valid, these comparisons should bear out predicted differences between the experimental and control groups.

The classical experimental design is outlined in Table 8.2. In the table, $O$ stands for observation or measurement, $X$ for administration of the experimental treatment, $c$ for control group, $e$ for experimental group, 1 for pretest, and 2 for posttest.

**TABLE 8.2**
Classical Experimental Design

| Group | Observation 1 | Treatment | Observation 2 | Comparison |
|---|---|---|---|---|
| Experimental | $O_{e1}$ | $X$ | $O_{e2}$ | $O_{e2} - O_{e1}$ |
| Control | $O_{c1}$ | | $O_{c2}$ | $O_{c2} - O_{c1}$ |

Intuitively, we know that the strength of experimental research designs with respect to internal validity arises from the fact that when these experiments are conducted properly, the experimental and control groups are identical except for a single factor—exposure to the experimental treatment. Thus, if at the conclusion of the experiment, the former group is significantly different than the latter with respect to the dependent variable, the cause *must* be the treatment or the independent variable. After all, this factor was the only one that distinguished the two groups.

The strength of the experimental design in internal validity can be shown more formally in connection with the elements of causality discussed before. First, consider the criterion of time order. Because the researcher controls administration of the experimental stimulus and measurements are obtained prior to and after its introduction, the time order of variables is clear. Through exposure to the stimulus, the level of the independent variable is first altered (for subjects in the experimental group) and then, through pretest-posttest comparison, any resulting changes in the dependent variable are readily observed.

Second, consider the criterion of covariation. If the independent variable is the cause of the dependent variable, then subjects exposed to higher levels of the former should manifest greater change in the latter. Operationally, this means that the experimental group should show greater change in the dependent variable than does the control group—or, equivalently, that exposure to the experimental treatment *covaries* with change in the dependent variable. The analyst can establish covariation by comparing pretest and posttest scores (if both are available) or by comparing the posttest scores alone.

Third, consider the criterion of nonspuriousness. As noted earlier, if the experimental and control groups are identical, with the exception of exposure to the treatment, then observed differences between the groups with respect to changes in the dependent variable can reliably be attributed to the independent variable rather than to other potential causes.

You may ask why the control group should manifest *any* changes in the dependent variable, since these subjects are denied exposure to the experimental treatment. It is in this area especially that the advantages of the control group become apparent. With the passage of time, subjects in both the experimental and control groups may show changes in the dependent variable for reasons quite unrelated to the independent variable. For example, subjects may develop biologically and emotionally; they may react to the fact that they are being observed or measured; they may learn of dramatic events that transpire outside of the experimental setting. The general name for developments like these that could potentially jeopardize the causal inference is "threats to internal validity." The three threats just delineated refer to the threats of "maturation," "reactivity," and "history," respectively. (This listing is illustrative; refer to research design texts for a more complete inventory.)

The impact of these threats may be felt in any experiment, but assuming that the experimental and control groups are equated to begin with (through a procedure such as random assignment of subjects to groups), there is no reason to suspect that the threats should affect the groups differently. Hence, when the measurements of the two groups are compared, these effects should *cancel* one another. However, if the independent variable is a cause of the dependent variable, the effect of the treatment should be manifested in an *additional* increment of change in the dependent variable—but only in the experimental group. Thus although both groups may exhibit change, the experimental group should demonstrate greater change. In this manner, the control group serves as an essential baseline for interpreting and evaluating change in the experimental group.

Care must be taken in assembling experimental and control groups that are as comparable as possible. In particular, assigning subjects to the experimental or control groups arbitrarily, or segregating them according to scores on a criterion (low achievers versus high achievers, regular voters versus occasional voters), or allowing them to volunteer for either group creates obvious selection biases that result in a priori differences between the groups. Consequently, if the experiment reveals a difference on the dependent variable between the experimental group and the control group, the researcher cannot rule out the possibility that it was the initial differences between the groups—rather than the experimental stimulus (independent variable)—that led to this result. Because the causal inference is thereby weakened, these selection procedures must be avoided.

**random assignment**

The technique of choice in constructing equivalent experimental and control groups is **random assignment** of subjects to those groups. Random assignment removes *any* systematic difference between the groups. Randomization is an extremely powerful technique, for it controls for factors both known *and* unknown to the researcher. For good reason, then, random assignment is the foremost method for equating experimental and control groups.

Random assignment does not mean haphazard or arbitrary assignment. It has a precise statistical meaning: Each subject or case has an equal chance of being assigned to the experimental group or to the control group. As a result, the groups will have very similar (if not equivalent) composition and characteristics, within the limits of statistical probability. It is this quality that leads to the comparability of the experimental and control groups. If you ever need to draw a random sample for research or other purposes, consult a table of random numbers (contained in the appendices of most statistics texts) or an expert in the field of sampling.

The final criterion of causality is theory. Unfortunately, no research design— and no statistical technique—can establish a causal relationship as substantively meaningful, credible, or important. This evaluation must be made on other grounds, such as logic, experience, and previous research. The criterion of theory reinforces the adage that statistics is no substitute for substantive knowledge of a field.

## EXTERNAL VALIDITY

The preceding discussion supports the conclusion that experimental designs of research are relatively strong with respect to internal validity—the causal inference based on the experimental setting and the selected sample of subjects. However, they are not as strong with respect to external validity—the ability to generalize the results of a study to other settings, other times, and other populations. There are primarily two factors that limit the external validity of experimental designs.

**context**

The first is the **context** of these designs. To isolate subjects from extraneous variables, experimenters frequently place them in a laboratory setting. Although the laboratory works admirably in sealing off subjects from possibly confounding factors, it also removes them from a real-life setting, to which the researcher usually seeks to generalize results. Thus, one can question how closely the situation simulated in the laboratory resembles the processes of everyday life. For example, as part of the experimental treatment, the researcher may systematically expose subjects to new ideas, problems, information, or people. However, in the normal course of events, people exercise a great deal more personal choice and control regarding their exposure to and handling of these influences. Consequently, the results obtained in the experiment may hold under the experimental conditions, but their application to less artificial (more realistic) situations may be problematic.

Closely related to this type of difficulty is the argument that because premeasurement (pretesting) may sensitize subjects to the experimental treatment, results may apply only to pretested populations. This problem, however, is more tractable than the first. If the experimental and control groups have been randomly assigned, then the researcher can eliminate the pretest procedure altogether, since random assignment should remove any initial differences between the groups; a posttest is then sufficient to assess the effect of the experimental treatment. This research design is called the "posttest only–control group design." Or, if time and resources allow, an additional set of experimental and control groups that are *not* pretested can be incorporated into the classical experimental design. With this addition, it is possible to determine not only whether the experimental stimulus has an effect on nonpretested samples, but also the magnitude of any reactive effects of premeasurement. This design is known as the "Solomon four-group design." Letting $O$ stand for observation or measurement, $X$ for administration of the experimental treatment, $R$ for a group chosen at random from available subjects, $c$ for control group, $e$ for experimental group, and $p$ for pretest, these two experimental designs can be outlined as shown in Tables 8.3 and 8.4.

**TABLE 8.3**

Posttest Only–Control Group Design

| Group | Randomization | Treatment | Observation 1 |
|-------|---------------|-----------|---------------|
| Experimental | $R_e$ | $X$ | $O_{e1}$ |
| Control | $R_c$ | | $O_{c1}$ |

**TABLE 8.4**

Solomon Four-Group Design

| Group | Randomization | Observation 1 | Treatment | Observation 2 |
|-------|---------------|---------------|-----------|---------------|
| Experimental | $R_{ep}$ | $O_{ep1}$ | $X$ | $O_{ep2}$ |
| Control | $R_{cp}$ | $O_{cp1}$ | | $O_{cp2}$ |
| Experimental | $R_e$ | | $X$ | $O_{e2}$ |
| Control | $R_c$ | | | $O_{c2}$ |

The second factor that threatens the external validity of experimental designs of research is the sample of subjects upon which findings are based. Because of ethical and financial considerations, experiments conducted on a random sample of individuals drawn from a well-defined population (such as U.S. citizens) have been rare. Funding authorities tend to take a dim view of experimentation on human subjects and frown on the use of deception, which may be employed in order to make an experimental setting seem more realistic to participants. Sometimes the potential knowledge to be gained by the experiment is judged so vital that these objections are put aside (as with medical research on life-threatening diseases). In addition, the cost and practical problems of conducting an experiment on a random sample of subjects can be prohibitive. As a result, experiments traditionally have been conducted on "captive" populations—prison inmates, hospital patients, and especially students. The correspondence between these groups and more heterogeneous, "natural" populations is necessarily problematic, thus threatening the external validity of many experiments.

It is important to note, however, that this situation is beginning to change. As social science researchers have grown more familiar with the use and advantages of experimental designs, they have become attuned to naturally occurring experiments—such as changes in traffic laws and their enforcement, the institutionalization of government programs, and so on. With adequate foreknowledge of such developments, the severity of threats to the external validity of experimental designs posed by problems of sampling and context can be attenuated significantly. In the future, social science researchers will probably become increasingly adept at warding off threats to the external validity of experiments.

## Quasi-EXPERIMENTAL DESIGNS OF RESEARCH

### INTERNAL VALIDITY

The most fundamental difference between quasi-experimental research designs and experimental designs centers on the ability of the researcher to control exposure to the experimental treatment or independent variable. This control is much greater in experimental designs than in quasi-experimental designs. This section discusses the internal validity of several of the most common quasi-experimental designs.

**cross-sectional study**

**case study**

**panel study**

**trend study**

Perhaps the most widely used quasi-experimental design is the **cross-sectional** or **correlational study**. This type of study is based on data obtained at one point in time, often from a large sample of subjects. Most surveys of public opinion are cross-sectional studies. A **case study** is an in-depth examination of an event or locale, usually undertaken after something dramatic has transpired (such as the Cuban missile crisis or Three Mile Island). Although a case study may rest (at least partially) on data obtained from a random sample of respondents, more often the researcher relies on information from carefully selected individuals ("informants") and archival records. A **panel study** is a series of cross-sectional studies based on the same sample of individuals over time; that is, a group of individuals is surveyed repeatedly over time. An examination of the effects of college that followed incoming students until their graduation would be a panel study. Finally, **trend studies** monitor and attempt to account for over-time shifts in various indicators, such as GNP, unemployment, attitude toward the president, and so on. Examples are plentiful; regularly published reports chart the course of myriad economic measures (consumer price index, inflation rate), as well as indicators of public opinion (Harris poll, Gallup poll).

These quasi-experimental research designs can be evaluated with respect to three of the four criteria for establishing a relationship as causal (internal validity): covariation, time order, and nonspuriousness. The remaining criterion is theory. As discussed before, the substantive plausibility of a causal relationship stands apart from considerations of research design or statistical techniques. Examples of these four quasi-experimental designs are diagrammed in Table 8.5. In the table, $X$ represents the independent variable, $O$ stands for observation or measurement, and the subscripts 1, 2, 3, ... refer to time points at which relevant variables are measured.

**TABLE 8.5**

Some Common Quasi-Experimental Designs of Research

| Design | Design Diagram |
|---|---|
| Cross-sectional study | $X \quad O$ |
| Case study | $X \quad O$ |
| Panel study | $O_1 \quad X \quad O_2$ |
| Trend study | $O_1 \quad O_2 \quad O_3 \quad X \quad O_4 \quad O_5 \quad O_6$ |

Quasi-experimental designs are relatively strong in demonstrating covariation between independent and dependent variables. Many statistics have been developed for assessing the magnitude of covariation or association between two variables (see Chapters 13–16). As long as the independent and dependent variables are measured across a sample of subjects, the researcher can use statistics to assess the degree of covariation.

An exception to this general conclusion should be noted. Because most case studies are based on a single unit of analysis (the case), establishing covariation may be problematic. For example, in a given case study, both the independent and the dependent variables may assume high values, thus tempting the researcher to conclude that one is the cause of the other. However, since other cases in which the independent variable takes on different values are *not* examined, it is not possible to observe how the dependent variable changes with changes in the independent variable—the essence of the concept of covariation. This situation resembles an experiment in which a control group is mistakenly omitted: without the control group, it is very difficult to evaluate the effect of the experimental treatment on the dependent variable.

In quasi-experimental designs that employ repeated measurements over time—called *longitudinal studies*—the time order of the independent and dependent variables is relatively clear. Thus, in panel studies, the criterion of time order for demonstrating causality is usually substantiated, since changes can be tracked over time. In-depth studies that seek to reconstruct the chronology of important events may also be able to establish time order.

This conclusion does *not* hold for static or single-point-in-time studies, however. In cross-sectional studies especially, because of the lack of over-time data, except in the most obvious cases (relationships between ascribed characteristics such as sex or race and various attitudes and behaviors), the time order of a relationship may be a matter of faith or assumption (such as relationships between attitudes or between attitudes and behaviors). As a consequence, in many static studies the causal inference is weakened. For example, if all variables are measured just once, it is unclear whether employee work motivation leads to self-confidence or vice versa, or whether either variable is the cause or the result of employee productivity.

The major threat to the internal validity of quasi-experimental designs is nonspuriousness. This criterion requires that the relationship between the independent variable and the dependent variable hold in the presence of all third variables. In experimental designs, control over exposure to the experimental treatment, random assignment of subjects to experimental and control groups, and isolation of subjects from extraneous influences enhance significantly the ability of the researcher to satisfy this condition. In quasi-experimental designs, circumstances are not as fortuitous. Exposure to the independent variable is beyond the control of the investigator; there is no reason to assume that those exposed are otherwise identical to those not exposed; and in the real world, confounding factors abound.

For example, a researcher interested in the determinants of efficiency in public organizations may conduct a survey of state agencies. The results of the survey may show that efficiency covaries with agency size, measured according to personnel and budget. Might this relationship be causal? The answer is complicated. Many other variables covary with efficiency and may be responsible for the observed relationship. The type of technology used in an agency will affect both its efficiency and its size. Similarly, the training of agency employees will affect how efficiently the agency operates and the amount of personnel and budget needed. The structure of the agency may influence the degree of efficiency attained, as well as the level of personnel and budget. In order to determine whether the relationship between agency size and efficiency is nonspurious, the researcher would have to show that even after the effects of third variables such as agency technology, employee training, and organization structure have been taken into account, this relationship persists in the survey data. Chapter 15 presents an extensive discussion of nonspuriousness and appropriate statistical procedures.

To test for nonspuriousness in a quasi-experimental design, researchers attempt to compensate statistically for their lack of control over the actual situation. They employ *statistical control techniques* that assess the magnitude of relationship between the independent and dependent variables, taking into account (controlling for) the effects of plausible third variables (see Chapters 15 and 19). Unfortunately, these techniques are complex. Also, it is not possible *logically* to eliminate all third variables as the putative cause of an observed relationship. Moreover, to control statistically for their effects, the researcher must hypothesize in advance the likely third variables and collect data on them. This task is difficult, time-consuming, and expensive—but essential nonetheless. Because statistical control techniques require data from several cases or subjects, case studies are especially vulnerable with respect to the nonspuriousness criterion of causality.

## EXTERNAL VALIDITY

Although quasi-experimental designs of research must overcome serious challenges to internal validity, they tend to be relatively strong with respect to external validity. Two major reasons account for this fact. First, it is easier to obtain representative samples of the population for quasi-experimental designs. Consequently, in these designs more confidence can be placed in inferring findings from sample to population.

Second, in general, quasi-experimental designs are conducted in more natural (less artificial) settings than are experimental designs. Experiments often place subjects in a contrived environment controlled and monitored by the researcher. In contrast, in quasi-experimental designs, subjects may not realize that they are the focus of study (as in the use of highly aggregated statistics pertaining to the economy, traffic fatalities, and so on), or relevant information may be ascertained from them in comfortable and familiar surroundings (as in surveys of public attitudes and behaviors administered in the home or office). Whereas few would contend that these settings are totally free of bias, there is consensus that they are less reactive than most experimental designs—subjects are less likely to react to the context of the study itself. Hence, the results obtained are more likely to hold outside the study in other settings, thereby increasing external validity.

Again, exceptions must be appended to these conclusions. Since in panel studies the same respondents are interviewed repeatedly over time, they may grow sensitized to the fact that they are under study and thus become less typical of the population they were originally chosen to represent. This problem may be alleviated by limiting participation in the panel to a short period of time. Case studies are less tractable with respect to external validity. The case is usually selected precisely because there is something distinctive, atypical, or particularly interesting about it. As a consequence, it is difficult to judge the extent to which the results of a case study have relevance for other cases. Case study researchers should devote serious attention to considering the population of cases to which they may legitimately generalize their results. Unfortunately, researchers and readers alike often are so captivated by the details of an arresting case that they fail to ask the important question, what can be learned from this case to apply to other cases?

# RESEARCH DESIGNS
# AND VALIDITY

In the discussion of research design, two general points stand out. First, there is a trade-off between internal and external validity. In a given design, it is very difficult to increase one type of validity without decreasing the other. In experimental designs, although the control exercised by the researcher enhances internal validity, it jeopardizes external validity. In quasi-experimental designs, more natural settings and representative samples contribute to external validity, but these same factors make it more difficult to establish internal validity. In a given study, the researcher should work to achieve an acceptable balance between the two types of validity.

Second, drawing reliable causal inferences is a serious, painstaking, and difficult enterprise. For example, after decades of research and thousands of studies on job attitudes and performance, experts continue to disagree over the causes and effects. This instance is not an isolated one; in many other fields in the social sciences, the causes of important phenomena remain elusive. By contrast, in everyday life one hears a great deal of loose talk regarding the cause or causes of an event or a phenomenon. Most of it is just that—talk. Nevertheless, critical decisions are often made on this basis. Remember that the same criteria used to establish a relationship as causal in research apply as well *outside* this environment. Unless these criteria are reasonably satisfied, one can—and should—question the causal inference.

## CHAPTER SUMMARY

Research design concerns setting up a research project so that research questions can be answered as unambiguously as possible. The objective of a good research design is to establish causal relationships and to assess their generalizability.

The basic building block in constructing causal explanations is the concept, which pinpoints an idea or element thought to be essential in accounting for the class of events under study. Concepts are defined in two ways: with a nominal definition, which is the standard dictionary definition, and with an operational definition, which translates the nominal definition into a form in which the concept can be measured empirically. Once concepts have been operationalized and measured in a sample of data, they are called variables. The two major types of variables are independent (anticipated causes) and dependent (the variables thought to be affected by them). A hypothesis formally proposes an expected relationship between an independent and dependent variable.

Social scientists have identified four criteria as necessary for establishing a relationship as causal: time order, covariation, nonspuriousness, and theory. A research design is a program for evaluating empirically proposed causal relationships. The evaluation is based on two criteria: internal validity (did the independent variable lead to changes in the dependent variable?) and external validity (can the results obtained in the study be generalized to other settings?). Two types of research design were outlined: experimental designs and quasi-experimental designs. Both types were evaluated with regard to the four criteria for causal relationships that define internal validity and with regard to external validity. Briefly, the experimental design has its primary strengths in internal validity, and the quasi-experimental design has its strengths in external validity.

## PROBLEMS

**8.1**  A researcher asserts that the relationship between *attitude toward the field of public administration* and *taking courses in a public administration degree program* is causal.

    **(a)** What evidence must the researcher provide about this relationship to prove that it is causal?

    **(b)** Given your answer, what aspects of the researcher's argument are likely to be strongest, and what aspects of her argument are likely to be weakest? Your discussion should include clear definitions of each element of a causal relationship.

**8.2**  Develop a model that includes at least four concepts. Elaborate any theoretical or literature support underlying it. Present the model in an arrow diagram that shows schematically the relationships the model proposes. Provide operational definitions for all concepts, and state hypotheses derived from the model.

    **(a)** Which types of research design would be best suited to testing the model?

    **(b)** Which types of research design would be least suited to testing the model?

**8.3**  Professor George A. Bulldogski has taught social graces to athletic teams at a major southeastern university for the past fifteen years. Based on this experience, he insists that table manners are causally related to leadership. Professor Bulldogski has data showing that athletes who have better table manners also demonstrate greater leadership in athletic competition. The university gymnastics coach, who wants to build leadership on her team, is considering asking Professor Bulldogski to meet regularly with her team. She hopes that by having him teach table manners to team members, they will become better leaders. Should she invite Professor Bulldogski to meet with the gymnastic team? If she does so, can she expect his involvement to develop greater leadership on the team? Explain your answers.

# PART IV

# INFERENTIAL

# STATISTICS

## CHAPTER 9

# INTRODUCTION TO

# INFERENCE

When statistics are used to summarize the distribution of a given population, we call this summarizing **descriptive statistics**. In descriptive statistics, we use statistical techniques to describe and to summarize data. **Inferential statistics** is the use of quantitative techniques to generalize from a sample to a population. In short, with inferential statistics, we hope to use a small subset of data to infer what all the data look like.

**descriptive statistics**

**inferential statistics**

For example, the city fathers of Normal, Oklahoma, would like to know how pleased Normal citizens are with their new bus service. The best way to do this would be to ask every citizen of Normal how he or she feels about the transit system. Since Normal has 70,000 people, this interviewing could take forever (not to mention that it would cost more to do that than to run the transit system). An alternative is to randomly select a subset of persons (say 100), and ask them about the mass transit system. From this sample, we will infer what the people of Normal think.

In this chapter, we will begin the presentation of inferential statistics by reviewing some basic definitions and describing some simple inferential techniques.

## SOME DEFINITIONS

A **population** is the total set of items that we are concerned about. In the preceding example, the population is all the persons who live in Normal, Oklahoma.

**population**

A measure that is used to summarize a population is called a **parameter**. For example, the mean education level in Normal is 12.9 years. This measure is a parameter. Thus far in this book, we have discussed a variety of parameters including the mean, the median, and the standard deviation.

**parameter**

**sample**      A **sample** is a subset of a population. In this text, we will assume that all samples are selected randomly. A random sample is a sample in which every member of the population has an equal chance of being included.

**statistic**      A **statistic** is a measure that is used to summarize a sample. The mean, the standard deviation, and the median of a sample are all statistics.

To create a bit more complexity in the interests of clarity, statisticians use different symbols for the mean and the standard deviation, depending on whether they are parameters or statistics. Table 9.1 illustrates the symbols.

**TABLE 9.1**

Symbols for Parameters and Statistics

| Measure | Population Parameter | Sample Statistic |
|---|---|---|
| Mean | $\mu$ | $\overline{X}$ |
| Standard deviation | $\sigma$ | $s$ |
| Number of cases | $N$ | $n$ |

The mean is always calculated the same way, whether the data are taken from a sample or a population. The standard deviation, however, is calculated differently. Recall that the formula for calculating the standard deviation is

$$\sigma = \sqrt{\frac{\sum_{i=1}^{N}(X_i - \mu)^2}{N}}$$

The formula for the standard deviation of a sample is similar, with one slight twist:

$$s = \sqrt{\frac{\sum_{i=1}^{n}(X_i - \overline{X})^2}{n - 1}}$$

The difference here is that the sum of the squared deviations from the mean is divided by $n - 1$ rather than by $N$. Later in this chapter, we will explain why this correction is made.

# ESTIMATING A
# POPULATION MEAN

The best estimate of the population mean $\mu$ is the mean of the sample $\overline{X}$. To illustrate why this is true, we will use the data in Table 9.2, which lists the number of arrests by all ten Yukon, Oklahoma, police officers in 1991.

The mean number of arrests by Yukon police officers is 15.0. But in circumstances where the population parameter cannot be calculated, either because the population is too large or because the data are not available, the mean of a sample can be used to estimate the population mean.

**TABLE 9.2**

Number of Arrests by Police Officers in Yukon, Oklahoma, 1991

| Police Officer | Number of Arrests, 1991 |
|----------------|--------------------------|
| 1 | 14 |
| 2 | 16 |
| 3 | 10 |
| 4 | 18 |
| 5 | 8 |
| 6 | 15 |
| 7 | 17 |
| 8 | 20 |
| 9 | 19 |
| 10 | 13 |

Assume that we took a random sample of five Yukon police officers and calculated the mean for those five as follows (the sample was selected by using a random number table):

| Officers in Sample | Arrests | Mean |
|--------------------|---------|------|
| 1, 3, 2, 8, 4 | 14, 10, 16, 20, 18 | 15.6 |

The sample mean is one estimate of the population mean. Note that although our estimate is close (15.6 compared to 15.0), it is not exact. This discrepancy occurs because of sampling error—that is, our sample is not perfectly representative of the population. We would expect, however, that if we took numerous samples of five, the average sample mean would approach the population mean. Let's try it. The data and calculations are shown in Table 9.3.

Notice how the average sample mean quickly approaches the population mean and fluctuates around it. Statisticians have worked out this general problem and have logically demonstrated that the average sample mean over the long run will equal the population mean. The best estimate of the population mean, therefore, is the sample mean.

## ESTIMATING A POPULATION STANDARD DEVIATION

The best estimate of the population standard deviation $\sigma$ is the sample standard deviation $s$. Remember that $s$ has $n - 1$ as a denominator rather than N. Again, let's use the Yukon police arrests example to illustrate the estimating accuracy of the sample standard deviation. The population standard deviation is 3.7. (If you do not believe us, calculate it from the data in Table 9.2.)

Drawing a sample of five officers, we get the estimate of the standard deviation shown in Table 9.4 (note that we use the same sample in this illustration that we used before).

**TABLE 9.3**

Calculating the Average Sample Mean from Samples of Five

| Officers in Sample | Number of Arrests | Sample Mean | Average Mean |
|---|---|---|---|
| 1, 3, 2, 8, 4 | 14, 10, 16, 20, 18 | 15.6 | 15.6 |
| 1, 6, 8, 3, 4 | 14, 15, 20, 10, 18 | 15.4 | 15.5 |
| 7, 4, 1, 5, 9 | 17, 18, 14, 8, 19 | 15.2 | 15.4 |
| 2, 10, 7, 4, 6 | 16, 13, 17, 18, 15 | 15.8 | 15.5 |
| 7, 10, 3, 6, 5 | 17, 13, 10, 15, 8 | 12.6 | 14.9 |
| 10, 7, 2, 1, 4 | 13, 17, 16, 14, 18 | 15.6 | 15.0 |
| 10, 3, 7, 4, 2 | 13, 10, 17, 18, 16 | 14.8 | 15.0 |
| 10, 3, 8, 9, 4 | 13, 10, 20, 19, 18 | 16.0 | 15.1 |
| 6, 4, 8, 9, 10 | 15, 18, 20, 19, 13 | 17.0 | 15.3 |
| 2, 8, 4, 1, 5 | 16, 20, 18, 14, 8 | 15.2 | 15.3 |
| 8, 3, 9, 10, 5 | 20, 10, 19, 13, 8 | 14.0 | 15.2 |
| 2, 3, 7, 5, 1 | 16, 10, 17, 8, 14 | 13.0 | 15.0 |
| 10, 8, 5, 6, 4 | 13, 20, 8, 15, 18 | 14.8 | 15.0 |
| 9, 3, 6, 2, 7 | 19, 10, 15, 16, 17 | 15.4 | 15.0 |
| 9, 8, 10, 4, 3 | 19, 20, 13, 18, 10 | 16.0 | 15.1 |

**TABLE 9.4**

Calculating $s$ for a Sample of Five

| Officer | Arrests | Arrests – Mean | Squared |
|---|---|---|---|
| 1 | 14 | –1.6 | 2.56 |
| 3 | 10 | –5.6 | 31.36 |
| 2 | 16 | .4 | .16 |
| 8 | 20 | 4.4 | 19.36 |
| 4 | 18 | 2.4 | 5.76 |
| | | | 59.20 sum of squares |

$$s = \sqrt{59.2 \div 4} = 3.85$$

Our estimate of the population standard deviation is 3.85, which is close to the population value of 3.7. Note that had we divided by $n$ rather than by $n - 1$, the standard deviation estimate would have been 3.4. Dividing by $n$ gives us a consistently low estimate of the population standard deviation. For this reason, the estimate *always* is made with a denominator of $n - 1$. If you want to know why this is true, consult an advanced statistics text (Ott, 1977).

## THE STANDARD ERROR

If you reported that the mean arrests per police officer in Yukon was 15.6, your superior might ask you if the mean was exactly 15.6. Your answer would be that you do not know, but that your best estimate of the mean is 15.6. Your superior might then ask, how good an estimate is 15.6? What your superior wants to know is, what is the range of values that the mean must fall within—that is, how much error can the mean estimate contain?

One way to answer this question is to take numerous samples, calculate a mean for each sample, and show the supervisor the range of mean estimates. If you wanted to be more sophisticated, you might calculate a standard deviation for all the mean estimates. The standard deviation for mean estimates has a special name; it is called the **standard error of the mean**.

**standard error of the mean**

Fortunately for the sanity of most management analysts, one does not need to take numerous samples, calculate a mean for each sample, and then calculate a standard deviation for the mean estimates to find the standard error of the mean. Statisticians have demonstrated that a good estimate of the standard error of the mean can be made with the following formula:

$$\text{s.e.} = \frac{\sigma}{\sqrt{n}}$$

where s.e. is the standard error of the mean, $\sigma$ is the standard deviation of the population, and $n$ is the sample size. Since we rarely know the population standard deviation, the estimated standard deviation can be used in computations.

In our present example, we have a mean estimate of 15.6, a standard deviation estimate of 3.85, and a sample size of 5. Substituting these values into the equation for standard error, we get

$$\text{s.e.} = \frac{3.85}{\sqrt{5}} = \frac{3.85}{2.236} = 1.7$$

Sample estimates of a population mean are normally distributed if the sample size is greater than 30 or if the population is normally distributed. Let's assume that this is the case in our example. (For instructions about what to do when the population is not normally distributed *and* the sample size is less than 30, see Chapter 12. To avoid any problems, always use a sample of more than 30 when you feel that the population is not normally distributed.) Since the standard error of the mean is equivalent to the standard deviation of mean estimates, we know from Chapter 5 that 68.26% of all mean estimates will fall within one standard error in either direction. In this case, 68% of the mean estimates will fall between 13.9 (15.6 − 1.7) and 17.3 (15.6 + 1.7). We also know that 95.44% of all mean estimates will fall within two standard errors of the estimated mean, that is, between 12.2 and 19.0. Given our knowledge of probability, we can say that we are 95.44% sure that the mean number of arrests by Yukon police officers is between 12.2 arrests and 19.0 arrests.

## AN EXAMPLE

Several years ago, the Wiese school system was criticized because the average Wiese High School graduate could only read at the ninth-grade level. After this report was made, a special reading program was established to upgrade skills. The WHS principal wants to know if the reading program worked. If it has, he will request that an accreditation team visit the school. If the program has not improved the reading level to at least 10.0 (sophomore level), the administrator would like to avoid the embarrassment of a poor review.

To determine the average reading level of the senior class, we select ten seniors at random. We assume that reading scores are normally distributed. The reading scores for these ten seniors are shown in Table 9.5. We proceed as follows:

**TABLE 9.5**
Reading Scores

| Senior | Reading Score |
|--------|---------------|
| 1 | 13.4 |
| 2 | 12.1 |
| 3 | 11.4 |
| 4 | 10.6 |
| 5 | 10.3 |
| 6 | 10.2 |
| 7 | 9.8 |
| 8 | 9.7 |
| 9 | 9.4 |
| 10 | 8.6 |

**STEP 1**   Estimate the population mean. Calculate the sample mean reading score in the space provided next to Table 9.5. The answer should be 10.6.

**STEP 2**   Estimate the population standard deviation. In this case, the estimated standard deviation is 1.4. Calculate in the space next to the table.

**STEP 3**    Calculate the standard error of the mean.

$$\text{s.e.} = \frac{\sigma}{\sqrt{n}} = \frac{1.4}{\sqrt{10}} = \frac{1.4}{3.16} = .44$$

**STEP 4**    Provide an **interval estimate** of the mean. An interval estimate is an **interval estimate** interval such that the probability that the mean falls within the interval is acceptably high. The most common interval is the 95% confidence interval (we are 95% sure the mean falls within the interval). The $z$ score for 95% confidence limits is 1.96 (.475 on each side of the mean; see Table 1 in the Appendix). Using this $z$ score, we find that the 95% confidence interval is equal to

$$10.6 \pm 1.96 \times .44$$

$$10.6 \pm .86$$

$$9.7 \text{ to } 11.5$$

We are 95% sure that the mean reading level falls within the range of 9.7 to 11.5 years of school.

This answer bothers the principal because he wants to be certain that the mean is above 10.0. The principal wants us to calculate the probability that the population mean is 10.0 or less. Another way to ask this question is, if $\mu$ is 10.0 or less, what is the probability of drawing a sample with a mean of 10.6? This probability can be determined easily, since we have both a mean and a standard error. We convert 10.6 into a $z$ score:

$$z = \frac{\overline{X} - \mu}{\text{s.e.}} = \frac{10.6 - 10.00}{.44} = \frac{.6}{.44} = 1.36$$

Looking up a $z$ score of 1.36 in the normal table, we find a probability of .087. In other words, the probability is .087 that with a mean of less than 10.0 we could get a sample mean estimate of 10.6.

The principal decides that he would like to be more certain. Greater certainty can be achieved if the standard error of the mean can be reduced. The formula for the standard error of the mean

$$\text{s.e.} = \frac{\sigma}{\sqrt{n}}$$

shows that the standard error can be reduced if the standard deviation can be reduced (not likely, since this is a function of the population) or if the sample size can be increased. Let's increase the sample size to 100. By a quirk of fate, our sample of 100 has a mean of 10.6 and a standard deviation of 1.4. In the space provided, calculate the new standard error.

If you found the standard error to be .14, congratulations.

In the space provided, calculate the new 95% confidence limits for the Wiese High School senior class reading scores.

From this new information, what can you tell the principal?

## CHAPTER SUMMARY

Whenever someone wants to say something about a group of items or people, based on a subset of those items or people, that person wants to engage in inference. Inferential statistics use quantitative techniques to generalize from a sample (with summary measures called *statistics*) to a population (with summary measures called *parameters*). This chapter illustrates how to infer (by using estimates) population means and standard deviations from a sample. The standard error of the mean tells us how much error is contained in the estimate of the mean—that is, how good the estimate is.

## PROBLEMS

**9.1**   George Fastrack, head of the Bureau of Obfuscation's United Way drive, wants to know the average United Way pledge among Obfuscation Bureau employees (pledges are normally distributed). George takes a sample of ten and gets the results shown in the accompanying table. What is George's best estimate of the mean donation? What is George's best estimate of the standard deviation of the donations? Between what two values can George be 95% sure the mean value lies?

| Person | Pledge |
| --- | --- |
| 1 | $ 25 |
| 2 | 0 |
| 3 | 35 |
| 4 | 100 |
| 5 | 0 |
| 6 | 0 |
| 7 | 15 |
| 8 | 50 |
| 9 | 25 |
| 10 | 50 |

**9.2**   Captain E. Garth Beaver has been warned by Colonel Sy Verleaf that if the mean efficiency rating for the 150 platoons under Verleaf's command falls below 80, Captain Beaver will be transferred to Minot Air Force Base (a fate worse than Diego Garcia). Beaver wants to know in advance what his fate will be, so he knows whether to send change-of-address cards to all his magazine subscriptions. Beaver takes a sample of 20 platoons and finds the following:

$$\overline{X} = 85 \qquad s = 13.5$$

Would you advise Beaver to send change-of-address cards? (Assume that efficiency ratings are normally distributed.)

**9.3** Last year, sanitation engineer crews in Normal, Oklahoma, collected 124 tons of trash per day. This year, larger, more efficient trucks were purchased. A sample of 100 truck-days shows that a mean of 130 tons of trash were collected, with a standard deviation of 30 tons. What is the probability that a sample with this mean could be drawn if the new trucks are no improvement (that is, the population mean = 124)?

**9.4** Current Tinderbox Park water pumps can pump 2000 gallons of water per minute. The park tests ten new Fastwater brand pumps and finds a mean of 2200 and a standard deviation of 500. What is the probability that the Fastwater pumps were selected from a population with a mean no better than that of the present pumps?

**9.5** If the absenteeism rates for a school district rise above 10%, the state reduces its aid to the school district. Stermerville Independent School District takes a sample of five schools within the district and finds the following absenteeism rates: 5.4%, 8.6%, 4.1%, 8.9%, 7.8%. What is your best estimate of the absenteeism rate in Stermerville? What is the probability that the absenteeism rate is greater than 10%?

**9.6** The Department of Animal Husbandry at State University believes that adding cement to cattle feed will increase the cattle's weight gain. The average weekly gain for State U cattle last year was 12.7 pounds. A sample of 30 cattle are fed cement-fortified feed with the following results:

$$\overline{X} = 14.1 \text{ pounds} \qquad s = 5.0$$

What can you tell the department?

**9.7** Last year, Groton, Georgia, had 512 burglaries. The police chief wants to know the average economic loss associated with burglaries in Groton and wants to know it this afternoon. Since there isn't time to analyze all 512 burglaries the department's research analyst selects ten burglaries at random, which show the following losses:

| | |
|---|---|
| $ 550 | $ 874 |
| $ 675 | $ 595 |
| $ 324 | $ 835 |
| $ 487 | $ 910 |
| $1246 | $ 612 |

What is the best estimate of the average loss on a burglary? Place 80% confidence limits around this estimate.

**9.8** Last year, the Department of Vocational Rehabilitation was able to place people in jobs with an average salary of $10,600. This year, placement is handled by a private agency that charges $200 per placement. What can you tell the department based on the following placement figures for this year (sample of 100):

$$\overline{X} = \$10,900 \qquad s = 2000$$

**9.9** The General Accounting Office is auditing Branflake International Airways, a company that flies numerous charters for the government. The contract with Branflake specifies that the average flight can be no more than 15 minutes late. A sample of twenty flights reveals the results in the accompanying table. Write a brief memo interpreting this information.

| Flight Number | Status |
|---|---|
| 217 | On time |
| 167 | 20 minutes late |
| 133 | 17 minutes late |
| 207 | 64 minutes late |
| 219 | On time |
| 457 | 96 minutes late |
| 371 | 30 minutes late |
| 612 | On time |
| 319 | 6 minutes late |
| 423 | 12 minutes late |
| 684 | 11 minutes late |
| 661 | 61 minutes late |
| 511 | On time |
| 536 | On time |
| 493 | 17 minutes late |
| 382 | 12 minutes late |
| 115 | 6 minutes late |
| 107 | 3 minutes late |
| 19 | 26 minutes late |
| 123 | 19 minutes late |

**9.10** The secretary of welfare hypothesizes that the average district office has 5% or fewer fraudulent or ineligible recipients. A sample of ten offices reveals a mean of 4.7% with a standard deviation of 1.2%. What can be said about the secretary's hypothesis?

**9.11** The Department of Health and Human Services wants to know the average income of general assistance recipients. A sample of sixty recipients shows a sample mean of $4400 with a standard deviation of $2500. Place a 90% confidence limit around your best estimate of the average income of general assistance recipients. What is the probability that the average income could be $6000 or more? What is the probability that the average might be as low as $4000?

**9.12** As an analyst for the Overseas Private Investment Corporation, you are required to report to Congress about guaranteed loans to companies doing business in Central American countries. You do not have time to find all the loans, so you take a sample of six loans. The loans have the following values, in millions of dollars:

223     247     187     17     215     275

Use this information to calculate a mean, and put 90% confidence limits around your estimate.

**9.13** Complaints about how long it takes the city of Shorewood to pay its bills have reached the city manager. City policy requires that bills be paid within 30 days. A sample of 100 bills shows a mean of 34 days with a standard deviation of 15. Is it possible that a sample mean of 34 days could be generated from a population with a true mean of 30?

**9.14** Last year, the Texas State Penitentiary averaged 14.1 violent incidents per day in its prisons. At the end of last year, the federal courts held that inmates could not supervise other inmates. Warden John Law thinks that this ruling will generate more violent incidents, because in the past inmates used the supervision hierarchy to maintain a pecking order inside the prison. A sample of 40 days of records reveals a mean of 17.5 and a standard deviation of 2.0. What can you tell Warden Law?

**9.15** The Metro City Bus system is concerned about the number of people who complain about the service. They suspect that many people do not know how to complain. Last year, complaints averaged 47.3 per day. This year, bus systems manager Ralph Kramden has posted a sign in all buses listing a number to call with complaints. Ralph would like to know if this effort has generated any additional complaints. He takes a sample of 50 days, and finds a mean of 54.7 and a standard deviation of 25.4. What can you tell Ralph?

## CHAPTER 10

# HYPOTHESIS

# TESTING

A manager is often faced with decisions about program effectiveness, personnel productivity, and procedural changes. Decisions on such matters are based on the information relevant to them. Is the Chicago-area Head Start program upgrading the educational skills of its participants? Is Robert Allen an effective first-line supervisor? Will redesigning form SKL473/26 result in faster processing of equal employment complaints? Questions that seek information about managerial problems are called **hypotheses**. When phrased as a statement rather than as a question, a hypothesis is nothing more than a statement about the world that may be either true or false. Some examples of hypotheses are these:

**hypotheses**

Following the Connecticut Highway Patrol's crackdown on speeders, the number of highway accident fatalities dropped.

The average number of tons of trash collected by Normal, Oklahoma, sanitation engineer crews is 247 tons per week.

After implementing the project team's management strategy, the productivity of the England County Welfare Department has increased.

Hypotheses are traditionally presented in the negative. For example,

Following the Connecticut Highway Patrol's crackdown on speeders, the number of highway accident fatalities *has not dropped*.

In the space provided, present the Normal and England County hypotheses in the negative.

**null hypothesis**

A hypothesis expressed in the negative is referred to as the **null hypothesis** (the hypothesis that nothing happened). As this chapter will illustrate, null hypotheses are easier to use in inferential statistics than are other types of hypotheses.

This chapter will cover the logic of hypothesis testing. It will also illustrate the process of testing hypotheses with both population parameters and sample statistics.

## STEPS IN HYPOTHESIS TESTING

The logic of hypothesis testing is fairly simple.

**STEP 1**   Formulate the hypothesis. Suppose that you have a research assistant, Thurman Truck, who is preparing a lengthy research report. Based on Thurman's assurances, you hypothesize that he will complete the report by August. The null hypothesis is that Thurman will not complete the research report by August.

**STEP 2**   Collect data relevant to the hypothesis. You know that to complete the research report by August, Thurman must complete a prospectus by January 15. On January 15, Thurman tells you the prospectus will be done January 22. On January 21, Thurman promises you the prospectus on January 28. On January 27, Thurman swears that the prospectus will be on your desk by February 5. On February 4, Thurman ceases to come to work.

**STEP 3**   Evaluate the hypothesis in light of the data. Are the data consistent with the hypothesis? Does Thurman's behavior indicate that the research report will not be completed by August (the null hypothesis)?

**STEP 4**   Accept or reject the hypothesis. In this situation, you must accept the null hypothesis that Thurman will not finish his research report by August.

**STEP 5**   Revise your decisions in light of this new information. In this case, you decide to transfer Mr. Truck to your regional office in Lubbock, Texas, as a punishment for nonperformance.

## TESTING HYPOTHESES WITH POPULATION PARAMETERS

If the manager has access to population parameters, then hypothesis testing is as easy as deciding whom to start at running back if Christian Okoye plays for your team. As an illustration, suppose that Jerry Green, governor of a large eastern state, wants to know if a former governor's executive reorganization had any impact on the state's expenditures. After some meditation, he postulates the following null hypothesis:

State expenditues did not decrease after the executive reorganization,
    compared to the state budget's long-run growth rate.

Governor Green stated the null hypothesis in this way so that the test would be fair. He reasoned that one could not expect an absolute decrease in expenditures because the state's population was growing (and thus generating greater demands for state services). The average growth rate of state expenditures appears to provide a reasonable test.

A management review shows that the state's expenditures grew at the rate of 10.7% per year before the reorganization and 10.4% after the reorganization. What do these figures say about the null hypothesis? Since 10.4% is less than 10.7%, we reject the null hypothesis and conclude that the growth rate in state expenditures declined after the reorganization.

You may have objected to the preceding conclusion, thinking that a .3% decrease in the growth rate of expenditures was not significant. If you meant statistically significant, you were incorrect. Since these are exact population parameters, statistical significance has no meaning (the probability that the state reduced its growth rate in expenditures is 1.0, or nearly so). If by significance you meant that the decrease was trivial, you are correct. Remember, however, that the hypothesis did not state that the change would be large, only that there would be a change.

Notice that we did not conclude that the reorganization resulted in a decline in the state budget's growth rate. Statistics cannot come to this conclusion. Statistics can only determine if the expenditure rate after the reorganization was less than the rate before the reorganization. To conclude that the reorganization resulted in the reduced rate, the manager must determine that no other variable could have caused the decline. This assessment is an evaluation of the research design. Finally, the manager must make a managerial assessment of this question based on the risks the manager wishes to sustain.

To avoid overstepping the limits of statistics, we suggest you approach all statistical problems in three steps.

**STEP 1**    The statistics step: did the growth rate in the budget decline after the reorganization?

**STEP 2**    The research design step: could things other than the reorganization have caused the decline?

**STEP 3**    The managerical step: what can I confidently conclude about the reorganization and the budget growth rate?

## HYPOTHESIS TESTING
## WITH SAMPLES

In most managerial situations, population parameters are not available. This absence is the result of cost, inaccessibility, and a variety of other factors that prevent gathering data on the entire population. Although population parameters are the ideal data to use in hypothesis testing, circumstances often dictate the use of sample statistics. The Food and Nutrition Service of the Department of Agriculture, for example, may want to know the impact of food stamps on family nutrition. (The null hypothesis is that they have no impact.) Although the service might prefer data on all food stamp recipients, costs of gathering the data restrict the Food and Nutrition Service to testing with samples.

Hypothesis testing with a sample can best be illustrated with an example. The police chief of Prudeville, Oklahoma, has received several complaints from the city council about prostitution in Prudeville. The council members all suggest a crackdown. The police chief issues orders to make more prostitution arrests and asks the department's research analyst to gather some data. After a month, the council is still upset and calls the police chief in to appear before the council. The chief asks his research assistant to assess the effectiveness of the crackdown so that the chief can present these data to the council.

Before the crackdown on prostitution, the Prudeville vice squad was making 3.4 prostitution arrests per day (arrests are normally distributed). The research assistant forms the following null hypothesis:

Following the Prudeville prostitution crackdown, prostitution arrests
  were not greater than 3.4 per day.

Since there is not enough time before the city council meeting to analyze all the data, the research analyst randomly selects ten days of arrests for analysis. The data are given in Table 10.1.

**TABLE 10.1**

Sample Data for Prostitution Arrests

| Day | Prostitution Arrests |
|-----|----------------------|
| 1   | 3                    |
| 2   | 5                    |
| 3   | 7                    |
| 4   | 2                    |
| 5   | 3                    |
| 6   | 6                    |
| 7   | 4                    |
| 8   | 3                    |
| 9   | 6                    |
| 10  | 1                    |

The analyst proceeds by the following steps.

**STEP 1**   Estimate the population mean after the crackdown. Since the best estimate of the population mean is the sample mean, the analyst calculates
the mean. His figure is 4.0.

**STEP 2**   Estimate the population standard deviation. In this example the estimated standard deviation is 1.94. (**Hint:** divide by $n - 1$.)

**STEP 3**   Calculate the standard error of the mean. Since we only have a sample,
the mean estimate may be in error. As a result, we need to know how
good an estimate of the mean we have. We use the formula

$$\text{s.e.} = \frac{\sigma}{\sqrt{n}} = \frac{1.94}{\sqrt{10}} = .61$$

The standard error is .61.

**STEP 4**   Test the hypothesis. Answer the following question: What is the probability of drawing a sample of ten with a mean of 4.0 if the population
mean is 3.4? This question can be answered by coverting 4.0 into a $z$
score and using the normal table (arrests are normally distributed).

$$z = \frac{\overline{X} - \mu}{\text{s.e.}} = \frac{4.0 - 3.4}{.61} = .98$$

Looking up a $z$ score of .98 in the normal table, we find that the probability of a sample of ten with a mean of 4.0 coming from a population
with a mean of 3.4 is .16 (rounded off from .1635).

The research assistant decides to accept the null hypothesis because he feels
.16 is too large a probability to reject the null hypothesis. The police chief
overrules the research assistant because he wants to show positive results. He
argues before the city council that this improvement in arrest rates has only a
one-in-six chance of happening by chance. The research assistant is fired later
that day.

Does the criterion used (arrest rates per day) accurately measure what the
city council is concerned about? What does the city council want stopped? How
could you measure this? How valid are the findings above given what you said
about these measurements? Apply the research design step.

## How Sure Should A Person Be?

In the preceding example, a research analyst felt that a probability of .16 was
not sufficient to reject a null hypothesis, whereas the police chief felt that it was.

Political considerations aside, how sure should a person be before rejecting the null hypothesis? In the words of Harvey Sherman, "It all depends." It all depends on how sure one needs to be to make a decision confidently.

Social scientists routinely accept a probability of .05 for rejecting the null hypothesis. But in many management situations, a .05 probability may be too great a risk. A rape crisis center may decide that the probability that one staff member cannot handle all the possible rape calls in any given day is .05. This means, however, that one day in twenty, or once every thee weeks, the rape crisis center will fail to meet a crisis. In this situation, a .05 level is too great a risk. A .001 level, one failure in three years, may be more acceptable.

A police department, on the other hand, may be able to accept a .05 probability that one of its cars will be out of service. But the fire department may require a probability of only .0001 that a fire hose will fail to operate.

In short, the decision on how certain one must be to reject a null hypothesis depends on the importance of the question involved. A manager should never let his or her analyst make this decision. The analyst should provide the probability; it is the function of the manager to decide if the proability is sufficient to reject the null hypothesis given the circumstances that are involved in the decision.

## ONE- AND TWO-TAILED TESTS

Determining the probability of an event is another way of assessing the statistical significance of an event. Another way of saying that the probability of event A is .01 is to say that A is statistically significant at the .01 level (that is, the probability that event A would occur by chance is .01). A significance test, therefore, is nothing more than a determination of the probability of an event.

Most statistics texts devote an extended discussion to one-tailed versus two-tailed tests of significance. This book will describe both briefly, but will focus on the one-tailed test because it has much greater utility than the two-tailed test. A **one-tailed test** is applied whenever the hypothesis under consideration specifies a direction. In the previous Prudeville prostitution problem, the null hypothesis was that the arrest rate did not increase. We call this a one-tailed test because we are concerned with only one tail of the normal curve, the tail larger than 3.4 (see Figure 10.1).

one-tailed test

A one-tailed test affects the probability assigned to the null hypothesis. Since we are interested only in values greater than 3.4, an $\overline{X}$ of 4.0 has a probability of .16. (**Reasoning:** if $\mu = 3.4$, 34% of all sample means fall between 3.4 and 4.0; 50% of all sample means fall below 3.4; this means 16% of all sample means fall at 4.0 or above; thus the probability is .16.)

In rare circumstances, a public manager is interested in situations that differ greatly from the mean in either direction. For example, the Federal Railroad

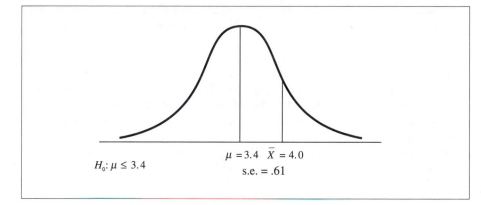

$H_0: \mu \leq 3.4$

$\mu = 3.4 \quad \bar{X} = 4.0$
s.e. = .61

**FIGURE 10.1**
A One-Tailed Test

Administration is purchasing railroad ties to recondition a railroad line from Bessmer, Michigan, to Rolla, Missouri. (Many of Bessmer's finest serve at Fort Leonard Wood, Missouri.) Because the railroad bed is unstable, only ties between 10 and $10\frac{1}{2}$ feet long can be used. The FRA administrator must inspect railroad tie shipments and decide whether they meet these standards. Because the FRA administrator cannot measure every tie, he decides to have a random sample of ten pulled from every shipment. Any shipment of ties in which more than 20% of the ties are either too large or too small will be rejected. From past experience, the administrator knows that the standard deviation of machine-cut ties is 1 inch. Based on the mean of each sample of ten, how can the administrator decide whether or not to accept a shipment?

Since this problem does not specify a direction for the hypothesis, it requires a **two-tailed test**. The first step is to determine the maximum mean value so that less than 10% of all ties are more than 10 feet 6 inches long. (We use 10% because, if 10% are too large and 10% are too small, 20% cannot be used.) To do this, look up a value of .4000 in the $z$ score table (Table 1) (10% = .5000 − .4000). The $z$ score is 1.28. If the mean sample is within 1.28 standard deviations of 10 feet 6 inches, then the shipment should be rejected. Converting this figure to a length in feet, we have

$$X = 10 \text{ feet } 6 \text{ inches} - (1.28 \times 1 \text{ inch}) = 10 \text{ feet } 4.72 \text{ inches}$$

In any sample whose mean is greater than 10 feet 4.72 inches, probably 10% of the ties are longer than 10 feet 6 inches.

Similarly, if the mean of the sample is 1.28 standard deviations from the lower limit of 10 feet, less than 10% of the ties will be too short. The lower limit for sample means then should be 10 feet 1.28 inches. We now have a decision rule:

If the mean length of ten ties is between 10 feet 1.28 inches and 10 feet 4.72 inches, accept the shipment; if not, reject the shipment.

If shipments have a mean length of 10.3 inches and are normally distributed, using this decision rule will result in less than 20% of ties that are too long or too short. No more than 10% of the ties will be too long, and no more than 10% will be too short.

Although this problem uses both tails of the normal curve, it could easily be transformed into two separate problems, each with a one-tailed test. Because most management problems in the public sector can be transformed into one-tailed problems, we suggest that you concentrate on learning how one-tailed tests are made. The only exception to this rule is when you want to know the optimal sample size so that you are 95% (or some other percentage) sure that a mean falls between two numbers (see below).

## ERRORS

**type 1 error**

When testing a null hypothesis, there are two possible errors you can make. You can reject the null hypothesis even though the null hypothesis is true. This is called a **type 1 error**. For example, let us assume that the Federal Highway Administration wants to determine whether Oklahoma is enforcing the 65-mile-per-hour speed limit. If the average speed of Oklahoma cars is 65 or less, the FHA will concede that Oklahoma is enforcing the law. If the average speed is more than 65 mph, then the FHA will begin proceedings to cut off Oklahoma's federal transportation funds. Since this is a serious step to take, FHA officials want to be 99% sure before they act to cut off funds. Cost restrictions limit the sample of cars to be clocked to 100 cars.

Given this problem, the FHA analyst takes a preliminary survey and finds the standard deviation of Oklahoma car speeds to be 17.4 miles per hour. With a sample of 100, the standard error of any mean estimate would be

$$\text{s.e.} = \frac{\sigma}{\sqrt{n}} = \frac{17.4}{\sqrt{100}} = \frac{17.4}{10} = 1.74$$

For a 99% confidence limit, the analyst scans the normal table for a value of .4900. This corresponds to a $z$ score of 2.33. The analyst knows that if the sample mean of Oklahoma cars is 2.33 standard errors greater than 65, then he is 99% sure that Oklahoma cars' average speed exceeds 65 miles per hour.

Translating this into a decision rule, he finds

$$X = 65 + (2.33 \times 1.74) = 65 + 4.05 = 69.05$$

If the sample average speed is 69.05 miles per hour or above, the FHA will conclude that Oklahoma cars' average speed is greater than 65 miles per hour and will begin withholding funds.

To illustrate the possibility of a type 1 error, consider the following hypothetical situation. The average speed in Oklahoma is 65 miles per hour, but due to sampling error, the sample mean is 69.1. This situation will happen once every 100 samples. The hypothesis of 65 miles per hour was rejected when it was actually true.

The second type of error, called, quite appropriately, a **type 2 error**, occurs when you accept the null hypothesis as true when in fact it is false. Suppose that in the preceding example the population mean is 67 miles per hour and a sample revealed a mean of 67 miles per hour. (Clearly this can happen.) In this situation, you would conclude that Oklahoma cars' average speed does not exceed 65 miles per hour when in fact it does.

**type 2 error**

The probability of committing either a type 1 or type 2 error always exists. The probability of committing a type 1 error can be reduced by increasing the probability required to reject the null hypothesis (for example, .001 or .0001). Unfortunately, this increases the probability of a type 2 error. This trade-off is resolved by deciding whether it would be worse to make a type 1 or a type 2 error. Is it worse to cut off Oklahoma's federal aid when it is complying with the law, or to continue to aid Oklahoma if it is violating the law? Clearly the former is more dangerous in a political sense, so one would try to minimize type 1 errors.

A method of minimizing type 2 errors is to increase sample size. All things being equal, the larger the sample size, the smaller is the standard error of the mean and, therefore, the smaller is the likelihood of rejecting a true hypothesis. The data in Table 10.2 illustrate this. Clearly the certainty of the analyst is increased by the larger sample. The probability of rejecting a true hypothesis with a sample mean of 67 is much less with a sample of 500 than with 100.

**TABLE 10.2**

Calculations for Two Different Sample Sizes

| Statistic | Sample 1 | Sample 2 |
|---|---|---|
| $n$ | 100 | 500 |
| $\overline{X}$ | 67.0 | 67.0 |
| $\sigma$ | 17.4 | 17.4 |
| s.e. | 1.74 | .78 |
| probability $X < 65$ | .119 | .0051 |

## DETERMINING SAMPLE SIZE

Another research problem facing management analysts is deciding how large a sample is necessary to adequately test the hypothesis. For example, the Wisconsin State Welfare Department may want to know the average income of all Wisconsin welfare recipients. It would like to be 95% certain that its estimate of the average income is within $100 of the actual average (this information is needed for federal forms). Using a sample, we can get an estimate of the mean by using the sample mean. A 95% confidence interval can be placed around this estimate by adding and subtracting a number equal to 1.96 standard errors from the mean estimate (1.96 is the 95% confidence limit $z$ score):

$$\overline{X} \pm 1.96 \times \text{s.e.}$$

The amount of error in the estimate is represented by that part of the computation to the right of the plus or minus sign (1.96 × s.e.). Our problem is this: how large a sample is needed to reduce this error to $100? Mathematically, we can determine this by setting 1.96 × s.e. equal to $100.

$$100 = 1.96 \times \text{s.e.}$$

But

$$\text{s.e.} = \frac{\sigma}{\sqrt{n}}$$

so

$$100 = \frac{1.96\sigma}{\sqrt{n}}$$

$$\sqrt{n} = \frac{1.96\sigma}{100}$$

$$n = \left(\frac{1.96\sigma}{100}\right)^2$$

These calculations show that, with an estimate of the standard deviation, we can calculate the desired sample size.

To estimate the standard deviation, the analyst takes a small sample of Wisconsin welfare recipients. The data of Table 10.3 result. In the space to the right of the data, calculate the standard deviation.

If you performed the calculations correctly, your answer should be 442. Substituting this value into the equation, we have

$$n = \left(\frac{1.96 \times 442}{100}\right)^2 = \left(\frac{866.3}{100}\right)^2 = (8.7)^2 = 75.7$$

The optimum sample size in this situation is 76 people. This size should provide an estimate of the average income of Wisconsin welfare recipients to within $100.

To generalize this problem, the ideal sample size for any problem is a function of (1) the amount of error that can be tolerated, (2) the confidence one wants to

**TABLE 10.3**

Data from a Sample of
Wisconsin Welfare
Recipients

| Recipient | Income |
|-----------|--------|
| 1 | $1500 |
| 2 | 1700 |
| 3 | 2600 |
| 4 | 1800 |
| 5 | 1200 |
| 6 | 2400 |
| 7 | 1300 |
| 8 | 1700 |
| 9 | 2000 |
| 10 | 1800 |

have in the error estimate, and (3) the standard deviation of the population. Symbolically, this can be expressed as follows:

$$n = \left(\frac{z \times \sigma}{E}\right)^2$$

where $n$ is the sample size, $z$ is the $z$ score associated with the desired confidence limit, $\sigma$ is the population standard deviation, and $E$ is the amount of error that can be tolerated.

For example, if you wanted to be 95% certain that the analyst's estimate in the previous example was within $50, you would perform the following calculations:

$$n = \left(\frac{1.96 \times 442}{50}\right)^2 = \left(\frac{866.3}{50}\right)^2 = (17.3)^2 = 300$$

The optimum sample size is 300 persons. (Always round up for sample sizes.)

## CHAPTER SUMMARY

Hypothesis testing is determining whether a statement is true or false. There are five steps involved: (1) formulate the hypothesis; (2) collect the relevant data; (3) evaluate the hypothesis in light of the data; (4) accept or reject the hypothesis; (5) revise your decisions in light of the new information.

Hypotheses can be tested by using population parameters or sample statistics, and hypothesis tests can be either one-tailed or two-tailed. When statistics are used, the techniques of inference are needed to test hypotheses.

This chapter also discusses the size of samples needed for ensuring only a given amount of error—that is, the sample size necessary to adequately test the hypothesis.

## PROBLEMS

**10.1**  Last year, Normal, Oklahoma, had all car maintenance on the city's automobiles done by the city maintenance pool. The cost was $364 per car. This year, the city fathers fired all the workers in the maintenance pool and are using Jack's Crash Shop to perform the maintenance. The city fathers would like to know, without a complete audit, if Jack is saving them money. A random sample of 36 cars showed a mean repair cost of $330, with a standard deviation of $120. What can you tell the city fathers?

**10.2**  The average grass maintenance engineer mows 1.4 acres of grass per day in Barron, Montana. Because labor costs are increasing, the city decides to try a new brand of mower. Ten randomly selected engineers are given these new mowers. After a test period, these ten engineers cut an average of 2.1 acres per day, with a standard deviation of .6 acre. If the costs are similar, should the city purchase more new mowers?

**10.3**  It is contract negotiation time, and the Oklahoma teachers union wants to argue that its salaries are the lowest in the region. Since the union has 20,000 members, it must rely on a survey. If the union wants to estimate its members' mean salary and be 95% sure that the estimate is within $200 of the real mean, how large a sample should the union use? Assume that a preliminary survey estimates the mean as $15,000, with a $1000 standard deviation.

**10.4**  The departments at Bufford State University publish an average of 5.1 professional articles a year. The sociology department regularly averages about 3.5. The chairman of the sociology department, Steig Willick, feels her department does less well because it is harder to publish in sociology. Willick takes a survey of 12 other sociology departments and finds the following:

$$\overline{X} = 4.2 \qquad s = 1.6$$

What can Willick tell the Dean?

**10.5**  The police chief of Kramer, Texas, reads a report that says the police clear 46.2% of all burglaries that occur in Kramer. The chief would like to know how good this figure is. She randomly selects ten other Texas cities and asks them what percentage they clear. She gets the following numbers:

| 44.2% | 36.4% | 51.7% | 32.9% | 46.4% |
| 40.3% | 49.4% | 32.1% | 29.0% | 41.0% |

Is Kramer's clearance rate significantly different from those of other Texas cities?

**10.6** The average per capita annual health care cost for a sample of U.S. cities (50,000–200,000 population) is $586.00, with a standard deviation of $116.00 ($n = 378$). Cavileer, Oregon (population 175,000), contends that its new outpatient treatment program reduces annual health care costs to $525.00 per person. Is this a significant improvement?

**10.7** Refer to Problem 10.6. The average health care costs per year are $586.00. The Department of Health and Human Services has funded several Health Maintenance Organizations (HMOs). A sample of their average annual costs per person are as follows:

| $591 | $451 |
| $546 | $494 |
| $437 | $561 |
| $527 | $523 |
| $602 | $481 |

The hypothesis is that HMOs are an improvement. Are they?

**10.8** The National Welfare Recipients Organization has charged that state caseworkers are inexperienced. The Kansas State Welfare Department surveys its employees and finds that they have an average of 3.4 years of welfare experience ($s = 3.9$, $n = 200$). What can the Kansas State Welfare Department claim?

**10.9** The Bureau of Forms has replaced 12 employees with 20 mini-computers. The 12 employees cost $204,500 per year in salaries and fringe benefits. The minicomputers cost $74,000. Operation and maintenance costs, however, are high; a sample of 10 machines reveals an average annual cost of $5200, with a standard deviation of $2000. What can be said about the decision to purchase minicomputers? **Hint:** How much does the bureau save by replacing the employees with minicomputers? What is the savings per computer?

**10.10** The Whitehawk Indian Tribe wants to know the average number of absences for each student at the elementary school run by the Bureau of Indian Affairs (BIA). The tribe members believe that the number of absences is at least 12 per student. A sample of 150 students reveals

$$\overline{X} = 11.8 \qquad s = 4.3$$

What can you tell from this information about the Whitehawk hypothesis?

**10.11**   The Bureau of Administration is concerned with high levels of employee absenteeism. Last year, the average employee missed 12.8 workdays. This year, there is an experimental program in which the agency pays employees for each sick day or personal day that they do not use. A preliminary survey of 20 persons reveals a mean of 8.7 days missed and a standard deviation of 4.6. Present a hypothesis, a null hypothesis, and evaluate them. State a conclusion in plain English.

**10.12**   The state of Michigan has just changed one of its toll roads from human collection of tolls to machine collection. The idea behind the change was to allow traffic to flow more smoothly through the toll plaza. With human attendants, the mean number of cars passing through the toll plaza was 1253 per hour. A random sample of 100 hours under the new machine system of toll collection shows a mean of 1261, with a standard deviation of 59. Present a hypothesis, a null hypothesis, and evaluate them. State a conclusion in plain English.

**10.13**   The Iowa State University Agriculture Research Team is concerned about the impact of the recent drought on the productivity of the state's corn crop. During the last ten years, Iowa's corn crop has averaged 32.4 bushels per acre per year. Final figures on this year's yields will not be in for another 6 months, but the team needs to estimate yields now in case the governor decides to apply for federal disaster aid. A sample of 100 acres reveals a mean of 22.4 bushels, with a standard deviation of 15.7. Based on this sample, present a hypothesis, a null hypothesis, and evaluate them. In plain English, state a conclusion of what you have found. Then place an 80% confidence limit around your best estimate of the mean yield.

**10.14**   The We Are Saved Christian Elementary School has decided to examine whether or not using biblical materials to teach reading has an impact on reading levels. Last year, a test revealed that the average sixth-grade student read at the 5.7 grade level. This year, after all secular humanist material was deleted from the curriculum, a 20-person sample of the sixth-grade student body was tested, with the following results:

$$\text{mean} = 6.4 \qquad \text{standard deviation} = 1.9$$

Present a hypothesis, a null hypothesis, and evaluate them. Present your conclusion in plain English.

**10.15**   The Wisconsin State Court system wants to assess the impact that punitive damages have on large tort awards. Using the court system's computer, 16 cases were selected at random from all those cases in which damages of $1 million or more were awarded. The sample revealed the following about the punitive damages in these cases:

mean $= \$74,500$     standard deviation $= 55,000$

Place a 99% confidence limit around your best estimate of the punitive damages for this type of case. One concern is that punitive damages for these cases might be in excess of $100,000. Present a hypothesis, a null hypothesis, and evaluate your hypothesis. Finish with a conclusion that a judge could understand.

## CHAPTER 11

# ESTIMATING

# POPULATION

# PROPORTIONS

Often a manager does not want to know the mean score of some population but rather the percentage of some population that does something. A Department of Transportation official, for example, might want to know the proportion of motor vehicles that pass a state's vehicle inspection. A criminal justice planner might want to know what percentage of persons released from prison will be arrested for another criminal act within one year. The police chief in a city might want to know the proportion of robberies that are not solved within one year. All these situations require the analyst to estimate a population proportion rather than a population mean.

This chapter will illustrate the procedure for estimating population proportions and will demonstrate how to test hypotheses using proportions.

## ESTIMATING A POPULATION PROPORTION

The procedure for estimating a population proportion and placing confidence limits around that estimate is relatively similar to that for estimating a population mean. We will illustrate this process with an example.

The warden of Ramsey Prison wants to know the prison's recidivism rate. The warden wants to know this information because he believes that the Ramsey rehabilitation program is a rousing success that others might want to copy. If the recidivism rate is fairly low (say, under 70%), the warden will write an article on the Ramsey rehabilitation program for the *Journal of Law 'n Order*. (The Ramsey rehabilitation program involves teaching each inmate a skill, such as making license plates, and then finding the inmate a job making license plates in the outside world.)

Since Ramsey is a large institution, calculating the recidivism rate for all past inmates would be difficult. The warden takes a sample of 100 former inmates who went through the rehabilitation program. These inmates are traced through the FBI's data system to find out whether they were re-arrested within a year of release. The warden considers anyone arrested within a year a failure. The FBI search reveals that 68 of the 100 inmates became inmates again.

**QUESTION 1** What is the best estimate of the proportion of recidivists in this situation? The sample of 100 can be interpreted as 100 samples of 1. The mean of these 100 samples is .68, which is the best estimate of the population proportion. In other words, the best estimate of a population proportion is the sample proportion.

**QUESTION 2** What is the standard deviation of the population? Recall that the standard deviation for a binomial probability distribution is

$$\sigma = \sqrt{n \times p \times (1 - p)}$$

where $p$ is the probability and $n$ is the number of trials.

If we treat this situation as a probability distribution, with $p = .68$ and 1 trial, the standard deviation is

$$\sigma = \sqrt{1 \times .68 \times .32} = \sqrt{.2176} = .47$$

The standard deviation is .47. In fact, this is how the standard deviation of a proportion is defined:

$$\sigma = \sqrt{p \times (1 - p)}$$

where $\sigma$ is the standard deviation of the proportion and $p$ is the proportion.

Actually, the standard deviation of a proportion makes no sense at all. All elements in the set have a value of 1 (recidivist) or 0 (not a recidivist). This means that the usual interpretation of a standard deviation as telling us the degree of clustering about the mean has little value. We calculate the standard deviation, however, because it permits us to calculate the standard error of the proportion.

**QUESTION 3** What is the standard error of the proportion? The standard error of a proportion has the same formula as the standard error of the mean:

$$\text{s.e.} = \frac{\sigma}{\sqrt{n}}$$

where $n$ is equal to the sample size. In our example we have

$$\text{s.e.} = \frac{.47}{\sqrt{100}} = \frac{.47}{10} = .047$$

**QUESTION 4**  What are the 95% confidence limits of the proportion? (Although proportions cannot be normally distributed—since individuals are either recidivists or not—in this case the sample size is larger than 30, so the normal curve can be used.) Since we have a mean (read "proportion") and a standard error of the estimate, we can easily construct a 95% confidence limit. In this situation, the 95% confidence limits are

$$p \pm z \times \text{s.e.}$$

$$.68 \pm 1.96 \times .047$$

$$.68 \pm .092$$

$$.59 \text{ to } .77$$

Using this 95% confidence limit, should the warden submit an article to the *Journal of Law 'n Order*?

# PROPORTIONS

Proportions problems have the same logic as means problems, and both are solved in a similar manner. For example, city council member Liver Smith argues that a majority of the people in Normal oppose the continued funding of the Normal Transit Bus System. Liver bases this argument on a random sample of 30 Normal residents. Twenty-one residents opposed continued funding of the bus system. For Liver's data, what is the probability that this sample could be drawn if a majority of residents favor continuing the bus system?

This problem can be interpreted as an example of hypothesis testing. Liver's hypothesis is that the proportion of Normal residents opposing the bus system is greater than .5:

$$H_1: p > .5$$

The null hypothesis may be expressed as

$$H_0: p \leq .5$$

or "the proportion of Normal residents who oppose the bus system is less than .5." Clearly this hypothesis can be tested.

**STEP 1**    Estimate the population proportion. In this case, it is .7 (21 ÷ 30).

**STEP 2**    Estimate the population standard deviation. Since we are given a hypothetical population proportion ($p = .5$), that proportion (not the sample proportion) should be used to estimate the standard deviation:

$$\sigma = \sqrt{p \times (1 - p)} = \sqrt{.5 \times .5} = .50$$

**STEP 3**    Estimate the standard error of the proportion.

$$\text{s.e.} = \frac{\sigma}{\sqrt{n}} = \frac{.50}{\sqrt{30}} = \frac{.50}{5.5} = .091$$

**STEP 4**    Test the hypothesis. What is the probability that a sample of 30 would result in a proportion estimate of .7 or greater if the true proportion were .5? Use a normal table and convert .7 to a $z$ score.

$$z = \frac{X - \mu}{\text{s.e.}} = \frac{.7 - .5}{.091} = \frac{.2}{.091} = 2.20$$

Looking up a $z$ score of 2.20 in the normal distribution table, we find a tabulated value of .4861, which means that the probability is .0139 of obtaining a sample that has a proportion of .7 or greater, if the true proportion is .5 (.5 − .4861 = .0139).

## A Digression

Before examining some other uses of proportions, a digression is in order. (Digressions are in order only after a $z$ score of 2.0 or more.) The perceptive reader might have seen another way to solve the previous problem. Another way to phrase the problem is this: if the probability of finding a person opposed to the Normal Bus System is .5, what is the probability that 21 or more of 30 randomly selected persons will oppose the bus system?

This problem is a binomial distribution problem, where $n = 30$, $r = 21$ or more, and $p = .5$. The mean in this case (or the expected value) is

$$\mu = n \times p = 30 \times .5 = 15$$

The standard deviation is

$$\sigma = \sqrt{n \times p \times (1 - p)} = \sqrt{30 \times .5 \times .5} = \sqrt{15 \times .5} = \sqrt{7.5} = 2.7$$

Converting $r$ to a $z$ score, we have

$$z = \frac{r - \mu}{\sigma} = \frac{21 - 15}{2.7} = \frac{6}{2.7} = 2.22$$

This $z$ score corresponds to a probability of .0132 that 21 or more of 30 people oppose the bus system if $p = .5$. Although this probability is not the same as the probability found earlier (.0139), the two probabilities are fairly close. The differences are the result of rounding error.

## DETERMINING SAMPLE SIZE

The director of the Office of Human Development wants to know the proportion of welfare recipients who own cars. She needs to know this information to refute the common myth about welfare Cadillacs. She wants to know the proportion within 2% and wants to be 95% sure. Determine the sample size necessary to find out this information.

This problem is identical to any other sample size problem. Remember from Chapter 10 that sample size is determined by the following formula:

$$n = \left( \frac{z \times \sigma}{E} \right)^2$$

where $E$ is the amount of error tolerated. Because the director specified a 95% confidence limit and a 2% error, this formula becomes

$$n = \left( \frac{1.96 \times \sigma}{.02} \right)^2$$

The only thing we need to know in order to calculate sample size is the standard deviation. Although we could take a preliminary sample and estimate the standard deviation, there is an easier way. Statisticians have discovered that the standard deviation from a proportion is greatest when the proportion is equal to .5. You may verify this in a barefoot way by calculating the standard deviations for the listed proportions in Table 11.1.

**TABLE 11.1**

When Is the Standard Deviation Greatest?

| Proportion | Standard Deviation | Proportion | Standard Deviation |
|---|---|---|---|
| $p$ | $\sqrt{p(1 - p)}$ | .5 | |
| .1 | | .6 | |
| .2 | | .7 | |
| .3 | | .8 | |
| .4 | | .9 | |

If you calculated the correct standard deviations, the largest deviation is .50 for a proportion of .5. This fact means that if we do not know a population proportion and we need to estimate a sample size, .5 is the best proportion estimate to use. Since all other proportions have smaller standard deviations, they will require smaller samples to have the same accuracy. So, in this case, we assume a proportion of .5 and thus, a standard deviation of .5. Substituting into the formula, we get

$$n = \left( \frac{1.96 \times .5}{.02} \right)^2 = \left( \frac{.98}{.02} \right)^2 = 49^2 = 2401$$

To be 95% confident that the proportion of welfare Cadillacs is within 2% of the estimate, a sample of 2401 is required.

To illustrate the need for a smaller sample if the proportion is smaller (or larger), assume that an earlier survey revealed that 10% of all welfare recipients owned Cadillacs. In this case, our estimate of the standard deviation is .3. Substituting this value into the sample size formula, we get

$$n = \left( \frac{1.96 \times .3}{.02} \right)^2 = (29.2)^2 = 864$$

If interview costs run approximately $20 per interview, why is it sometimes helpful to estimate the population proportion in advance?

## DECISION MAKING

John Johnson, the warden at the Maxwell Federal Penitentiary, is considering a novel rehabilitation program. He believes that if certain types of nonviolent offenders are released early, they will have a very low recidivism rate. John considers a recidivism rate of 50% an acceptably low rate. John would like to try the program for a few years and then, based on data from samples of inmates, decide whether or not to continue it. Because of the sensitive nature of experiments that release prisoners early, John wants to be 99% sure of his decision and can only afford a sample of 100. Given this information, construct a decision rule.

The procedure for a decision rule in this case is much like a decision rule based on means.

If $\mu > .5$, then eliminate the program.
If $\mu < .5$, then keep the program.

Translating this to a sample of 100 with 99% confidence, we have

If $\overline{X} + z \times$ s.e. $< .5$, then keep the program.

(Note that we only need to consider the "keep the program" option because the greatest danger is in keeping a program that lets hardened criminals loose on the streets. This means that we are interested in only one tail of the curve, so we look up a probability of .49 in the $z$ table.)

Since a 99% confidence limit has a $z$ score of 2.33, and since the largest standard deviation possible is for $p = .5$ ($\sigma = .5$), we can substitute in these values.

$$\overline{X} + 2.33 \times \left( \frac{.5}{\sqrt{100}} \right) < .5$$

$$\overline{X} + 2.33 \times .05 < .5$$

$$\overline{X} + .1165 < .5$$

$$\overline{X} < .3835$$

From these calculations, we can formulate a new decision rule in which we have 99% confidence. Stated in terms of percentages:

If $\overline{X} < 38.35$, then keep the program.
If $\overline{X} > 38.35$, then terminate the program.

Therefore, whenever a sample of 100 inmates reveals a recidivism rate of 38.35% or more, the release program should be terminated.

## CHAPTER SUMMARY

Often the analyst will not have means but only proportions from the sample data. Proportions can be used to estimate parameters and to test hypotheses in processes very similar to those used for means. The problems and pitfalls remain basically the same. In addition, the sample size needed for a particular problem involving proportions can be determined in a manner similar to that shown in the previous chapter for means.

## PROBLEMS

**11.1** The personnel department of a large government agency needs to know the percentage of employees who will retire this year. This information is essential to agency recruitment personnel. The agency determines this information with a random sample. If the agency wants to be 90% sure that its estimate of the retirement percentage is within 2%, how large a sample should it take?

**11.2** If 33% of the members of the Sweetheart Union sign petitions to decertify the union, the National Labor Relations Board (NLRB) will call an election to determine whether Sweetheart will remain the exclusive bargaining agent. The union leadership takes a random sample survey of 40 and finds that 8 persons will sign the petition. What can you tell the union?

**11.3** After a massive inventory, Central Library finds 12% of its volumes missing. As a result, Central institutes new procedures to prevent theft. After instituting these procedures for one year, Central Library wants to know whether they are working, but it cannot afford the cost of a complete inventory. The library takes a sample of 200 books and cannot locate 14 of them. These 14 are assumed to be lost to theft. What can you say about the new procedures?

**11.4** Last year, 30% of all Wheezer School children missed class during March because of illness. This year, the school board requires all teachers to dispense vitamin C tablets during the morning milk break. A sample of 60 children reveals that only 12 missed school during March. What can be said about the differences in absentee rates?

**11.5** According to the Department of Transportation, 74% of all cars on Interstate 35 were exceeding the 55-mile-per-hour speed limit. The department runs a series of public service ads, and then takes a sample of 2000 cars. It finds that 72% of the cars are exceeding the 55 limit. Write a memo discussing the possible impact of the department's ad program.

**11.6** Bernie Belfry, District 7 state legislator, wants to know the percentage of his constituents who support the Equal Rights Amendment (ERA). Belfry wants to be 99% certain that he is within 10 percentage points of the population percentage. How large a sample does Belfry need?

**11.7** Refer to Problem 11.6. If an earlier survey revealed that 70% of District 7 supported the ERA, how large a sample should Belfry use?

**11.8** The Department of Fish and Wildlife is under pressure to use poisons to kill coyotes. The department feels that poison will only kill those coyotes that would be killed by predators and harsh weather anyway. According to their records, an estimated 28% of all coyotes live through the winter. A pilot project is tried with poisons in the Lupus Wildlife Refuge. Of the 214 coyotes released there in the fall, 51 are found alive in the spring. What can you tell the department about the experiment?

**11.9** Refer to Problem 9.9. What is your best estimate of the proportion of Branflake International flights that arrive on time?

**11.10** City council member William Phogbound has charged that 50% of all Normal policemen are overweight. A survey of 16 reveals that 7 are overweight. What can be said about Phogbound's assertion?

**11.11** If the error rate for AFDC payments is greater than 5%, the federal government will cut off funding to the state of Wisconsin. To see whether this is a problem, the agency director takes a sample of 250 welfare recipients and finds that errors have been made in 18 cases. What is your best esimate of the error rate in Wisconsin? Place a 90% confidence limit around this estimate. Present a hypothesis, a null hypothesis, and evaluate them. State a conclusion in plain English.

**11.12** The Milwaukee Independent School District is concerned with white flight—the withdrawal of white students from MISD. Last year, 63% of all MISD students were white. To get a quick reading of the situation this year, a sample of 100 students is selected; 52 of those students are white. What is your best estimate of the proportion of white students in MISD? Present a hypothesis, a null hypothesis, and evaluate them. Present a conclusion in plain English.

**11.13** The village of Whitefish Bay uses a private insurance carrier to cover its automobile fleet. The carrier contends that it pays 90% of all claims within 30 days after the claims are filed. The department wants to check this out without going through a complete audit. Analyst Melinda Ann Gann takes a sample of 100 claims from last year and finds that 82 were paid within 30 days. Present a statistical evaluation of these results.

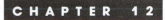

## CHAPTER 12

# TESTING THE DIFFERENCE BETWEEN TWO GROUPS

Often a public administrator will have two samples and will want to know whether the values measured for one sample are different from those of the other sample. For example, a school administrator might want to know whether the reading levels of high school seniors improved after a special reading seminar was given: he wants a before-after comparison. A librarian might want to know whether advertising affects circulation and thus might set up an experiment in which some branches advertise and others do not. In situations such as these, where one wants to know whether two samples are different or if two sample means are different, the appropriate technique to use is analysis of variance. In this chapter, we will present the basic technique of analysis of variance and discuss some of its applications.

## ANALYSIS OF VARIANCE PROCEDURE

The best way to illustrate **analysis of variance** is with an example.

**analysis of variance**

The Ware County librarian wants to increase circulation from the Ware County bookmobiles. The librarian thinks that poster ads in areas where the bookmobiles stop will attract more browsers and increase circulation. To test this idea, the librarian sets up an experiment. Ten bookmobile routes are selected at random; on those routes, poster ads are posted with bookmobile information. Ten other bookmobile routes are randomly selected; on those routes, no advertising is done. In effect, the librarian has set up the following experiment:

experimental group → place ads → measure circulation
control group ———→ no ads ——→ measure circulation

After a week-long experiment, the information listed in Table 12.1 is available to the librarian.

**TABLE 12.1**
Librarian's Data

|  | Experimental Group | Control Group |
|---|---|---|
| Mean | 526 books | 475 books |
| Standard deviation | 125 | 115 |

The null hypothesis is that the mean circulation of the experimental group is not higher than the mean circulation of the control group. Testing the difference between two means tells us the probability that both groups could be drawn from the same population. The procedure is as follows.

**STEP 1**    Calculate the mean and standard deviation for each group. This has already been done in Table 12.1.

**STEP 2**    Calculate the standard error of the mean estimate for each group.

$$\text{s.e.} = \frac{\sigma}{\sqrt{n}}$$

Experimental group:

$$\text{s.e.} = \frac{125}{\sqrt{10}} = 39.5$$

Control group:

$$\text{s.e.} = \frac{115}{\sqrt{10}} = 36.4$$

**STEP 3**    Calculate an overall standard error for both groups. The overall standard error is equal to the square root of the sum of the squared standard errors for each group. Symbolically, this can be expressed as

$$\text{s.e.}_{\text{overall}} = \sqrt{\text{s.e.}_1^2 + \text{s.e.}_2^2}$$

For the present example, we have

$$\text{s.e.} = \sqrt{39.5^2 + 36.4^2} = \sqrt{1560.25 + 1324.96} = \sqrt{2885.21} = 53.7$$

**STEP 4**   Since we want to know the probability that the groups could be drawn from the same population, and since we have a mean estimate and a standard error, we can calculate the following $z$ score (if we assume that the data are normally distributed):

$$z = \frac{\overline{X}_1 - \overline{X}_2}{\text{s.e.}_{\text{overall}}}$$

where $\overline{X}_1$ is the control group mean, $\overline{X}_2$ is the experimental group mean, and s.e. is the overall standard error. In the present example we have

$$z = \frac{475 - 526}{53.7} = \frac{-51}{53.7} = -.95$$

Looking up a $z$ score of $-.95$ in the normal table, we find a probability of .17. Statistically we can say that there is one chance in six that the two samples could be drawn from the same population (that is, there is no difference). If the research design shows no other possible causes, what can the librarian say managerially about the program?

# PROPORTIONS

Analysis of variance is a technique that can be used both for the difference between two sample means and for the difference between two sample proportions. For example, the Morgan City parole board has been running an experimental program on one-third of their parolees. The parolees in the experimental program are placed in halfway houses run by social workers to ease their adjustment to society. All other parolees are simply released and asked to check in with their parole officer once a month. The parole board wanted to evaluate the experimental program and decided that if the experimental program significantly reduced the recidivism rate of parolees, then the program would be declared a success. A random sample of 100 parolees who were placed in halfway houses is selected. These people's names are traced through the Nationwide Criminal Data System (NCDS); 68 have been arrested again and convicted. Two hundred randomly selected parolees who were not assigned to halfway houses were also traced through the NCDS, and 148 of these were in jail. Is the recidivism rate for parolees sent to halfway houses lower than the rate for other parolees?

The process of analysis of variance for proportions is identical to that for sample means.

**STEP 1**   Calculate the sample proportions (means) and standard deviations. For the experimental group we have

$$p = \frac{68}{100} = .68$$

$$\sigma = \sqrt{p(1 - p)} = \sqrt{.68 \times .32} = .47$$

For the control group, we have

$$p = \frac{148}{200} = .74 \quad \text{and} \quad \sigma = \sqrt{.74 \times .26} = .44$$

**STEP 2**  Calculate the standard error of the proportion estimate for each group.

$$\text{s.e.} = \frac{\sigma}{\sqrt{n}}$$

Experimental group:

$$\text{s.e.} = \frac{.47}{\sqrt{100}} = .047$$

Control group:

$$\text{s.e.} = \frac{.44}{\sqrt{200}} = .031$$

**STEP 3**  Calculate an overall standard error for both groups.

$$\text{s.e.}_{\text{overall}} = \sqrt{\text{s.e.}_1^2 + \text{s.e.}_2^2} = \sqrt{.047^2 + .031^2} = \sqrt{.00317} = .056$$

**STEP 4**  Convert the difference between the experimental and control groups into a $z$ score.

$$z = \frac{p_1 - p_2}{\text{s.e.}_{\text{overall}}} = \frac{.74 - .68}{.056} = \frac{.06}{.056} = 1.07$$

The probability that the two samples could be drawn from a single population is .14.

Since neither analysis of variance problem provided a statistically significant difference, let us look at one more example. Suppose the Morgan City parole board had a second experimental parole program in which parolees are found a job before they are granted parole. A sample of 100 of these parolees reveals 60 recidivists. Is the second experiment successfully reducing the recidivism rate in comparison to the control group? The calculations follow.

| Experimental Group | Control Group |
|---|---|
| $n = 100$ | $n = 200$ |
| $p = .60$ | $p = .74$ |
| $\sigma = .49$ | $\sigma = .44$ |
| s.e. $= .049$ | s.e. $= .031$ |

$$\text{s.e.}_{\text{overall}} = \sqrt{.049^2 + .031^2} = .058$$

$$z = \frac{.74 - .60}{.058} = 2.41$$

The probability that the samples could be drawn from the same population is .008. What can you say from a research design perspective? From a management perspective?

## ANALYSIS OF VARIANCE
## APPLICATIONS

Analysis of variance is not limited to control and experimental groups of the kind just illustrated. For example, analysis of variance can be used when a group is tested on some criterion, then some new experiment is introduced, and then the group is retested on the same criterion. To determine if a new training program is improving the ability of workers to process a given form, you could test workers before and after the training program. Analysis of variance can then be used to determine if the workers' processing ability changed significantly.

If the situation arises in which analysis of variance must be applied to more than two groups, the public administrator has two options. First, consult a statistics text (see Blalock 1972) or a statistician. Second, read Chapter 17 in this textbook, which discusses regression extensions. In Chapter 17, we show how analysis of variance can be performed with a regression program. In Chapter 19, analysis of variance with more than two groups is shown to be a special case of multiple regression.

## *t* TESTS

We have consistently assumed in this text either that our population was normally distributed or that we had a sample of more than 30. The purist rarely ever assumes that a distribution is normal. Rather than using a $z$ score and the normal curve to determine significance, the purist uses a $t$ score and a $t$ test. A **$t$ score** is calculated the same way that a $z$ score is. The **$t$ distribution**, however, is flatter than the normal curve, so $t$ values must be larger than $z$ scores to be

*t* score

*t* distribution

significant. The larger the sample size, the more the $t$ distribution resembles the normal distribution. When $n$ is greater than 30, the normal distribution closely approximates the $t$ distribution. So when $n$ is greater than 30, use the normal distribution. The $t$ distribution is reproduced in the Appendix as Table 3.

To illustrate the $t$ test, an example is in order. The Fair Employment Practices Commission (FEPC) recently changed its internal administrative procedures because it had been accused of being slow to respond to discrimination charges. The FEPC contends that the new procedures will improve its response time. Response time is not normally distributed. A sample of ten cases before and after the change reveals the data shown in Table 12.2.

**TABLE 12.2**
Data for the FEPC

|  | Before | After |
|---|---|---|
| Average time to process a case | 227 days | 145 days |
| Standard deviation | 100 days | 60 days |
| $n$ | 10 | 10 |
| Standard error | 31.6 | 19.0 |
| Overall standard error | 36.9 | |

The $t$ score is calculated in the same way as the $z$ score is.

$$t = \frac{\overline{X}_1 - \overline{X}_2}{\text{s.e.}} = \frac{227 - 145}{36.9} = 2.22$$

To use Table 3, you need to know both a $t$ score and the degrees of freedom (df in the table). In a situation having two samples, df equals the size of one sample plus the size of the other sample minus 2. In this case, df = 18 (for single samples df = $n - 1$).

Along the left column of Table 3, find the df value of 18. The line of figures next to 18 contains $t$ scores that we compare to our $t$ score of 2.22. The first $t$ score is 1.33, which is associated with a probability of .10 (note the column head). Since 2.22 is larger than 1.33, the probability in our example is less than .10. Proceeding along the row, we find a $t$ score of 1.734 (associated with $p = .05$), which is also less than 2.22. The next $t$ score is 2.552 (associated with $p = .01$), which is larger than 2.22. In the present situation, therefore, a $t$ score of 2.22 has a probability of less than .05 and more than .01. Often, to save space, we simply say the probability is less than .05 that the two samples could have been drawn from the same population (and, therefore, have the same population mean).

Whenever you have small samples from distributions that are not normal, use the $t$ distribution.

## CHAPTER SUMMARY

Often a manager has samples from two groups (experimental and control, before and after, and so on) and wants to determine whether the two samples could be drawn from the same population (and hence not be significantly different). This chapter illustrates the process of testing two sample means or two sample proportions to determine if they could have been drawn from the same population. The procedure is a simplified version of analysis of variance and basically involves four steps. First, calculate the mean and standard deviation for each group. Second, calculate the standard error of the mean estimate for each group. Third, calculate an overall standard error for the groups. Finally, calculate a $z$ score and find its associated probability from the normal table.

In the preceding chapters, we have assumed either that the population was normally distributed or that we had a sample of more than 30. When neither of these assumptions is met, the $t$ distribution is used, not the normal distribution. A $t$ score is calculated in the same way that a $z$ score is. The $t$ curve, however, is flatter than the normal curve, so that $t$ values must be larger than $z$ scores to be significant.

## PROBLEMS

**12.1** John Johnson, the local sheriff, suspects that many of his city's residents are operating motor vehicles without current inspection stickers. To determine whether this is true, John has his boys, John, H. R., and Charles, randomly stop 100 cars. Of these 100 cars, 43 do not have current inspection stickers. John decides to put the fear of God into drivers and launches a public relations campaign threatening to crack down. A month later, John wants to know whether the program worked. A random sample of 100 cars showed that 21 did not have valid inspection stickers. What can you tell John about the program (ask the statistical, research design, and management questions)?

**12.2** Art Howe decides to see whether batting practice has any impact on the Houston Astros' hitting. Twenty Astros take batting practice; they are randomly selected (the control group). Ten Astros, randomly selected, take no batting practice. After 25 games the figures shown in the accompanying table are available. What can you tell Art about his experiment, statistically and managerially?

|  | Batting Practice Group | No Practice Group |
|---|---|---|
| Mean | .212 | .193 |
| Standard deviation | .026 | .047 |

12.3   The police chief wants to know whether the city's blacks feel that the police are doing a good job. In comparison to whites' evaluations, this information will tell the police if they have a community relations problem in the black community. A survey reveals the information in the accompanying table. What can you tell the police chief?

| Opinion | Race | |
|---|---|---|
| | *Black* | *White* |
| Feel police do good job | 74 | 223 |
| Do not feel police do good job | 76 | 73 |

12.4   General Kleinherbst is concerned with the VD epidemic among soldiers in Europe. At a nonroutine inspection of 100 troops, 31 were found to have VD. Kleinherbst requires all troops to view the award-winning film "VD: Just Between Friends." At another inspection 180 days later, Kleinherbst finds 43 of the 200 troops inspected have VD. What can you say about the program, statistically, managerially, and from a research design point of view?

12.5   Morgan City Fire Chief Sidney Pyro is concerned about the low efficiency scores that his firefighters receive at the state testing institute. Chief Pyro believes that these scores result because some firefighters are not in good physical condition. Pyro orders 75 randomly selected firefighters to participate in an hour of exercise per day. Another 200 firefighters have no required exercise. After 60 days, all firefighters are tested again by the state; the results are shown in the accompanying table. What can you tell the chief from this information?

| | Exercise Group | No Exercise Group |
|---|---|---|
| Mean | 74.5 | 70.6 |
| Standard deviation | 31.4 | 26.3 |

12.6   Two hundred people on the welfare rolls in Deadbeat County are randomly selected. One hundred are required to do public service work for the county; the other one hundred continue as before. After six months, 63 of the public service workers are still on welfare, as are 76 of the control group. What can you say about the effectiveness of this program? What facts may explain these results?

12.7   Normal City Maintenance Chief Leon Tightwad wants to cut back the costs of maintaining the city automobile fleet. Since city cars are kept for only one year, Leon feels that the city's periodic maintenance schedule may cost more than it is worth. Leon randomly selects 75 cars out of 300 and performs no maintenance on these cars unless they break down. At the end of the year, Leon finds the results shown in the accompanying table. What can you tell Leon about his experiment?

|  | Maintained Cars | No Maintenance |
| --- | --- | --- |
| Mean | $625 | $575 |
| Standard deviation | 150 | 200 |

**12.8** Refer to Problem 12.7. Charlie Hustle is in charge of selling Normal's cars after they have been used one year. He believes that Leon's policy costs the city money, and he presents the figures on the cars' sales prices, shown in the accompanying table. Does Charlie have an argument? On an overall basis, who will save the city the most money, Leon Tightwad or Charlie Hustle?

|  | Maintained Cars | No Maintenance |
| --- | --- | --- |
| Mean | $3456 | $3121 |
| Standard deviation | 250 | 200 |

**12.9** Both the Brethren Charity and the Lost Soul's Mission are operating marriage counseling programs. The Brethren program has a man-woman team to counsel people, whereas Lost Soul's uses single counselors. Last year, 12 of 84 randomly selected couples receiving counseling at Brethren ended up divorced. Ten of the 51 randomly selected couples at Lost Soul's were divorced. As a policy analyst, what can you say about the programs?

**12.10** The William G. Harding School of Public Affairs would like to evaluate its affirmative action program for students. After extended discussion, the faculty decides that all students will take the federal PACE exam, and the scores on this exam will be used as the criterion of success. Write a memo discussing the results shown in the accompanying table.

|  | Regular Students | Affirmative Action Students |
| --- | --- | --- |
| Mean | 86.4 | 84.1 |
| Standard deviation | 17.3 | 28.2 |
| $n$ | 44 | 19 |

**12.11** A professor thinks that MPA students at the University of Wisconsin (UW) are brighter than those at the University of Oklahoma (OU). To examine this hypothesis, he gives the same midterm to UW students that he gave to OU students the previous year. He finds the following results:

|        | UW   | OU   |
|--------|------|------|
| Mean   | 83.1 | 88.7 |
| std dev | 11.4 | 7.8 |
| $n$    | 36   | 24   |

Present a testable hypothesis, a null hypothesis, and evaluate them. Present a conclusion in plain English.

**12.12**  The state personnel bureau wants to know whether people resign if they are not promoted during the year. They take a sample of 30 people who are promoted and find that 6 of them resigned; a sample of 45 people who were not promoted includes 15 who resigned. State a hypothesis, a null hypothesis, and test them. State your conclusion in plain English.

**12.13**  The state of Wisconsin has decided to run a quasi-experiment in regard to its workfare program and the program's impact on incentives. Officials think that workfare increases the incentives to individuals to earn more money in addition to welfare. Two hundred recipients are selected; 120 are randomly assigned to a workfare program and 80 are assigned to a control group. By follow-up interviews, the state finds out how much outside income per week is earned by each individual with the following results:

|        | Workfare | Control |
|--------|----------|---------|
| Mean   | $142.50  | $97.30  |
| $s$    | 137.00   | 85.00   |

Present a hypothesis, a null hypothesis, and evaluate them. State a conclusion in plain English.

**12.14**  The Beaver Dam Job Placement Center wants to evaluate the quality of its program. One hundred unemployed individuals are selected at random. Sixty of these are run through the Beaver Dam program; the others serve as a control group. Sixty percent of the Beaver Dam program group get jobs; the average salary of those jobs is $12,847 (with a standard deviation of $1,800). Of the control group, 30% get jobs; the average salary of those jobs is $14,567 (standard deviation $3,600). This program can be evaluated by two different criteria. Perform the calculations for both criteria, and present your conclusions.

**12.15**  Enormous State University has an MPA program. The MPA director is concerned with the small number of MPA students who are being awarded Presidential Management Internships. She thinks that this might be because MPA students lack interviewing skills. To experiment with this notion, ten of the twenty PMI nominees are sent to a special interviewing workshop; the other ten do not attend the workshop. Seven of the ten attending the workshop receive PMIs, and three of those not attending the workshop receive PMIs. Present a hypothesis, a null hypothesis, and evaluate them. Present a conclusion in plain English.

**12.16**   The Department of Human Services has contracted with the Institute for Research on Poverty to run an experimental job training program. A group of 200 individuals are randomly selected from among the hard-core unemployed. A control group of 50 is selected at the same time. The 200 individuals in the experimental group are assigned to a program that attempts to place them in jobs. DHS has defined placement of the individual in a job for six months as a success. Of this group, 38 are still employed after six months. Of the control group, 11 are employed after six months. Present a hypothesis, a null hypothesis, and test them. Present a conclusion in plain English.

**12.17**   As an NIH administrator, you wish to evaluate an experiment at the University of Illinois concerning the impact of exercise on individuals with high-cholesterol diets. The Illinois researchers take 25 pigs that have high-cholesterol diets; 10 of these are randomly selected and made to jog on a treadmill for 2 miles a day. The other 15 pigs do not jog (although they might play golf or get exercise in other ways). After 6 months, each pig is tested for cholesterol in the blood stream (measured in parts per million) with the following results:

|                 | Exercise Group | Others |
|-----------------|:--------------:|:------:|
| Mean            | 160            | 210    |
| Std. deviation  | 40             | 60     |

Present a hypothesis, a null hypothesis, and evaluate them. Present a statistical conclusion in plain English.

**12.18**   The Austin Independent School District wants to know if the LBJ magnet school for the sciences is improving student performance. One hundred students were admitted as sophomores last year to the LBJ school. These students scored a mean of 14.7 on the junior year math achievement test (14 years 7 months, or about a college sophomore level) with a standard deviation of 1.1. Twenty-three of these students play football. Education researcher Lana Stein selects a control group of students who, in their sophomore year, performed comparably to the LBJ students in their sophomore year. These 144 students did not attend a magnet school. Their junior math achievement test produced a mean of 13.6 and a standard deviation of 2.9. Their mean IQ score was 117. Present a hypothesis, test this hypothesis, and present a conclusion in plain English regarding the magnet school students.

**12.19**    The legislature is considering a mandatory seat belt law. What legislators don't know is whether the law would encourage more people to use seat belts. Senator I. C. Probability tells you that Minnesota has a law similar to the one that Wisconsin is considering. He would like you to compare the use of seat belts in Minnesota and Wisconsin. A survey is taken in both states resulting in the statistics presented below. Present a hypothesis, a null hypothesis, and test them. Present your conclusion in plain English.

|                       | Minnesota | Wisconsin |
| --------------------- | --------- | --------- |
| $n$                   | 75        | 110       |
| Number using seat belts | 37      | 28        |

**12.20**    Paul Sabatier, a human relations theorist working for Warm and Fuzzy Inc., believes that workers who work in cooperatives are more satisfied with their jobs than workers who do not. He surveys 50 cab drivers who work in cooperatives and 30 cab drivers who do not work in cooperatives. All are asked whether they are satisfied with their job. From the data in the following table, what can you conclude?

| Job Satisfaction | Company Type | |
| ---------------- | ----------- | -------------- |
|                  | *Cooperative* | *Noncooperative* |
| Satisfied        | 21          | 17             |
| Not satisfied    | 29          | 13             |

**12.21**    The Big State University's MPA program is running an experiment concerning the mental health of its students. Unknown to the students, they have been randomly assigned to two groups. Group A takes Statistics for Public Administration; there are 10 students in this group. Five suffer breakdowns before midterm. The 15 students in Group B take Sensitivity Training for Public Managers. Four students in this group suffer breakdowns. Is there a relationship between breakdowns and class assignments? Present a hypothesis, a null hypothesis, and evaluate them.

**12.22**    Madonna Lewis' job in the Department of Sanitary Engineering is to determine whether new refuse collection procedures have improved the public's perception of the department. Public opinion surveys were taken both before and after the new procedures were implemented. The results are as follows:

|                                        | Before | After |
|----------------------------------------|--------|-------|
| The department is doing a good job     | 23     | 47    |
| The department is doing a poor job     | 79     | 73    |

Present a hypothesis, a null hypothesis, and evaluate the hypothesis.

**12.23**  Edinburg attorney J. L. "Bubba" Pollinard is collecting data for a discrimination suit. He asks 500 Latino people if they believe that the city is biased against them; 354 say it is. Bubba asks 300 Anglo residents the same question, and 104 state the city is biased against them. Present a hypothesis, a null hypothesis, test the hypothesis, and present a conclusion in plain English.

**12.24**  The Postal Service recently compared newly hired employees who tested "drug free" with those who tested "drug positive" after six months on the job. They wanted to see whether more drug users than drug-free employees would be fired during their 6-month probation period. Research analyst Stephanie Larson presents a report with the following data:

|            | Total Hired | Total Fired | % Fired |
|------------|-------------|-------------|---------|
| Drug free  | 3340        | 319         | 9.5     |
| Drug users | 315         | 42          | 13.3    |

Present a hypothesis, a null hypothesis, and test them. What do these data mean? Could you design a more meaningful test?

# PART V

# ANALYSIS OF
# NOMINAL AND
# ORDINAL DATA

## CHAPTER 13

# CONSTRUCTION

# AND ANALYSIS OF

# CONTINGENCY

# TABLES

Chapter 7 introduced the three levels of measurement (nominal, ordinal, and interval) and discussed the measures of central tendency that can be used to describe and summarize variables of each type. Although this information provides a useful guide to the treatment of single variables, ordinarily such univariate statistics constitute only the first step in data analysis—and in the job of the public administrator.

For example, imagine for a moment that you work in the department of public affairs for a large public agency. The department has just finished conducting its annual survey of public opinion toward the agency. Some of the initial results show that most of the people interviewed now feel that the agency is doing a "very poor job," and the median opinion is not very cheery either—a "poor job." This assessment represents a dramatic downturn in public opinion compared to previous years. To be sure, this is important information, but obviously it is not the kind of news that you would want to give to your boss or to the mayor and the budget-minded city council *without some idea of how the public image of the agency might be improved*. But how might this goal be attained?

One way to approach this question is to consider *why* public support has fallen. There may be several reasons. Perhaps the agency has cut a popular program that it used to administer in Avery County. If the loss of this program is responsible for the drop in public prestige, then you would expect to find a lower level of public favor in Avery County than in the other counties, where it has not been necessary to cut programs. Or perhaps the fall in public esteem is a result of the recent appointment of a new director of the agency, whose past political exploits received rough treatment in the local press. If so, then you would hypothesize (make an educated guess) that those citizens who disapproved of the appointment would be more critical of the job performance of the agency than would those who approved of the appointment. Fortunately, the survey of public opinion conducted by the agency elicited information pertaining to citizen residence and attitude toward the new director, so both of these ideas can be checked out.

These proposed explanations for the decline in public opinion carry different implications for public policy. If data analysis yielded support for the first of these, then the chief executive could be informed (gently!) that, although public opinion of the agency is low, there is evidence that it could be improved through restoration of the program that had been cut in Avery County. On the other hand, if the data showed support for the second explanation, the chief executive might advise the director of the agency to clear the air about her past through public speeches and press conferences—or the chief executive might decide that less pleasant steps are necessary.

Regardless of which (if either) explanation proves correct, the important point to bear in mind is that data analysis has moved from a concern with a single variable—public opinion toward the performance of the agency—to a focus on *relationships between variables*. This sequence is typical in the analysis of data. Generally, we would like to know not only the distribution of scores or responses on a variable of interest, but also an explanation for this distribution. Is there a relationship between the county of residence of a citizen and attitude toward the agency? Is there a relationship between citizens' attitudes toward the new director and their attitudes toward the agency?

This chapter begins the development of statistical methods to answer such questions. It is concerned with relationships between variables measured at the nominal and ordinal levels. (Relationships between interval level variables are the subject of Part VI.) The method that is generally employed to examine these relationships is called *contingency table analysis*. In this chapter, we show how to set up a contingency table—cross-tabulating the responses to a pair of nominal or ordinal variables—and how to interpret it. Subsequent chapters elaborate on this topic: Chapter 14 presents aids to the interpretation of contingency tables, such as "measures of association" between variables. Chapter 15 discusses a procedure called control table analysis, or statistical controls, through which the relationships among three or more variables may be examined.

## PERCENTAGE DISTRIBUTIONS

Before we can treat the construction and interpretation of contingency tables, it is necessary to review *percentage distributions* (see Chapter 1). A percentage distribution is simply a frequency distribution that has been converted to percentages. Consider the distribution of responses of a sample of individuals to a standard survey question that asks respondents to consider whether there are too many bureaucrats in the federal government. The distribution is shown in Table 13.1.

**TABLE 13.1**
Distribution of Responses

To what extent would you agree or
disagree with the following statement?
There are currently too many bureaucrats
working for the federal government.

| Response | Number of People |
| --- | --- |
| Strongly agree | 686 |
| Agree | 979 |
| Neutral | 208 |
| Disagree | 436 |
| Strongly disagree | 232 |

As it stands, this table is difficult to interpret. Although it is evident that the modal opinion is "agree," the table does not give a clear presentation of this opinion's popularity. Is it held by half of the people interviewed? A third? Nor does the table communicate the relative frequency of occurrence of the other opinions (strongly disagree, disagree, and so on). What proportion of the sample voiced these responses?

Without this informaton, it is difficult not only to comprehend this distribution of responses, but also to *compare* it with other distributions of attitudes. For example, it would be interesting to know how this particular distribution of opinion toward federal bureaucrats compares with distributions obtained when the question was put to different samples and at different times. Has there been a trend over time toward the view that there are too many federal bureaucrats? Does the public feel the same way about local bureaucrats or state bureaucrats?

The raw response figures displayed in Table 13.1 cannot answer these questions. In order to address them, data analysts conventionally convert the raw figures to *percentages*.

## STEPS IN PERCENTAGING

The procedure for converting raw figures to percentages involves three steps.

**STEP 1**  Add the number of people (frequencies) giving each of the responses. In Table 13.1, this sum is equal to $686 + 979 + 208 + 436 + 232 = 2541$.

**STEP 2**  Divide each of the individual frequencies by this total and multiply the result by 100. For example, for the response "strongly agree" in Table 13.1, we divide 686 by 2541 and obtain .26997. Then multiply this result by 100, yielding 26.997. This figure is the *percentage* of the people interviewed who gave the response "strongly agree." Repeat the procedure for each of the other response categories.

**STEP 3**     Round each of the percentages to one decimal place. If the second place to the right of decimal point is greater than or equal to 5, add 1 to the first place to the right of the decimal. In this procedure, .16 becomes .2, .43 becomes .4, and 26.997 becomes 27.0. Table 13.2 shows the percentage distribution.

**TABLE 13.2**
Percentage Distribution

To what extent would you agree or disagree with the following statement? There are currently too many bureaucrats working for the federal government.

| Response | Frequency | | Percentage |
|---|---|---|---|
| Strongly agree | 686 | $(686 \div 2541) \times 100 =$ | 27.0 |
| Agree | 979 | $(979 \div 2541) \times 100 =$ | 38.5 |
| Neutral | 208 | $(208 \div 2541) \times 100 =$ | 8.2 |
| Disagree | 436 | $(436 \div 2541) \times 100 =$ | 17.2 |
| Strongly disagree | 232 | $(232 \div 2541) \times 100 =$ | 9.1 |
| Total | 2541 | | 100.0 |

## DISPLAYING AND INTERPRETING DISTRIBUTIONS

The table should display the percentage of respondents giving each of the answers. The sum of the percentages should be presented directly beneath the column of these figures at the foot of the table. Normally this sum will equal 100.0%, but due to rounding error, the sum may vary between 99% and 101%; don't worry about it. The only *frequency* that should be presented in the table is the total. It is usually abbreviated **N** and displayed in parentheses, also at the foot of the table. The total frequency helps the reader evaluate the distribution of responses. In general, the larger the number of cases upon which the percentages are based, the greater the confidence in the results. For example, you would normally have more confidence in a distribution based on 2541 respondents than in one based on 541. Table 13.3 shows the final percentaged table.

The percentage distribution facilitates interpretation and comparison. It is clear from the percentage distribution in Table 13.3 that approximately 40% of those interviewed (the mode) "agree" that there are currently too many federal bureaucrats, and that 65.5% (27.0% + 38.5% = 65.5%), or nearly two-thirds, express agreement with this notion (either "strongly agree" or "agree"). The extent of agreement far outweighs the extent of disagreement—65.5% versus 26.3% (the percentage indicating either "disagree" or "strongly disagree"; 17.2% + 9.1% = 26.3%)—and that only a small proportion (8.2%) remain "neutral."

**TABLE 13.3**
Percentage Distribution

To what extent would you agree or disagree with the following statement? There are currently too many bureaucrats working for the federal government.

| Response | Percentage |
| --- | --- |
| Strongly agree | 27.0 |
| Agree | 38.5 |
| Neutral | 8.2 |
| Disagree | 17.2 |
| Strongly disagree | 9.1 |
| Total | 100.0 |
| | (N = 2541) |

These percentages can be compared with those obtained in other surveys of public opinion, particularly those taken at other points in time, to determine whether attitudes toward bureaucrats are changing. For instance, if five years ago a similar survey of public opinion indicated that only 40% of the public expressed agreement that there are too many federal bureaucrats, it would be evident that public opinion is becoming more negative.

## COLLAPSING PERCENTAGE DISTRIBUTIONS

Often, researchers combine or *collapse* several of the original response categories in order to form a smaller number of new categories and to calculate percentages based on the new categories. For example, in the preceding discussion, the response categories "strongly agree" and "agree," and the categories "strongly disagree" and "disagree," were collapsed into broader categories of "agreement" and "disagreement," respectively.

To calculate percentages in a collapsed distribution, you employ the procedure elaborated earlier: (1) compute the total frequency, (2) divide the frequency of each of the new categories by this total and multiply by 100, and (3) round to the first decimal place. Alternatively, if the percentage distribution for the variable has already been computed based on the *original response categories*, the percentages for the new collapsed categories can be found by adding the percentages for the categories that have been collapsed. (The percentages for categories that have not been collapsed will not change.) The latter method was employed in the preceding discussion. For example, since 27.0% of the sample stated that they "strongly agree" that there are too many federal bureaucrats and 38.5% "agree," then a total of 65.5% fall into the new collapsed category of "agree." The first of these methods for percentaging a collapsed distribution is illustrated in Table 13.4.

**TABLE 13.4**

Collapsed Percentage Distribution

To what extent would you agree or disagree with the following statment? There are currently too many bureaucrats working for the federal government.

| Original Response Categories | (Original) Frequency | Collapsed Response Categories | (Collapsed) Frequency | | Percentage |
|---|---|---|---|---|---|
| Strongly Agree | 686 ⎫ | Agree | 1665 | $(1665 \div 2541) \times 100 =$ | 65.5 |
| Agree | 979 ⎭ | | | | |
| Neutral | 208 | Neutral | 208 | $(108 \div 2541) \times 100 =$ | 8.2 |
| Disagree | 436 ⎫ | Disagree | 668 | $(668 \div 2541) \times 100 =$ | 26.3 |
| Strongly Disagree | 232 ⎭ | | | | |
| Total | 2541 | Total | 2541 | | 100.0 |

There are two primary reasons for presenting the percentage distribution in collapsed form. First, it is easier to interpret a distribution based on a few response categories than one based on many. In many instances, such as the preparation of memoranda, the collapsed distribution presents all the information readers need to know, without burdening them with unnecessary complexity. Second, often in social science research and particularly in the assessment of attitudes, the researcher is not confident that the distinction between some response categories is very clear or meaningful; that is, the researcher is usually much more confident that, *in all*, 65.5% of those interviewed agree with a proposition than he or she is that *exactly* 27.0% "strongly agree" and *exactly* 38.5% "agree." In order to avoid communicating a false sense of precision, categories may be collapsed.

When you collapse response categories of a variable, the collapsing must not pervert the meaning of the original categories. Response categories should be collapsed only if they are close in substantive meaning. Whereas the kind of collapsing we have done here—strongly agree and agree, strongly disagree and disagree—is justified, collapsing the categories of "disagree" and "neutral" would not be.

The major exception to this rule occurs in distributions of *nominal* variables that have many response categories. Frequently only a few of the categories will have a large percentage of cases, whereas most of the categories will have only trivial numbers. In this situation, the analyst may choose to present each of the categories containing a substantial percentage and a category labeled "other," formed by collapsing all the remaining categories. For example, consider the variable "religion." In a given sample, the distribution of religion may be 62% Protestant, 22% Catholic, 13% Jewish, 1% Shinto, .5% Buddhist, .6% Hedonist, .5% Janist, and .4% Central Schwenkenfelter. To summarize this distribution, the analyst may present the percentages as shown in Table 13.5.

**TABLE 13.5**

Collapsed Percentage Distribution for Religion

| Religion | Percentage |
|---|---|
| Protestant | 62 |
| Catholic | 22 |
| Jewish | 13 |
| Other | 3 |
| Total | 100 |
| | (N = 1872) |

An exercise is in order. The Shawnee Heights Independent Transit System has commissioned a poll of 120 persons to determine where Shawnee citizens do most of their shopping. This is important information in determining future routes in Shawnee Heights. The transit planners receive the data shown in Table 13.6.

**TABLE 13.6**

Data for Shawnee Poll

| Main Store Named | Number of Persons |
|---|---|
| Cleo's (neighborhood store) | 5 |
| Morgan's (downtown) | 18 |
| Wiese's (eastern shopping center) | 12 |
| Cheatham's (neighborhood store) | 2 |
| Shop City (eastern shopping center) | 19 |
| Food-a-Rama (western shopping center) | 15 |
| Stermer's (downtown) | 7 |
| Binzer's (neighborhood store) | 2 |
| England's (western shopping center) | 1 |
| Bargainville's (eastern shopping center) | 26 |
| Whiskey River (downtown) | 13 |
| | 120 |

In the space provided, construct a collapsed percentage distribution of the data in Table 13.6.

# CONTINGENCY TABLE
# ANALYSIS

Analysis of contingency tables or cross-tabulations is the primary method researchers use to examine relationships between variables measured at the ordinal and nominal levels. The remainder of the chapter discusses the construction and interpretation of contingency tables. As you will see, the methods for percentaging are instrumental to this type of analysis.

### CONSTRUCTING CONTINGENCY TABLES

**contingency table**

**univariate**

**bivariate**

A **contingency table** or **cross-tabulation** is a bivariate frequency distribution. We have dealt with **univariate** or single-variable frequency distributions in examples in this chapter and in previous chapters. A univariate frequency distribution simply presents the number of cases (or frequency) taking each value of a given variable. Analogously, a **bivariate** or two-variable frequency distribution presents the number of cases that fall into each possible pairing of the values or categories of two variables. This definition is more readily visualized in a concrete example.

Consider the cross-tabulation of the variables race (white, black) and sex (male, female). As these variables are defined here, there are four possible pairings: white and male, white and female, black and male, and black and female. The cross-tabulation of these two variables displays the number of cases that fall into each of the race-sex combinations. For example, in a sample of respondents composed of 142 white males, 67 white females, 109 black males, and 133 black females, we would obtain the contingency table of Table 13.7. This type of table is called a cross-tabulation because it crosses (and tabulates) each of the categories of one variable with each of the categories of a second variable.

**TABLE 13.7**

Contingency Table

| Sex | Race | | |
|---|---|---|---|
| | *White* | *Black* | *Total* |
| Male | 142 | 109 | 251 |
| Female | 67 | 133 | 200 |
| Total | 209 | 242 | 451 |

At this point, some terminology is useful. The cross-classifications—white-male, white-female, black-male, black-female—are called the **cells** of the table. **cells** The cell frequencies indicate the number of cases fitting the description specified by the categories of the row and column variables. The total number of respondents who are white or black is presented at the foot of the "white" and "black" columns, respectively. Similarly, the total number of respondents who are male or female is presented at the far right of the respective rows. In reference to their position around the perimeter of the table, these total frequencies are called **marginals** (or marginal frequencies). These totals are calculated by adding the **marginals** frequencies in the appropriate column or row. Finally, the **grand total**—the total number of cases represented in the table—is displayed conventionally in **grand total** the lower right corner of the table. (The symbol for this number is **N**.) It can be found by adding the cell frequencies, or the row marginals, or the column marginals. You should satisfy yourself that all three of these additions give the same result. You should also make certain that you understand what each number in Table 13.7 means.

To ensure that you can assemble a cross-tabulation, fill in the cell, marginal, and grand total frequencies in Table 13.8. The variables of interest are "type of employment" (public sector, private sector, nonprofit sector) and "attitude toward balancing the federal budget" (disapprove, approve). The cell frequencies are as follows: public-disapprove 126; public-approve 54; private-disapprove 51; private-approve 97; nonprofit-disapprove 25; nonprofit-approve 38.

**TABLE 13.8**

Relationship Between Type of Employment and Attitude Toward Balancing the Federal Budget

| Attitude Toward Budget Balancing | Type of Employment | | | |
|---|---|---|---|---|
| | *Public* | *Private* | *Nonprofit* | *Total* |
| Disapprove | | | | |
| Approve | | | | |
| Total | | | | |

**RELATIONSHIPS BETWEEN VARIABLES**

**statistical relationship**

Researchers assemble and examine cross-tabulations because they are interested in the relationship between two ordinal or nominal level variables. A **statistical relationship** may be defined as a recognizable pattern of change in one variable as the other variable changes. In particular, the type of question that is usually asked is: As one variable increases in value, does the other also increase? Does it decrease?

The cell frequencies of a cross-tabulation provide some information regarding whether changes in one variable are associated statistically with (related to) changes in the other variable. The cross-tabulation presented in Table 13.9 of "education" (high school or less, more than high school) with "performance on the civil service examination" (low, high) illustrates this idea.

**TABLE 13.9**
Relationship Between Educational Level and Performance on Civil Service Examination

| Performance on Civil Service Examination | Education | | |
|---|---|---|---|
| | *High School or Less* | *More Than High School* | *Total* |
| Low | 100 | 200 | 300 |
| High | 150 | 800 | 950 |
| Total | 250 | 1000 | 1250 |

At first glance, the table seems to indicate that as education *increases* from high school or less ("low") to more than high school ("high"), performance on the civil service examination *decreases*, for twice as many individuals with high education (200) received low scores on the test than did those with low education. Because we would anticipate that education would *improve* scores on the examination, this initial finding seems counterintuitive. In fact, it is not only counterintuitive, but also incorrect.

The reason for the faulty interpretation is that we have failed to take into account the *total number* of individuals who have low as compared to high education. Note that although this sample contained only 250 people with a high school education or less, 1000 individuals—four times as many—had more than a high school education. Thus, when these figures are put in perspective, there are *four* times as many people with high education than low education in the sample—yet only *twice* as many of the former as the latter received low scores on the civil service examination. These data suggest that in contrast to our initial interpretation of the table, more highly educated people do earn *higher* scores on the civil service examination than do the less educated. This finding accords with intuition and is the primary conclusion supported by the table—when it has been analyzed correctly.

How does one do so? There are three major steps. The problem with the initial interpretation of the contingency table was that it overlooked the relative number of cases in the categories of education. This problem can be remedied by percentaging the table appropriately, which is the key to analyzing and understanding cross-tabulations. The steps in the analysis process are as follows:

**STEP 1** Determine which variable is *independent* and which is *dependent*. As explained in Chapter 8, the independent variable is the anticipated causal variable, the one that is supposed to lead to changes or effects in the dependent or response (criterion) variable. In the present example of the relationship between education and performance on the civil service examination, it is expected that higher education leads to improved performance on the test. Stated as a hypothesis: the higher the education, the higher the expected score on the civil service examination. Hence, education is the independent variable, and performance on the civil service examination is the dependent variable.

**STEP 2** Calculate percentages within the categories of the *independent* variable—in this case, education. We would like to know the percentage of people with high school education or less (low education) who received high scores on the civil service examination, and the percentage of people with more than a high school education (high education) who received high scores. Then it would be possible to compare these percentages in order to determine whether those with high education receive higher scores on the examination than do those with low education. This comparison allows us to evaluate, *on the basis of the data,* whether the expectation or hypothesis stated previously is correct— that is, that education leads to improved scores on the civil service examination.

The procedure used to calculate percentages within the categories of education is the same as the univariate procedure elaborated earlier in the chapter. We are interested first in the percentage of people with high school education or less who received high scores on the civil service examination. Table 13.9 indicates that a total of 250 people fall into this category of education, and of these, 150 received high scores on the test. Thus we find that $(150 \div 250) \times 100 = 60\%$ of those with low education earned high scores on the civil service examination. (Note that this is also the probability of receiving a high score on the exam given low education; see Chapter 5.) The other 100 of the 250 people with low education received low scores on the test; converting to a percentage, we find that $(100 \div 250) \times 100 = 40\%$ of those with low education earned low test scores.

Moving to those with more than a high school education, Table 13.9 shows that 800 of the 1000 people with this level of education—or 80%

(800 ÷ 1000 × 100)—received high scores on the civil service examination, and the other 200—or 20% (200 ÷ 1000 × 100)—earned low scores. All percentages have now been calculated. The cross-tabulation percentaged within the categories of education is presented in Table 13.10.

**TABLE 13.10**

Percentage Distribution for Data of Table 13.9

| Performance on Civil Service Examination | Education | | | |
|---|---|---|---|---|
| | *High School or Less* | | *More Than High School* | |
| Low | (100 ÷ 250) × 100 = | 40% | (200 ÷ 1000) × 100 = | 20% |
| High | (150 ÷ 250) × 100 = | 60% | (800 ÷ 1000) × 100 = | 80% |
| Total | ($n = 250$) | 100% | ($n = 1000$) | 100% |

**STEP 3** Compare the percentages calculated within the categories of the *independent variable* (education) across *one* of the categories of the *dependent variable* (performance on civil service examination). For example, whereas 80% of those with high education earned high scores on the civil service examination, only 60% of those with low education did so. Thus our hypothesis is supported by these data. In general, those with high education received higher scores on the examination than did those with low education. As hypothesized, the higher the education, the higher is the score on the civil service examination.

**percentage difference**     To summarize the relationship between two variables in a cross-tabulation, researchers often calculate a **percentage difference** across one of the categories of the dependent variable. In the present case, the percentage difference is equal to 80% minus 60%, or 20% (the percentage of those with high education who earned high scores on the test minus the percentage of those with low education who did so). The conclusion, then, is that education appears to make a difference of 20% in performance on the civil service examination.

**EXAMPLE: AUTOMOBILE MAINTENANCE IN BERRYSVILLE**

The city council of Berrysville, Oklahoma, has been under considerable pressure to economize. Last year, the council passed an ordinance authorizing an experimental program for the maintenance of city-owned vehicles. The bill stipulates that, for one year, a random sample of 150 of the city's 400 automobiles will receive no preventive maintenance and will simply be driven until they break down. The other 250 automobiles will receive regularly scheduled preventive maintenance. The council is interested in whether the expensive program of preventive maintenance actually reduces the number of breakdowns. After a year under the experimental maintenance program, the city council was presented the data in Table 13.11, which summarizes the number of automobile breakdowns under the no maintenance and preventive maintenance conditions. You are to analyze the data for the city council and make a recommendation as to whether the program should be continued (and/or expanded) or terminated.

**TABLE 13.11**
Automobile Maintenance Data

| Automobile Breakdowns | Automobile Maintenance | | |
|---|---|---|---|
| | *None* | *Regularly Scheduled* | *Total* |
| No breakdown | 72 | 194 | 266 |
| Breakdown | 78 | 56 | 134 |
| Total | 150 | 250 | 400 |

**STEP 1**  Determine which variable is independent and which is dependent. There should be no doubt that automobile maintenance is expected to affect the number of breakdowns. Therefore, "maintenance" is the independent variable and "breakdowns" is the dependent variable. Stated as a hypothesis, we have the following: the greater the maintenance, the fewer are the breakdowns.

**STEP 2**  Calculate percentages within the categories of the independent variable, "automobile maintenance." The calculations are shown in Table 13.12.

**TABLE 13.12**
Percentage Distribution for Data of Table 13.11

| Automobile Breakdowns | Automobile Maintenance | | | |
|---|---|---|---|---|
| | *None* | | *Regularly Scheduled* | |
| No breakdown | $(72 \div 150) \times 100 =$ | 48% | $(194 \div 250) \times 100 =$ | 77.6% |
| Breakdown | $(78 \div 150) \times 100 =$ | 52% | $(56 \div 250) \times 100 =$ | 22.4% |
| Total | $(n = 150)$ | 100% | $(n = 250)$ | 100% |

**STEP 3**  Compare percentages across one of the categories of the dependent variable. Although over half (52%) of the automobiles that received no maintenance broke down during the one-year experimental program, only 22.4% of the automobiles that received regularly scheduled main-

tenance did so. This is a difference of 29.6% (52 minus 22.4). Thus automobile maintenance appears to make nearly a 30% difference in the number of breakdowns. The data show support for the hypothesis: as maintenance increases, the number of breakdowns decreases by almost 30%. From these data, should you recommend that the city council continue or terminate the experimental maintenance program?

**Note:** when these data were released to the public, the Berrysville press made great sport of the folly of the city council for experimenting with the "dang fool" maintenance program. The members of the city council who had voted for the program were soundly defeated in the next election. In the first meeting of the new city council, the researcher who had compiled and analyzed the automobile maintenance data was awarded a substantial raise in salary. There may be a moral to this story.

## LARGER CONTINGENCY TABLES

With a single exception, the examples of contingency tables presented in this chapter have consisted of "two-by-two" tables—cross-tabulations in which both variables comprise just two response categories. Cross-tabulations may and often do consist of variables with a greater number of response categories. For example, Table 13.13 presents the cross-tabulation of "income" (low, medium, high) and "job satisfaction" (low, medium, high)—How satisfied are you with your job?—for the employees of the Maslow City Post Office.

**TABLE 13.13**

Relationship Between Income and Job Satisfaction

| Job Satisfaction | Income | | | |
|---|---|---|---|---|
| | *Low* | *Medium* | *High* | *Total* |
| Low | 100 | 30 | 10 | 140 |
| Medium | 60 | 80 | 15 | 155 |
| High | 40 | 40 | 50 | 130 |
| Total | 200 | 150 | 75 | 425 |

Although the analysis becomes more complicated, *contingency tables based on variables with many response categories are analyzed in the same way as are the smaller two-by-two tables.* Start by determining which variable is independent and which is dependent. In the present example, you would expect income to lead to job satisfaction: the higher the income, the higher would be the job satisfaction. "Income" is the independent variable and 'job satisfaction" is the dependent variable. Therefore, the table should be percentaged within the categories of income; percentaging the cross-tabulation appropriately is the second step. Table 13.14 presents the percentaged cross-tabulation.

**TABLE 13.14**

Percentage Distribution for Data of Table 13.13

| Job Satisfaction | Income | | | | | |
|---|---|---|---|---|---|---|
| | *Low* | | *Medium* | | *High* | |
| Low | $(100 \div 200) \times 100 =$ | 50% | $(30 \div 150) \times 100 =$ | 20% | $(10 \div 75) \times 100 =$ | 13.3% |
| Medium | $(60 \div 200) \times 100 =$ | 30% | $(80 \div 150) \times 100 =$ | 53.3% | $(15 \div 75) \times 100 =$ | 20% |
| High | $(40 \div 200) \times 100 =$ | 20% | $(40 \div 150) \times 100 =$ | 36.7% | $(50 \div 75) \times 100 =$ | 66.7% |
| Total | $(n = 200)$ | 100% | $(n = 150)$ | 100% | $(n = 75)$ | 100% |

The third and final step in the analysis of contingency tables is to compare percentages across one of the categories of the dependent variable. Although the choice of a category in two-by-two tables is not a critical decision—both categories of the dependent variable will yield the *same* percentage difference—in larger tables, the selection of a category of the dependent variable for purposes of percentage comparison requires more care. In general, you should *not* choose an *intermediate* category, such as "medium" job satisfaction, for this purpose. Choice of either of the *endpoint* categories—"low" or "high" job satisfaction—will result in clearer understanding and interpretation of the contingency table.

Once the (endpoint) category of the dependent variable has been selected, compare the percentages calculated for the *endpoint* categories of the independent variable. Again, avoid intermediate categories for this purpose. In Table 13.14, this rule suggests that we compare the percentage of those with low income who have high job satisfaction (20%) with the percentage of those with high income who have high job satisfaction (66.7%). Alternatively, we could compare the percentage of those with low income who express low job satisfaction (50%) with the percentage of those with high income who express low job satisfaction (13.3%).

Which percentage comparison(s) should the researcher use to summarize the relationship found in the cross-tabulation? The percentage difference calculation can and typically does yield different results depending on the endpoint category of the dependent variable chosen. In the present case, the percentage difference based on high job satisfaction is 66.7% − 20.0% = 46.7%, whereas the percentage difference for low job satisfaction is 50.0% − 13.3% = 36.7%. Probably the best course of action for the researcher is to report *both* figures. They show that those with high income indicated high job satisfaction more often than did those with low income (by 47%), and conversely that those with low income indicated low job satisfaction more often than did their counterparts (by 37%). Thus, income appears to make a difference of 37% to 47% in job satisfaction. These figures provide support for the hypothesis that the greater the income, the greater is the expected job satisfaction.

## DISPLAYING CONTINGENCY TABLES

A set of conventions has been developed for presenting contingency tables. First, contingency tables are very rarely presented simply as bivariate frequency distributions. Instead, you should display the table in *percentaged* form, in which the percentages have been obtained according to the procedures described in the preceding section (do *not* show the percentage calculations in the final report). Second, the *independent* variable is placed along the *columns* of the table, and the *dependent* variable is positioned down the *rows*. Third, the substantive meaning of the categories of the independent variable should show a progression from least to most moving from left to right across the columns, and the categories of the dependent variable should show the same type of progression moving down the rows. In other words, the categories should be listed in the order "low," "medium," "high"; or "disapprove," "neutral," "approve"; or "disagree," "neutral," "agree"; and so on. This procedure greatly facilitates the interpretation of measures of association (see Chapter 14). Table 13.14 provides an illustration. Fourth, the percentages calculated within categories of the independent variable are summed down the column, and the total for each category is placed at the foot of the respective column. The sum should equal 100%, but due to rounding error, it may vary between 99% and 101%. *Do not add the percentages across the rows of the table; this is a meaningless operation.* Finally, the total number of cases within each category of the independent variable is presented at the foot of the respective column. Usually, these totals are enclosed in parentheses and contain the notation $n = \underline{\hspace{1cm}}$. Table 13.15 presents schematically a contingency table displayed according to the conventional rules.

Two problems arise regarding the conventional display of contingency tables. First, although these rules are widely accepted, some researchers violate them. Thus in reading and studying contingency tables presented in books, journals, reports, memoranda, magazines, newspapers, and so on, you cannot assume that the independent variable is along the columns or that the dependent variable is down the rows. Nor can you assume that the categories of the variables are ordered in the table according to the conventions. Instead, you should examine the table, deciding which variable is independent and which is dependent, checking to see whether the percentages have been calculated within the categories of the independent variable, and verifying whether the author has compared percentages appropriately. You should recognize these procedures as the steps already elaborated for analyzing and interpreting cross-tabulations. Cultivation of this habit will not only increase your understanding of contingency table results but also sharpen your analytical skills.

**TABLE 13.15**

Format for a Contingency Table

| Dependent Variable | Independent Variable | | | |
|---|---|---|---|---|
| Substantive meaning of categories increases ↓ | Substantive meaning of categories increases ————————————→ | | | |
| | ——% ——% ⋮ | ——% ——% ⋮ | ——% ——% ⋮ | ——% ——% ⋮ |
| Total | 100.0% (n = ____) | 100.0% (n = ____) | 100.0% (n = ____) | 100.0% (n = ____) |

The second problem arises as a consequence of computer utilization. It is likely that you will be dealing with contingency tables constructed and percentaged by a computer. Not only is the computer oblivious to the distinction between independent and dependent variables, the ordering of response categories of variables, and so on, but also most computers are programmed to print out *three different sets of percentages:* percentages calculated (1) within categories of the row variable; (2) within categories of the column variable; and (3) according to the total number of cases represented in the contingency table, usually called *corner* percentaging. It is up to you as the data analyst to determine which set of percentages is meaningful and, if necessary, to reconstruct the contingency table by hand from the computer printout according to conventional form. If you follow the steps for the analysis of contingency tables developed here, this task should not be difficult.

This chapter has elaborated a general method for determining whether two variables measured at the nominal or ordinal levels are related: contingency table analysis. However, it has not addressed the question of *how strongly* two variables are related. This question serves as the focus for the next chapter.

## CHAPTER SUMMARY

Contingency tables are tables used to demonstrate the relationship between two variables measured at the nominal or ordinal levels. The simplest and often most useful technique for analyzing contingency tables is to compare percentages through the use of percentage distributions appropriately calculated.

This chapter illustrates the analysis of contingency tables. A contingency table is a bivariate—or two-variable—frequency distribution. It presents the number of cases that fall into each possible pairing of the values of two variables. There are three major steps in the analysis process. First, determine which variable is independent and which is dependent. Second, calculate percentages within the categories of the independent variable. Finally, compare the percentages calculated within the categories of the independent variable across one of the categories of the dependent variable, and interpret the results. Contingency tables for variables with more than two response categories are analyzed using the same basic approach as for two-by-two tables.

## PROBLEMS

**13.1**  The Lebanon postmaster suspects that working on ziptronic machines is the cause of high absenteeism. More than ten absences from work without business-related reasons is considered excessive absenteeism. A check of employee records shows that 26 of the 44 ziptronic operators had 10 or more absences and 35 of 120 nonziptronic workers had 10 or more absences. Construct a contingency table for the postmaster. Does the table support the postmaster's suspicion that working on ziptronic machines is related to high absenteeism?

**13.2**  During last year's budget crunch, several deserving employees of the Bureau of Procedures were denied promotions. This year, an unusual number of BP employees retired. The bureau chief suspects that the denial of promotions resulted in increased retirements. Of the 115 employees denied promotion, 32 retired. Of the 58 employees promoted, 9 retired. Present a contingency table, and analyze this information.

**13.3**  The Egyptian Air Force brass believe that overweight pilots have slow reaction times. They attribute the poor performance of their air force in recent war games in the Sinai to overweight pilots. The accompanying data were collected for all pilots. Analyze these data for the Egyptian Air Force brass.

| Reaction Time | Pilot Weight | | |
|---|---|---|---|
| | *Normal* | *Up to 10 Pounds Overweight* | *More Than 10 Pounds Overweight* |
| Poor | 14 | 36 | 45 |
| Adequate | 35 | 40 | 33 |
| Excellent | 46 | 25 | 15 |
| Total | 95 | 101 | 93 |

**13.4**  Auditors for the Military Airlift Command (MAC) are checking the arrival times of the three charter airlines they used in the Pacific last year. Branflake Airways flew 135 flights and was late 78 times. Flying Armadillo Airlines flew 94 flights and was late 35 times. Air Idaho flew 115 flights, with 51 late arrivals. Set up a contingency table, and analyze it for MAC.

**13.5**  The state personnel office oversees the state's tuition assistance program, which pays the tuition of civil servants taking courses for an MPA. Only two schools offer an MPA degree in the state capital, Capital College of Law and East Winslow State University. Some concern is expressed by legislators that many tuition-assisted students do not graduate. Analyze the data in the accompanying table for the personnel office.

| Status | Students Assisted for MPA Tuition | |
|---|---|---|
| | *Capital* | *East Winslow* |
| Did not graduate | 69 | 83 |
| Graduated | 23 | 37 |

**13.6**  Hyram Drant, research analyst for the city fire department, suspects that old water pumps are more likely to fail. From the data in the accompanying table, construct a contingency table and check Drant's suspicion. How else could this problem be analyzed?

Age (in years) of Pump

| *Pump Failed* | *Pump Did Not Fail* | |
|---|---|---|
| 23 | 15 | 7 |
| 47 | 6 | 9 |
| 11 | 9 | 4 |
| 53 | 33 | 19 |
| 26 | 26 | 36 |
| 15 | 17 | 47 |
| 42 | 9 | 31 |
| 37 | 12 | 23 |
| | 31 | 6 |
| | 46 | 9 |
| | 15 | 3 |

**13.7**  As head scheduler of special events for the Incomparable Myriad (the city arena), your task is to schedule events that make a profit so that the city need not subsidize the arena. Analyze the data in the accompanying table, which is based on last year's data, and write a report to the city council.

| Status | Type of Event | | | | |
|---|---|---|---|---|---|
| | *Hockey Games* | *Religious Rallies* | *Basketball Games* | *Rock Concerts* | *Public Administration Conventions* |
| Not profitable | 24 | 4 | 21 | 2 | 3 |
| Profitable | 18 | 32 | 6 | 8 | 0 |

**13.8**   As newly appointed head of evaluation for the state agriculture experiment station, you are asked to evaluate the relative effectiveness of corn hybrids AX147 and AQ49. Of 32 test plots, AX147 had high yields on 21. AQ49 had high yields on 17 of 28 test plots. Construct a contingency table and make a recommendation.

**13.9**   The Cancer Institute is evaluating an experimental drug for controlling lip cancer. Eighty lip cancer victims are randomly selected and given the drug for one year. Sixty other lip cancer victims are randomly selected and given a placebo for a year. From the data in the accompanying table, what would you conclude?

| Cancer Status | Drug Group | Placebo Group |
|---|---|---|
| Active | 58 | 42 |
| Remission | 22 | 18 |

**13.10**  A supervisor in the Department of Rehabilitative Services is critical of the performance of one of her counselors. The counselor is expected to arrange job training for those in need of vocational rehabilitation so that they may find employment. Yet the counselor has managed to place just 35% of his clients. The counselor argues that he is actually doing a good job and that the reason for his overall low rate of placement is that most of his clients are severely disabled, which makes them very difficult to place. The counselor's case load is presented in the accompanying table. Percentage the table appropriately, and evaluate who is correct—the supervisor or the counselor.

| Job Placement | Disability | | |
|---|---|---|---|
| | *Not Severely Disabled* | *Severely Disabled* | *Total* |
| Not placed | 17 | 118 | 135 |
| Placed | 47 | 26 | 73 |
| Total | 64 | 144 | 208 |

**13.11**  A professor of public administration has kept records on the class participation of his students over the past several years. He has a strong feeling (hypothesis) that class participation is related to grade in the course. For this analysis he classifies course grades into two categories, fail and pass. He operationalizes class participation as "low" if the student participated in class discussion in fewer than 25% of class periods, and "high" if the student participated in 25% or more of the periods.

Based on these definitions, he has assembled the cross-tabulation below. Does a relationship exist between class participation and course grades?

| Grade in Course | Class Participation | |
|---|---|---|
| | *Low* | *High* |
| Fail | 56 | 15 |
| Pass | 178 | 107 |

**13.12** Susan Wolch and John Komer are interested in determining which of two books is more effective in teaching statistics to public administration students. They randomly assign a pool of 50 students to two groups of 25 students each. One group uses Meier and Brudney, *Applied Statistics for Public Administration.* The other group uses Brand *X.* Their criterion for measuring success is student grades in the course. They get the results shown in the accompanying table. Evaluate these data and make a recommendation.

| Grade | Book Used in Class | |
|---|---|---|
| | *Brand X* | *Meier and Brudney* |
| Students receiving C's, D's, or F's | 18 | 9 |
| Students receiving A's or B's | 7 | 16 |
| Total | 25 | 25 |

**13.13** Madonna Lewis' job in the Department of Sanitary Engineering is to determine if new refuse collection procedures have improved the public's perception of the department. A public opinion survey was taken both before and after the new procedures were implemented. The results appear in the accompanying table. Analyze the table, and evaluate whether public perception of the Department appears to have improved over time.

| Opinion | Survey | |
|---|---|---|
| | *Before* | *After* |
| Department is doing a poor job | 79 | 73 |
| Department is doing a good job | 23 | 47 |

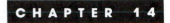

## CHAPTER 14

# AIDS FOR THE INTERPRETATION OF CONTINGENCY TABLES

Chapter 13 developed methods for constructing and analyzing contingency tables or cross-tabulations. It focused on procedures for percentaging these tables and determining whether two variables measured at the nominal or ordinal levels are associated statistically.

This chapter begins where the previous one concluded. It elaborates methods for assessing the strength of a relationship between a pair of nominal or ordinal variables. It is important to recognize that these techniques are not substitutes but *supplements* to those presented in Chapter 13. All these procedures are useful for understanding the relationship between two variables.

The chapter is divided into two major segments. The first part is devoted to the chi-square test. The chi-square is a test of statistical significance (see Chapter 9) for relationships between variables measured at the nominal or ordinal levels. The second portion of the chapter develops methods for evaluating the strength of the relationship between two variables. The most straightforward of these techniques is the percentage difference, and it is discussed first. The idea of measures of association—single statistics that summarize the strength of a relationship demonstrated in a cross-tabulation—is then introduced. The chapter concludes with a detailed development of frequently used measures of association: lambda and Cramér's $V$ for nominal-level variables; and gamma, Kendall's *tau-b* and *tau-c*, and Somers' $d_{yx}$ and $d_{xy}$ for ordinal-level variables.

## THE CHI-SQUARE TEST: STATISTICAL SIGNIFICANCE FOR CONTINGENCY TABLES

Chapter 9 introduced the issue of the correspondence between results obtained in a sample of data and the actual situation in the population that the sample is intended to represent. *Statistical significance* is a procedure for establishing the degree of confidence that one can have in making an inference from a sample to its parent population.

**chi-square test**

The **chi-square test** is a procedure for evaluating the level of statistical significance attained by a bivariate relationship in a cross-tabulation. The chi-square test procedure assumes that there is no relationship between the two variables in the population and determines whether any apparent relationship obtained in a sample cross-tabulation is attributable to chance. This procedure involves three steps. First, *expected frequencies* are calculated for each cell in the contingency table predicated upon the assumption that the two variables are unrelated in the population. Second, based on the difference between the expected frequency and the actual frequency observed in each table cell, a test statistic called the *chi-square* is computed. Since the expected frequencies are premised on the assumption of no relationship, the greater the deviation between them and the actual frequencies, the greater is the departure of the observed relationship from the null hypothesis—and hence the greater is the confidence in inferring the existence of a relationship between the two variables in the population. Third, the chi-square value computed for the actual data is compared with a table of theoretical chi-square values calculated and tabulated by statisticians. This comparison allows the analyst to determine the precise degree of confidence that he or she may have in inferring from the sample cross-tabulation that a relationship exists in the parent population.

### EXAMPLE: INCOMPETENCE IN THE FEDERAL GOVERNMENT?

A disgruntled official working in the personnel department of a large federal bureaucracy is disturbed by the level of incompetence she perceives in the leadership of the organization. She is convinced that incompetence rises to the top, and she shares this belief with a co-worker over lunch. The latter challanges her to substantiate her claim.

In order to do so, she selects from her personnel files a random sample of 400 people employed by the organization. From the formal education and civil service examination scores of these people, she classifies them into three levels of competence (low, medium, high); and from their GS ratings and formal job descriptions, she classifies them into three categories of hierarchical position in the organization (low, medium, high). The cross-tabulation of these two variables for the sample of employees appears in Table 14.1. She would like to know whether she can legitimately infer from this sample cross-tabulation that a relationship exists between competence and hierarchical position in the population of all workers in the organization. Accordingly, she decides to perform the chi-square test; the steps in this procedure follow.

**expected frequencies**

**STEP 1**    Compute **expected frequencies** for each cell of the cross-tabulation based on the null hypothesis that competence and hierarchical position are not related in the population. (**Note:** if the table has been percent-

**TABLE 14.1**

Cross-Tabulation of Competence and Hierarchy

| Hierarchy | Competence | | | |
| | Low | Medium | High | Total |
|---|---|---|---|---|
| Low | 113 | 60 | 27 | 200 |
| Medium | 31 | 91 | 38 | 160 |
| High | 8 | 8 | 24 | 40 |
| Total | 152 | 159 | 89 | 400 |

aged, then the data must be converted to raw frequencies before calculation of the expected frequencies. Expected frequencies must be
calculated on the basis of the raw figures.)

If these two variables were unrelated, then we would expect to find
the same distribution of hierarchical position in each category of competence as in the sample as a whole. For each level of competence, the
percentages of hierarchical position would be identical. In that case,
competence would have no impact on hierarchy; there would be percentage differences of 0% for each category of the dependent variable,
indicating that the two variables are totally unrelated.

Although calculation of the expected frequencies is a bit cumbersome, it is not difficult. Consider the distribution of hierarchical position. Of the 400 people in the sample, 200 (50%) rank low in position;
160 (40%) hold medium-level positions; and the remaining 40 (10%) are
at the top. The hypothetical no relationship cross-tabulation is displayed in Table 14.2. Assuming that the null hypothesis of no relationship between competence and hierarchy is true, we would expect to find
this same distribution of hierarchical position in each of the categories
of competence. For example, of the 152 employees ranking low in competence, you would expect to find 50%, or 76.0, in low hierarchical
positions ($.50 \times 152 = 76.0$); 40%, or 60.8, in medium positions ($.40 \times
152 = 60.8$); and 10%, or 15.2, in high positions ($.10 \times 152 = 15.2$).
These are the expected frequencies for the low-competence category.

**TABLE 14.2**

Hypothetical No Relationship Cross-Tabulation for Chi-Square

| Hierarchy | Competence | | | |
| | Low | Medium | High | Total |
|---|---|---|---|---|
| Low | 50% | 50% | 50% | 50% |
| Medium | 40% | 40% | 40% | 40% |
| High | 10% | 10% | 10% | 10% |

The expected frequencies for the medium- and high-competence categories are found analogously. Table 14.3 presents the detailed calculations.

**TABLE 14.3**

Calculations for Expected Frequency and Chi-Square

| Table Cell | | Observed Frequency | Expected Frequency | $\dfrac{(\text{Observed} - \text{Expected})^2}{\text{Expected}}$ |
|---|---|---|---|---|
| *Competence* | *Hierarchy* | | | |
| Low | Low | 113 | .50 × 152 = 76.0 | 18.01 |
| Low | Medium | 31 | .40 × 152 = 60.8 | 14.61 |
| Low | High | 8 | .10 × 152 = 15.2 | 3.41 |
| Medium | Low | 60 | .50 × 159 = 79.5 | 4.78 |
| Medium | Medium | 91 | .40 × 159 = 63.6 | 11.80 |
| Medium | High | 8 | .10 × 159 = 15.9 | 3.93 |
| High | Low | 27 | .50 × 89 = 44.5 | 6.88 |
| High | Medium | 38 | .40 × 89 = 35.6 | .16 |
| High | High | 24 | .10 × 89 = 8.9 | 25.62 |
| | Total | 400 | 400.0 | 89.20 = chi-square |

**chi-square statistic**

**STEP 2** Compute the value of chi-square for the cross-tabulation. The **chi-square statistic** compares the frequencies actually observed with the expected frequencies throughout the contingency table. The value of chi-square is found by (1) taking the difference between the observed and expected frequencies for each table cell, (2) squaring this difference, (3) dividing this result by the expected frequency, and (4) summing these quotients across all cells of the table. For example, in the low-competence–low-hierarchy cell of Table 14.1, the observed frequency is 113, as compared to an expected frequency of 76.0. Thus $(113 - 76.0)^2/76.0 = 18.01$, as shown in the last column of Table 14.3. Although in themselves these calculations are not likely to make a great deal of sense to you, their virtue is that they yield a sum—the value of chi-square—whose theoretical distribution is well known and can be used to evaluate the statistical significance of the relationship found in the contingency table. Table 14.3 indicates that the value of chi-square for the competence-hierarchy cross-tabulation is 89.20.

**STEP 3** Compare the value of chi-square computed for the actual cross-tabulation with the appropriate value of chi-square tabulated in the table of theoretical values. The table of chi-square values is presented in Table 4 in the Appendix of this book.

To find the appropriate theoretical value of chi-square in this table for an actual contingency table, two pieces of information must be supplied: (1) the *degrees of freedom* associated with the table; and (2) the *level of statistical significance* desired. The **degrees of freedom** is simply a number that indicates some idea of the size of the empirical contingency table under study. It is found by multiplying one less than the number of rows in the table by one less than the number of columns (discounting both marginal rows and columns). In the present example, since the number of rows and the number of columns are both equal to 3, there are $(3 - 1) \times (3 - 1) = 2 \times 2 = 4$ degrees of freedom. In the Appendix, Table 4, the degrees of freedom (abbreviated df) are printed down the far left column of the table.

**degrees of freedom**

The **level of statistical significance** is determined by the researcher. It is the exact probability of error that he or she is willing to tolerate in making an inference from the sample cross-tabulation to the parent population. For example, if the frequently used level of .05 is selected by the researcher, then there is a probability of 5% that an incorrect inference will be made that a relationship exists in the population when in fact it does not. In Table 4, the level of statistical significance (abbreviated $P$, for probability) is printed along the top of the table; these values cut off the specified area of the curve. Turning to this table, you should find that the theoretical value of chi-square for 4 degrees of freedom, allowing a probability of error of 5% (that is, a level of statistical significance of .05), is equal to 9.49.

**level of statistical significance**

Now that the appropriate theoretical vaue of chi-square has been determined, it is possible to make the critical decision whether, based on the sample cross-tabulation between competence and hierarchical position, the existence of a relationship can be inferred in the population of all agency employees. The table of theoretical values (Appendix, Table 4) consists of *minimum* values of chi-square that must be obtained in empirical contingency tables in order to infer, with a given level of confidence (statistical significance), that a relationship exists in the population. In the present case, since the value of chi-square calculated for the cross-tabulation (89.20) is far greater than the appropriate minimum value stipulated by Table 4 (9.49), allowing a 5% chance of error, we can infer that a relationship *does exist* between competence and hierarchical position in the population. Had the calculated value of chi-square failed to surpass this minimum, the null hypothesis of no relationship in the population could *not* be rejected.

## LIMITATIONS OF THE CHI-SQUARE TEST

The preceding example illustrates well one of the primary limitations of the chi-square test. The test procedure led to the conclusion that a relationship does exist between competence and hierarchical position in the population of agency employees. However, recall that the researcher in this example hypothesized that this relationship is *inverse*: that is, the less the competence of the employee, the higher is the level of the position attained in the hierarchy of the organization. In fact, when the cross-tabulation of these two variables in the sample of employees (Table 14.1) has been percentaged appropriately (see Chapter 13), the relationship between competence and hierarchical position is found to be *positive*. The percentaged cross-tabulation, presented in Table 14.4, shows that as competence increases, position in the hierarchy also increases. Thus, whereas the existence of a relationship can be inferred in the population, it is in the *opposite* direction of the one hypothesized by the researcher. Therefore, her hypothesis is incorrect.

**TABLE 14.4**

Percentaged Cross-Tabulation for Competence-Hierarchy Relationship

| Hierarchy | Competence | | |
|---|---|---|---|
| | *Low* | *Medium* | *High* |
| Low | 74% | 38% | 30% |
| Medium | 21% | 57% | 43% |
| High | 5% | 5% | 27% |
| Total | 100% | 100% | 100% |
| | (*n* = 152) | (*n* = 159) | (*n* = 89) |

The important point illustrated by this example is *not* that the chi-square test yields fallacious information, but that it yields information of only a *limited* kind. The test is based solely on the deviation of an observed cross-tabulation from the condition of no relationship or statistical independence. It is totally insensitive to the nature and direction of the relationship actually found in the contingency table. Too often, researchers jump to the conclusion that a significant value of chi-square calculated in a table indicates that the two variables are related in the hypothesized manner in the population. It may—and it may not. Supplementary analytical procedures, such as percentaging the contingency table and computing a measure of association, are necessary to answer this question.

The other limitations of the chi-square test are typical of tests of statistical significance in general, including tests of the $t$ and $z$ statistics (see Chapter 9). First, the chi-square test requires a method of sampling from the population— simple random sampling—that sometimes cannot be satisfied. Second, the value of chi-square calculated in a cross-tabulation is markedly inflated by sample size. As a result, in large samples, weak relationships are usually found to be statistically significant. Hence, the test is not very discriminating.

Finally, although the chi-square test is frequently *misinterpreted* as a measure of strength of relationship, it does *not* assess the magnitude or substantive importance of empirical relationships. Instead, it provides information pertaining only to the probability of the *existence* of a relationship in the population. To be sure, this is valuable information, but it ignores the issue of size of relationship. (Later, we present a measure of association derived from chi-square: Cramér's *V*.) For this reason, we strongly encourage you to use the chi-square test in combination with other statistical procedures, especially those designed to evaluate strength of relationship.

# ASSESSING THE STRENGTH OF A RELATIONSHIP

## THE PERCENTAGE DIFFERENCE

Two transportation planners are locked in debate regarding the measures that should be implemented to increase ridership on public transportation, particularly line buses. The first insists that the major reason that people do not ride the bus to work is that they have not heard about it. Thus, she argues that the way to increase ridership is to advertise the availability of public transportation. The second planner contends that the situaton is neither that simple nor that inexpensive. He believes that the primary obstacle to the success of public transportation is that it is not readily accessible to great masses of potential riders. People will not leave their cars for a system they are unable to reach conveniently. From this point of view, the way to increase ridership is to expand existing bus routes and to design and implement new ones so that public transportation is more accessible.

Since the measures proposed by the two transportation planners carry dramatically different implications—as well as price tags—for public policy, the federal government has decided to fund a study to evaluate the relative validity of their claims. Data were collected from a random sample of 500 individuals. Among other questions, these individuals were asked whether they (1) rode the bus regularly to work, (2) had learned of the existence of public transportation through advertising, and (3) lived in close proximity to a bus stop (defined as within three blocks).

Table 14.5 presents the cross-tabulations between riding the bus to work and each of the other two variables. Both the raw, or nonpercentaged, tables and the percentaged tables are displayed. You should practice deriving the percentages from the raw figures. If any aspect of this process remains mysterious to you, you should review the steps for percentaging contingency tables elaborated in Chapter 13 before proceeding further.

Table 14.5 provides support for the hypotheses of both transportation planners. As hypothesized by the first, advertising is related positively to ridership. Whereas 33% of those who had heard advertising about public transportation rode the bus regularly to work, only 25% of those who had not heard such advertising did so. Thus, advertising was associated with an 8% increase in

**TABLE 14.5**

Data for Bus Survey

| | Raw Data | | | | | | |
|---|---|---|---|---|---|---|---|
| Ride Bus | Heard Advertising | | | Ride Bus | Bus Accessible | | |
| | *No* | *Yes* | *Total* | | *No* | *Yes* | *Total* |
| No | 225 | 134 | 359 | No | 269 | 90 | 359 |
| Yes | 75 | 66 | 141 | Yes | 81 | 60 | 141 |
| Total | 300 | 200 | 500 | Total | 350 | 150 | 500 |

| | Percentaged Cross-Tabulations | | | | | |
|---|---|---|---|---|---|---|
| Ride Bus | Heard Advertising | | Ride Bus | Bus Accessible | |
| | *No* | *Yes* | | *No* | *Yes* |
| No | 75% | 67% | No | 77% | 60% |
| Yes | 25% | 33% | Yes | 23% | 40% |
| Total | 100% | 100% | Total | 100% | 100% |
| | ($n = 300$) | ($n = 200$) | | ($n = 350$) | ($n = 150$) |

ridership. Similarly, as predicted by the second planner, accessibility is related positively to ridership; 40% of those living in close proximity to a bus stop rode the bus regularly, compared to only 23% of those for whom the bus was less convenient. Thus, accessibility was associated with a 17% increase in ridership.

These results raise the question of which proposal is likely to have the greater impact on increasing ridership of public transportation. Since accessibility made a difference of 17% in ridership and advertising made a difference of 8%, the former has the larger impact; that is, changes in accessibility apparently lead to a larger change in ridership than do changes in advertising. Stated another way, accessibility is related *more strongly* to ridership than is advertising. *In general, the greater the percentage difference, the stronger is the relationship between two variables.* Accordingly, if the federal government intends to adopt one or the other of the two proposals (but not both) as a measure to increase the ridership of public transportation, these data suggest that improving accessibility is to be preferred.*

---

*To have greater confidence in this conclusion, one must examine the effects on ridership of advertising and accessibility *simultaneously*. However, the techniques necessary to do this—statistical controls—lie beyond the scope of the present chapter. They are elaborated in Chapter 15.

## PERFECT AND NULL RELATIONSHIPS

In a cross-tabulation, the percentage difference within a given category of the dependent variable may range from 0 to 100%. Percentage differences of 100 within each of the categories of the dependent variable indicate that the two variables are associated *perfectly*. If you are given the score of a case on the independent variable, it is possible to predict the score on the dependent variable with certainty.

As shown in Table 14.6, the relationship between two ordinal variables is perfect if all cases are located in the diagonal cells of the contingency table. Assuming that the table has been constructed according to the usual conventions and consists of ordinal variables (see Chapter 13), the relationship is perfect in the *positive* direction if all cases fall into the diagonal cells sloping downward to the right. This configuration would indicate that, as scores on the independent variable increase, the scores on the dependent variable also increase. In contrast, if all cases fall into the diagonal cells sloping downward to the left, the relationship is perfect in the *negative* direction. This pattern would

**TABLE 14.6**

Perfect Relationships

| Perfect Positive Relationship | | | | |
|---|---|---|---|---|
| Dependent Variable | Independent Variable | | | |
| | *Category 1* | *Category 2* | ... | *Category n* |
| Category 1 | 100% | 0% | ... | 0% |
| Category 2 | 0% | 100% | ... | 0% |
| ⋮ | ⋮ | ⋮ | | ⋮ |
| Category n | 0% | 0% | ... | 100% |
| Total | 100% | 100% | ... | 100% |

| Perfect Negative Relationship | | | | |
|---|---|---|---|---|
| Dependent Variable | Independent Variable | | | |
| | *Category 1* | *Category 2* | ... | *Category n* |
| Category 1 | 0% | 0% | ... | 100% |
| Category 2 | ⋮ | ⋮ | | ⋮ |
| ⋮ | 0% | 100% | ... | 0% |
| Category n | 100% | 0% | ... | 0% |
| Total | 100% | 100% | ... | 100% |

indicate that, as scores on the independent variable increase, the scores on the dependent variable decrease. *The closer the resemblance of an actual cross-tabulation to either of these configurations, the stronger is the association between the two variables.* Because changes in the independent variable are hypothesized to be accompanied by changes in the dependent variable, this pattern is called the *covariation model* of relationship.

At the other extreme in a cross-tabulation, percentage differences of 0% within each of the categories of the dependent variable indicate that the two variables are *not* associated. The more similar the distribution of the dependent variable across each of the categories of the independent variable, the less strongly two variables are related. As was explained above in the discussion of the chi-square test, the strength of relationship between two variables reaches its lowest point when those distributions are identical. In that situation the variables are totally unrelated or independent. Table 14.2, which was developed in conjunction with the chi-square test, provides an example. Note that knowing the value of the independent variable (competence) in the table does not help in predicting values of the dependent variable (hierarchy) because the percentages are the same for each category of the independent variable. Table 14.7 illustrates

**TABLE 14.7**

No Relationship

|  | No Association: General Model $(a\% + b\% + c\% = 100\%)$ | | |
|---|---|---|---|
| Dependent Variable | Independent Variable | | |
|  | *Category 1* | *Category 2* | *Category 3* |
| Category 1 | $a\%$ | $a\%$ | $a\%$ |
| Category 2 | $b\%$ | $b\%$ | $b\%$ |
| Category 3 | $c\%$ | $c\%$ | $c\%$ |
| Total | 100% | 100% | 100% |

No Association: Empirical Examples

| Dependent Variable | Independent Variable | | | Dependent Variable | Independent Variable | | |
|---|---|---|---|---|---|---|---|
|  | *Category 1* | *Category 2* | *Category 3* |  | *Category 1* | *Category 2* | *Category 3* |
| Category 1 | 50% | 50% | 50% | Category 1 | 7% | 7% | 7% |
| Category 2 | 25% | 25% | 25% | Category 2 | 90% | 90% | 90% |
| Category 3 | 25% | 25% | 25% | Category 3 | 3% | 3% | 3% |
| Total | 100% | 100% | 100% | Total | 100% | 100% | 100% |

that in contrast to the single model of perfect association, there are many empirical models of no association.

In evaluating the strength of relationship between two variables, the critical question is, where on the continuum between the poles of no association and perfect association do the actual data fall? Do they more closely resemble the model in Table 14.7 or the model in Table 14.6? The more that they correspond to the model of perfect association, the more strongly they are said to be related.

This discussion of extreme values of association raises a problem with respect to the percentage difference as a measure of strength of relationship. Since the models of perfect and null association are based on all cells of the cross-tabulation, it seems reasonable that a desirable quality of a measure intended to assess strength of relationship is that it take into account the configuration of data in the entire contingency table. Because it is based on only one or both of the endpoint categories of the dependent variable, the percentage difference does not satisfy this desideratum; it takes into account only a portion of the data in the table (see Chapter 13). As a result, in larger cross-tabulations, the choice of the dependent variable category not only is somewhat arbitrary but also can lead to *different* results representing the strength of relationship between two variables in the *same* table. Depending upon one's point of view, the category selected may understate or overstate the actual degree of relationship in the cross-tabulation. Accordingly, we recommended (in Chapter 13) that you calculate and report both percentage differences.

It is important to place these points in perspective. In spite of its flaws, the percentage difference is perhaps the most widely used and certainly the most easily understood measure of strength of relationship. Used in combination with the other measures elaborated in this chapter, it can be extremely helpful for evaluating the nature and strength of relationship between two nominal- or ordinal-level variables. It is a hard fact of quantitative life that all statistics have flaws. An inevitable consequence of describing or summarizing or distilling a distribution into a single representative number or statistic is that some features of the data are captured very well, whereas others are slighted or overlooked completely. For this reason, this chapter is intended to encourage you to think of the measures presented for understanding bivariate relationships as complementary rather than exclusive. In actual data analysis situations, use those measures that best elucidate the relationship under study.

# MEASURES OF
# ASSOCIATION

**Measures of associaton** are single statistics whose magnitude and sign (positive or negative) provide information about the extent and direction of relationship between two variables in a cross-tabulation. In contrast to the percentage difference, measures of association are calculated on the basis of—and take into

**measures of
association**

account—all data in the contingency table. These statistics are designed to indicate where an actual relationship falls on the scale from perfect to null.

To facilitate interpretation, statisticians define measures of association so that they follow these four conventions:

1. If the relationship between the two variables is perfect, the measure equals $+1.0$ (positive relationship) or $-1.0$ (negative relationship).
2. If there is no relationship between the two variables, the measure equals $0.0$.
3. The stronger the relationship between the two variables, the greater is the magnitude (absolute value) of the measure.
4. The sign of the measure indicates the direction of the relationship. A value greater than zero (a positive number) corresponds to a positive relationship; a value less than zero (a negative number) corresponds to a negative relationship.

Because the concept of direction (or sign) of relationship assumes that the categories of the variables are ordered (that is, they increase or decrease), this concept can be applied only to relationships between variables measured at the *ordinal or interval* levels. Direction of relationship has no meaning for nominal variables. Based on the properties of measurement for each type of variable (see Chapter 7), different measures of association have been developed. Thus there are interval measures of association, ordinal measures, and nominal measures. Some interval measures are considered in Chapters 16 and 17. The remainder of this chapter describes several ordinal and nominal measures of association and provides examples illustrating their use.

## AN ORDINAL MEASURE OF ASSOCIATION: GAMMA

It is extremely cumbersome to compute any of the ordinal measures of association by hand, even with the aid of a (nonprogrammable) calculator. If these measures are essential to a report or analysis, the best strategy is to obtain access to a computer or a programmable calculator.

We will illustrate the computation of one of the more easily calculated ordinal measures of association, gamma. As will be shown, several other of the most frequently used measures of ordinal association (the tau statistic of Kendall and the *d* statistics of Somers) have a similar development. Gamma will be used to assess the strength of relationship between education and seniority in a small sample of 50 civil service employees. These variables are cross-tabulated in Table 14.8.

**paired**
**observations**

To calculate the gamma statistic, we must first introduce the idea of **paired observations**. Consider two data cases in Table 14.8, one of an individual in the low-education–low-seniority cell, and the other of an individual in the high-education–high-seniority cell. With respect to one another, this pair of cases is ranked consistently on education and seniority—that is, for this pair of cases, as education increases, seniority increases. Thus this pair provides support for the existence of a *positive* relationship between the two variables. This situation is called a **concordant pair** of cases.

**concordant pair**

**TABLE 14.8**

Cross-Tabulation of Education and Seniority

| Seniority | Education | | Total |
|---|---|---|---|
| | *Low* | *High* | *Total* |
| Low | 20 | 10 | 30 |
| High | 5 | 15 | 20 |
| Total | 25 | 25 | 50 |

Now consider two different data cases in Table 14.8, one of an individual in the low-education–high-seniority cell, and the other of an individual in the high-education–low-seniority cell. In contrast to the first pair of cases, with respect to one another, this pair of cases is ranked inconsistently on education and seniority—that is, as education increases, seniority decreases, and vice versa. This pair provides support for the existence of a negative relationship between the two variables. It is called a **discordant pair**.

**discordant pair**

What **gamma** (and many other ordinal measures of association) does is to take the *difference* between the number of concordant or consistently ordered pairs and the number of discordant or inconsistently ordered pairs in the cross-tabulation. *This difference indicates the relative support in the contingency table for a positive as opposed to a negative relationship between the two variables.* If the number of concordant pairs exceeds the number of discordant pairs, then, on balance, there is greater support for a positive relationship in the table. In that case the difference between them will be positive, and the gamma statistic will have this sign. On the other hand, if the number of concordant pairs is less than the number of discordant pairs, there is greater support for a negative relationship. The difference between them will be negative, and this will be reflected in the (negative) sign of gamma. Regardless of the direction of the relationship, the larger the difference between the number of concordant and the number of discordant pairs, the greater is the association between the two variables, and the greater is the magnitude of gamma.

**gamma**

In a small cross-tabulation such as in Table 14.8, calculation of the numbers of concordant and discordant pairs is not difficult. Consider first the concordant pairs. There are 20 cases in the low-education–low-seniority cell of the table. With respect to this group, the set of cases that is ordered consistently on both variables is the set of 15 observations in the high-education–high-seniority cell. Since each pairing of cases from these two table cells yields a concordant pair, in all there are $20 \times 15 = 300$ concordant pairs in Table 14.8.

The number of discordant pairs is found analogously. There are ten cases in the high-education–low-seniority cell of Table 14.8. With respect to this set, the group of cases that is ordered inconsistently on the variables is the group of five observations in the low-education–high-seniority cell of the table. Since each pairing of cases from these two table cells gives a discordant pair, there are $10 \times 5 = 50$ discordant pairs in Table 14.8.

At this point, it is evident that the relationship between education and seniority presented in Table 14.8 is positive. The difference between the number of concordant pairs and the number of discordant pairs is $300 - 50 = 250$. However, this simple difference is not very meaningful for interpreting relative strength of a relationship. For example, it would be misleading to compare the difference obtained in this contingency table with that obtained in larger tables or in tables with many more cases, in order to determine which table demonstrates the largest relationship.

For this reason, statisticians have *standardized* gamma (as well as the other measures of association) so that it will vary between $-1.0$ and $+1.0$. Standardization is accomplished by dividing the difference between concordant and discordant pairs by a well-defined quantity based on the contingency table under study. In the case of gamma, this quantity is the *sum of the number of concordant and the number of discordant pairs in the table.* Thus

$$\text{gamma} = \frac{\text{number of concordant pairs} - \text{number of discordant pairs}}{\text{number of concordant pairs} + \text{number of discordant pairs}}$$

Accordingly, the value of gamma for Table 14.8 is equal to

$$\frac{300 - 50}{300 + 50} = \frac{250}{350} = .71$$

This value of gamma indicates a relatively strong positive relationship between education and seniority in the sample of employees. When the original table has been percentaged, as shown in Table 14.9, further support is found for this conclusion. The percentaged table shows that education made a difference of 40% in seniority.

**TABLE 14.9**

Percentaged Cross-Tabulation of Education and Seniority

| Seniority | Education | |
|---|---|---|
| | *Low* | *High* |
| Low | 80% | 40% |
| High | 20% | 60% |
| | ($n = 25$) | ($n = 25$) |

## OTHER ORDINAL MEASURES OF ASSOCIATION: KENDALL'S *tau-b* AND *tau-c*, AND SOMERS' $d_{yx}$ AND $d_{xy}$

Several other commonly used measures of association for ordinal-level variables have a derivation and interpretation similar to gamma's. These include Kendall's *tau-b* and *tau-c*, and Somers' $d_{yx}$ and $d_{xy}$. Since these measures are similar and easy for the computer to calculate, many statistical package programs have been designed to compute and print them routinely. Because they are very cumbersome to calculate by hand, however, we will not do so here, but will only explain their use and interpretation.

Like gamma, all of these measures are based on comparing the number of concordant pairs with the number of discordant pairs in the contingency table. Yet they differ from gamma, for they take into account pairs of observations in the table that are tied on one or both of the variables. For example, a case in the low-education–low-seniority cell of the table is tied with a case in the low-education–high-seniority cell with respect to education, since both cases have the same rank on education. Similarly, a case in the low-education–high-seniority cell is tied with a case in the high-education–high seniority cell with respect to seniority, since they both have the same rank on seniority.

Gamma takes into account only concordant and discordant pairs; it ignores tied pairs completely. The other measures of association do not. Instead, they are based on a more stringent conception of the types of data patterns in a contingency table that constitute a perfect relationship. In particular, they will yield lower values for a contingency table to the extent that the table contains pairs of cases tied on the variables. For this reason, unless a contingency table has no tied pairs (a very rare occurrence), gamma will always be greater than *tau-b*, *tau-c*, $d_{yx}$, and $d_{xy}$.

**Kendall's *tau-b*** is an appropriate measure of strict linear relationship for "square tables"—tables with the same number of rows and columns. The calculation of *tau-b* takes into account pairs of cases tied on each of the variables in the contingency table. For the education-seniority cross-tabulation in Table 14.8, the calculated value of *tau-b* is .41. **Kendall's *tau-c*** is an appropriate measure of strict linear relationship for "rectangular tables"—tables with different numbers of rows and columns. In the present example, *tau-c* is .40 (*tau-b* is preferred, since the table is square). **Somers' $d_{yx}$** presumes that seniority is the dependent variable and yields lower values to the degree that cases are tied on this variable only. The logic is that a tie on seniority indicates that a change in the independent variable (education) does not lead to a change in seniority as a perfect relationship would predict. Here, Somers' $d_{yx}$ is .40. Conversely, **Somers' $d_{xy}$** presumes that education is the dependent variable and yields lower values to the degree that cases are tied on education only. The reasoning is that a tie on the dependent variable (now education) indicates that a change in the independent variable, now seniority, does not lead to a change in education, as a

**Kendall's *tau-b***

**Kendall's *tau-c***

**Somers' $d_{yx}$**

**Somers' $d_{xy}$**

perfect relationship would predict. In this example, Somers' $d_{xy}$ is .42, but would not be the statistic of choice because the hypothesis was that education (independent variable) leads to seniority (dependent variable), not the reverse.

Note that the gamma calculated for Table 14.8 is .71, which is much greater than the calculated value of any of the other measures of association. This situation is not at all unusual in the analysis of contingency tables. Among the measures of association, gamma will typically yield the largest value, whereas the others will be more modest. Which measure(s) should you use and interpret? In general, the *tau* measures are used more commonly than are the Somers' *d* measures. Many managers prefer to use both gamma and either *tau-b* or *tau-c*, depending upon whether the contingency table is square or rectangular. In this manner, the measures of association give a good idea of the magnitude of the relationship found in the table evaluated, according to more as well as less stringent standards.

## A NOMINAL MEASURE OF ASSOCIATION: LAMBDA

Ordinal measures of association are based on a covariation model of relationship. To the extent that two variables change together, or *covary*, they are considered associated or related. Measures of covariation such as gamma assess the extent to which increases in one variable are accompanied by increases (positive relationship) or decreases (negative relationship) in a second variable.

Because nominal variables do not consist of ordered categories (the categories lack any sense of magnitude or intensity), application of the covariation model of association to relationships between nominal variables is precluded. Therefore, a different model of association is required. A frequently used model of association for nominal variables is called the *predictability* model, or the model of *predictive association*. It is based on the ability to predict the category of the dependent variable based on knowledge of the category of the independent variable.

**lambda**

One of the most helpful and frequently used nominal measures of association premised on the predictability model is lambda. **Lambda** is defined as the proportional reduction in error gained in predicting the category of the dependent variable when the value of the independent variable is taken into account. That is, lambda evaluates the extent to which prediction of the dependent variable is improved when the value of the independent variable is known. Since the worst case is one in which the independent variable provides no (zero) improvement in predicting the dependent variable, lambda cannot be negative, but ranges from 0.0 to +1.0. Measures of association that incorporate the proportional reduction in error interpretation are sometimes abbreviated PRE statistics.

An example will illustrate the calculation and interpretation of lambda. Consider the relationship between race (white, black) and whether an individual made a contribution to the Bureau of Obfuscation's United Way drive. These variables are cross-tabulated for a random sample of 500 employees in Table 14.10.

**TABLE 14.10**

Cross-Tabulation of Race and Contribution

| Contribution | Race | | |
| --- | --- | --- | --- |
| | *White* | *Black* | *Total* |
| No | 100 | 125 | 225 |
| Yes | 200 | 75 | 275 |
| Total | 300 | 200 | 500 |

To calculate the value of lambda for the relationship shown in Table 14.10, we first disregard totally the race of the employee (independent variable). If race is disregarded, how many errors will we make in predicting whether or not the employee made a contribution to the United Way (dependent variable)? Since more employees made a contribution than did not, our best prediction is "contributed." This prediction is correct for 275 of the 500 employees in the sample, but it is in error for the remaining 225 who did not contribute. Thus, when the value of the independent variable is not taken into account (disregarded), the proportion of errors made in predicting the dependent variable is 225 ÷ 500 = .45.

If the race of the employee is now introduced, how much better can contributions to the United Way be predicted? If we knew that an employee was white, our best prediction would be that he or she made a contribution. We would be correct for 200 of the 300 whites in the sample, but we would make errors in predicting for the other 100 cases. If an employee is black, we would predict that he or she did not make a contribution. We would be correct for 125 of the 200 blacks, leaving 75 errors in prediction. Thus knowing the race of the employee we would make a total of 100 + 75 = 175 errors in predicting contributions to the United Way in a sample of 500 employees. This is a proportion of error equal to 175 ÷ 500 = .35.

We began with a proportion of error in predicting the dependent variable of .45, not taking into account the independent variable. By introducing the independent variable, we were able to reduce the proportion of error to .35. Compared to the original proportion, this is a rate of improvement in predicting the dependent variable—or proportional reduction in error—of

$$\frac{.45 - .35}{.45} = .22$$

which is the value of lambda for Table 14.10. This value suggests a weak predictive relationship between race and contributions to the United Way.

An alternative way to understand and compute lambda is to consider that, without knowing the value of the independent variable, we made 225 errors in predicting the dependent variable; and knowing the independent variable, we made 175 errors, a reduction of 50 errors. Thus errors in prediction were reduced by the proportion $50 \div 225 = .22$, which again is the value of lambda for Table 14.10. Based on this logic, the formula for lambda can be written

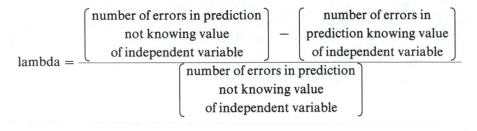

$$\text{lambda} = \frac{\begin{bmatrix} \text{number of errors in prediction} \\ \text{not knowing value} \\ \text{of independent variable} \end{bmatrix} - \begin{bmatrix} \text{number of errors in} \\ \text{prediction knowing value} \\ \text{of independent variable} \end{bmatrix}}{\begin{bmatrix} \text{number of errors in prediction} \\ \text{not knowing value} \\ \text{of independent variable} \end{bmatrix}}$$

## A NOMINAL MEASURE OF ASSOCIATION BASED ON CHI-SQUARE: CRAMÉR'S *V*

The chi-square test of statistical significance elaborated at the outset of this chapter is a measure of the existence of a relationship, not its strength. A variety of measures of association for nominal-level variables have been developed based on the chi-square. The measures include Pearson's contingency coefficient *C*, phi-square, Tschuprow's *T*, and Cramér's *V*. These measures are all related, and many computer statistical packages have been programmed to calculate and print them routinely.

Cramér's *V*      Probably the most useful (and most often used) of the measures is **Cramér's** *V*. It is given by the formula

$$V = \sqrt{\frac{\text{chi-square}}{m\mathbf{N}}}$$

where chi-square = value of chi-square calculated for the contingency table, $m$ = (number of rows in the table − 1) or (number of columns in the table − 1) whichever is smaller, and $\mathbf{N}$ = size of sample. Although the formula may seem complicated, it is easy to calculate Cramér's *V*, and we do so now for the cross-tabulation in Table 14.1.

**STEP 1**    Calculate the value of chi-square for the cross-tabulation. For the data in Table 14.1, the value of chi-square is 89.20 (Table 14.2 shows the calculations).

**STEP 2**    Calculate *m*. Determine which is smaller, the number of rows or the number of columns in the cross-tabulation, and subtract 1 from this number. Because Table 14.1 has the same number of rows as columns (3), this choice does not matter in the present example. Subtracting 1 from 3 yields a difference of 2, which is the value of *m*.

**STEP 3**   The remainder of the formula indicates that we must multiply $m$ times $N$, divide chi-square (from Step 1) by this product, and take the square root of the result. In this example, $m = 2$ and $N = 400$, so $m \times N = 2 \times 400 = 800$. Dividing chi-square (89.20) by this product $= 89.20 \div 800 = 0.1115$; taking the square root of $0.1115 = 0.33$, which is the value of Cramér's $V$ for Table 14.1.

Like all measures of association for nominal level variables, Cramér's $V$ is always positive (remember that direction of relationship has no meaning for nominal data). The measure ranges from 0.0, indicating no relationship between variables, to 1.0, indicating a perfect relationship.

## USE OF NOMINAL MEASURES OF ASSOCIATION WITH ORDINAL DATA

For the analysis of relationships between variables measured at the ordinal level, researchers generally use ordinal measures of association. However, if the analyst anticipates that the relationship is not one of covariation but of predictability, a nominal measure of association such as lambda can be employed. For example, one might hypothesize that, because jobs at the bottom of the organizational hierarchy tend to be low paying and those at the top tend to be quite stressful, middle-level officials may have the highest level of job satisfaction. An empirical example is presented in Table 14.11.

**TABLE 14.11**
Percentaged Cross-Tabulation of Hierarchy and Job Satisfaction

| Job Satisfaction | Hierarchy | | |
|---|---|---|---|
| | *Low* | *Middle* | *High* |
| Low | 75% | 10% | 20% |
| Medium | 15% | 10% | 70% |
| High | 10% | 80% | 10% |
| Total | 100% | 100% | 100% |
| | ($n = 200$) | ($n = 200$) | ($n = 200$) |

Because the cross-tabulation in Table 14.11 does not demonstrate a consistent pattern of increase in job satisfaction (dependent variable) with an increase in hierarchy (independent variable), the value of an ordinal measure of association predicated on the covariation logic will be small. In contrast, since job satisfaction is highly predictable based on the categories of hierarchy, the value of lambda will be large. Whether a researcher would consider these variables strongly related depends on the underlying substantive hypothesis.

## MEASURES OF ASSOCIATION FOR LARGER TABLES

We have illustrated the calculation and interpretation of measures of association for contingency tables with two rows and two columns, so-called 2-by-2 tables. The interpretation of the measures of association for larger tables is analogous, but the calculation is much more involved. Here we illustrate the calculation of gamma and lambda for the 3-by-3 cross-tabulation in Table 14.11. This example will show how useful it can be to apply different measures of association to a contingency table.

To begin, because measures of association are calculated from the raw frequencies rather than from percentaged data, we must convert the percentages in Table 14.11 to frequencies. Table 14.12 shows the result.

As explained before, *gamma* is based on the number of concordant pairs of cases versus the number of discordant pairs in the table; the concordant pairs demonstrate support for a positive relationship, whereas the discordant pairs show support for a negative relationship. To find the number of concordant pairs, work through the table, moving downward and to the right simultaneously. Begin with the cell in the top row and left column of the table. All table cells both below and to the right of this cell form concordant pairs with it. Four cells satisfy this condition: the middle-row–middle-column cell of the table, the middle-row–right-column cell, the bottom-row–middle-column cell, and the bottom-row–right-column cell. Sum the frequencies of the four cells (20 + 140 + 160 + 20 = 340); multiply the result by the frequency in the top-row–left-column cell (150). This multiplication gives the number of concordant pairs that can be formed with the top-row–left-column cell, 150 × 340 = 51,000 pairs [see part (a) of Figure 14.1].

**TABLE 14.12**
Cross-Tabulation of Hierarchy and Job Satisfaction (Frequencies)

| Job Satisfaction | Hierarchy | | | |
|---|---|---|---|---|
| | *Low* | *Medium* | *High* | *Total* |
| Low | 150 | 20 | 40 | 210 |
| Medium | 30 | 20 | 140 | 190 |
| High | 20 | 160 | 20 | 200 |
| Total | 200 | 200 | 200 | 600 |

Move to the top-row–middle-column cell of the table. Cells forming concordant pairs are again down and to the right: the middle-row–right-column cell and the bottom-row–right-column cell. Sum the frequencies in these two cells (140 + 20 = 160) and multiply by the frequency in the top-row–middle-column cell (20). This multiplication gives the number of concordant pairs that can be formed with the top-row–middle-column cell, 20 × 160 = 3200 pairs [see part (b) of Figure 14.1].

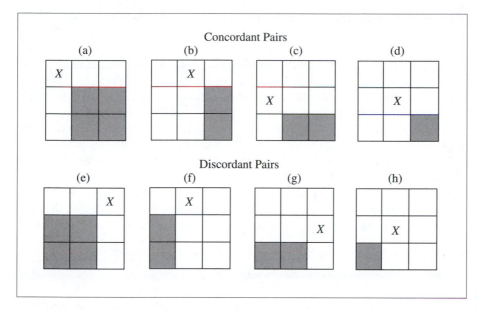

**FIGURE 14.1**

Concordant and Discordant Pairs

Since no table cells are *both* to the right and below the top-row–right-column cell of the table, it forms no concordant pairs. Instead, move to the middle-row–left-column cell of the table. Concordant pairs are formed with the cells below and to the right: the bottom-row–middle-column cell and the bottom-row–right-column cell. Sum these two cell frequencies ($160 + 20 = 180$) and multiply by the frequency in the middle-row–left-column cell (30). This multiplication gives the number of concordant pairs that can be formed with this cell, $30 \times 180 = 5400$ pairs [see part (c) of Figure 14.1].

Move to the middle-row–middle-column cell of the table. With which cells does it form concordant pairs? Just one—the bottom-row–right-column cell. Multiply the two cell frequencies to find the number of concordant pairs, $20 \times 20 = 400$ [see part (d) of Figure 14.1].

You may not realize it, but you have now found all concordant pairs in the table. Because no table cell is *both* below and to the right of the middle-row–right-column cell, no concordant pairs can be formed with it. Similarly, since no table cell is both below and to the right of the cells in the bottom row of the table, no concordant pairs can be formed with any of them. The total number of concordant pairs is equal to the sum of the four sets of concordant pairs that we have calculated: $51,000 + 3200 + 5400 + 400 = 60,000$.

To find the number of discordant pairs, the procedure is analogous to that for concordant pairs, except that you must start with the top-row–right-column cell of the table and move downward and to the left simultaneously to form the pairs. Parts (e) through (f) of Figure 14.1 show the procedure schematically. To begin, multiply the frequency in the top-row–right-column cell (40) by the sum of the frequencies in the cells both below and to the left $(20 + 30 + 160 + 20 = 230)$, yielding 9200 pairs. Move to the top-row–middle-column cell; multiply this frequency (20) by the sum of the frequencies in the cells both below and to the left $(30 + 20 = 50)$, giving 1000 pairs. Move to the middle-row–right-column cell of the table, and multiply this frequency (140) by the sum of the cell frequencies below and to the right $(160 + 20 = 180)$, yielding 25,200 pairs. Finally, the discordant pairs for the middle-row–middle-column cell are formed with the bottom-row–left-column cell only; multiplying the relevant cell frequencies yields $20 \times 20 = 400$ pairs. The total number of discordant pairs in the contingency table is the sum of these four sets of pairs: $9200 + 1000 + 25,200 + 400 = 35,800$ pairs.

Recall that gamma is equal to the difference between the number of concordant pairs and the number of discordant pairs in the contingency table, divided by their sum. Thus, for the cross-tabulation in Table 14.12, gamma is equal to

$$\frac{60,000 - 35,800}{60,000 + 35,800} = \frac{24,200}{95,800} = .25$$

The gamma value suggests a modest degree of covariation or relationship between the level in the hierarchy and job satisfaction.

Note how important it is to set up a table in the standard format displayed in Table 13.15 in Chapter 13. Had the ordering of the categories for either variable in the contingency table been reversed, concordant pairs would have been misidentified as discordant pairs, and vice versa. For calculating measures of association, whether by hand or by computer, the presumption is that the table has been set up in the standard format.

*Lambda* is a measure of association for nominal or higher levels of measurement that is based on the ability to predict values of the dependent variable. Lambda is a proportional reduction in error statistic: The formula for lambda indicates that we must (1) determine the number of errors in predicting the value of the dependent variable without knowledge of the independent variable, (2) subtract from this number the number of errors that we would make with knowledge of the independent variable to inform our predictions, and (3) see by what proportion the errors in predicting values of the dependent variable are reduced by introducing knowledge of the independent variable.

In Table 14.12, which category of job satisfaction would you predict that most employees have, if you did not know their level in the organizational hierarchy? Your best guess is low job satisfaction, because more employees gave this response than any other (210). You would make the correct prediction for these 210 employees, but you would be incorrect in making this prediction for employees with medium satisfaction (190) or high satisfaction (200). In all, you would make a total of $190 + 200 = 390$ errors in predicting values of the dependent variable if you do not consider employees' position in the organizational hierarchy (the independent variable).

Now, introduce knowledge of the independent variable. For each category of hierarchy, select the category of the dependent variable that will minimize the number of errors in predicting employee job satisfaction. For employees who are low in the organizational hierarchy, what is your best guess of their level of job satisfaction? You should guess low satisfaction, because most employees low in the hierarchy gave this response (150). You would be correct in predicting the job satisfaction of these 150 employees, but you would make errors in prediction for the 30 employees low in the hierarchy who have medium job satisfaction, and for the 20 who have high satisfaction—a total of 50 errors in prediction.

Which category of job satisfaction yields the fewest errors in prediction for the employees in the middle ranks of the organizational hierarchy? The best prediction is high job satisfaction. This prediction would be correct for 160 of the employees in the middle ranks, but it would be in error for the 20 employees with medium job satisfaction and for the 20 with low satisfaction in the middle of the hierarchy—a total of 40 errors.

Finally, for employees high in the organizational hierarchy, the best prediction of job satisfaction is medium. The prediction is correct for 140 employees, but in error for 60 employees—the 40 with low job satisfaction and the 20 with high satisfaction in this category of hierarchy. In all, then, given knowledge of employees' standing in the organizational hierarchy (the independent variable), the total number of errors in predicting job satisfaction is 50 + 40 + 60 = 150.

Lambda evaluates how much prediction of the dependent variable has improved by introducing knowledge of the independent variable. In this example, we began with 390 errors in predicting employees' levels of job satisfaction, absent knowledge of their position in the organizational hierarchy. Introducing this knowledge, we made only 150 errors in prediction. By what proportion has our prediction been improved? The formula for lambda provides the answer:

$$\frac{390 - 150}{390} = \frac{240}{390} = .62$$

The value of lambda suggests a much stronger relationship between hierarchy and job satisfaction than does gamma (.25). Because the percentaged cross-tabulation (Table 14.11) does not reveal a consistent pattern of increase or decrease in employee job satisfaction across levels of the organizational hierarchy, measures of association based on covariation—such as gamma—will be small (Kendall's *tau* and Somers' *d* would have been even smaller). By contrast, this relationship has high predictability, the model of association tapped by lambda. Given knowledge of employees' position in the organizational hierarchy, job satisfaction can be predicted very well. As this example shows, a good strategy with table analysis is to use and interpret not only the percentaged cross-tabulation, but also several measures of association.

## CHAPTER SUMMARY

This chapter introduces three aids for interpreting contingency tables. The chi-square test is a significance test that determines whether a distribution could have occurred by chance. It involves three steps. First, compute expected frequencies for each cell of the cross-tabulation based on the null hypothesis that the variables are not related. Second, compute the value of chi-square for the cross-tabulation. Finally, compare the value of the computed chi-square with an appropriate value in the chi-square table of theoretical values, and evaluate the result.

The strength of a relationship can be assessed by using percentage differences. The strength will range from a perfect relationship (percentage differences of 100) to a null relationship (percentage differences of 0).

Measures of association are single statistics used to determine the extent and direction of a relationship between two variables in a contingency table. Gamma, which uses paired observations, is a measure of association for ordinal data. It indicates the relative support in the contingency table for a positive, as opposed to a negative, relationship between two variables. Related measures of association for ordinal-level variables are Kendall's *tau-b* and *tau-c*, and Somers' $d_{yx}$ and $d_{xy}$.

Models of predictive association are used for nominal-level data. Lambda is a measure of association for nominal-level data. Lambda evaluates the extent to which prediction of the dependent variable is improved when the value of the independent variable is taken into account. Cramér's $V$ is another measure of association for nominal-level variables.

# PROBLEMS

**14.1**  The police chief wants to know if the city's blacks feel that the police are doing a good job. In comparison to whites' evaluations, this information will tell the police if they have a community relations problem in the black community. A survey reveals the data in the accompanying table. What can you tell the police chief? Base your statements on what you have learned in this chapter.

| Attitude Toward Police | Race | | |
|---|---|---|---|
| | *Black* | *White* | *Total* |
| Police do not do good job | 76 | 73 | 149 |
| Police do good job | 74 | 223 | 297 |
| Total | 150 | 296 | 446 |

**14.2**  For the competence-hierarchy example discussed earlier in the chapter, percentage the accompanying table and calculate gamma. Discuss the relationship between competence and level of organizational hierarchy.

| Hierarchy | Competence | | | |
|---|---|---|---|---|
| | *Low* | *Medium* | *High* | *Total* |
| Low | 113 | 60 | 27 | 200 |
| Medium | 31 | 91 | 38 | 160 |
| High | 8 | 8 | 24 | 40 |
| Total | 152 | 159 | 89 | 400 |

**14.3** Compute the value of chi-square for the data in the accompanying table, and percentage the cross-tabulation. From these data, would you say that the relationship between proximity of residence to hospital and the frequency of visits to the hospital for care is weak or strong? Explain your answer.

| Frequency of Visits | Proximity to Hospital | | |
|---|---|---|---|
| | *Close* | *Medium* | *Far* |
| Low | 1000 | 1030 | 1050 |
| Medium | 525 | 520 | 515 |
| High | 475 | 450 | 435 |

**14.4** Two scholars are locked in debate regarding the interpretation of the accompanying data. One insists that the relationship between the age of a child and the child's perception of the parents is very strong; the other argues that no relationship exists. Why do the two scholars reach different conclusions? Analyze the table and resolve the dilemma. Is there a relationship between the age of a child and the child's perception of the parents?

| Child's Perception of Parents | Age of Child (Years) | | |
|---|---|---|---|
| | *5–15* | *16–27* | *28 and Older* |
| Negative | 11% | 53% | 23% |
| Neutral | 18% | 27% | 59% |
| Positive | 71% | 20% | 18% |
| Total | 100% | 100% | 100% |

**14.5** Devise a hypothesis of interest to you. Using percentages, construct cross-tabulations that show (a) perfect support for the hypothesis, and (b) no support for the hypothesis. Construct three additional tables that show (c) strong, (d) medium, and (e) weak support for the hypothesis. After you have constructed the percentaged tables, make up marginal frequencies for each category of the independent variable and convert the percentages in the table cells to frequencies.

**14.6** The city parks commission has decided to redevelop a community park. Some members of the commission feel that refurbishment of existing park facilities is sufficient to meet the needs of the community and, therefore, they advocate minimal redevelopment. Other members feel that such a small-scale project is pointless. They contend that improvement of the park will create greater public satisfaction with the park and, thus, will draw many more people than use it presently. An increase in patrons could exhaust existing facilities, thus necessitating further redevelopment. To resolve this disagreement, the commission hires a consultant to conduct a survey of community opinion. Among the questions asked are these: Do you regularly use the park? Do you consider park facilities satisfactory or unsatisfactory? From the cross-tabulation of these questions presented in the accompanying table, what should the consultant recommend to the commission?

| Use Park | Park Facilities | | |
|---|---|---|---|
| | *Unsatisfactory* | *Satisfactory* | *Total* |
| No | 401 | 107 | 508 |
| Yes | 180 | 50 | 230 |
| Total | 581 | 157 | 738 |

**14.7** The director of the state department of motor vehicles is concerned about the high level of employee dissatisfaction in the department. To alleviate this problem, he hires a statistical analyst to investigate the attitudes of employees. The analyst believes that the primary source of dissatisfaction is the type of job held by the employee—hourly wage or salary. To test this hypothesis, she obtains data pertaining to whether the employee is paid hourly or is salaried and whether he or she is satisfied or dissatisfied with the job. These data are cross-tabulated in the accompanying table. Percentage the table and calculate gamma. Is there a relationship between type of job and job satisfaction?

| Attitude Toward Job | Type of Job | | |
|---|---|---|---|
| | *Hourly* | *Salary* | *Total* |
| Dissatisfied | 194 | 54 | 248 |
| Satisfied | 278 | 85 | 363 |
| Total | 472 | 139 | 611 |

**14.8** The data analyst from Problem 14.7 also obtained information regarding whether the employee was on a standard eight-hour shift or on flextime. The cross-tabulation between these two variables appears below. Percentage the table and calculate gamma. Is there a relationship between the employment status of employees (shift versus flextime) and job satisfaction?

| Attitude Toward Job | Employment Status | | Total |
|---|---|---|---|
| | *Shift* | *Flextime* | *Total* |
| Dissatisfied | 194 | 55 | 249 |
| Satisfied | 186 | 176 | 362 |
| Total | 380 | 231 | 611 |

**14.9**  The personnel department of a small city has compiled the accompanying data regarding city employees. The data consist of the age of employees and the probability of their receiving a job promotion. On the basis of these data, how should the department advise job applicants who seek employment with the city?

| Probability of Promotion | Age | | |
|---|---|---|---|
| | *30 or Less* | *31–50* | *51 or Greater* |
| Low | 17% | 9% | 65% |
| Medium | 56% | 15% | 22% |
| High | 27% | 76% | 13% |
| Total | 100% | 100% | 100% |

**14.10**  A Ph.D. student in public administration has studied the relationship between the quality of municipal bureaucracy and the economic development of cities. She hypothesizes that the higher the quality of the city bureaucracy (as measured by such factors as innovativeness, efficiency, and responsiveness), the greater the economic development. By this hypothesis, she assumes that bureaucratic quality leads to economic development. In order to test this hypothesis, she sent out questionnaires to a random sample of 120 cities with a population between 50,000 and 100,000. Based on these data, she assembles the accompanying cross-tabulation.

| Bureaucratic Quality | Economic Development | | |
|---|---|---|---|
| | *Low* | *Medium* | *High* |
| High | 6 | 8 | 16 |
| Medium | 12 | 16 | 22 |
| Low | 16 | 14 | 10 |

Reorganize this table into the standard format. Percentage the table and calculate gamma. Is there a relationship between bureaucratic quality and economic development?

**14.11** In her dissertation, the Ph.D. student from Problem 14.10 writes that the relationship between the quality of a municipal bureaucracy and the economic development of a city is causal, that is, that higher quality bueaucracy leads to higher economic development. Evaluate her claim of causality. What conditions would have to be met in order to establish that this relationship is causal? Does the cross-tabulation between the two variables (presented in standard format) bear on the question of causality? How? Explain your answer. (Hint: See Chapter 8.)

**14.12** Paul Sabatier, a human relations theorist working for Warm and Fuzzy, Inc., believes that workers who work in cooperatives are more satisfied than workers who do not. He surveys 50 cab drivers who work in cooperatives and 30 cab drivers who do not work in cooperatives. All are asked whether they are satisfied with their job. From the data in the accompanying table, calculate the percentage difference, gamma, lambda, and chi-square. What do you conclude?

| Job Satisfaction | Type of Organization | |
|---|---|---|
| | *Noncooperative* | *Cooperative* |
| Not satisfied | 13 | 29 |
| Satisfied | 17 | 21 |

**14.13** Organizational analyst Paula McClain is examining the Peter Principle, which contends that people will rise in an organization until they reach their level of incompetence. She feels that this means that proportionately more competent people will be found at the lower level of the organization. To test this question, she decides to ask students to rate assistant professors, associate professors, and full professors; based on these ratings, she classified the competence of professors as high, medium, or low (deans are excluded to avoid biasing the results). Interpret the accompanying table; calculate any necessary statistics.

| Competence | Academic Rank | | | |
|---|---|---|---|---|
| | *Assistant* | *Associate* | *Full* | *Total* |
| Low | 27 | 38 | 24 | 89 |
| Medium | 60 | 91 | 8 | 159 |
| High | 106 | 38 | 8 | 152 |
| Total | 193 | 167 | 40 | 400 |

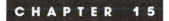

## CHAPTER 15

# STATISTICAL

# CONTROL TABLE

# ANALYSIS

The previous two chapters have discussed methods for examining the relationship between two variables measured at either the ordinal or the nominal level. In that discussion, when a pair of variables were found to be associated statistically, we inevitably assumed that they were in fact related, in the sense that changes in one could be expected to lead to changes in the other. Conversely, when the variables were not associated statistically, we assumed that the opposite was true.

Unfortunately for the data analyst, this is not always a correct assumption. A simple example should persuade you how this assumption can lead you astray.

Suppose that you are a staff analyst working for the police department of a fairly large community. The mayor is concerned with a recent upsurge in juvenile crime and asks that you prepare a report advising him how the increase in crime may be combated. In researching the issue, you discover an interesting phenomenon. In those precincts of the city in which ice-cream consumption is high, the rate of juvenile crime is low; and in the precincts in which consumption is low, juvenile crime reaches high levels. Thus, across the precincts of the city, the higher the ice-cream consumption, the lower is the rate of juvenile crime. As Table 15.1 shows, according to any measure of association, this relationship is strong.

Using these data, should you advise the mayor that you have found the answer to the crime problem—to subsidize the sale of ice cream so that it may be offered at bargain prices to the rampaging juvenile hordes? Is satisfying their hunger for ice cream likely to appease their appetite for more costly antisocial behavior? After all, the data indicate that ice-cream consumption and juvenile crime are strongly associated inversely.

Even though Table 15.1 would seem to support this policy response, somehow the proposed solution does not sit well. You would probably feel more than

**TABLE 15.1**

Relationship Between Juvenile Crime and Ice-Cream Consumption

| Rate of Juvenile Crime | Ice-Cream Consumption | |
|---|---|---|
| | *Low* | *High* |
| Low | 25% | 80% |
| High | 75% | 20% |
| Total | 100% | 100% |
| | ($n$ = 20 precincts) | ($n$ = 25 precincts) |

a little silly—not to mention fearful for your job—were you to inform the mayor that a scoop of chocolate (or perhaps rocky road or vanilla) is the answer to the problem of juvenile crime. But if ice cream is not the answer, then what is? And why are ice-cream consumption and juvenile crime rates associated statistically, when in fact one almost certainly has nothing whatever to do with the other?

The answers to these two questions are interrelated. First, one variable that may bear on the rate of juvenile crime is the socioeconomic status (SES) of the precincts across the city. SES is a social science concept intended to assess the social status of a precinct based on the income, education, and occupational prestige of its residents (SES can also be measured at the level of individual respondents). For a number of reasons (such as stable home life, access to better education and job opportunities), juveniles living in high-SES precincts—those in which income, education, and occupational status are high—commit fewer crimes than do their peers living in less fortunate circumstances in low-SES precincts. As for the second question, since in high-SES precincts parents and children have more money to purchase ice cream than do their counterparts living in low-SES precincts, ice-cream consumption is higher in the former areas than in the latter. Note the circumstance created by these two relationships. In high-SES precincts, youths both eat more ice cream *and* commit fewer crimes than do youths living in low-SES precincts. Thus, because of the relationship of each variable to the SES of the precinct, ice-cream consumption and the rate of juvenile crime *appear* to be related, when in fact they are quite independent of one another. These relationships can be depicted graphically:

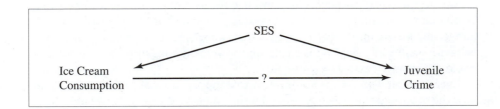

The type of reasoning illustrated in this example is typical of the data analysis process. The analyst finds that two variables are associated statistically (ice-cream consumption and juvenile crime). She then tries to understand *why* the variables are associated. (Recall from Chapter 8 how important theory—a meaningful substantive explanation—is to understanding and interpreting a statistical relationship.) Are the two variables actually related in the sense that changes in one are likely to produce changes in the other, or is their apparent relationship attributable to the action of a *third* variable (SES of the precinct)? To address this question, the researcher must introduce the third variable explicitly into the analysis. She then reexamines the relationship between the original two variables, taking into account the effect of the third variable. The technique used to incorporate a third variable into the analysis is called *controlling for* or *holding constant* the third variable (controlling for SES or holding constant SES), or more simply, **statistical controls**.

This chapter elaborates statistical control techniques for the analysis of relationships between three or more variables measured at the ordinal or nominal levels. The chapter both explains the use of these techniques and illustrates several likely results of introducing a third variable into the examination of a two-variable relationship. Different possible results are illustrated in a series of examples.

**statistical controls**

# Controlling for
## a Third Variable

The procedure by which the researcher controls for the effect of a third variable on a bivariate relationship is deceptively simple. *He or she examines the relationship between the original two variables within each of the categories of the control variable and compares the results across the categories of the control.* The examples that follow illustrate the procedure.

### EXAMPLE 1: ALCOHOLISM IN THE POSTAL SERVICE—THE EFFECT OF HIERARCHICAL POSITION

The Post Office Department has become alarmed by recent unsubstantiated reports from employees that the pressures of the workplace, such as large volumes of mail and very short time deadlines, contribute to alcoholism. The Post Office Department has commissioned a (Pabst) blue ribbon panel to investigate the problem. The panel collected data from post office employees working in offices in Ripple, Montana; Thunderbird, New Mexico; and Gallo, Mississippi.

As a first step the panel hypothesized a positive relationship between position of the employee in the Post Office hierarchy and rate of alcoholism. They reasoned that those holding supervisory positions were under greater pressure than those holding nonsupervisory jobs and, therefore, would be more likely to turn to alcohol to relieve tensions of work. The measure of alcoholism used by the study team is called the Harris Test. The test identifies with 95% accuracy whether the respondent is an alcoholic or a nonalcoholic. The relationship between hierarchical position (nonsupervisor, supervisor) and alcoholism (alcoholic, nonalcoholic) found by the study team is displayed in Table 15.2 in both raw (nonpercentaged) and percentaged form.

**TABLE 15.2**

Relationship Between Hierarchy and Alcoholism

| Raw Data | | | |
|---|---|---|---|
| Alcoholism | Hierarchy | | |
| | *Nonsupervisor* | *Supervisor* | *Total* |
| Nonalcoholic | 115 | 60 | 175 |
| Alcoholic | 5 | 20 | 25 |
| Total | 120 | 80 | 200 |

| Percentaged Data | | |
|---|---|---|
| Alcoholism | Hierarchy | |
| | *Nonsupervisor* | *Supervisor* |
| Nonalcoholic | 96% | 75% |
| Alcoholic | 4% | 25% |
| Total | 100% | 100% |
| | ($n = 120$) | ($n = 80$) |

Since the table shows that supervisors are more likely than are nonsupervisors to be alcoholics by 21% (25% − 4%), most members of the panel feel that these data offer support for the hypothesis that hierarchical position is related to alcoholism. However, one investigator is not convinced. He maintains that it is not hierarchical position at all that leads Post Office employees to drink; rather, it is whether they are made to operate the ziptronic machine—a demonic device that puts high stress on the operator to identify zip codes printed on letters at an extremely rapid rate. Because supervisors operate the ziptronic more frequently than do nonsupervisors, he argues that it only appears that hierarchical position leads to alcoholism. In fact, if one were to control for the effects of operating the ziptronic, one would find no relationship between hierarchy and alcoholism. His argument can be depicted graphically:

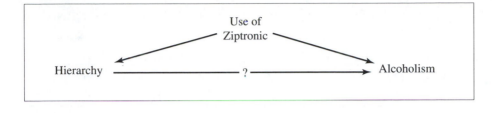

There are three major steps in the statistical control process.

**STEP 1**    Partition the sample according to the categories of the control variable. In the present example, 90 postal employees have operated the ziptronic and the remaining 110 have not.

**STEP 2**    Prepare the cross-tabulation between the original two variables for each of the subsamples defined by the control variable in Step 1. Percentage each of these tables separately (refer to Chapter 13 if you do not recall how to percentage a table). In this example, the researcher would construct two distinct cross-tabulations between hierarchical position and alcoholism: one for those employees who have operated the ziptronic, and the second for those who have not operated the ziptronic. Table 15.3 presents the results obtained according to this procedure for the Post Office data. Both the nonpercentaged and the percentaged cross-tabulations are displayed in the table.

It is important to recognize that the data presented in Table 15.3 are simply an *elaboration* of the cross-tabulation displayed in Table 15.2. Table 15.3 shows how the sample of 200 postal employees is distributed with respect to operation of the ziptronic (have operated the ziptronic, have not operated the ziptronic). For example, Table 15.2 shows that, in all, there are 175 nonalcoholics in the sample; Table 15.3 indicates that 74 of these employees have operated the ziptronic and the remaining 101 have not. Similarly, of the total of 25 alcoholics in the sample (Table 15.2), 16 have operated the ziptronic and 9 have not (Table 15.3). With respect to hierarchical position, of the total of 120 nonsupervisors in the sample (Table 15.2), 30 have operated the ziptronic whereas the other 90 have not (Table 15.3). Finally, of the 80 supervisors in the sample (Table 15.2), 60 have operated the ziptronic and the remaining 20 have not (Table 15.3).

Because Table 15.3 elaborates the original cross-tabulation presented in Table 15.2, this research method is sometimes called the *elaboration model*. Make sure that you can follow the correspondences relating the two tables outlined in the previous paragraph. You should

**TABLE 15.3**

Cross-Tabulation of Subsamples

| | | Raw Data | | | | | | |
|---|---|---|---|---|---|---|---|---|

**Employees Who Have Operated Ziptronic** $(n = 90)$ | | | Employees Who Have Not Operated Ziptronic $(n = 110)$

| Alcoholism | Hierarchy | | | Alcoholism | Hierarchy | | |
|---|---|---|---|---|---|---|---|
| | Non-super-visor | Super-visor | Total | | Non-super-visor | Super-visor | Total |
| Nonalcoholic | 29 | 45 | 74 | Nonalcoholic | 86 | 15 | 101 |
| Alcoholic | 1 | 15 | 16 | Alcoholic | 4 | 5 | 9 |
| Total | 30 | 60 | 90 | Total | 90 | 20 | 110 |

Percentaged Data

| Alcoholism | Hierarchy | | Alcoholism | Hierarchy | |
|---|---|---|---|---|---|
| | Nonsupervisor | Supervisor | | Nonsupervisor | Supervisor |
| Nonalcoholic | 96% | 75% | Nonalcoholic | 96% | 75% |
| Alcoholic | 4% | 25% | Alcoholic | 4% | 25% |
| Total | 100% | 100% | Total | 100% | 100% |
| | $(n = 30)$ | $(n = 60)$ | | $(n = 90)$ | $(n = 20)$ |

be able to see that the figures displayed in the cross-tabulations of Table 15.3 are perfectly consistent with those of Table 15.2.

**STEP 3**    Interpret the cross-tabulations obtained for each of the categories of the control variable. This step is by far the most difficult in the statistical control procedure, but a modicum of reasoning will greatly simplify matters.

Consider the argument made by the investigator on the study team who introduced the issue of the ziptronic machines. If he is correct in his hypothesis that operating the ziptronic (rather than hierarchical position) is the actual cause of alcoholism among postal employees, then once the effect of the ziptronic has been taken into account, hierarchical position should make no difference in the rate of alcoholism. Another way of stating this conclusion is that, within the categories of the control variable (have operated the ziptronic, have not operated the ziptronic), one should find the same rate of alcoholism for supervisors and nonsupervisors. In other words, supervisory and nonsupervisory personnel who have operated the ziptronic *should not differ* in rate of alcoholism. Similarly, supervisors and nonsupervisors who have operated the ziptronic also should not differ in rate of alcoholism. These data would indicate that after taking into account (controlling for) the effect of operating the ziptronic, hierarchical position bears no relationship to the rate of alcoholism.

This logic encapsulates one side of the picture. The expectation is that operating the ziptronic machine, rather than hierarchical position, is the actual cause of alcoholism among postal employees. What would one expect to find if the *opposite* is the case—that hierarchical position, rather than operation of the ziptronic, causes alcoholism? Since the operation of the ziptronic is not related to alcoholism, then one would expect to find the same relationship between hierarchical position and alcoholism as displayed in the original cross-tabulation (Table 15.2)— regardless of whether the employees have operated the ziptronic machine. Operationally, in each of the control tables (the separate tables cross-tabulating hierarchical position and alcoholism within each category of the control variable, operation of the ziptronic—Table 15.3), one should find that the relationship between hierarchical position and alcoholism is identical to that found in Table 15.2. These data would indicate that even when the effect of operating the ziptronic has been taken into account, hierarchical position and alcoholism remain related.

These two data expectations outline polar explanations for the causes of alcoholism among Post Office personnel. According to the first, if operation of the ziptronic machine (rather than hierarchical position) is the actual cause of alcoholism, then when the effect of operating the ziptronic is taken into account, the original relationship between hierarchy and alcoholism should disappear. That is, when use of the ziptronic is considered, hierarchical position is found to make no difference in the rate of alcoholism. According to the second, if hierarchical position (rather than operation of the ziptronic machine) is the actual cause of alcoholism, then when the effect of operating the ziptronic is taken into account, the original relationship between hierarchy and alcoholism should persist. Therefore, even when use of the ziptronic is considered, hierarchy continues to make a difference in the rate of alcoholism.

With these expectations in mind, we can interpret the data displayed in Table 15.3. To which polar situation do the percentaged cross-tabulations more closely correspond? These data show overwhelming support for the second explanation. When the effects of operation of the ziptronic have been controlled, hierarchical position is related to alcoholism in exactly the same manner as in the original, uncontrolled cross-tabulation in Table 15.2. Regardless of whether they have used the ziptronic machines, 25% of the supervisors are alcoholics, as compared with only 4% of the nonsupervisors, a difference of 21%. Since the relationship between hierarchy and the rate of alcoholism is unaffected by the introduction of the ziptronic variable into the analysis, these data lend support to the conclusion that hierarchical position (rather than operation of the ziptronic) is a cause of alcoholism among postal employees. This finding offers some evidence of a nonspurious relationship between these two variables (see Chapter 8).

## EXAMPLE 2: PERFORMANCE ON THE CIVIL SERVICE EXAMINATION—DOES RACE MAKE A DIFFERENCE?

The Civil Service Commission has become concerned about charges that its examination discriminates against minorities, particularly blacks. To examine these charges, a staff analyst obtains data from a random sample of 335 applicants. Table 15.4 displays the cross-tabulation between race (black, white) and performance on the examination (no pass, pass) for these individuals.

**TABLE 15.4**

Relationship Between Test Performance and Race

| Raw Data | | | |
|---|---|---|---|
| Test Performance | Race | | |
| | Black | White | Total |
| No pass | 70 | 70 | 140 |
| Pass | 60 | 135 | 195 |
| Total | 130 | 205 | 335 |

| Percentaged Data | | |
|---|---|---|
| Test Performance | Race | |
| | Black | White |
| No pass | 54% | 34% |
| Pass | 46% | 66% |
| Total | 100% | 100% |
| | (n = 130) | (n = 205) |

Naturally, the analyst is disturbed by these data. In this sample, blacks failed the civil service examination 20% more frequently than did whites (54% − 34%). However, the analyst suspects that a third variable may be affecting this relationship: *education.* She hypothesizes that education affects performance on the test; she feels that the only reason that whites appear to perform better than blacks do on the test is that they are more likely to have completed a college education and, of course, college-educated people are more likely to pass the examination. To test these ideas empirically, she intends to introduce education into the analysis. The anticipated relationships among the three variables are shown in the following diagram.

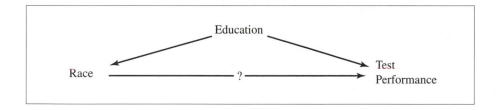

**STEP 1**  Partition the sample according to the categories of the control variable. In this example, education is the control variable and consists of two categories: those who are college graduates and those who are not. Of the 335 individuals in the sample, 200 are college graduates, and the remaining 135 are not.

**STEP 2**  Assemble the cross-tabulation between the original two variables for each of the subsamples defined by the control variable in Step 1. Percentage each of these tables separately according to the procedure outlined in Chapter 13. In the present instance, two cross-tabulations between race and test performance would be obtained: the first based on those individuals who are college graduates, and the second based on those individuals who are not. Table 15.5 displays the results obtained according to this procedure in the sample of civil service applicants.

You should satisfy yourself that the elaboration of Table 15.4 presented in the cross-tabulations of Table 15.5 is perfectly consistent with the original data.

**STEP 3**  Interpret the cross-tabulations obtained for each of the categories of the control variable. The logic of this process is precisely the same as that elaborated in the previous example (hierarchy-ziptronic-alcoholism).

If education (rather than race) is the actual cause of performance on the civil service examination, then when the effect of education is taken into account, the original relationship between race and test performance should disappear; that is, when the effect of education has been controlled, race should make no difference in test performance. Conversely, if race (rather than education) is the actual cause of performance on the examination, then when education is taken into account,

**TABLE 15.5**

Cross-Tabulation of Subsamples

| | Raw Data | | | | | | |
|---|---|---|---|---|---|---|---|
| | College Graduates ($n = 200$) | | | | Not College Graduates ($n = 135$) | | |
| Test Performance | Race | | | Test Performance | Race | | |
| | Black | White | Total | | Black | White | Total |
| No pass | 10 | 40 | 50 | No pass | 60 | 30 | 90 |
| Pass | 30 | 120 | 150 | Pass | 30 | 15 | 45 |
| Total | 40 | 160 | 200 | Total | 90 | 45 | 135 |

| | Percentaged Data | | | | | |
|---|---|---|---|---|---|---|
| Test Performance | Race | | Test Performance | Race | | |
| | Black | White | | Black | White | |
| No pass | 25% | 25% | No pass | 67% | 67% | |
| Pass | 75% | 75% | Pass | 33% | 33% | |
| Total | 100% | 100% | Total | 100% | 100% | |
| | ($n = 40$) | ($n = 160$) | | ($n = 90$) | ($n = 45$) | |

the original relationship found between race and test performance in Table 15.4 should persist; that is, even when the effect of education has been considered, race should continue to make a difference in performance on the civil service examination.

The percentaged cross-tabulations presented in Table 15.5 show that once education has been controlled, blacks and whites fail the civil service examination with equal frequency. Among the college graduates, 25% of both blacks and whites fail the exam; and among the noncollege graduates, 67% of both blacks and whites fail. Thus, since within the categories of education race makes no difference in test performance, these data warrant the conclusion that race and performance on the civil service examination are not related. (If they were related, one would expect that race would make a difference in test performance even when education was taken into account.)

Although race *appeared* to affect test performance in the original bivariate cross-tabulation (Table 15.4), the introduction of the control variable (education) made the relationship disappear. Thus, in this example, race is not a cause of test performance. Instead, race is a *spurious* variable—one that initially appears to be related to the dependent variable but whose effect vanishes in the presence of the control variable.

Table 15.5 also demonstrates that, regardless of race, the percentage of college graduates failing the examination (25%) is much smaller than the percentage of nongraduates who fail (67%). This finding indicates that it is *education* that leads to test performance. For both races, the higher the education, the better is the performance on the examination. The strength of this relationship can be seen in Table 15.6, which cross-tabulates education and performance on the civil service examination. This cross-tabulation is constructed from the control tables in Table 15.5. The relationship between education and test performance persists even when the effect of race has been controlled.

**TABLE 15.6**

Relationship between Education and Test Performance

|  | Raw Data | | |
|---|---|---|---|
| Test Performance | Education | | |
|  | *Not College Graduate* | *College Graduate* | *Total* |
| No pass | 90 | 50 | 140 |
| Pass | 45 | 150 | 195 |
| Total | 135 | 200 | 335 |
|  | Percentaged Data | | |
| Test Performance | Education | | |
|  | *Not College Graduate* | *College Graduate* | |
| No pass | 67% | 25% | |
| Pass | 33% | 75% | |
| Total | 100% | 100% | |
|  | ($n = 135$) | ($n = 200$) | |

## EXAMPLE 3: GUARANTEED ANNUAL INCOME— A CASE OF INTERACTION

The previous two examples have illustrated polar data analysis situations. In the first, introduction of a control variable (operation of the ziptronic) into the analysis had no effect on the original bivariate relationship (hierarchy versus alcoholism). In the second, the control variable (education) was totally responsible for the apparent—but not actual—relationship originally found between two variables (race and test performance).

A third situation that frequently occurs in the analysis of data is called *interaction* or *specification*. In this situation, the relationship between two variables changes markedly depending on the category of the control variable; that is, the categories of the control variable specify the nature of the relationship between the two variables.

There are several types of interactive relationships. For example, in one category of a control variable, there may be no relationship between two other variables of interest; whereas in the second category of the control, there may be a strong positive or negative relationship. As an illustration, consider the likely effect on personal assertiveness of attending feminist meetings, controlling for the sex of the individual. Among the women, one is likely to find a positive relationship between attending the meetings and personal assertiveness; however, among the men, one is likely to find no relationship.

In a second type of interaction, the relationship between two variables can change direction (positive to negative or vice versa) contingent on the category of the control variable. The following example elaborates a three-variable relationship of this kind.

The federal government has been experimenting with a guaranteed annual income program (GAI). Volatile policy debate centers around the effects of this federal largesse. When people are guaranteed an income, are they more likely to spend all the money or to save at least a portion of it? To examine the effects of GAI, a staff analyst is appointed. He assembles data from 200 individuals who have participated in GAI and a matching sample of 200 who have not.

His first concern is whether those who participated in the GAI were more likely to save money than those who did not. Therefore, he cross-tabulates participation in GAI (no, yes) with money saved during the program (no, yes). The results are presented in Table 15.7.

This table reveals no relationship between participation in the GAI program and saving behavior. Those who participated in the program were just as likely to save (or not save) money as those who did not. However, the analyst is curious about the effect on this relationship of the individual's past history of saving money. He believes that the ability to save money is learned over time; therefore, he reasons that those who have a past history of saving money will do so again under the GAI. Those who lack this history (or "learning") will fail in this pursuit once again. This hypothesis calls for the introduction of the saving history of the respondent (have saved in the past, have not saved in the past) into the analysis as a control variable. We omit detailed elaboration of the first two steps of the control procedure and simply present in Table 15.8 the two cross-tabulations obtained when this control variable is introduced. (If these steps remain unclear to you, review the first two examples developed in the chapter.)

**TABLE 15.7**

Relationship Between GAI and Saving Money

| | Raw Data | | |
|---|---|---|---|
| | Guaranteed Annual Income (GAI) | | |
| Saved Money | *No* | *Yes* | *Total* |
| No | 100 | 100 | 200 |
| Yes | 100 | 100 | 200 |
| Total | 200 | 200 | 400 |

| | Percentaged Data | |
|---|---|---|
| | Guaranteed Annual Income (GAI) | |
| Saved Money | *No* | *Yes* |
| No | 50% | 50% |
| Yes | 50% | 50% |
| Total | 100% | 100% |
| | (*n* = 200) | (*n* = 200) |

The control tables presented in Table 15.8 resemble neither of the polar situations developed in the first two examples. Instead, Table 15.8 shows that the past history of saving *specifies* the relationship between participation in the GAI program and saving money. Among the individuals who had a past history of saving money, participation in the program is related positively to saving. Note that program participants saved money more frequently over the period of the study than did nonparticipants. In the subsample of respondents with a past history of saving, 64% of participants in the GAI saved money, compared to 55% of the nonparticipants. These data suggest that for this subsample, the GAI encouraged and led to saving behavior.

In contrast, for those individuals who had no past history of saving money, participation in the GAI had exactly the opposite effect. In this subsample of respondents, participants in the program saved money less frequently than did nonparticipants, 33% versus 44%, a difference in saving behavior of 11%. Thus among those who had not saved money in the past, participation in the GAI is related negatively to saving during the period of the study. In this subsample, the GAI seemed to discourage saving behavior. In an interactive relationship such as this one, the control variable must be taken into account in order to understand the relationship between the independent and dependent variables.

This example is important not only because it demonstrates an interactive

**TABLE 15.8**

Cross-Tabulation of Subsamples

| | | | | | | | |
|---|---|---|---|---|---|---|---|
| | | | Raw | Data | | | |
| Have Saved in Past ($n = 220$) | | | | Have Not Saved in Past ($n = 180$) | | | |
| Saved Money | GAI | | | Saved Money | GAI | | |
| | *No* | *Yes* | *Total* | | *No* | *Yes* | *Total* |
| No | 50 | 40 | 90 | No | 50 | 60 | 110 |
| Yes | 60 | 70 | 130 | Yes | 40 | 30 | 70 |
| Total | 110 | 110 | 220 | Total | 90 | 90 | 180 |

| | | | | | | |
|---|---|---|---|---|---|---|
| | | Percentaged | Data | | | |
| Saved Money | GAI | | Saved Money | GAI | |
| | *No* | *Yes* | | *No* | *Yes* |
| No | 45% | 36% | No | 56% | 67% |
| Yes | 55% | 64% | Yes | 44% | 33% |
| Total | 100% | 100% | Total | 100% | 100% |
| | ($n = 110$) | ($n = 110$) | | ($n = 90$) | ($n = 90$) |

relationship, but also because it shows that a relationship between two variables may not be manifest *unless* a control variable is incorporated into the analysis. In the original, noncontrolled cross-tabulation displayed in Table 15.7, participation in the Guaranteed Annual Income program does *not* appear to be related to saving behavior. Participants in the program were just as likely to save (or not save) money as were nonparticipants. However, the controlled cross-tabulations presented in Table 15.8 indicate that, when the effect of past history of saving is considered, participation in the GAI is clearly related to saving behavior. Among individuals who had saved in the past, the GAI led to further saving; among those who had no past history of saving, just the opposite was true.

Thus, in data analysis, a cross-tabulation that reveals no relationship between two variables cannot ensure that the two variables are unrelated. As in this example, failure to take into account a control variable can suppress an actual relationship between two other variables. For this reason this type of situation is sometimes called a *suppressor* relationship. The converse is also true: A cross-tabulation that demonstrates a statistical association between two variables cannot ensure that the two variables are actually related. It was on this point that the chapter began. Whereas ice-cream consumption appeared to be related to juvenile crime, controlling for the socioeconomic status (SES) of the precinct will cause this relationship to disappear. In fact, SES—not ice-cream consumption—is a cause of juvenile crime. Ice-cream consumption only appeared to be related to crime, because individuals living in high-SES precincts are likely both to eat more ice cream and to commit fewer crimes than are those living in low-SES precincts. (Another example of such a spurious relationship was elaborated earlier, based on the relationships between race, education, and performance on the civil service examination.) It is these kinds of complexities that make data analysis exciting and frustrating at the same time.

## EXAMPLE 4: SUPPORT FOR PERFORMANCE-BASED PAY—EVIDENCE OF JOINT CAUSATION

The mayor of the city of Athenia has proposed to the city council that Athenia change compensation systems. As do many cities in the southeastern United States, Athenia determines employee pay primarily on the basis of years (seniority) in government service, in a grade-and-step system. The mayor believes that motivation and productivity of city workers would improve if Athenia were to shift to a performance-based pay system. Under the mayor's plan, supervisors would meet annually with individual employees to set performance goals; employees would be evaluated one year later on accomplishment of the objectives; and pay increases would be tied to the performance evaluation. The city council is impressed with the pay plan, but before taking action, it authorizes the mayor to conduct a study of employee reaction to the plan and to report back with the results.

The mayor appoints two top MPAs in her office, Megan Samantha and Philip Joseph, to carry out the study. Because performance-based pay is thought to increase employee morale—because employees have greater involvement in establishing work goals and can move up the pay ladder more quickly than in a grade-and-step system—the mayor expects to find strong support for her plan. Samantha and Joseph decide to survey a representative sample of 212 Athenia employees to ascertain their attitudes and opinions toward the mayor's proposal. They are surprised to find that only a bare majority of city workers, 52% ($n = 111$), favor the mayor's plan, whereas 48% ($n = 101$) oppose it. Good analysts that they are, Samantha and Joseph decide to undertake further study.

They believe that prior experience in the private sector may help to explain the results. Performance-based pay systems are much more common in private business than in government. Thus, Samantha and Joseph cross-tabulate support for performance-based pay (coded "no"/"yes") in the Athenia sample by whether the employee has had work experience in the private sector (also coded "no"/"yes"). They anticipate that city workers with a background in the private sector will be more favorable toward the new pay plan. Table 15.9 displays the cross-tabulation.

**TABLE 15.9**

Relationship Between Employee Experience in the Private Sector and Support for Performance-Based Pay

| | Raw Data | | |
|---|---|---|---|
| Support for Performance-Based Pay | Private Sector Experience | | |
| | *No* | *Yes* | *Total* |
| No | 55 | 46 | 101 |
| Yes | 50 | 61 | 111 |
| Total | 105 | 107 | 212 |

| | Percentaged Data | |
|---|---|---|
| Support for Performance-Based Pay | Private Sector Experience | |
| | *No* | *Yes* |
| No | 52% | 43% |
| Yes | 48% | 57% |
| Total | 100% | 100% |
| | ($n = 105$) | ($n = 107$) |

Just as Samantha and Joseph had expected, support for performance-based pay is higher by 9% for employees who have work experience in the private sector (57%) than for those who do not (48%). Still, the researchers would like to identify other factors that may account for the attitudes of Athenia workers and that would help them to devise a strategy for building employee acceptance.

One variable that occurs to them is job classification as either supervisory or nonsupervisory personnel. The mayor's pay plan would add to the burden on supervisors by giving them a larger role in setting goals for employees and, especially, in evaluating their performance. Although Athenia supervisory personnel already have evaluation responsibilities, according to city records, over 95% of the time, supervisors give employees performance ratings in the highest two categories. Samantha and Joseph would like to think that Athenia city government has a superior workforce—but they doubt that it's that good. Instead, they suspect that, since performance appraisal is not tied strongly to pay, it has become largely a pro forma exercise for supervisors and employees. By linking pay raises to performance, however, the mayor's plan could radically

**TABLE 15.10**

Cross-Tabulation of Subsamples

| | | | | Raw Data | | | | |
|---|---|---|---|---|---|---|---|---|
| | Supervisory Personnel (n = 40) | | | | Nonsupervisory Personnel (n = 172) | | | |
| Support for Performance-Based Pay | Private Sector Experience | | | | Support for Performance-Based Pay | Private Sector Experience | | |
| | *No* | *Yes* | *Total* | | | *No* | *Yes* | *Total* |
| No | 13 | 11 | 24 | | No | 42 | 35 | 77 |
| Yes | 7 | 9 | 16 | | Yes | 43 | 52 | 95 |
| Total | 20 | 20 | 40 | | Total | 85 | 87 | 172 |

| | | Percentaged Data | | | | |
|---|---|---|---|---|---|---|
| Support for Performance-Based Pay | Private Sector Experience | | | Support for Performance-Based Pay | Private Sector Experience | |
| | *No* | *Yes* | | | *No* | *Yes* |
| No | 65% | 55% | | No | 49% | 40% |
| Yes | 35% | 45% | | Yes | 51% | 60% |
| Total | 100% (n = 20) | 100% (n = 20) | | Total | 100% (n = 85) | 100% (n = 87) |

alter the nature of evaluation: not only would it increase the workload on supervisors, but also (with pay at stake) it could make the process more confrontational and open the door to much-dreaded litigation. Of course, it might just as well produce greater teamwork and collaboration between supervisors and employees; yet Samantha and Joseph realize that when organizations introduce change without laying the appropriate groundwork, members often fear the worst. Their next step is to compare support for performance-based pay for supervisory versus nonsupervisory personnel, again taking into account work experience in the private sector, which has been shown to have an effect on these attitudes (Table 15.9). Table 15.10 presents the cross-tabulation of support for performance-based pay and work experience in the private sector, controlling for employee status as supervisory or nonsupervisory.

The percentaged data in the control tables lend insight into the attitudes of the Athenia employees. First, the tables show that even when job classification as supervisory versus nonsupervisory is taken into account (controlled statistically), prior work experience in the private sector continues to have the same effect on support for performance-based pay. Whether the employee is a supervisor or not, private-sector job experience increases support for the proposed pay system by 10% and 9%, respectively. These findings reinforce the original relationship investigated in Table 15.9, which also yielded a 9% difference. Thus, the control tables provide evidence that the relationship between private sector work experience and support for performance-based pay is *nonspurious*; that is, in the presence of a third variable, employee job classification, the relationship persists. (The control tables cannot prove nonspuriousness, however, because other variables may turn out to be responsible for the relationship observed in Table 15.9).

What about the effect of the job classification variable on support for performance-based pay? Samantha and Joseph had anticipated that supervisors would be less receptive to the new pay plan than would nonsupervisory personnel. Comparing supervisors with nonsupervisors across the two control tables, Samantha and Joseph find that the latter group is considerably more favorable. Among those without background in the private sector, nonsupervisors are more supportive of performance-based pay 51% to 35%, a difference of 16%. Similarly, among city employees who have worked in the private sector, nonsupervisors are again more favorable than supervisors by a margin of 15% (60% − 45%). For job classification, too, the table gives evidence of a *nonspurious* relationship: classification produces substantial differences in support for performance-based pay, both for employees who have and for employees who do not have prior work experience in the private sector. (As before, the control tables cannot prove that this relationship is nonspurious, for other variables may account for the association found.) Stated in another (equivalent) way, controlling for private sector work experience, supervisory status appears to decrease support for performance-based pay—just as Samantha and Joseph had expected.

Samantha and Joseph could proceed with further analysis of the employee survey data, identifying other variables that may affect employee attitudes on this dimension. In the present instance, the strength of the original relationship between prior work experience in the private sector and support for performance-based pay (Table 15.9) is maintained when supervisory status is introduced (Table 15.10): city employees with work experience in the private sector remained more favorable toward the mayor's pay plan by 9% to 10%. Had prior work experience (independent variable) been related to supervisory status (control variable), however, the control tables would very likely have shown an attenuation in the original relationship. In that case, the issue the analyst would have to consider is whether the percentage differences produced by the independent variable on the dependent variable, though reduced, are still large enough to conclude that the independent variable has an effect on the dependent variable. If, when the control variable is introduced, these percentage differences should fall close to zero, the control tables give evidence of a spurious relationship (see, for example, Table 15.5), rather than of joint causation.

# RESULTS AND IMPLICATIONS OF CONTROL TABLE ANALYSIS

It is now possible to summarize four sets of possible empirical results—and their implications for further data analysis—of introducing a third (control) variable into a bivariate relationship. These sets are explained in Table 15.11. Examples of all four types of three-variable relationships have been elaborated in this chapter.

**TABLE 15.11**

Effect and Interpretation of Introducing a Third (Control) Variable into a Bivariate Relationship

| Empirical Effect of Introduction of Control Variable | Substantive Interpretation | Implications for Further Analysis |
|---|---|---|
| Relationship between independent and dependent variables remains virtually unchanged (evidence of nonspuriousness). | Evidence that independent variable is related to dependent variable and that control variable is not related to dependent variable. | Eliminate control variable from further analysis. Continue analysis of relationship between independent and dependent variables. |
| Relationship between independent and dependent variables virtually disappears (spurious). | Evidence that independent variable is not related to dependent variable and that control variable is related to dependent variable. | Eliminate independent variable from analysis. Control variable becomes new independent variable in further analysis. |
| Relationship between independent and dependent variables changes markedly, depending on the category of the control variable (interaction). | Relationship between the three variables is interactive. Control variable specifies relationship between independent and dependent variables. | Both independent and control variables must be considered in further analysis. |
| Relationship between independent and dependent variables persists or is only somewhat attenuated in each control table; control variable is related to dependent variable (evidence of joint causation). | Evidence that both independent and control variables are related to dependent variable. | Both independent and control variables must be considered in further analysis. |

# LIMITATIONS OF THE
# CONTROL TABLE TECHNIQUE

## MULTIVARIATE RELATIONSHIPS

Control table analysis is a relatively tractable procedure for the analysis of three-variable relationships. However, beyond three variables, its utility as an analytical tool rapidly dissipates. For example, if a researcher is interested in the determinants of performance on the civil service examination, she might hypothesize that not only race and education but also sex and motivation might have an impact. To assess the effect of each of these variables on test performance, she would have to examine the relationship between performance and one of the independent variables—say race—controlling simultaneously for the other two independent variables—sex and motivation. At a minimum, this procedure will generate four control tables: the cross-tabulation between race and test performance for (1) males with high motivation, (2) males with low motivation, (3) females with high motivation, and (4) females with low motivation. If the motivation variable consists of three categories (such as low, medium, high) rather than two, six control tables will result. The number of control tables is equal to the product of the number of categories of each of the control variables. Just as in the three-variable case, which has been the focus of this chapter, each of these control tables must be analyzed, compared, and interpreted for evidence not only of the simple effects of independent variables, but also of possible interactions among them. Obviously the number of control tables quickly becomes unwieldy. In addition, each control table requires sufficient cases for reliable analysis. As a result, the total number of cases necessary in the sample grows larger and, hence, more expensive to collect.

For these reasons, control table analysis is performed only rarely for more than three variables simultaneously and almost never for more than four variables. Instead, in the face of multivariate complexity, researchers typically turn to more powerful, parsimonious methods, especially regression analysis (see Chapter 19). Although regression analysis is predicated on the interval measurement of variables, many researchers feel that advantages of this technique more than compensate for any problems occasioned by treating ordinal data as interval (see Chapter 17). Another statistical technique useful for examining multivariate relationships is analysis of variance, introduced in Chapter 12. Consult an advanced statistics text for a full treatment.

## THE SOURCE OF CONTROL VARIABLES

The examples presented in this chapter have begun with plausible relationships between two variables and then introduced sensible control variables. An issue that has been ignored in this process is, where do control variables originate?

Without question, the best source of meaningful control variables is good theory. Substantive theory intended to explain a given phenomenon will identity the crucial variables that must be considered in data analysis. In Chapter 8, theory was discussed as an essential component in drawing correct causal infer-ences. Other valuable sources of control variables are creative intuition, experi-ence, previous research and published literature in an area, and expert opinion—including your boss's or your instructor's, even if you do not consider them experts.

This issue should be put in proper perspective. The source of appropriate control variables is a limitation of not only control table analysis but also all other forms of data analysis. The most powerful statistical techniques cannot compensate for a lack of solid substantive ideas and insights. Statistics is an excellent tool for testing hypothesized substantive relationships, but it is a poor one for suggesting these hypotheses.

# CHAPTER
# SUMMARY

Control table analysis is used to determine if a third variable is responsible for the association between two variables. Control techniques illustrated in this chapter use percentage differences. Basically, one examines the relationship be-tween the original two variables within each of the categories of the control variable and compares the results across the categories of the control. The process involves three steps. First, partition the sample according to the categories of the control variable. Second, assemble the cross-tabulation be-tween the original two variables for each of the subsamples defined by the control; percentage each of these tables separately. Third, interpret and compare the cross-tabulations obtained for each of the categories of the control variable.

The control table technique can diagnose the four major types of statistical effects emanating from the introduction of a control variable into a bivariate relationship: evidence of (1) nonspuriousness, (2) spuriousness, (3) interaction or specification, and (4) joint causation. The general approach can be used with other analysis aids discussed in Chapter 14, such as chi-square and measures of association.

# PROBLEMS

**15.1** General Halftrack suspects that Colonel Sy Verleaf is discriminating in his promotions by promoting more whites than blacks. The following table illustrates this hypothesis.

| Status | Race | | |
| --- | --- | --- | --- |
| | *Black* | *White* | *Total* |
| Passed over | 23 | 14 | 113 |
| Promoted | 27 | 86 | 37 |
| Total | 50 | 100 | 150 |

When called in to explain, Colonel Verleaf presents the following table.

| Status | Non–West Pointers Race | | Status | West Pointers Race | |
|---|---|---|---|---|---|
| | *Blacks* | *Whites* | | *Blacks* | *Whites* |
| Passed over | 20 | 12 | Passed over | 3 | 2 |
| Promoted | 19 | 12 | Promoted | 8 | 74 |

Analyze the preceding tables and present a brief statement to General Halftrack about Colonel Verleaf's activities.

**15.2**   The Department of Defense is concerned about the number of Harrier crashes. The Air Force argues that the crashes result because many of these planes are piloted by marines. The data for this claim are shown in the following table.

| Result | Pilot | | |
|---|---|---|---|
| | *Marine* | *Air Force* | *Total* |
| Crash | 46 | 32 | 78 |
| Did not crash | 187 | 155 | 342 |
| Total | 233 | 187 | 420 |

When the number of flight hours of the pilot is controlled, the following pattern appears.

| Result | Less Than 200 Hours Pilot | | | More Than 200 Hours Pilot | | |
|---|---|---|---|---|---|---|
| | *Marine* | *Air Force* | *Total* | *Marine* | *Air Force* | *Total* |
| Crash | 36 | 26 | 62 | 10 | 6 | 16 |
| Did not crash | 62 | 51 | 113 | 125 | 104 | 229 |
| Total | 98 | 77 | 175 | 135 | 110 | 245 |

Analyze these tables and present your findings.

**15.3**   The health inspectors in a large city are trying to isolate the sources of health problems in the city. Some debate centers on whether health problems are related to family income or to frequency of city garbage collection. The accompanying tables display data for each neighborhood in the city regarding average income of residents (low, high), frequency of city garbage collection (once per week, twice per week), and frequency of health problems reported in the neighborhood (low, high).

Analyze these data and discuss the sources of health problems in the city.

| Frequency of Health Problems | Average Income | |
|---|---|---|
| | *Low* | *High* |
| Low | 103 | 180 |
| High | 147 | 120 |

Garbage Collection Once per Week

| Frequency of Health Problems | Average Income | |
|---|---|---|
| | *Low* | *High* |
| Low | 25 | 10 |
| High | 56 | 12 |

Garbage Collection Twice per Week

| Frequency of Health Problems | Average Income | |
|---|---|---|
| | *Low* | *High* |
| Low | 78 | 170 |
| High | 91 | 108 |

**15.4** A researcher is conducting an experiment to determine support for the feminist movement. The experimental procedure consists of playing a tape recording of a meeting of a feminist organization for a group of subjects, and then comparing their attitudes with those of a matched control group of subjects who are not exposed to the tape. At the conclusion of the experiment, the researcher is amazed to find that the tape recording apparently made no difference in attitude toward the feminist movement. Check this result in the following table.

| Attitude Toward Feminist Movement | Listened to Tape Recording | |
|---|---|---|
| | *No* | *Yes* |
| Not favorable | 40 | 39 |
| Favorable | 40 | 41 |

The researcher then decides to take into account the sex of the subjects and obtains the following tables.

| Men | | | Women | | |
|-----|---|---|-------|---|---|
| Attitude Toward Feminist Movement | Listened to Tape Recording | | Attitude Toward Feminist Movement | Listened to Tape Recording | |
| | *No* | *Yes* | | *No* | *Yes* |
| Not favorable | 21 | 24 | Not favorable | 19 | 15 |
| Favorable | 19 | 16 | Favorable | 21 | 25 |

Did the tape recording have an effect on attitude toward the feminist movement? Explain your answer.

**15.5** A national commission has been appointed to try to reduce crime in the United States. The commission has assembled data for 400 randomly selected cities. These data include whether police walk or do not walk a beat in the city, whether the city has fewer than the average number or more than the average number of streetlights for cities of the same size, and whether its crime rate is below the average or above the average for cities of the same size. For the accompanying data, what should the commission recommend in order to combat crime? Explain your answer.

| Crime Rate | Streetlights | |
|------------|--------------|---|
| | *Below Average* | *Above Average* |
| Below average | 98 | 114 |
| Above average | 102 | 86 |

| Police Do Not Walk Beat | | | Police Walk Beat | | |
|-------------------------|---|---|------------------|---|---|
| Crime Rate | Streetlights | | Crime Rate | Streetlights | |
| | *Below Average* | *Above Average* | | *Below Average* | *Above Average* |
| Below average | 83 | 16 | Below average | 15 | 98 |
| Above average | 91 | 18 | Above average | 11 | 68 |

**15.6** A consumer advocate is trying to get legislation passed that will protect the environment of a large city. To increase the probability of success, the advocate researches the history of all legislation introduced in the city council in the last five years. She records whether the bill was favorable or not favorable to industry, whether the bill was introduced by a member of the city council or by the mayor, and whether it passed or was defeated. These variables are cross-tabulated in the accompanying tables. From these cross-tabulations, whom should she try to persuade to introduce her legislation in the city council? Explain your answer.

| Bill | Favorable to Industry | |
|---|---|---|
| | *No* | *Yes* |
| Defeated | 132 | 43 |
| Passed | 138 | 87 |

Bill Introduced by Mayor

| Bill | Favorable to Industry | |
|---|---|---|
| | *No* | *Yes* |
| Defeated | 64 | 22 |
| Passed | 67 | 44 |

Bill Introduced by Member of City Council

| Bill | Favorable to Industry | |
|---|---|---|
| | *No* | *Yes* |
| Defeated | 68 | 21 |
| Passed | 71 | 43 |

**15.7** A city intends to construct a new museum. The city is concerned that the museum be a success in the sense of drawing many patrons. The city has compiled data from 549 cities regarding how frequently museum collections are changed (infrequently, frequently), the size of the museum and surrounding grounds (small, large), and yearly attendance (low, high). From these data (see the accompanying cross-tabulations), what recommendations should be made to the city about constructing and maintaining the new museum?

| Attendance | Size | |
|---|---|---|
| | *Small* | *Large* |
| Low | 135 | 87 |
| High | 165 | 162 |

Infrequent Collection Changes

| Attendance | Size | |
|---|---|---|
| | *Small* | *Large* |
| Low | 78 | 47 |
| High | 82 | 51 |

Frequent Collection Changes

| Attendance | Size | |
|---|---|---|
| | *Small* | *Large* |
| Low | 57 | 40 |
| High | 83 | 111 |

**15.8**  A state welfare department has commissioned a survey to investigate the attitudes of its clients toward the department. For one week, upon completing a visit to the department, clients were asked whether they thought that they had to complete too many forms, whether they had to wait too long in line for service, and whether they felt the agency was run efficiently or inefficiently. For the accompanying cross-tabulations of their responses, what can the welfare department do to improve its image with clients?

| Opinion | Too Many Forms | |
|---|---|---|
| | *No* | *Yes* |
| Inefficient | 192 | 182 |
| Efficient | 128 | 78 |

| Not Too Long in Line | | | | Too Long in Line | | |
|---|---|---|---|---|---|---|
| Opinion | Too Many Forms | | | Opinion | Too Many Forms | |
| | *No* | *Yes* | | | *No* | *Yes* |
| Inefficient | 96 | 62 | | Inefficient | 96 | 120 |
| Efficient | 96 | 49 | | Efficient | 32 | 29 |

**15.9**  A school district is experimenting with two different methods of instruction to improve the performance of elementary school students. The first "traditional" method emphasizes learning through memorization, and the second "modern" method emphasizes learning through individual discovery. As the first cross-tabulation indicates, the two methods seem to be equally effective in their impact on student performance. Some educators, however, dispute this result; they argue that the best method depends on the intelligence of the student. To test this hypothesis, they examine the relationship between instructional method and performance in each of three groups—students with low, medium, and high intelligence. Do the accompanying cross-tabulations support this hypothesis? Which method should the school district employ for which type of student? Explain your answer. (**Hint:** Although this example has three control tables, the procedures used in analysis are analogous to those used in the case of two control tables, which were discussed at length in this chapter. The analyst must examine the relationship between the original two variables within each category of the third or control variable, and note how the control tables differ from one another and from the original table. You can interpret the result according to the guidelines presented in Table 15.11.)

| Performance | Method | |
|---|---|---|
| | *Traditional* | *Modern* |
| Low | 268 | 269 |
| High | 272 | 271 |

| | Low Intelligence | | | | Medium Intelligence | | |
|---|---|---|---|---|---|---|---|
| Performance | Method | | | Performance | Method | | |
| | *Traditional* | *Modern* | | | *Traditional* | *Modern* | |
| Low | 68 | 120 | | Low | 78 | 79 | |
| High | 102 | 70 | | High | 102 | 101 | |

| | High Intelligence | |
|---|---|---|
| Performance | Method | |
| | *Traditional* | *Modern* |
| Low | 122 | 70 |
| High | 68 | 100 |

**15.10** The MPA director at a large university is interested in the factors that lead to successful placement of MPA students in employment. She defines successful placement of an MPA student as being offered the position that was his or her first choice for employment after completing the program. From student transcripts, she has classified students' grade point averages in the MPA program into two categories: 3.0 or below, and above 3.0 (on a 4.0 scale). From the transcripts, she also has determined whether the student took the courses in the quantitative concentration in the MPA program (which use a familiar statistics book). These data appear in the accompanying tables. Based on the data, how should the MPA director advise students about how to receive successful placements?

| Placement | Grade Point Average | |
|---|---|---|
| | *3.0 or Below* | *Above 3.0* |
| Not successful | 78 | 97 |
| Successful | 104 | 184 |

Did Not Take Quantitative Concentration

| Placement | Grade Point Average | |
|---|---|---|
| | *3.0 or Below* | *Above 3.0* |
| Not successful | 44 | 58 |
| Successful | 44 | 79 |

Did Take Quantitative Concentration

| Placement | Grade Point Average | |
|---|---|---|
| | *3.0 or Below* | *Above 3.0* |
| Not successful | 34 | 39 |
| Successful | 60 | 105 |

**15.11** A researcher is interested in how agency and bureau directors can achieve stronger control over their organizations. Using data from 500 of these organizations, she finds a relationship between type of budget and control. By a large percentage difference, directors claim to have stronger control with a line-item budget than with any other type. This relationship persists even when she introduces the third (control) variables of size of agency or bureau and number of hierarchical levels in the organization. Accordingly, she concludes that the relationship between type of budget and director control must be causal. Explain why you agree or disagree with her conclusion.

# PART VI

# REGRESSION

# INTRODUCTION TO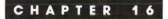

# REGRESSION

# ANALYSIS

Often a public manager wants to know whether two variables are related but is unwilling to collapse information into categories (see Chapters 13–15). In general, an analyst should never take interval level data and use ordinal or nominal level techniques. Treating interval information as ordinal loses much of the information that the data contain. Just as the analyst should never calculate the mean and standard deviation for grouped data when the ungrouped data are available, an analyst should never take interval data (number of cars, revenue, highway speeds, crime rates) and collapse them into categories for analysis purposes. (Collapsing data to present simple tables is permissible.)

A variety of public management problems can be interpreted as relationships between two variables. For example, the director of the highway patrol might want to know if the average speed of motorists on a stretch of highway is related to the number of patrol cars on that stretch of highway. Knowing this information would allow the director to decide rationally whether or not to increase the number of patrol cars. In other situations, the public manager might want to know the relationship between two variables for prediction purposes. For example, a southwestern state is considering a sales tax on beer and would like to know how much revenue the tax would raise in the state. An analyst's strategy might be to see if there was a relationship between a state's population and its tax revenues from beer sales. If a relationship is found, the analyst could then use the state's population to predict its potential revenue from a beer sales tax.

This chapter will provide an introduction to the techniques of simple linear regression.

## RELATIONSHIPS BETWEEN VARIABLES

Relationships between two variables can be classified in two ways: as causal or predictive *and* as functional or statistical. In our first example, the relationship between police cars on the road and motorists' average speed, we have a causal relationship. The implicit hypothesis is that increasing the number of patrol cars on the road will reduce average speeds. In the beer sales tax example, a state's population will predict, or determine, tax revenues from beer sales. The variable that is predicted or is caused is referred to as the *dependent* variable (this variable is usually called $Y$). The variable that is used to predict or is the cause of change in another variable is called the *independent* variable (this variable is usually called $X$).

In the following examples, determine which variable is the dependent variable and which is the independent variable.

A police chief believes increasing expenditures for police will reduce crime.

independent variable _____

dependent variable _____

A librarian feels that circulation is related to advertising.

independent variable _____

dependent variable _____

MPA candidates make good summer interns.

independent variable _____

dependent variable _____

Batting averages are affected by batting practice.

independent variable _____

dependent variable _____

If you said the dependent variables were crime, circulation, good performance, and batting averages, congratulations.

**functional relationship**

Relationships may also be functional or statistical. A **functional relationship** is a relationship in which one variable ($Y$) is a direct function of another ($X$). For example, Russell Thomas, longtime head of the city motor pool, believes that there is some type of relationship between the number of cars he sends over to Marquette's Tune-up Shop for tune-ups and the amount of the bill that he receives from Marquette's. Russell finds the information in Table 16.1 for the last five transactions with Marquette's.

Russell knows the first step in determining whether two variables are related is to graph the two variables. When graphing two variables, the independent

**TABLE 16.1**

Data from Marquette's

| Number of Cars | Amount of Bill |
| --- | --- |
| 2 | $ 64 |
| 1 | 32 |
| 5 | 160 |
| 4 | 128 |
| 2 | 64 |

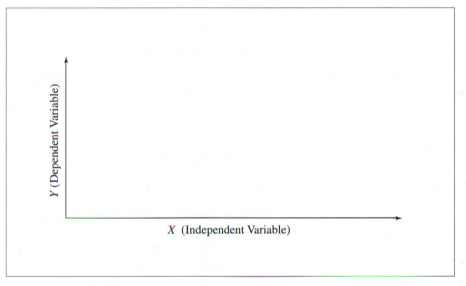

$X$ (Independent Variable)

**FIGURE 16.1**
The Horizontal Axis
Is for $X$

variable ($X$) is always graphed along the bottom and the dependent variable ($Y$) is always graphed along the side. See Figure 16.1.

On the axes presented in Figure 16.2, graph the points representing the two variables.

If you look carefully at the points you graphed in Figure 16.2, you will see that they fall without any deviation along a single line. This is a characteristic of a functional relationship. If someone knows the value of the independent variable, the value of the dependent variable can be predicted exactly. In the preceding example, Marquette's charges the city $32 to tune a car, so the bill is simply $32 times the number of cars.

Unfortunately, very few of the important relationships that a public manager must consider are functional. Most relationships are statistical. In a statistical relationship, knowing the value of the independent variable lets us estimate a

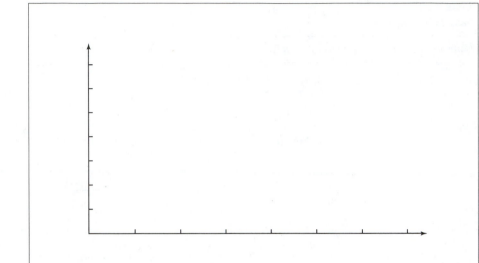

**FIGURE 16.2**
Graph Data Here

value for the dependent variable, but the estimate is not exact. One process of determining the exact nature of a statistical relationship is called *regression*. We will illustrate how regression can be used to describe relationships with an example.

The Normal, Illinois, traffic commissioner believes that the average speed of motorists along Highway 35 within the city limits is related to the number of police cars patrolling that stretch. Average speed is measured by a stationary, unmanned radar gun. The experiment spans two months, with measurements taken daily. For a sample of five days, the results of the commissioner's experiment are as shown in Table 16.2.

**TABLE 16.2**
Commissioner's Data

| Number of Police Cars | Average Speed of Motorists |
| --- | --- |
| 3 | 64 |
| 1 | 71 |
| 4 | 61 |
| 5 | 58 |
| 7 | 56 |

The first step in determining whether a relationship exists is to plot the data on a graph. Plot the given data on the graph in Figure 16.2. After the data are plotted, the analyst can eyeball the data to see whether there is a relationship

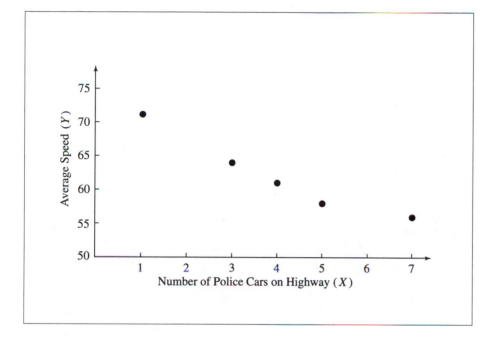

**FIGURE 16.3**
Graph of Traffic
Speed Data

between the number of cars and the average speed. The graph of the data is shown in Figure 16.3.

Clearly, the graph shows a relationship between the number of police cars on this highway and the motorists' average speed: the more cars on the highway, the lower the average speed. This is termed a negative relationship because the dependent variable (speed) decreases as the independent variable increases.

Our hypothetical situation in which state population is compared with sales tax revenues from beer sales illustrates a positive relationship (see Table 16.3).

**TABLE 16.3**

Relationship Between Tax Revenues and Population

| State | Population (millions) | Beer Revenue (millions) |
|-------|----------------------|-------------------------|
| TX    | 12.4                 | 146                     |
| LA    | 6.1                  | 85                      |
| AK    | 2.4                  | 21                      |
| KS    | 4.3                  | 47                      |
| MO    | 9.5                  | 115                     |
| CO    | 7.6                  | 90                      |

The graph of these data is shown in Figure 16.4. From the graph, we see that as states' populations increase, so do the states' sales tax revenues from beer

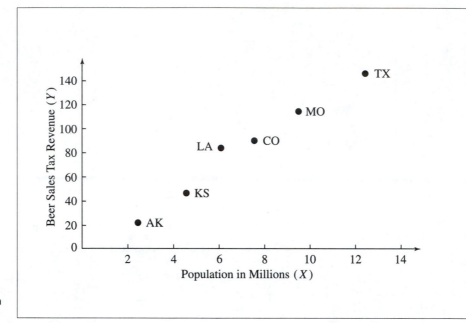

**FIGURE 16.4**
Relationship
Between Population
and Tax Revenue

sales. Since both variables increase (or decrease) at the same time, the relationship is positive.

In many cases (far too many for most managers), no relationship exists between two variables. In Table 16.4, the number of police cars patrolling the streets of Normal is contrasted with the number of arrests for indecent exposure in Kansas City.

**TABLE 16.4**
Patrol Cars and Number of Arrests

| Day | Cars on Patrol in Normal | Arrests for Indecent Exposure in Kansas City |
|---|---|---|
| Monday | 2 | 27 |
| Tuesday | 3 | 12 |
| Wednesday | 3 | 57 |
| Thursday | 7 | 28 |
| Friday | 1 | 66 |
| Saturday | 6 | 60 |

A note of explanation is in order. On Wednesday, a regional public administration conference opened in Kansas City. Since suspects are held for 24 hours, this also explains the Friday figures. Most of the Saturday incidents occurred at the airport.

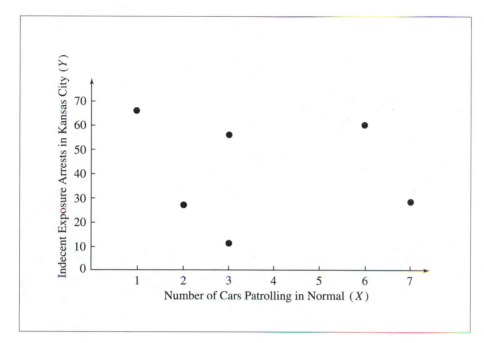

**FIGURE 16.5**
Relationship
Between Number of
Patrol Cars and
Indecent Exposure
Arrests

The data are graphed in Figure 16.5. Clearly no relationship exists between the number of police cars patrolling the streets of Normal and arrests for indecent exposure in Kansas City.

# ODE TO

# EYEBALLING

When an analyst has only a few data points, the relationship between two variables can be determined visually. When the data sets become fairly large, however, eyeballing a relationship is extremely inaccurate. What is needed are statistics that summarize the relationship between two variables. One variable, of course, can be summarized by a set of single figures, say, the mean and the standard deviation. *The relationship between two variables can be summarized by a line.*

For our example of cars patrolling a stretch of Highway 35 and the average speed of traffic on that portion of highway, a straight line can be drawn that represents the relationship between the data (see Figure 16.6). The line generally follows the pattern of the data, sloping downward and to the right.

Any line can be described by two numbers, and the line describing the relationship between two variables is no exception. Lines *a*, *b*, and *c* in Figure 16.7 differ from each other in terms of how steeply the lines slant from left to right.

The slant of a line is referred to as its slope. The **slope** of any line is defined to be how much the line rises or falls relative to the distance it travels horizontally.

**slope**

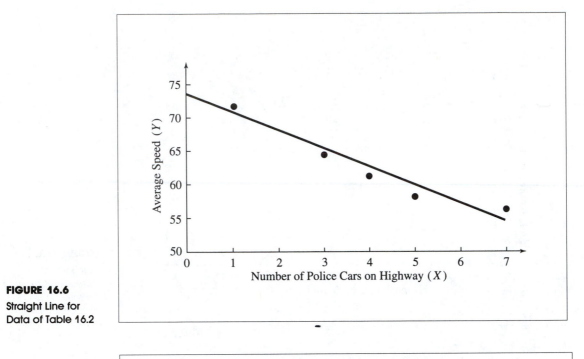

**FIGURE 16.6**
Straight Line for
Data of Table 16.2

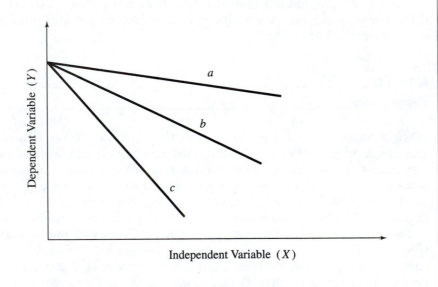

**FIGURE 16.7**
The Lines Differ
in Their Slopes

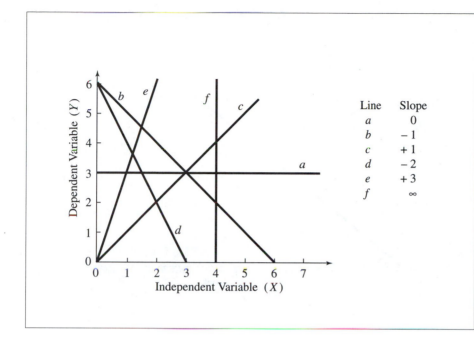

**FIGURE 16.8**
Several Different
Slopes

Symbolically,

$$\beta = \frac{\Delta Y}{\Delta X}$$

where $\beta$ (Greek letter beta) is the slope of a line, $\Delta Y$ (Greek letter delta) is the change in the $Y$ (dependent) variable, and $\Delta X$ is the change in the $X$ (independent) variable.

Another way to express this formula is to say that the slope of a line is equal to the ratio of the change in $Y$ for a given change in $X$ (rise over run, for you geometry buffs). The graph in Figure 16.8 shows the slopes of several hypothetical lines.

The second number used to describe a line is the point where the line intersects the $Y$-axis (called the **intercept**). The graph in Figure 16.9 shows several lines with the same slopes but with different intercepts. The intercept, referred to as $\alpha$ (Greek letter alpha) by statisticians, is the value of the dependent variable when the independent variable is equal to zero.

**intercept**

Any line can be fully described by its slope and its intercept:

$$Y = \alpha + \beta X$$

A line describing the relationship between two variables is represented by

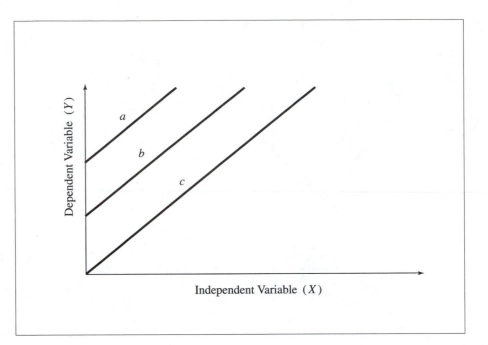

**FIGURE 16.9**

The Lines Have the
Same Slope but
Different Intercepts

$$\hat{Y} = \alpha + \beta X$$

**predicted value**    $\hat{Y}$ is a statistician's symbol for the **predicted value** of $Y$ (called "$Y$ hat"). $\hat{Y}$ for any value of $X$ is a function of the intercept ($\alpha$) and the slope ($\beta$), and it may or may not be equal to the actual value of $Y$.

To illustrate, let us return to our example of traffic speeds and patrol cars. The line drawn through the data in Figure 16.10 represents the relationship between the two variables. If we had only the line, what could we say about the expected average speed if three cars were on the road? $\hat{Y}$, the expected speed, is 65 miles per hour. (To find this number, draw a line straight up from the three-cars point to the relationship line. From the point where your line touches the relationship line, draw a line parallel to the $X$-axis to the speed limit line. Your line should touch the $Y$-axis at 65. This value is $\hat{Y}$.)

Note that the actual value of $Y$ on the one day when three cars were on the road is 64 miles per hour. This fact illustrates the following:

predicted value of $Y$ = real value of $Y$ + some error

$$\hat{Y}_i = Y_i + e_i$$

or

$$e_i = (\hat{Y}_i - Y_i)$$

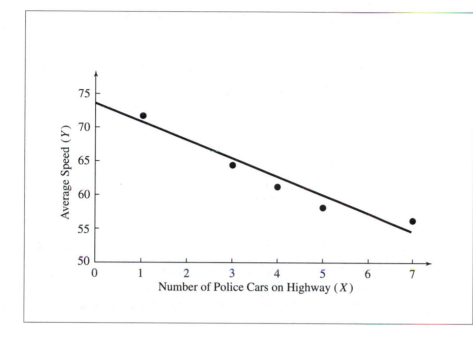

**FIGURE 16.10**
Straight Line for
Data of Table 16.2

Another way of expressing this is that every value of $Y$ is equal to some predicted value of $Y$ based on $X$ plus some error.*

## LINEAR REGRESSION

The pitfall of just drawing in a line to summarize a relationship is that numerous lines will look as if they summarize the relationship between two variables. Statisticians have agreed that the best line to use to describe a relationship is the line that minimizes the squared errors—that is, makes the sum of all $(\hat{Y}_i - Y_i)^2$ the smallest possible number. This form of **regression** (or fitting a line to data) is called ordinary **least squares,** or you may call it just **linear regression.**

Linear regression using the principle of minimizing squared errors allows us to find one value of $\alpha$ and one value of $\beta$ so that a unique regression line of the form $\hat{Y} = \alpha + \beta X$ can be found. The calculations necessary to find $\alpha$ and $\beta$ will be illustrated with an example.

Through some heavy mathematics based on calculus, statisticians have found that the formula for $\beta$ is as follows:

**regression**

**least squares**

**linear regression**

---

* We assume that error can be either negative or positive, so that it does not matter whether error is added to $\hat{Y}_i$ (or $Y_i$) or subtracted from $\hat{Y}_i$ (or $Y_i$).

$$\beta = \frac{\Sigma(X_i - \bar{X})(Y_i - \bar{Y})}{\Sigma(X_i - \bar{X})^2}$$

When taken a piece at a time, this formula is rather simple. We will use the police cars and average speed data to calculate $\beta$ (see Table 16.5).

**TABLE 16.5**

Relationship Between Police Cars and Average Speed

| Number of Police Cars ($X$) | Average Speed ($Y$) |
| --- | --- |
| 3 | 64 |
| 1 | 71 |
| 4 | 61 |
| 5 | 58 |
| 7 | 56 |

**STEP 1** Calculate the mean for both the dependent variable ($Y$) and the independent variable ($X$). Do this in the space provided next to the table. If you have forgotten how to calculate a mean, reread Chapter 2. The mean for $Y$ is 62, and the mean for $X$ is 4.

**STEP 2** Subtract the mean of the dependent variable from each value of the dependent variable, yielding ($Y_i - \bar{Y}$). Do the same for the independent variable, yielding ($X_i - \bar{X}$).

| $X_i - \bar{X}$ | $Y_i - \bar{Y}$ |
| --- | --- |
| $3 - 4 = -1$ | $64 - 62 = \phantom{-}2$ |
| $1 - 4 = -3$ | $71 - 62 = \phantom{-}9$ |
| $4 - 4 = \phantom{-}0$ | $61 - 62 = -1$ |
| $5 - 4 = \phantom{-}1$ | $58 - 62 = -4$ |
| $7 - 4 = \phantom{-}3$ | $56 - 62 = -6$ |

**STEP 3** Multiply ($Y_i - \bar{Y}$) times ($X_i - \bar{X}$). That is, multiply the value that you get when you subtract the mean from $Y_i$ by the value you get when you subtract the mean from $X_i$.

| $(X_i - \bar{X}) \times (Y_i - \bar{Y})$ | | |
| --- | --- | --- |
| $-1$ | $\times \phantom{-}2$ | $= -2$ |
| $-3$ | $\times \phantom{-}9$ | $= -27$ |
| $0$ | $\times -1$ | $= \phantom{-}0$ |
| $1$ | $\times -4$ | $= -4$ |
| $3$ | $\times -6$ | $= -18$ |

**STEP 4**   Sum all the values of $(Y_i - \overline{Y})(X_i - \overline{X})$. You should get a sum of $-51$. This is the numerator of the formula for $\beta$.

**STEP 5**   Use the $(X_i - \overline{X})$ column in Step 3 and square each of the values found in the column.

| $(X_i - \overline{X})$ | $(X_i - \overline{X})^2$ |
| --- | --- |
| $-1$ | 1 |
| $-3$ | 9 |
| 0 | 0 |
| 1 | 1 |
| 3 | 9 |

**STEP 6**   Sum the squared values of $(X_i - \overline{X})$. The answer is 20.

**STEP 7**   Divide $\Sigma(Y_i - \overline{Y})(X_i - \overline{X})$, or $-51$, by $\Sigma(X_i - \overline{X})^2$, or 20. This number $(-2.55)$ is beta.

Alpha (or the intercept) is much easier to calculate. Statisticians have discovered that

$$\alpha = \overline{Y} - \beta\overline{X}$$

Substituting in the values of 62, $-2.55$, and 4 for $\overline{Y}$, $\beta$, and $\overline{X}$, respectively, we find

$$\alpha = 62 - (-2.55) \times 4 = 62 - (-10.2) = 62 + 10.2 = 72.2$$

The regression equation that describes the relationship between the number of patrol cars on a stretch of Highway 35 and the average speed of motorists on that stretch of highway is

$$\hat{Y} = 72.2 - 2.55X$$

All regressions are of the general form

$$\hat{Y} = \alpha + \beta X$$

In English, the predicted value of $Y(\hat{Y})$ is equal to $X$ times some constant $(\beta)$ plus another constant $(\alpha)$. Either constant may be negative.

## SOME APPLICATIONS

The regression equation provides a wealth of information. Suppose the traffic commissioner wants to know the estimated average speed of traffic if six patrol cars are placed on duty. Another way of stating this question is, What is the value of $\hat{Y}$ (the estimated average speed) if the value of $X$ (the number of cars) is 6? Using the formula

$$\hat{Y} = 72.2 - 2.55X$$

substitute 6 for $X$ to obtain

$$\hat{Y} = 72.2 - 2.55 \times 6 = 72.2 - 15.3 = 56.9$$

The best estimate of the average speed for all cars on a stretch of Highway 35 is 56.9 if six patrol cars are placed on that stretch.

**regression coefficient**

How much would the mean speed for all cars decrease if one additional patrol car were added? The answer is 2.55 miles per hour. The **regression coefficient,** beta, is the ratio of change in $\hat{Y}$ to the change in $X$. Where the change in $X$ is 1 (car), the change in $\hat{Y}$ is $-2.55$ (miles per hour). In a management situation, this is how beta should be interpreted. Beta is how much $\hat{Y}$ will change if $X$ is changed (increased) 1 unit.

What would the average speed be if no patrol cars were on the road? Substituting 0 into the regression equation, we find

$$\hat{Y} = 72.2 - 2.55X = 72.2 - 2.55(0) = 72.2$$

When $X$ is 0, the value of $\hat{Y}$ is 72.2, or the intercept. The intercept is defined as the value of $\hat{Y}$ when $X$ is equal to zero.

## AN EXAMPLE

Most analysts rely on computer programs to calculate regression equations. The authors expect that you will do so. However, just for practice, we ask you to calculate the regression equation for the population and beer sales tax example. Recall that for six states, the data are as given in Table 16.6.

**TABLE 16.6**
Relationship Between Tax Revenues and Population

| Population, $X$ (millions) | Beer Revenue, $Y$ (millions) |
| --- | --- |
| 12.4 | 146 |
| 6.1 | 85 |
| 2.4 | 21 |
| 4.3 | 47 |
| 9.5 | 115 |
| 7.6 | 90 |

In the space provided, calculate the slope and the intercept of the regression line.

$$\bar{X} = \underline{\hspace{2cm}} \qquad \bar{Y} = \underline{\hspace{2cm}}$$

| $X_i - \bar{X}$ | | | $(X_i - \bar{X})^2$ | $Y_i - \bar{Y}$ | | |
|---|---|---|---|---|---|---|
| 12.4 − | = | | | 146 − | = | |
| 6.1 − | = | | | 85 − | = | |
| 2.4 − | = | | | 21 − | = | |
| 4.3 − | = | | | 47 − | = | |
| 9.5 − | = | | | 115 − | = | |
| 7.6 − | = | | | 90 − | = | |

$$(X_i - \bar{X}) \times (Y_i - \bar{Y})$$

$$\underline{\hspace{2cm}} \times \underline{\hspace{2cm}} = \underline{\hspace{2cm}}$$
$$\underline{\hspace{2cm}} \times \underline{\hspace{2cm}} = \underline{\hspace{2cm}}$$
$$\underline{\hspace{2cm}} \times \underline{\hspace{2cm}} = \underline{\hspace{2cm}}$$
$$\underline{\hspace{2cm}} \times \underline{\hspace{2cm}} = \underline{\hspace{2cm}}$$
$$\underline{\hspace{2cm}} \times \underline{\hspace{2cm}} = \underline{\hspace{2cm}}$$
$$\underline{\hspace{2cm}} \times \underline{\hspace{2cm}} = \underline{\hspace{2cm}}$$

$$\Sigma(X_i - \bar{X})(Y_i - \bar{Y}) = \underline{\hspace{2cm}}$$

$$\Sigma(X_i - \bar{X})^2 = \underline{\hspace{2cm}}$$

$$\beta = \frac{\Sigma(X_i - \bar{X})(Y_i - \bar{Y})}{\Sigma(X_i - \bar{X})^2} = \underline{\hspace{2cm}}$$

$$\alpha = \bar{Y} - \beta\bar{X} = \underline{\hspace{2cm}}$$

The answer to this exercise is presented at the end of the chapter following the problems.

What would be the best estimate of Oklahoma's beer sales tax revenue if it had such a tax and had 5.5 million people?

# MEASURES OF _____
# GOODNESS OF FIT _____

Any relationship between two variables can be summarized by linear regression. A regression line per se, however, does not tell you how well the regression line summarizes the data. To illustrate, the two sets of data in Figure 16.11 can both be summarized with the same regression line. In the graph of part (b), however,

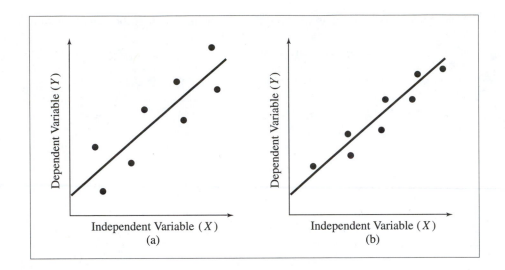

**FIGURE 16.11**

Differences in
Goodness of Fit

the data points cluster closely about the line; in the graph of part (a), the data points are much farther from the line. We can say that the regression line of (b) fits the data better than does the regression line of (a).

**error**

The distance a point is from the regression line is referred to as **error**. Recall that the regression line gives the value of $\hat{Y}_i$, whereas the data point represents $Y_i$. In the following sections, we will discuss various ways that statisticians have devised to measure the goodness of fit of the regression line to data. All these methods are based on the error.

## THE STANDARD ERROR OF
## THE ESTIMATE

**residual
variation**

Statisticians commonly use three measures of fit. The first, called the **residual variation,** or the variance of the estimate, is equal to the sum of the squared error divided by $n - 2$. Symbolically,

$$S_{y|x}^2 = \frac{\Sigma(Y_i - \hat{Y}_i)^2}{n - 2}$$

$S_{y|x}^2$ is called the residual variance of $Y$ given $X$.

**standard error of
the estimate**

Another way of stating what $S_{y|x}^2$ represents is that it is the average squared error of the regression estimates. Although the residual variation is rarely used as a measure of fit, its square root ($S_{y|x}$) is. This measure, called the **standard error of the estimate,** is an estimate of the variation in $\hat{Y}$, the predicted value of

*Y.* The standard error of the estimate can be used to place confidence intervals around an estimate that is based on a regression equation.

To illustrate the utility of this measure of regression line fit, we need to calculate the residual variance for a set of data. We will use the police cars and speed data of Table 16.5. In the worked-out example presented earlier, we found that the number of patrol cars on the highway was related to the average speed of all cars and that

$$\overline{X} = 4 \qquad \overline{Y} = 62 \qquad \hat{Y} = 72.2 - 2.55X$$

To calculate the residual variation, follow these steps:

**STEP 1**    Using the values of *X* and the regression equation, calculate a $\hat{Y}$ value for every *X* value.

| $X \times$ | $\beta$ | $X\beta$ | $+ \alpha =$ | $\hat{Y}$ |
|---|---|---|---|---|
| 3 × | −2.55 | −7.65 | + 72.2 = | 64.6 |
| 1 × | −2.55 | −2.55 | + 72.2 = | 69.7 |
| 4 × | −2.55 | −10.2 | + 72.2 = | 62.0 |
| 5 × | −2.55 | −12.75 | + 72.2 = | 59.5 |
| 7 × | −2.55 | −17.85 | + 72.2 = | 54.4 |

**STEP 2**    Using the $\hat{Y}$ values and the *Y* values, calculate the total error for each value of *Y*.

| $Y -$ | $\hat{Y}$ | | |
|---|---|---|---|
| 64 − | 64.6 | = | −.6 |
| 71 − | 69.7 | = | 1.3 |
| 61 − | 62.0 | = | −1.0 |
| 58 − | 59.5 | = | −1.5 |
| 56 − | 54.4 | = | 1.6 |

**STEP 3**    Square the errors found in Step 2, and then sum these squares.

| $(Y - \hat{Y})^2$ | |
|---|---|
| .36 | |
| 1.69 | $\Sigma(Y - \hat{Y})^2 = 7.86$ |
| 1.00 | |
| 2.25 | |
| 2.56 | |

**STEP 4**    Divide the sum of the squared errors by *n* − 2 to find the residual variation (or average squared error).

$$S^2_{y|x} = \frac{7.86}{3} = 2.62$$

**STEP 5**   Take the square root of this number to find the standard error of the estimate.

$$S_{y|x} = \sqrt{2.62} = 1.62$$

The standard error of the estimate may be interpreted as the amount of error that one makes when predicting a value of $Y$ from a value of $X$. Suppose the highway commissioner wanted to predict the average speed of all cars when four patrol cars were on the road. Using the regression equation, he would find

$$\hat{Y} = 72.2 - 2.55(4) = 72.2 - 10.2 = 62.0$$

This estimate of the average speed is not exact; it can be in error by a certain amount. The amount of error is equal to the standard deviation of $\hat{Y}$, or the standard error of the esimated $Y$. With this number, we can place a 90% confidence limit around $\hat{Y}$ by using the $t$-distribution with three degress of freedom (df for a simple regression is $n - 2$):

$$\hat{Y} \pm t \times S_{y|x}$$

$$62.0 \pm 2.35 \times 1.62$$

$$62.0 \pm 3.8$$

$$58.2 \text{ to } 65.8$$

We can be 90% sure that the mean speed of all cars (when four patrol cars are on the road) is between 58.2 and 65.8 miles per hour.

# THE COEFFICIENT OF DETERMINATION

The second goodness of fit measure adjusts for the total variation in $Y$. This measure, the coefficient of determination, is the ratio of the explained variation to the total variation in $Y$. Explained variation is nothing more than the total variation in the dependent variable minus the error. Statisticians have defined the ratio of explained to unexplained variation as equal to

$$r^2 = \frac{\Sigma(\hat{Y}_i - \bar{Y})^2}{\Sigma(Y_i - \bar{Y})^2}$$

This measure is called the **coefficient of determination**, or $r^2$. The coefficient of    **coefficient of**
determination ranges from zero (the data do not fit the line at all) to one (the    **determination**
data fit the line perfectly).

The best way to interpret the coefficient of determination is as follows. If
someone wanted you to guess the next value of $Y$ but gave you no information,
your best guess as to what $Y$ is would be $\overline{Y}$, the mean. The amount of error in
this guess would be $(Y_i - \overline{Y})$. The total squared error for several guesses of $Y$
would be $\Sigma(Y_i - \overline{Y})^2$. If someone asked you to guess the next value of $Y$ and
gave you both the corresponding value of $X$ and a regression equation, your
best guess as to the value of $Y_i$ would be $\hat{Y}_i$. How much of an improvement
would this be over just guessing the mean? Obviously, it is $(\hat{Y}_i - \overline{Y})$, or the
difference between the estimated value of $Y_i$ (or $\hat{Y}_i$) and the mean. The total
improvement in squared error for several guesses would be $\Sigma(\hat{Y}_i - \overline{Y})^2$. As you
can tell, the coefficient of determination is the ratio of the reduction of the error
by using the regression line to the total error by guessing the mean.

To calculate the coefficient of determination, follow these steps:

**STEP 1**   Using the regression equation and each value of $X$, estimate a predicted
value of $Y(\hat{Y})$. Such estimates were just made in the previous problem;
they are:

| $X$ | $\hat{Y}$ |
|-----|-----|
| 3 | 64.6 |
| 1 | 69.7 |
| 4 | 62.0 |
| 5 | 59.5 |
| 7 | 54.4 |

**STEP 2**   From each value of $\hat{Y}$, subtract the mean value of $Y$ (in this case 62), and
square these differences.

| $\hat{Y} - \overline{Y} = (\hat{Y} - \overline{Y})$ | | $(\hat{Y} - \overline{Y})^2$ |
|-----|-----|-----|
| 64.6 − 62 = | 2.6 | 6.8 |
| 69.7 − 62 = | 7.7 | 59.3 |
| 62.0 − 62 = | .0 | .0 |
| 59.5 − 62 = | −2.5 | 6.3 |
| 54.4 − 62 = | −7.6 | 57.8 |

**STEP 3**   Sum these squared differences to find the numerator of the coefficient of
determination. In this case, the answer is 130.2.

**STEP 4**   Subtract the mean value of $Y$ from every individual value of $Y$, and
square these differences.

$$Y - \overline{Y} = (Y - \overline{Y}) \qquad (Y - \overline{Y})^2$$

| $Y - \overline{Y} = (Y - \overline{Y})$ | | $(Y - \overline{Y})^2$ |
|---|---|---|
| 64 − 62 = | 2 | 4 |
| 71 − 62 = | 9 | 81 |
| 61 − 62 = | −1 | 1 |
| 58 − 62 = | −4 | 16 |
| 56 − 62 = | −6 | 36 |

**STEP 5**    Sum these squared differences to get the denominator of the coefficient of determination. The answer is 138.

**STEP 6**    To find the coefficient of determination, divide the value found in Step 3 by the value found in Step 5.

$$r^2 = \frac{130.2}{138} = .94$$

To interpret the coefficient of determination, we can say that the number of patrol cars on a stretch of Highway 35 explains 94% of the variance in the average speed of cars on that stretch of highway.

Although simpler ways of calculating $r^2$ exist, we will not discuss them here, because most people will rely on computer programs to do these calculations. If you want to know the shortcut calculation methods, consult any statistics text.

**correlation coefficient**

The square root of the coefficient of determination is called the **correlation coefficient**, or $r$. The value of $r$ ranges from $-1.0$ for perfect negative correlation to $+1.0$ for perfect positive correlation. Despite its frequent use in many academic disciplines, the correlation coefficient has no inherent value because it is difficult to interpret. The coefficient of determination is far more useful.

## THE STANDARD ERROR OF THE SLOPE

**standard error of the slope**

The third measure of goodness of fit is the standard error of the slope. If we took several samples of two variables and calculated a slope for each sample, the sample slopes would vary somewhat. The standard deviation of these slope estimates is called the **standard error of the slope** estimate. The formula for the standard error of the slope estimate is

$$\text{s.e.}_\beta = \frac{S_{y|x}}{\sqrt{\Sigma(X_i - \overline{X})^2}}$$

The standard error of the slope can be used in the same manner as other standard errors—to place a confidence interval around the slope estimate. The standard error of the slope esitmate is calculated as follows:

**STEP 1**  Calculate $S_{y|x}$, the standard error of the estimate. If you turn back a few pages, you will find that $S_{y|x}$ for the data we have been considering is equal to 1.62.

**STEP 2**  From each value of $X$, subtract the value of $\overline{X}$, and square these differences.

| $X - \overline{X} = (X - \overline{X})$ | | $(X - \overline{X})^2$ |
|---|---|---|
| $3 - 4 =$ | $-1$ | $1$ |
| $1 - 4 =$ | $-3$ | $9$ |
| $4 - 4 =$ | $0$ | $0$ |
| $5 - 4 =$ | $1$ | $1$ |
| $7 - 4 =$ | $3$ | $9$ |

**STEP 3**  Sum all the squared differences: $\Sigma(X_i - \overline{X})^2 = 20$.

**STEP 4**  Take the square root of the number found in Step 3: $\sqrt{20} = 4.47$.

**STEP 5**  Divide the standard error of the estimate (1.62) by the number found in Step 4 to get the standard error of the slope estimate.

$$\text{s.e.}_\beta = \frac{1.62}{4.47} = .36$$

The standard error of the slope estimate can be used just like any other standard error. We can place 90% confidence limits around the slope estimates. To do so, we must distinguish between the sample slope and the population slope. Statisticians use the symbol $\beta$ when referring to the population slope and $b$ for reference to a sample slope (the population intercept is $\alpha$, and the sample intercept is $a$). The procedure for using the sample slope to place a 90% confidence limit around the slope estimate is

$$b \pm t \times \text{s.e.}_\beta, \qquad df = 3$$

$$-2.55 \pm 2.35 \times .36$$

$$-2.55 \pm .85$$

$$-3.40 \text{ to } -1.70$$

We can be 90% sure that the population slope falls between $-1.70$ and $-3.40$.

The standard error of the slope can also be used to answer the following question: What is the probability that one could draw a sample with a slope of $b$ given that the population slope equals zero? This is called *testing the significance of the slope*. If $\beta = 0$, then there is no relationship between the variables in the population. If it is probable that the sample was drawn from such a population, we could not reject the null hypothesis that no relationship exists.

To determine the probability in our example that a sample with a slope of $-2.55$ could have been drawn from a population where $\beta = 0$, we convert $b$ into a $t$ score by using 0 as the mean and by using the standard error of the slope.

$$t = \frac{X - \mu}{\sigma}$$

$$t = \frac{b - \beta}{\text{s.e.}_\beta} = \frac{-2.55 - 0}{.36} = -7.1$$

A $t$ value of 7.1 with 3 degrees of freedom is greater than the value for .005 ($t = 5.841$) but less than the value for .0005 ($t = 12.941$). The probability that a sample with a slope of $-2.55$ could have been drawn from a population with a slope of zero is less than .005. If there are no major research design problems (and there appear to be none), management would be justified in concluding that a relationship exists.

Sometimes the entire population is used to calculate a regression line. In such cases, the preceding exercise of testing for significance does not make theoretical sense. Many analysts do it anyway to illustrate that the relationship is not trivial. A manager must be aware that this is done.

# CHAPTER SUMMARY

Regression is a technique that can be used to describe the statistical relationship between two interval variables. This chapter illustrates the use of simple linear regression.

The relationship between two variables can be summarized by a line, and any line can be fully described by its slope and its intercept. The slope of a line is equal to the ratio of the change in $Y$ for a given change in $X$. The intercept of the line is the point where the line intersects the $Y$-axis. The technique of linear regression uses these concepts to find the best line to describe a relationship, which statisticians have agreed is the line that minimizes the squared errors. All regressions are of the general form $\hat{Y} = \alpha + \beta X$, where $\alpha$ is the intercept and $\beta$ is the slope. Calculations for slopes and intercepts are illustrated in the chapter.

Once the regression line has been found, we usually want to see how well that line summarizes the data. To do so, we use what statisticians call measures of the goodness of fit. Three common measures are used. The standard error of the estimate, $S_{y|x}$, is an estimate of the variation in $\hat{Y}$, the predicted value of $Y$. The coefficient of determination, $r^2$, adjusts for the total variation in $Y$. The standard error of the slope, s.e.$_\beta$, gives the standard deviation of the sample slope estimates. The standard error of the slope can also be used to test (with a $t$ test) the significance of the slope.

## PROBLEMS

**16.1**  The chief of automobile maintenance for the city of Normal feels that maintenance costs on high-mileage cars are much higher than those costs for low-mileage cars. The maintenance chief regresses yearly maintenance costs for a sample of 200 cars on each car's total mileage for the year. She finds the following:

$$\hat{Y} = \$50 + .030X \qquad S_{y|x} = \$150.00 \qquad \text{s.e.}_\beta = .0005 \qquad r^2 = .90$$

where $Y$ is maintenance cost (in dollars) for the year and $X$ is the mileage on a car.

**(a)** Is there a relationship between maintenance costs and mileage?

**(b)** What are the predicted maintenance costs of a car with 50,000 miles? Place a 95% confidence limit around this estimate.

**(c)** The maintenance chief considers $1000 in maintenance a year excessive. For this criterion, how many miles will generate maintenance costs of $1000?

**16.2**  James Jesse, head of the Bureau of Animal Husbandry, perceives that several agencies received large increases in appropriations last year because they encouraged interest groups to testify for them before the House Appropriations Committee. The accompanying sample data for five agencies similar to Jesse's were gathered. Using regression analysis, calculate a regression equation. Does a relationship exist? The Bureau of Animal Husbandry could pressure 15 groups to testify for it. What percentage increase would this number of groups predict? Place a 90% confidence interval around that estimate. How large an increase is each additional interest group worth?

| Interest Groups Testifying | Percentage Increase in Appropriation |
|:---:|:---:|
| 25 | 22 |
| 14 | 17 |
| 7 | 8 |
| 18 | 19 |
| 10 | 12 |

**16.3**  Martina Justice, head of the state Bureau of Criminal Justice, feels that she could significantly reduce the crime rate in the state if the state doubled expenditures for police. To support her argument, Martina runs a regression of state crime rates ($Y$) (in crimes per 100,000 population) on per capita police expenditures (in dollars). She finds the following:

$$\hat{Y} = 2475 + 5.1X \qquad S_{y|x} = 425 \qquad \text{s.e.}_\beta = 1.3 \qquad r^2 = .63 \qquad n = 50$$

What has Martina found? Interpret the slope, intercept, and $r^2$.

**16.4**    The South Dakota Department of Game and Fish (SDDGF) wants to lengthen the pheasant-hunting season to bring in more tourist revenue. SDDGF's thinking is that most pheasants are killed during the first two weeks of the season; therefore, a longer season will not deplete the bird population. Using sample data from all past hunting seasons, Rodney Ringneck, the SDDGF's data analyst, regresses the number of birds surviving the season on the length in days in the season. He finds

$$\hat{Y} = 547,000 - 214X \quad \text{s.e.}_\beta = 415 \quad r^2 = .15 \quad S_{y|x} = 15,000 \quad n = 35$$

What is Rodney's hypothesis? What did he find?

**16.5**    Lieutenant Edgar Beaver believes that officers who take master's level courses receive higher officer efficiency ratings (OERs). Using a sample of 100 officers, Beaver regresses OERs ($Y$—it ranges from 0 to 100) on the number of courses each officer took beyond the BA. He finds

$$\hat{Y} = 95 + .1X \quad S_{y|x} = 1.4 \quad \text{s.e.}_\beta = .07 \quad r^2 = .4$$

What can Beaver say based on these results? Beaver has a 10-course master's degree. What is the best estimate of his OER? Place a 90% confidence limit around this estimate.

**16.6**    The city of Newland owns and operatres the Newland Baseball Park, home of the Newland Nuggets (a minor league baseball team). The city is concerned with waste in the concessions areas. Too many precooked hot dogs are left over after a game. Heinz Canine, the city's research analyst, feels that hot dog consumption (and other concession sales) can be predicted by the number of advance sale tickets purchased for a game (attendance is usually twice advance sales). Heinz gathers the accompanying data for a sample of ten days. Run the regression for Heinz and tell him if his hypothesis is correct. Predict how many hot dogs will be sold if 1000 advance tickets are sold.

| Advance Sales | Hot Dog Sales |
| --- | --- |
| 247 | 503 |
| 317 | 691 |
| 1247 | 2638 |
| 784 | 1347 |
| 247 | 602 |
| 1106 | 2493 |
| 1749 | 3502 |
| 875 | 2100 |
| 963 | 1947 |
| 415 | 927 |

**16.7** The Nome City Personnel Office suspects that employees are staying home on cold days during the winter. The personnel office regresses the number of absences ($Y$) on the low temperature of the preceding night. Using a sample of 60 days, it finds

$$\hat{Y} = 485 - 5.1X \qquad \text{s.e.}_\beta = 1.1 \qquad S_{y|x} = 12.0 \qquad r^2 = .86$$

Interpret the intercept, the slope, and $r^2$. Is the relationship significant? How many people will miss work if the overnight low is $-20°$? Place 90% confidence limits around this estimate.

**16.8** Ridership on the North Salem Independent Transit System is increasing. The city's program evaluation office feels that the increase in the number of riders every day is due to the price of gasoline. Using data for the past three years, the evaluation office regresses daily ridership ($Y$) on the price of gasoline (in cents) for that day ($X$). It finds

$$\hat{Y} = 212 + 187X \qquad \text{s.e.}_\beta = 17.4 \qquad S_{y|x} = 206 \qquad r^2 = .91$$

Write a memo on the policy implications of a 50¢ increase in gasoline prices.

**16.9** The Environmental Protection Agency believes that the air quality in a city is directly related to the number of serious respiratory diseases. The agency regresses the number of reported cases of respiratory diseases per 1000 population on the city's air quality index (ranges from 0 to 100; high scores indicate pollution) for 150 cities. It finds

$$\hat{Y} = 15.7 + .7X \qquad \text{s.e.}_\beta = .04 \qquad S_{y|x} = 5.1 \qquad r^2 = .71$$

Write a memo interpreting these results. What other factors affect this relationship?

**16.10** The Office of Gerontology Policy is considering a lawsuit against the bureau of investigations for age discrimination. OGP wants to base its suit on the following regression of civil service exam scores ($Y$) on age of applicant ($X$) for the bureau of investigations. Write a memo evaluating OGP's case.

$$\hat{Y} = 92.4 - .3X \qquad \text{s.e.}_\beta = .007 \qquad S_{y|x} = 5.2 \qquad r^2 = .45 \qquad n = 500$$

**16.11** The Wisconsin Association of School Districts is interested in the relationship between school district population and funding for schools. From a sample of 300 school districts, the Association uses simple regression to predict total school district expenditures in dollars ($Y$) using the school district's population ($X$ = number of persons residing in the district). Calculate the following regression:

$$\hat{Y} = \$4{,}566 + \$824X$$

$$\text{s.e.}_\beta = 135 \qquad S_{y|x} = 34{,}788 \qquad r^2 = .78$$

$$t = 6.10 \qquad p < .0001$$

Express in plain English what the substantive interpretations of the following are:

1. the intercept
2. the slope
3. the coefficient of determination
4. the $t$-score and how it is calculated

16.12   Stanley Student is an MPA candidate at Big State University. Stanley is concerned about his performance in the BSU's quantitative methods class. The class has consisted of five quizzes and one midterm exam. Stanley is thinking of filing a civil rights suit against his professor because he did really well on the quizzes (a total of 45 points) but not as well on the midterm (75 points). He is thinking of using a unique application of the administrative law doctrine of collateral estoppel in his suit. Before filing suit he needs to know if there is a relationship between quiz grades and midterm grades. After stealing the instructor's grade book, Stanley runs the following regression, where $Y$ is the midterm grade and $X$ is the total points on the quizzes:

$$\hat{Y} = 52.5 + .78X$$

$$S_{y|x} = 8.46$$

$$r^2 = .71 \qquad \text{s.e.}_\beta = .0049 \qquad n = 40$$

Interpret this regression by explaining the meaning of the slope, intercept, and $r^2$, and test the slope for significance. Present, in plain English, a hypothesis concerning the relationship, and then a null hypothesis. What is your best estimate of the midterm grade that Stanley should have received given his quiz grade? Estimate the probability that Stanley would receive a 75 on the midterm given a quiz grade of 45.

16.13   The State Department of Mental Health is doing a study of the use of drugs to control violent behavior among its patients. The case histories of 75 patients are selected for analysis. For each patient two variables are collected: the number of violent incidents the patient was involved in during the previous three months and the daily dosage of Valium given to each patient in milligrams. A regression analysis results in the following:

$$\hat{Y} = 126.6 - .0138X$$

$$\text{s.e.}_{\beta} = .0053 \qquad S_{y|x} = 2.4 \qquad r^2 = .46$$

What is the department's hypothesis? Interpret this regression. Is the hypothesis supported? Esimate the number of violent incidents that would be expected if a patient were given 1000 milligrams of Valium per day. Put a 90 percent confidence limit around this estimate.

**16.14**  The Bureau of Personnel needs to predict how many employees will retire next month. Based on a sample of 35 past months, the bureau has run a regression using the number of employees older than age 60 as the independent variable and the number of retirements as the dependent variable. They calculate the following regression:

$$\hat{Y} = .21 + .04X$$

$$r^2 = .35 \qquad S_{y|x} = 4.5 \qquad \text{s.e.}_{\beta} = .006$$

Interpret the slope, intercept, and coefficient of determination, and test the slope for significance. What is your best estimate of the number of retirements next month if there are 620 employees older than 60. Could this number be as high as 30?

**16.15**  Dick Engstrom and Mike MacDonald are interested in the relationship between black representation on city councils and the structure of the electoral system. Their independent variable is the percentage of blacks in the population; their dependent variable is the percentage of seats on the city council that are held by blacks. Engstrom and MacDonald want to compare representation under single-member district election systems and under at-large election systems. They get the following results:

At-Large Systems

$$\hat{Y} = .348 + .495X$$

$$r^2 = .34 \qquad n = 128 \qquad \text{s.e.}_{\beta} = .061 \qquad S_{y|x} = 2.4$$

Single-Member District Systems

$$\hat{Y} = -.832 + .994X$$

$$r^2 = .816 \qquad n = 36 \qquad \text{s.e.}_{\beta} = .075 \qquad S_{y|x} = 2.1$$

For each equation, interpret the slope, intercept, and coefficient of determination. Test the slope to see if it could be zero. Get the predicted city council representation of a city with 25% black population under both systems. Place a 95% confidence limit around your estimates. Present a hypothesis about the relative impact of electoral systems. What can you say about the relative representation of blacks under each type of system?

**16.16**   Robert Stein of Brooklyn Associates argues that the per capita allocation of federal aid dollars to local governments is related to local needs. He measures *aid* as the number of dollars a city receives per person and *need* as the percentage of city residents that reside in poverty. For 1991, he gets the following results:

$$\hat{Y} = 27.81 + 339.10X$$

$$r^2 = .43 \qquad n = 243 \qquad \text{s.e.}_\beta = 93.4 \qquad S_{y|x} = 124.066 \qquad n = 147$$

Interpret this equation. Present a hypothesis and a null hypothesis, and evaluate the hypotheses based on this equation.

**16.17**   Presidential candidate Rebecca Hendrick wants to know if it would be worthwhile to challenge the incumbent next year. If she decides to run, she feels the key issue should be inflation, so she is interested in whether or not the inflation rate ($X$, in percentage increase in the CPI) is related to the percentage of the vote received by the presidential candidate of the party in power. Using twelve elections, the following regression is found:

$$\hat{Y} = 54.3 - .84X \qquad \text{s.e.}_\beta = .24 \qquad r^2 = .34 \qquad S_{y|x} = 1.9$$

Interpret this equation. Present a hypothesis and a null hypothesis, and test them. If inflation is 8%, predict the vote for the incumbent's party and place an 80% confidence limit around it.

## ANSWER TO REGRESSION PROBLEM

$$\overline{X} = 7.1 \qquad \overline{Y} = 84$$

| $X_i - \overline{X}$ | | $(X_i - \overline{X})^2$ | $Y_i - \overline{Y}$ | | $(X_i - \overline{X}) \times (Y_i - \overline{Y})$ | | |
|---|---|---|---|---|---|---|---|
| $12.4 - 7.1 =$ | 5.3 | 28.1 | $146 - 84 =$ | 62 | 5.3 × | 62 | = 328.6 |
| $6.1 - 7.1 =$ | $-1.0$ | 1.0 | $85 - 84 =$ | 1 | $-1.0$ × | 1 | $= -1.0$ |
| $2.4 - 7.1 =$ | $-4.7$ | 22.1 | $21 - 84 =$ | $-63$ | $-4.7$ × | $-63$ | = 296.1 |
| $4.3 - 7.1 =$ | $-2.8$ | 7.8 | $47 - 84 =$ | $-37$ | $-2.8$ × | $-37$ | = 103.6 |
| $9.5 - 7.1 =$ | 2.4 | 5.8 | $115 - 84 =$ | 31 | 2.4 × | 31 | = 74.4 |
| $7.6 - 7.1 =$ | .5 | .3 | $90 - 84 =$ | 6 | .5 × | 6 | = 3.0 |

$$\Sigma(X_i - \overline{X})(Y_i - \overline{Y}) = 804.7$$

$$\Sigma(X_i - \overline{X})^2 = 65.1$$

$$\beta = \frac{804.7}{65.1} = 12.4$$

$$\alpha = \overline{Y} - \beta\overline{X} = 84 - 12.4 \times 7.1 = 84 - 88.0 = -4.0$$

$$\hat{Y} = -4.0 + 12.4X$$

## CHAPTER 17

# THE ASSUMPTIONS

# OF LINEAR

# REGRESSION

The presentation in Chapter 16 did not discuss the assumptions and limitations of linear regression. In the real world, almost all analysts ignore these assumptions, but they do so at some managerial risk. All the manipulations presented in the previous chapter become less reliable when any of the assumptions is not met.

In Chapter 16, recall that our highway patrol example found that

$$\hat{Y} = 72.2 - 2.55X \qquad r^2 = .94$$

where $\hat{Y}$ is the predicted speed of all cars, and $X$ is the number of patrol cars. In our discussion in Chapter 16, we found that $\hat{Y}_i$ did not exactly equal the real value of $Y_i$. According to the coefficient of determination, we only accounted for 94% of the variation in $Y$ with $\hat{Y}$. What sort of other factors account for average car speed other than number of patrol cars on the road?

We can think of several factors. The weather conditions on any given day can slow traffic. The emergence and filling of potholes affect traffic speed. The number of other cars on the road restricts any one car's speed. The curves and hills on a stretch of highway affect traffic speed. These factors and others probably account for the difference between $Y_i$ and $\hat{Y}_i$. We could express this symbolically as

$$\hat{Y} = \alpha + \beta X + \beta_1(X_1, X_2, X_3, X_4)$$

where $X_1, X_2, X_3, X_4$ are the other factors, and $\beta_1$ is some weight.

To simplify matters, we generally refer to all the other factors as $e$, or error.

$$Y = \alpha + \beta X + e$$

That is, the value of $Y$ is equal to some constant ($\alpha$) plus a constant ($\beta$) times $X$ plus some error ($e$).

We introduce this terminology because most assumptions about linear regression are concerned with the error component. In this chapter, we will discuss the assumptions and limitations—the results of the error component—of linear regression.

# ASSUMPTION 1

For any value of $X$, the errors in predicting $Y$ are normally distributed with a mean of zero.

To illustrate, let us assume that we continue the Normal, Oklahoma, patrol car experiment for an entire year. Every day between one and seven cars are sent out to patrol the local highway, and the average speed of all cars is measured. At the end of the year, let us assume that the overall regression equation remains the same:

$$\hat{Y} = 72.2 - 2.55X$$

By the end of the year, we probably have 50 days when 4 patrol cars were on the road. The average speed for each of these 50 days is listed in Table 17.1 in a frequency distribution.

**TABLE 17.1**
Frequency Distribution for Patrol Cars and
Average Speeds (in mph)

| Average Speed | Number of Days |
|---|---|
| 58.5–59.0 | 1 |
| 59.0–59.5 | 2 |
| 59.5–60.0 | 2 |
| 60.0–60.5 | 4 |
| 60.5–61.0 | 4 |
| 61.0–61.5 | 6 |
| 61.5–62.0 | 6 |
| 62.0–62.5 | 6 |
| 62.5–63.0 | 6 |
| 63.0–63.5 | 4 |
| 63.5–64.0 | 4 |
| 64.0–64.5 | 2 |
| 64.5–65.0 | 2 |
| 65.0–65.5 | 1 |
| 65.5–66.0 | 0 |

Using the midpoint of the frequencies to represent each interval, we can calculate the error for each prediction, because we know that the predicted speed for 4 patrol cars is 62 miles per hour ($72.2 - 2.55 \times 4 = 62$). The error calculations are given in Table 17.2. The mean error for all 50 cars is 0 (add the last column and divide by 50) and is distributed fairly close to normal.

**TABLE 17.2**

Error Calculations

| Average Speed | − | Predicted Speed | = | Error | × | Frequency | = | Total Error |
|---|---|---|---|---|---|---|---|---|
| 58.75 | − | 62 | = | −3.25 | × | 1 | = | −3.25 |
| 59.25 | − | 62 | = | −2.75 | × | 2 | = | −5.50 |
| 59.75 | − | 62 | = | −2.25 | × | 2 | = | −4.50 |
| 60.25 | − | 62 | = | −1.75 | × | 4 | = | −7.00 |
| 60.75 | − | 62 | = | −1.25 | × | 4 | = | −5.00 |
| 61.25 | − | 62 | = | −.75 | × | 6 | = | −3.75 |
| 61.75 | − | 62 | = | −.25 | × | 6 | = | −1.50 |
| 62.25 | − | 62 | = | .25 | × | 6 | = | 1.50 |
| 62.75 | − | 62 | = | .75 | × | 6 | = | 3.75 |
| 63.25 | − | 62 | = | 1.25 | × | 4 | = | 5.00 |
| 63.75 | − | 62 | = | 1.75 | × | 4 | = | 7.00 |
| 64.25 | − | 62 | = | 2.25 | × | 2 | = | 4.50 |
| 64.75 | − | 62 | = | 2.75 | × | 2 | = | 5.50 |
| 65.25 | − | 62 | = | 3.25 | × | 1 | = | 3.25 |

Whenever $e$ has a mean of zero and is normally distributed, statisticians have found that sample slopes ($b$) have a mean equal to the population slope ($\beta$) and are distributed like the $t$ distribution with a standard deviation s.e.$_\beta$. When the sample size is fairly large ($N > 30$), then the $t$ distribution resembles the normal distribution, and $z$ scores can be used in place of $t$ scores. Since the $t$ distribution is flatter than the normal distribution, it behooves us to use large samples whenever possible.

## ASSUMPTION 2

The variance of the error term is constant, regardless of the value of $X$. In other words, errors do not get larger as $X$ gets larger. In Figure 17.1(a), errors have the same variance for all values of $X$; in Figure 17.1(b), the errors get larger as the value of $X$ increases.

If this assumption of linear regression is violated (statisticians call it *homoscedasticity*), then the slope coefficient will appear to be significant when in fact it may not be. Techniques exist for handling many types of nonhomoscedasticity, but they are fairly advanced. The term *homoscedasticity* is a good one to know. The manager can always disturb her statistician by asking her if the homoscedasticity assumption is met.

Although we have been discussing errors for which the size of the error is positively related to the value of $X$ (as $X$ increases, $e$ increases), the opposite

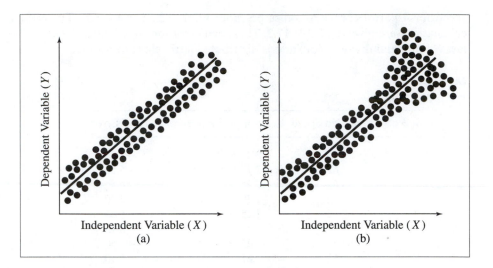

**FIGURE 17.1**

Errors and Their
Variance

situation is just as severe. If $e$ decreases as $X$ increases, the data are still nonhomoscedastic.

## ASSUMPTION 3

Assumption 3 is related to Assumptions 1 and 2. Assumption 3 is that the errors are independent of each other.

Another way of stating this assumption is to say that the size of one error is not a function of the size of any previous errors. We can test for nonindependent errors by examining the residuals (the predicted value of $Y$ minus the actual value of $Y$). If they appear to be random with respect to each other, then the errors are independent, and we need not worry. Computer programs exist that can determine whether errors are not random. If this problem ever exists, find a statistician or consult a textbook (see Nelson, 1973). This problem usually causes difficulty only when time series data are used (see Chapter 18). Chapter 20 includes some tests for nonrandom errors.

## ASSUMPTION 4

Both the independent and the dependent variables must be interval variables (see Chapter 7).

The purist position is that regression cannot be performed with nominal or ordinal data. In a practical situation, however, regression with nominal or ordinal dependent and independent variables is possible. First, we will illustrate regression with a nominal independent variable.

The Midwest City Parks superintendent wants to determine whether brand $X$ or brand $Y$ riding mowers are more efficient. He tries three of each, and tests them over normal city parks; he finds the data given in Table 17.3.

**TABLE 17.3**
Mower Brand and Acres of Grass Mowed

| Mower | Acres of Grass Mowed |
|-------|---------------------|
| Brand $X1$ | 52 |
| Brand $X2$ | 63 |
| Brand $X3$ | 71 |
| Brand $Y1$ | 54 |
| Brand $Y2$ | 46 |
| Brand $Y3$ | 38 |

If the independent variable (the type of mower) is coded 1 when brand $X$ is used and coded 0 when brand $Y$ is used, we have a nominal variable (nominal variables with values of 1 or 0 are called *dummy variables*).

| $X$ | $Y$ | $\bar{X} = .5$ | $\bar{Y} = 54$ |
|-----|-----|-----|-----|
| 1 | 52 | | |
| 1 | 63 | | |
| 1 | 71 | | |
| 0 | 54 | | |
| 0 | 46 | | |
| 0 | 38 | | |

Recall from Chapter 16 that the formula for the slope of a regression line is

$$\frac{\Sigma(X_i - \bar{X})(Y_i - \bar{Y})}{\Sigma(X_i - \bar{X})^2}$$

The calculations follow.

| $X_i - \bar{X} = (X_i - \bar{X})$ | | $(X_i - \bar{X})^2$ | $Y_i - \bar{Y} = (Y_i - \bar{Y})$ | |
|-----|-----|-----|-----|-----|
| $1 - .5 =$ | $.5$ | $.25$ | $52 - 54 =$ | $-2$ |
| $1 - .5 =$ | $.5$ | $.25$ | $63 - 54 =$ | $9$ |
| $1 - .5 =$ | $.5$ | $.25$ | $71 - 54 =$ | $17$ |
| $0 - .5 =$ | $-.5$ | $.25$ | $54 - 54 =$ | $0$ |
| $0 - .5 =$ | $-.5$ | $.25$ | $46 - 54 =$ | $-8$ |
| $0 - .5 =$ | $-.5$ | $.25$ | $38 - 54 =$ | $-16$ |

$$\Sigma(X_i - \bar{X})^2 = 1.50$$

$$(X_i - \overline{X}) \times (Y_i - \overline{Y}) = (X_i - \overline{X})(Y_i - \overline{Y})$$

| | | | | |
|---|---|---|---|---|
| .5 | × | −2 | = | −1 |
| .5 | × | 9 | = | 4.5 |
| .5 | × | 17 | = | 8.5 |
| −.5 | × | 0 | = | 0 |
| −.5 | × | 8 | = | 4.0 |
| −.5 | × | −16 | = | 8.0 |

$$\Sigma(X_i - \overline{X})(Y_i - \overline{Y}) = 24$$

$$b = \frac{24}{1.5} = 16$$

$$a = \overline{Y} - b\overline{X} = 54 - 16 \times .5 = 46$$

$$\hat{Y} = 46 + 16X$$

Since $X$ can be only two values, 0 and 1, $\hat{Y}$ can be only two values, 46 and 62. If we test for the significance of the regression slope, we will find whether the brand $X$ mowers cut significantly more grass than do the brand $Y$ mowers. Recall that the formula for the standard error of the slope is

$$\text{s.e.}_\beta = \frac{S_{y|x}}{\sqrt{\Sigma(X - \overline{X})^2}} = \frac{S_{y|x}}{\sqrt{1.5}} = \frac{S_{y|x}}{1.22}$$

Recall that $S_{y|x}$ can be calculated by the following formula:

$$S_{y|x}^2 = \frac{\Sigma(Y_i - \hat{Y}_i)^2}{n - 2}$$

The calculations follow.

| $Y_i - \hat{Y}_i = (Y_i - \hat{Y}_i)$ | | | $(Y_i - \hat{Y}_i)^2$ |
|---|---|---|---|
| 52 − 62 = | −10 | | 100 |
| 63 − 62 = | 1 | | 1 |
| 71 − 62 = | 9 | | 81 |
| 54 − 46 = | 8 | | 64 |
| 46 − 46 = | 0 | | 0 |
| 38 − 46 = | −8 | | 64 |

$$S_{y|x}^2 = \frac{\Sigma(Y_i - \hat{Y}_i)^2}{n - 2} = \frac{310}{4} = 77.5$$

$$S_{y|x} = 8.8$$

Substituting this value into the preceding formula yields

$$\text{s.e.}_{\beta} = \frac{8.8}{1.22} = 7.2$$

Converting $b = 16.0$ to a $t$ score, we have

$$t = \frac{16.0 - 0}{7.2} = 2.22$$

With a $t$ score of 2.22, the probability of brand $X$ being no better than brand $Y$ is approximately .05 ($t$ test, df $= 4$).

When the mower problem was first presented, you may have thought that this problem could have been solved with analysis of variance (see Chapter 12). Indeed, it can.

| Brand $X$ | Brand $Y$ |
|---|---|
| $\overline{X} = 62$ | $\overline{Y} = 46$ |
| $s = 9.5$ | $s = 8.0$ |
| s.e. $= 5.48$ | s.e. $= 4.61$ |

$$\text{s.e.}_{\text{overall}} = \sqrt{5.48^2 + 4.61^2} = 7.2$$

$$z = \frac{62 - 46}{7.2} = \frac{16}{7.2} = 2.22$$

Notice that we get the same answer that we obtained using regression. This result occurs because analysis of variance is similar to regression with dummy variables (a dummy variable is a nominal variable with codes 1 and 0). You should also note that the regression intercept (46) is the same value as one of the means; the slope (16) is equal to the difference between the means; and the standard error of the slope (7.2) is equal to the overall standard error in analysis of variance.

Regression can also be performed with a nominal dependent variable. Suppose a personnel office tests the typing skills of ten job applicants, who are then hired. After one year, five of these typists have been fired. A personnel manager hypothesizes that the typists were fired because they lacked good typing skills. The job situation and typing scores are listed in Table 17.4.

After subjecting these data to a regression program, the analyst found the following relationship:

$$\hat{Y} = -1.19 + .0248X \qquad \text{s.e.}_{\beta} = .009$$

$$S_{y|x} = .4 \qquad r^2 = .49$$

**TABLE 17.4**

Job Situation and Typing Score

| Job Situation, $Y$ (0 = fired; 1 = not fired) | Typing Score, $X$ (words per minute) |
|---|---|
| 1 | 85 |
| 0 | 48 |
| 1 | 63 |
| 0 | 57 |
| 1 | 94 |
| 0 | 56 |
| 1 | 65 |
| 0 | 58 |
| 0 | 72 |
| 1 | 82 |

Clearly a relationship exists ($t = 2.8$, df = 8). To interpret this regression, we must interpret $\hat{Y}$ as the probability that a typist is not fired. For example, substituting the first person's typing score into the regression equation, we find

$$\hat{Y} = -1.19 + .0248(85) = -1.19 + 2.11 = .92$$

The probability that the first person will not be fired is .92. Similar calculations could be made for all typists, and confidence limits could be placed around the probability by using the standard error of the estimate.

Regression with dummy dependent variables does have some pitfalls. If we substitute the typing score of the fifth person (94) into the regression equation, we find

$$\hat{Y} = -1.19 + .0248(94) = -1.19 + 2.33 = 1.14$$

The probability that this person will not be fired is 1.14, a meaningless probability. Using regression with dummy dependent variables often results in probabilities greater than 1 or less than 0. Managerially, we might want to interpret probabilities of more than 1.0 as equal to .99. Similarly, probabilities of less than 0 can be reset to .01. For most management situations, these adjustments will eliminate uninterpretable predictions. Special types of analysis called *probit and logit analysis* can be used to restrict probabilities to values between 0 and 1. These techniques are fairly sophisticated and, therefore, should not be used without expert assistance.

# ASSUMPTION 5

The final assumption of regression is that the relationships are linear.

Linear relationships are those that can be summarized by a straight line (without any curve). If linear regression is used to summarize a nonlinear rela-

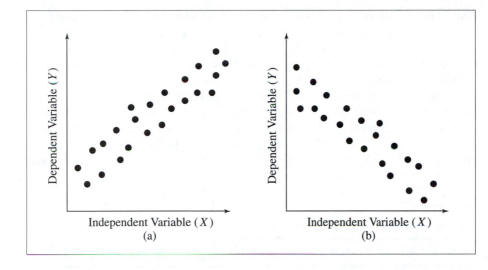

**FIGURE 17.2**
Linear Relationships

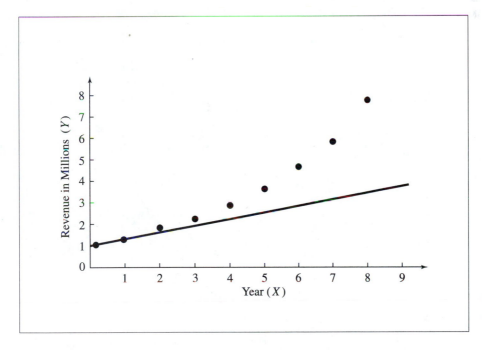

**FIGURE 17.3**
A Nonlinear
Relationship

tionship, the regression equation will be inaccurate. To determine if a relationship is linear, we must plot the data. The data plotted in Figure 17.2 represent linear relationships.

Unfortunately, many relationships that a manager must consider are not linear. For example, the city manager may want to project city revenues for next year. The growth of city revenues may well look like the graph in Figure 17.3. Revenues increase in this example faster than a linear relationship would predict. The graph represents a *logarithmic* relationship. Such relationships and how they can be treated in regression are the subject of the next chapter.

Another relationship sometimes found in the public sector is the *quadratic* relationship. In situations in which adding another worker will improve the productivity of all workers (because workers can then specialize and be more efficient), the relationship between the number of workers and total productivity may be quadratic. This idea is illustrated by the data in Table 17.5. Graphically, this relationship appears as shown in Figure 17.4. Quadratic relationships are discussed in Chapter 19.

**TABLE 17.5**

Data Representing a Quadratic Relationship

| Number of Welfare Workers ($X$) | Number of Cases Processed per Day ($Y$) |
|:---:|:---:|
| 1 | 1 |
| 2 | 4 |
| 3 | 9 |
| 4 | 16 |
| 5 | 25 |

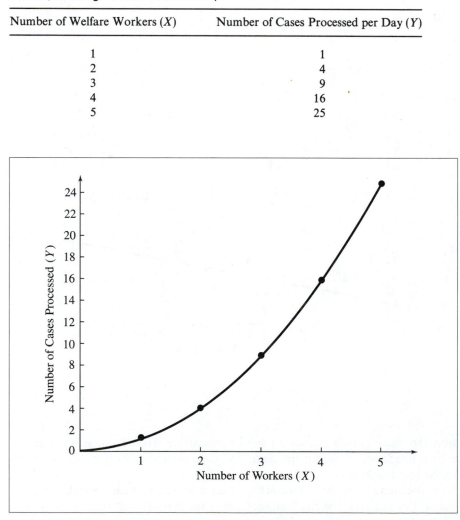

**FIGURE 17.4**

A Quadratic Relationship

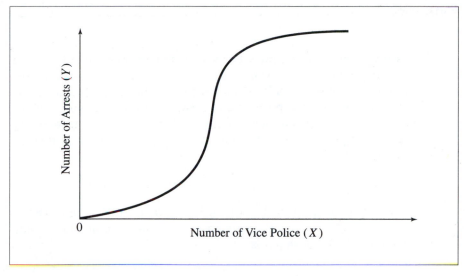

**FIGURE 17.5**
A Cubic
Relationship

Other relationships may be *cubic*. For example, the relationship of the total number of vice police to the number of prostitution arrests is probably cubic. The first few vice police will make very few arrests because they have so much territory to cover. Adding more vice police will raise the productivity of all vice police. As more and more vice police are added, the total arrests will level out (either because all possible prostitutes have been arrested or because they left town). The relationship would appear as shown in Figure 17.5. Cubic relationships will also be discussed in Chapter 19.

The important thing to remember about nonlinear relationships is that linear regression is not a good way to summarize them. Computers cannot (or, rather, usually do not) distinguish linear from nonlinear relationships; the onus is on the manager to discern nonlinear relationships.

## CHAPTER SUMMARY

This chapter discusses five assumptions made by simple linear regression and presents some of the problems associated with violating these assumptions. The assumptions are as follows: (1) all errors in prediction are normally distributed; (2) the distribution of the errors is constant regardless of the value of $X$; (3) the errors are independent of each other; (4) both variables are measured at the interval level; and (5) the relationship is linear. Almost all analysts ignore these assumptions in their day-to-day routine, but they do so at some managerial risk. All the analytical techniques presented in the previous chapter become less reliable when any of the assumptions is not met.

## PROBLEMS

**17.1** The Normal City police chief wants to know whether police car cruising has any impact on crime rates. Of the city's ten precincts, five are cruised regularly, and the other five are never cruised (police do respond to calls in these precincts). At the end of a test period, the police chief takes the crime rate $(Y)$ in each precinct and regresses it on a dummy variable coded 1 for cruising and coded 0 for no cruising $(X)$. From the following regression equation, what can you say about police cruising and crime rates in Normal?

$$\hat{Y} = 247.5 + 24X \qquad \text{s.e.}_\beta = 48 \qquad S_{y|x} = 35.0 \qquad r^2 = .12$$

**17.2** Take each set of data in the accompanying table and graph it. Determine whether the relationships are linear or nonlinear. If nonlinear, state what type of relationship it is.

| No. 1 | | No. 2 | | No. 3 | | No. 4 | |
|---|---|---|---|---|---|---|---|
| X | Y | X | Y | X | Y | X | Y |
| 2 | 1 | 2 | 1 | 1 | 5 | 1 | 15 |
| 5 | 3 | 5 | 3 | 4 | 8 | 2 | 11 |
| 7 | 6 | 8 | 5 | 7 | 11 | 4 | 6 |
| 9 | 10 | 11 | 9 | 10 | 14 | 6 | 4 |
| 14 | 15 | 14 | 14 | 13 | 17 | 9 | 3 |
| 17 | 16 | | | 16 | 20 | 15 | 2 |

**17.3** The city parks chief is concerned about sprinkler systems corroding in parks and failing to operate. Using a sample of 100 sprinklers in operation the previous year, the parks department regresses whether or not a sprinkler failed ($Y$, coded 1 for failure and 0 for no failure) on the age of the sprinkler system. The department gets the following regression equation ($X$ is age in years):

$$\hat{Y} = .06 + .016X \qquad \text{s.e.}_\beta = .0006$$

$$S_{y|x} = .04 \qquad r^2 = .56$$

**(a)** Is there a relationship?
**(b)** The sprinkler system in Frolic Park is 52 years old. What is the probability that this sprinkler system will fail?
**(c)** A sprinkler system that is only 2 years old fails in Barren Park. What is the probability that this will happen?
**(d)** What is the probability that the 65-year-old sprinkler system in Choirpractice Park will fail?

**17.4**  Too many U.S. Army mechanics are failing their yearly skills tests. Colonel Maxwell Brown believes that this failure rate results because mechanics do not learn anything from experience. His hypothesis is that time spent in an occupational specialty is unrelated to performance on the exam. He regresses whether or not a mechanic failed the test (0 = failure, 1 = no failure) on the mechanic's time as a mechanic ($X$) in years. For a sample of 400 troops, he finds

$$\hat{Y} = .63 + .03X \qquad S_{y|x} = .41 \qquad \text{s.e.}_\beta = .61 \qquad r^2 = .09$$

Evaluate Brown's argument by interpreting the regression.

**17.5**  Refer to Problem 17.4. Sergeant Desk believes the failures are related to reading ability. She regresses whether or not these same 400 troops failed ($Y$) on their reading test scores ($X$, scored in terms of school grade levels). She finds

$$\hat{Y} = .15 + .071X \qquad S_{y|x} = .06 \qquad \text{s.e.}_\beta = .011 \qquad r^2 = .80$$

Interpret Desk's regression. Compare her argument with that of Brown's. Can you reconcile them?

**17.6**  Refer to Problem 17.5. What is the probability that a troop reading at the fifth-grade level will pass the mechanics' exam? To be 80% sure that 75% of the mechanics pass the exam, what would the reading level need to be raised to? Comment on the validity of the mechanics' exam.

**17.7**  The Department of Health and Human Services (HHS) wants to compare average per capita health care costs for four cities that have health maintenance organizations (HMOs) with four similar cities that do not have HMOs. Using the accompanying data, run a regression, and prepare a brief memo to HHS about the findings.

| HMO Cities | Non-HMO Cities |
|---|---|
| $412 | $516 |
| $386 | $250 |
| $370 | $409 |
| $404 | $460 |

**17.8**  The Intercity Bus Company is concerned with the high cost of fuel. The company believes that fuel is being wasted because drivers are exceeding the speed limit. A series of tests ($N = 85$) shows the following relationship between bus speed ($X$) and miles per gallon of fuel ($Y$) for speeds between 35 and 85 miles per hour (mph):

$$\hat{Y} = 12.4 - .11X \qquad \text{s.e.}_\beta = .007 \qquad S_{y|x} = .41 \qquad r^2 = .98$$

Intercity is considering placing a governor on all buses, limiting their speed to 55 mph. At an average speed of 55 miles per hour (mph), how many miles per gallon would a bus get? Place a 95% confidence limit around this estimate.

**17.9** Refer to Problem 17.8. Intercity buses travel 8200 miles a week. Current miles per gallon for buses is 5.1. Provide an estimate of the amount of money that could be saved in a week (with a 55 mph governor) if fuel costs $2 per gallon. Place 95% confidence limits around this estimate.

**17.10** The White Hawk Indian Tribe wants to know whether their Head Start program is having any impact. To examine this question, an analyst regresses the reading scores in class grade equivalents of all fourth-grade students ($Y$) on whether the student was enrolled in a Head Start program ($1$ = enrolled; $0$ = not enrolled). Interpret the following regression for the tribe.

$$\hat{Y} = 3.2 + .06X \qquad \text{s.e.}_\beta = .1 \qquad S_{y|x} = 1.1 \qquad r^2 = .16$$

**17.11** The Wisconsin Insurance Commission wants to know whether states that have no-fault insurance for automobiles have lower insurance rates. The commission takes a survey of 20 states and asks whether they have a no-fault insurance law (coded 1 if they do) and determines the cost (in dollars) of an automobile insurance policy for a 30-year-old male driver who drives 15,000 miles per year and owns a 1985 Dodge Omni. It gets the following results:

$$\hat{Y} = \$265.00 - 74.33X$$

$$\text{s.e.}_\beta = 29.4 \qquad S_{y|x} = 14.9 \qquad r^2 = .34$$

Present a hypothesis, a null hypothesis, and evaluate them. Present a conclusion in plain English. Do not forget to interpret the regression.

**17.12** A study by the Occupational Safety and Health Administration seeks to know whether the probability that an industrial plant is inspected is affected by the number of accidents at the plant. An analyst regresses whether a plant is inspected ($1$ = inspected) on the number of accidents resulting in a lost day of work ($X$). He finds:

$$\hat{Y} = .04 + .012X$$

$$\text{s.e.}_\beta = .0021 \qquad S_{y|x} = .19 \qquad r^2 = .48 \qquad N = 320$$

Interpret this regression. If Ace Manufacturing has 14 accidents resulting in lost work days, what can you say about whether it will be inspected?

## CHAPTER 18

# TIME SERIES
# ANALYSIS

Any public manager who can accurately predict the future will become a member of the Senior Executive Service before he or she is 35 years old. In many situations, a manager must make decisions today that will not be implemented until next year, and the success of those decisions will depend on factors unknown at the time of the decision. A personnel manager needs to know the agency's total employment for next year to negotiate health care plans with private insurers. A city budget officer needs to know next year's revenue to make current budget decisions. A public works planner needs to know the demand for sewage disposal over the next 20 years so that disposal systems can be designed and constructed.

Projecting the future state of some managerially relevant variable is called **forecasting**. The major building block that permits data-based forecasting is called **time series analysis**. This chapter will illustrate a variety of time series techniques. First, the general principles of time series analysis will be noted. Second, simple time series linear regression models will be illustrated, followed by a more common logarithmic regression model. Third, the forecasting ability of these models will be illustrated. Finally, the bivariate time series model will be discussed.

**forecasting**

**time series analysis**

## INTRODUCTION TO
## TIME SERIES

A **time series** is nothing more than a sequence of observations on some variable ($Y$) when the observations occur at equally spaced time intervals. To illustrate the general principles of time series, we will use the following example. Kerry

**time series**

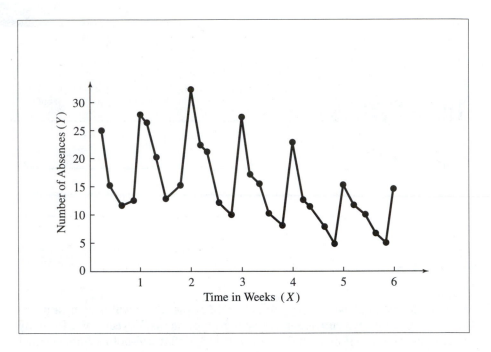

Jones, the head of the Normal City Public Works Department, needs to know the number of absences by sanitation engineers. Kerry uses this information to hire substitutes, who are then assigned to refuse policing units (garbage crews) when a member of the crew does not show up for work. Substitutes are assigned because the efficiency of a crew drops dramatically when the crew is short-handed. At the same time, Kerry announces an incentive program to reduce absenteeism. Any employee who does not use his or her sick leave by the end of the year will receive a cash payment. The graph in Figure 18.1 shows the number of absent sanitary engineers for the six weeks following the announcement of the incentive program.

**cyclical pattern**    The first noticeable aspect of the absenteeism graph is that a **cyclical pattern** based on the day of the week is present. Monday consistently has the second highest number of absentees. Absenteeism then drops on Tuesday and falls still further on Wednesday. After a slight increase on Thursday, absenteeism skyrockets to its weekly high on Friday. The cyclical pattern is the first important aspect that the analyst reports. It tells the analyst that absenteeism follows the same pattern for the public works department that it follows for most businesses and government (that is, much absenteeism appears to result from long weekends).

A second, perhaps more important, question for Kerry Jones is, did the absenteeism rate decline after the incentive system was introduced? This question is difficult to answer from the graph, because the day-to-day fluctuations (*short-term variation*) obscure any long-term trend. If the short-term fluctuations could be removed from the data, however, the long-term trend would be visible.

The accepted way to filter out a short-term fluctuation is by using a **moving average**. The first step is to determine how long the short-term cycle is. In this situation, the length of the short-term trend is obvious—five days. Absenteeism follows a five-day pattern, peaking on Mondays and Fridays. In this situation, then, a five-term moving average is needed.

**moving average**

To get a five-term moving average, simply take each day's number of absences and add the absences for the two previous days and the two following

**TABLE 18.1**

Calculations for Five-Term Moving Average

| Week | Day | Day Number | Absences (Y) | Sum | 5-Term Average | Fluctuation |
|------|-----|-----------|--------------|-----|----------------|-------------|
| 1 | M | 1 | 25 | | | |
| | Tu | 2 | 15 | | | |
| | W | 3 | 11 | 91 | 18.2 | −7.2 |
| | Th | 4 | 12 | 92 | 18.4 | −6.4 |
| | F | 5 | 28 | 97 | 19.4 | 8.6 |
| 2 | M | 6 | 26 | 98 | 19.6 | 6.4 |
| | Tu | 7 | 20 | 99 | 20.6 | −.6 |
| | W | 8 | 12 | 103 | 19.8 | −7.8 |
| | Th | 9 | 13 | 99 | 19.8 | −6.8 |
| | F | 10 | 32 | 100 | 20.0 | 12.0 |
| 3 | M | 11 | 22 | 100 | 20.0 | 2.0 |
| | Tu | 12 | 21 | 97 | 19.4 | 1.6 |
| | W | 13 | 12 | 93 | 18.6 | −6.6 |
| | Th | 14 | 10 | 88 | 17.6 | −7.6 |
| | F | 15 | 28 | 82 | 16.4 | 11.6 |
| 4 | M | 16 | 17 | 80 | 16.0 | 1.0 |
| | Tu | 17 | 15 | 78 | 15.6 | −.6 |
| | W | 18 | 10 | 73 | 14.6 | −4.6 |
| | Th | 19 | 8 | 68 | 13.6 | −5.6 |
| | F | 20 | 23 | 64 | 12.8 | 10.2 |
| 5 | M | 21 | 12 | 61 | 12.2 | −.2 |
| | Tu | 22 | 11 | 58 | 11.6 | −.6 |
| | W | 23 | 7 | 50 | 10.0 | −3.0 |
| | Th | 24 | 5 | 46 | 9.2 | −4.2 |
| | F | 25 | 15 | 48 | 9.6 | 5.4 |
| 6 | M | 26 | 11 | 47 | 9.4 | 1.6 |
| | Tu | 27 | 10 | 47 | 9.4 | .6 |
| | W | 28 | 6 | 46 | 9.2 | −3.2 |
| | Th | 29 | 5 | | | |
| | F | 30 | 14 | | | |

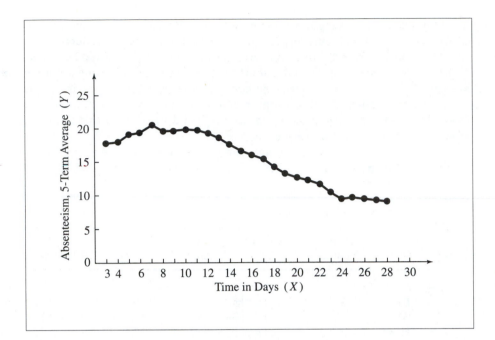

days. Divide this sum by 5. The resulting number is the five-term moving average. These calculations are performed in Table 18.1. (Note that the first two and the last two days in the table do not have five-term moving averages.) The five-term moving average can then be graphed to determine whether the absenteeism rate is declining. See Figure 18.2.

From the graph in Figure 18.2, we can clearly see a trend in absences. If Kerry were interested in a further specification of the relationship, he could apply regression analysis to the data. This result would tell him how strong the relationship between time and absenteeism is (or, within the context of this problem, how great a decline in absenteeism followed the incentive program).

Whenever the length of a short-term fluctuation is an odd number, computing a moving average is easy. In our example, the value for the third observation was the average of observations 1, 2, 3, 4, and 5. For a three-term moving average, the value of the third observation is the average of observations 2, 3, and 4. For a short-term fluctuation of an even number of terms, we run into a problem. Using the previous data for a four-term moving average model, we find that the first moving average is 15.8—but this is the value for the $2\frac{1}{2}$ observation. A $2\frac{1}{2}$ observation does not make sense. In this situation, we first calculate the four-term moving average for the $3\frac{1}{2}$ observation (16.5). Then we take the average of the $2\frac{1}{2}$ observation and the $3\frac{1}{2}$ observation and assign this value to the third observation [$(15.8 + 16.5) \div 2 = 16.2$)]. We continue this procedure for all items, as illustrated below.

| Observation: | 1 | 2 | 3 | 4 | 5 | 6 | 7 |
|---|---|---|---|---|---|---|---|
| Four-term Average: | | 15.8 | 16.5 | 19.3 | 21.5 | 21.5 | |
| Adjusted Average: | | | 16.2 | 17.9 | 20.4 | 21.5 | |

# FORECASTING WITHOUT
# FLUCTUATION

The chief personnel officer of Berryville needs to know approximately how many employees Berryville will have each year for the next five years. The only information that Ms. Jean Cruncher, the head personnel analyst, has is the city's employment figures since 1979. These data appear in Table 18.2.

Ms. Cruncher assumes that the same factors that have caused employment to increase in the past fifteen years (mandated federal programs, population growth, citizen demands for services, and so on) will continue to influence employment over the next five years. By assuming that the future will resemble the past, Ms. Cruncher can use some fairly simple techniques to forecast the city's employment in 1993, 1994, 1995, 1996, and 1997.

**TABLE 18.2**

Berryville Employment Data

| Year | Berryville City Employment Employees (thousands) |
|---|---|
| 1979 | 35.7 |
| 1980 | 38.8 |
| 1981 | 40.9 |
| 1982 | 43.4 |
| 1983 | 44.9 |
| 1984 | 47.2 |
| 1985 | 48.8 |
| 1986 | 50.8 |
| 1987 | 50.8 |
| 1988 | 50.7 |
| 1989 | 55.0 |
| 1990 | 55.3 |
| 1991 | 58.6 |
| 1992 | 59.9 |

**STEP 1** The first step in time series analysis (just like the first step in any bivariate analysis) is to plot the data. Employment should be considered the dependent variable, and the year should be considered the independent variable. See Figure 18.3.

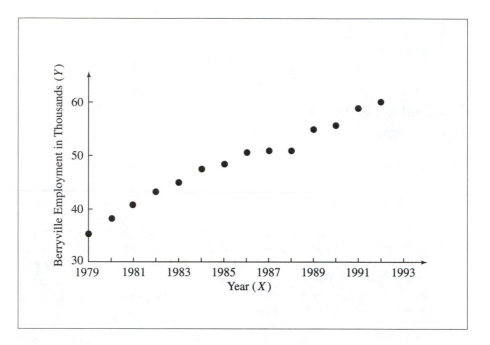

**FIGURE 18.3**

Berryville
Employment Data

**STEP 2**  Examine the plot of the data and determine if any short-term fluctuations exist. The data show no appreciable short-term fluctuation, so go
on to Step 4.

**STEP 3**  If the data show a cyclical trend, as the absenteeism data did, you will
need to determine the length of the short-term trend. Using this length
(*L*), construct an *L*-term moving average model. Short-term fluctuations create some problems in the next few steps; the problems will be
discussed later in this chapter.

**STEP 4**  Determine whether a relationship exists. From the data shown in Figure 18.3, you can discern a positive linear relationship between time
and employment in Berryville.

**STEP 5**  Use linear regression to estimate the relationship between time and the
variable that is being analyzed. To do this, label the first year (1979) as
1, the second year as 2, and so on. After this renumbering, we have the
following data set:

| X | Y |
|---|---|
| 1 | 35.7 |
| 2 | 38.8 |
| 3 | 40.9 |
| 4 | 43.4 |
| 5 | 44.9 |
| 6 | 47.2 |
| 7 | 48.8 |
| 8 | 50.8 |
| 9 | 50.8 |
| 10 | 50.7 |
| 11 | 55.0 |
| 12 | 55.3 |
| 13 | 58.6 |
| 14 | 59.9 |

Now perform linear regression, with $Y$ (employment) as the dependent variable. Regression produces the following results (if you do not believe us, feel free to calculate this yourself):

$$\hat{Y} = 35.04 + 1.79X \qquad \text{s.e.}_\beta = .07 \qquad S_{y|x} = 1.25 \qquad r^2 = .98$$

This informaton tells us that a strong relationship exists between time and city employment.

**STEP 6**  Using the regression equation, forecast employment figures for the years needed. Since 1992 is equivalent to an $X$ value of 14, then 1993, the first year to be forecast, has an $X$ value of 15. Entering 15 into the regression equation, we get

$$\hat{Y} = 35.04 + 1.79 \times 15 = 35.04 + 26.85 = 61.9$$

Our best estimate of the Berryville city employment for 1993 is 61,900. We can place 90% confidence limits around this estimate by using the standard error of the estimate and the $t$ score for 90% confidence with 12 degrees of freedom:

$$61.9 \pm 1.78 \times S_{x|y}$$

$$61.9 \pm 1.78(1.25)$$

$$61.9 \pm 2.23$$

$$59.68 \text{ to } 64.13$$

The 90% confidence limits on the Berryville city employment are 59,680 to 64,130.

A word of caution is in order. Forecasting forces us to go beyond the available data. Under normal circumstances, this process is to be avoided with regression models. Only if we can logically assume that the future will closely resemble the past can we forecast with confidence. In fact, the 90% confidence limits hold only if the future is an extrapolation of the past. If any major changes occur, the confidence limits are meaningless.

The Berryville city employment forecasts for 1994, 1995, 1996, and 1997 appear below:

| Year | $X \times b$ | $bX + a = \hat{Y}$ |
|------|--------------|---------------------|
| 1994 | $16 \times 1.79$ | $28.64 + 35.04 = 63.7$ |
| 1995 | $17 \times 1.79$ | $30.43 + 35.04 = 65.5$ |
| 1996 | $18 \times 1.79$ | $32.22 + 35.04 = 67.3$ |
| 1997 | $19 \times 1.79$ | $34.01 + 35.04 = 69.1$ |

The 90% confidence limits for these forecasts are

1994: 61.48 to 65.93

1995: 63.28 to 67.73

1996: 65.08 to 69.53

1997: 66.88 to 71.33

Ms. Cruncher can now use these forecasts to plan a variety of personnel decisions, including size of health care benefits, amount of money that needs to be set aside for pensions, and affirmative action goals.

## FORECASTING AN EXPONENTIAL TREND

B. Tom Line, chief budgeting officer for Normal, Oklahoma, needs to forecast city revenue for next year so that the city budget can be based on city revenue. The mayor also wants five years of revenue projections, because he wants to know whether sufficient revenue will be generated to purchase a $100,000 park without a bond issue. The current year's budget is $2.1 million, and current revenues are $2.138 million. The mayor tells Mr. Line to assume that past revenue trends will continue and that expenditures will increase 7% per year for the next five years. The question to be answered is, can Normal accumulate $100,000 in excess revenue (revenue saved last year cannot be used as part of the $100,000)? The revenue data are shown in Table 18.3.

Before forecasting revenue, Mr. Line needs a forecast of expenditures. The mayor said to assume a 7% annual increase. This growth rate results in the projections shown in Table 18.4.

**TABLE 18.3**

Normal Revenue Data

| Year | Revenue (thousands) |
|------|---------------------|
| 1979 | 678 |
| 1980 | 679 |
| 1981 | 743 |
| 1982 | 837 |
| 1983 | 949 |
| 1984 | 982 |
| 1985 | 1081 |
| 1986 | 1205 |
| 1987 | 1317 |
| 1988 | 1416 |
| 1989 | 1479 |
| 1990 | 1637 |
| 1991 | 1968 |
| 1992 | 2138 |

**TABLE 18.4**

Projected Expenditures

| Year | Expenditures (millions) |
|------|--------------------------|
| 1992 | 2.1 (actual) |
| 1993 | 2.247 |
| 1994 | 2.404 |
| 1995 | 2.573 |
| 1996 | 2.753 |
| 1997 | 2.945 |

Given the data in Table 18.4. Mr. Line follows the forecasting procedure outlined previously.

**STEP 1**   First, Mr. Line plots the data. The plot is shown in Figure 18.4.

**STEP 2**   Does a short-term fluctuation exist? None is apparent in the graph, so Mr. Line assumes that no short-term fluctuations exist. He skips to Step 4.

**STEP 4**   Does a time series relationship exist? Clearly one does. Unfortunately, the data do not appear to be linear; rather, they appear to increase a greater amount each year. For the moment, Mr. Line decides to ignore this fact and to proceed to Step 5.

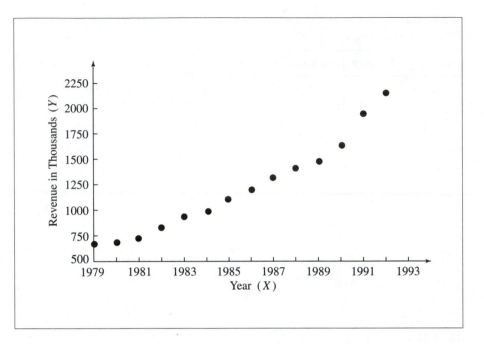

**FIGURE 18.4**

Yearly Revenue,
City of Normal

**STEP 5**     Using linear regression, Mr. Line estimates the equation for the line. To do this, he converts 1979 to year 1 and numbers all following years accordingly (1992 is year 14). He estimates the following regression line:

$$\hat{Y} = 459 + 103.1X \qquad \text{s.e.}_\beta = 6.9 \qquad S_{y|x} = 115.9 \qquad r^2 = .94$$

**STEP 6**     Using the regression equation, Mr. Line forecasts revenues for 1993–1997.

| Year | $X \times b$ | $bX + a = \hat{Y}$ |
|------|--------------|---------------------|
| 1993 | 15 × 103.1 | 1546.5 + 459 = 2005.5 |
| 1994 | 16 × 103.1 | 1649.6 + 459 = 2108.6 |
| 1995 | 17 × 103.1 | 1752.7 + 459 = 2211.7 |
| 1996 | 18 × 103.1 | 1855.8 + 459 = 2314.8 |
| 1997 | 19 × 103.1 | 1958.9 + 459 = 2417.9 |

Clearly something is wrong with the forecasts. Revenue for 1993 is forecast to be $100,000 less than 1992 revenue. When a time series that is not linear, such as this one, is estimated with linear regression, the forecasts will generally be underestimations. This results because linear regression cannot account for the upswing in revenues for the most recent few years. If Mr. Line's forecasts are compared to expenditures, the mayor will receive quite a shock (see Table 18.5).

**TABLE 18.5**

Revenue and Expenditures

| Projected Revenue | Expenditures | Debt |
|---|---|---|
| 2005.5 | 2247 | 242 |
| 2108.6 | 2404 | 296 |
| 2211.7 | 2573 | 361 |
| 2314.8 | 2753 | 438 |
| 2417.9 | 2945 | 527 |

The correct procedure to follow when the time series increases at a constant rate is to convert the time series variable into logarithms. (Those not familiar with logarithms should see Neter, Wasserman, and Whitmore 1978.) This conversion is done in Table 18.6.

Performing regression on the values of $X$ and $Y$ in Table 18.6, Mr. Line finds

$$\hat{Y} = 2.771 + .0384X \qquad \text{s.e.}_{\beta} = .00097 \qquad S_{y|x} = .01612 \qquad r^2 = .99$$

Notice that $r^2$ increased when a log transformation of $Y$ was regressed on time. This occurs because a log transformation bends the line upward to fit the values of the data.

How can the preceding regression line be interpreted? If we convert the regression slope into an antilog (in this case, the antilog of .0384 is 1.0885), and subtract 1 from the antilog, the resulting number tells us the percentage that $Y$ increases every year.

**TABLE 18.6**

Converting to Logarithms

| Year, $X$ | Revenue | Log (revenue), $Y$ |
|---|---|---|
| 1 | 678 | 2.831 |
| 2 | 679 | 2.832 |
| 3 | 743 | 2.871 |
| 4 | 837 | 2.923 |
| 5 | 949 | 2.977 |
| 6 | 982 | 2.992 |
| 7 | 1081 | 3.033 |
| 8 | 1205 | 3.081 |
| 9 | 1317 | 3.121 |
| 10 | 1416 | 3.152 |
| 11 | 1479 | 3.170 |
| 12 | 1637 | 3.215 |
| 13 | 1968 | 3.294 |
| 14 | 2138 | 3.330 |

$$1.0885 - 1.0 = .0885 \qquad \text{or} \qquad 8.9\%$$

Normal city revenues are increasing at a rate of 8.9% per year.

To forecast city revenues with a logarithmic regression, follow the usual procedure to get predicted logarithms of expenditures.

| Year | $X \times b$ | $bX + a = \hat{Y}$ |
|------|------|------|
| 1993 | $15 \times 0.384$ | $.576 + 2.771 = 3.347$ |
| 1994 | $16 \times .0384$ | $.614 + 2.771 = 3.385$ |
| 1995 | $17 \times .0384$ | $.653 + 2.771 = 3.424$ |
| 1996 | $18 \times .0384$ | $.691 + 2.771 = 3.462$ |
| 1997 | $19 \times .0384$ | $.730 + 2.771 = 3.501$ |

The predicted values $\hat{Y}$ must now be converted from logarithms to regular numbers (see Table 18.7).

**TABLE 18.7**

Converting $\hat{Y}$ to Revenue

| Year | $\hat{Y}$ | Projected Revenue |
|------|------|------|
| 1993 | 3.347 | 2230 |
| 1994 | 3.385 | 2430 |
| 1995 | 3.424 | 2660 |
| 1996 | 3.462 | 2900 |
| 1997 | 3.501 | 3170 |

Contrasting the revenue projections in Table 18.7 with expenditure predictions, we find the results shown in Table 18.8. The surplus figures show that Normal, Oklahoma, will accumulate the needed $100,000 for the park sometime early in 1996. The figures also show that the city will run a budget surplus of $225,000 in 1997 if no new programs are added and taxes are not cut. Why might this information be valuable to the mayor?

**TABLE 18.8**

Revenue and Expenditures

| Year | Revenue | Expenditures | Surplus |
|------|------|------|------|
| 1993 | 2230 | 2247 | −17 |
| 1994 | 2430 | 2404 | 16 |
| 1995 | 2660 | 2573 | 97 |
| 1996 | 2900 | 2753 | 147 |
| 1997 | 3170 | 2945 | 225 |

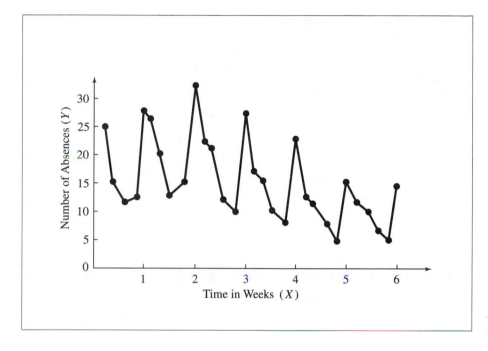

**FIGURE 18.5**
Number of
Absences for
Six Weeks

# FORECASTING WITH A
# SHORT-TERM FLUCTUATION

To this point, we have illustrated two fairly simple forecasts of trends. Neither set of data had any noticeable short-term fluctuation. To illustrate how forecasting is done when a time series contains some short-term fluctuation, let us return to our example of Normal Public Works Department absences introduced at the beginning of this chapter. Refer to Figure 18.5, which shows the number of absences from work for a six-week period.

**STEP 1**   The first step is to plot the data, as is done in Figure 18.5.

**STEP 2**   By examining the graph, determine whether any short-term fluctuation exists. In this instance, absences peak on Friday, remain high on Monday, drop on Tuesday and Wednesday, and show a slight increase on Thursday. Clearly a short-term trend exists.

**STEP 3**   Determine the length of the short-term fluctuation. In this example, the length of the short-term fluctuation is five days. To remove this short-term fluctuation, calculate a five-term moving average. These calculations, explained earlier in this chapter, are shown in Table 18.9.

**TABLE 18.9**
Calculations for Five-Term Moving Average

| Week | Day | Day Number | Absences (Y) | Sum | 5-Term Average | Fluctuation |
|------|-----|-----------|-------------|-----|---------------|-------------|
| 1 | M | 1 | 25 | | | |
| | Tu | 2 | 15 | | | |
| | W | 3 | 11 | 91 | 18.2 | −7.2 |
| | Th | 4 | 12 | 92 | 18.4 | −6.4 |
| | F | 5 | 28 | 97 | 19.4 | 8.6 |
| 2 | M | 6 | 26 | 98 | 19.6 | 6.4 |
| | Tu | 7 | 20 | 103 | 20.6 | −.6 |
| | W | 8 | 12 | 99 | 19.8 | −7.8 |
| | Th | 9 | 13 | 99 | 19.8 | −6.8 |
| | F | 10 | 32 | 100 | 20.0 | 12.0 |
| 3 | M | 11 | 22 | 100 | 20.0 | 2.0 |
| | Tu | 12 | 21 | 97 | 19.4 | 1.6 |
| | W | 13 | 12 | 93 | 18.6 | −6.6 |
| | Th | 14 | 10 | 88 | 17.6 | −7.6 |
| | F | 15 | 28 | 82 | 16.4 | 11.6 |
| 4 | M | 16 | 17 | 80 | 16.0 | 1.0 |
| | Tu | 17 | 15 | 78 | 15.6 | −.6 |
| | W | 18 | 10 | 73 | 14.6 | −4.6 |
| | Th | 19 | 8 | 68 | 13.6 | −5.6 |
| | F | 20 | 23 | 64 | 12.8 | 10.2 |
| 5 | M | 21 | 12 | 61 | 12.2 | −.2 |
| | Tu | 22 | 11 | 58 | 11.6 | −.6 |
| | W | 23 | 7 | 50 | 10.0 | −3.0 |
| | Th | 24 | 5 | 46 | 9.2 | −4.2 |
| | F | 25 | 15 | 48 | 9.6 | 5.4 |
| 6 | M | 26 | 11 | 47 | 9.4 | 1.6 |
| | Tu | 27 | 10 | 47 | 9.4 | .6 |
| | W | 28 | 6 | 46 | 9.2 | −3.2 |
| | Th | 29 | 5 | | | |
| | F | 30 | 14 | | | |

**STEP 4**   Graph the five-term moving average, since this represents the number of absences that occur each day when the short-term fluctuation is removed. Examining the graph in Figure 18.6, we see that a negative relationship exists between time and absenteeism. The absenteeism rate is clearly downward.

**STEP 5**   Using linear regression, estimate the relationship between time and the five-term moving average. In this case, use all values of $X$ from $X = 3$ to $X = 28$. The regression estimate of the relationship is

$$\hat{Y} = 23.35 - .512X \qquad \text{s.e.}_\beta = .0396 \qquad r^2 = .87 \qquad S_{y|x} = 1.513$$

where $X$ is the day and $Y$ is the number of absences.

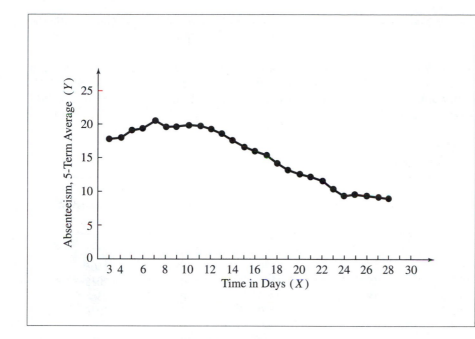

**FIGURE 18.6**

Five-Term Moving Average

You now have a forecast for the moving average of the number of absences. At this point, if you want to forecast specific days, the short-term fluctuation must be put back into the model. This procedure is fairly advanced and needs to be done with the assistance of a statistician (see Neter, Wasserman, and Whitmore 1978; Nelson 1973).

## BIVARIATE FORECASTING

In the previous three examples of forecasting, the independent variable was always time. This need not be the case. The independent variable can, in fact, be a variable that causes the dependent variable to vary. This section will illustrate forecasting when the independent variable is not time. Such forecasting is called **bivariate forecasting**.

**bivariate forecasting**

Stermerville is a bedroom suburb located 15 miles north of Normal. J. R. "Dusty" Rhodes, the Stermerville director of sewage treatment, wants to forecast the volume of sewage per day his plant will need to treat for the next five years. The Stermerville Treatment Plant has a capacity of 500 tons of sewage per day. At the present time, the plant is treating 375 tons per day. To expand the plant, it will take about four years (counting funding, EPA clearance, construction, and testing). For this reason Mr. Rhodes needs to forecast future demands on his sewage treatment plant. If demand will exceed 500 tons per day in the next five years, Mr. Rhodes must begin the process to expand the plant now.

Because Stermerville is a bedroom community with no industry and little commercial development, the volume of sewage is highly correlated with the number of households in Stermerville. Dusty's data analyst, Morticia "Severe" Storms, has discovered that she can accurately predict next year's sewage demand by combining the present number of houses in Stermerville with 90% of the number of building permits issued for new houses (90% is used because 10% of new houses for which permits are issued are not built). Severe gathers the data given in Table 18.10.

**TABLE 18.10**

Stermerville Data

| Year | Tons of Sewage per Day | Houses | Building Permits | Next Year's Projected Houses |
|------|------------------------|--------|------------------|------------------------------|
| 1979 |      | 1100 | 300 | 1370 |
| 1980 | 158  | 1370 | 150 | 1505 |
| 1981 | 188  | 1500 | 570 | 2018 |
| 1982 | 192  | 2000 | 600 | 2568 |
| 1983 | 230  | 2510 | 511 | 3028 |
| 1984 | 234  | 3000 | 754 | 3706 |
| 1985 | 252  | 3700 | 310 | 3979 |
| 1986 | 285  | 4050 | 680 | 4591 |
| 1987 | 293  | 4620 | 318 | 4877 |
| 1988 | 315  | 4885 | 815 | 5618 |
| 1989 | 335  | 5500 | 510 | 6077 |
| 1990 | 353  | 6040 | 603 | 6620 |
| 1991 | 358  | 6580 | 590 | 7151 |
| 1992 | 375  | 7150 | 475 | 7578 |

Severe explains what she wants to do. She wants to forecast next year's sewage demand in tons per day. Since the actual number of houses is highly correlated with sewage use, Severe needs an estimate of next year's number of houses to forecast next year's sewage use. This value appears in the "Projected Houses" column. Projected houses for 1980 (1370) is equal to the number of houses in 1979 (1100) plus 90% of the 1979 building permits (300 × .9 + 1100 = 270 + 1100 = 1370). Note that "Projected Houses" fairly accurately predicts the next year's total housing. Severe then aligns the variables in two columns so that sewage use for a given year is lined up with next year's projected houses for the previous year (that is, the value for 1979 projected houses is actually the projected number of houses for 1980; see Table 18.11). The number of projected houses for 1992 is withdrawn from the data set for the moment.

Severe then runs a regression of sewage in tons ($Y$) on the projected number of houses, with the following results:

$$\hat{Y} = 125.5 + .0350X \qquad r^2 = .98 \qquad \text{s.e.}_\beta = .00518 \qquad S_{y|x} = 10.6$$

Severe has no trouble using this information to project sewage demand for 1993,

**TABLE 18.11**
Sewage and Projected Houses

| Tons of Sewage per Day (Y) | Projected Houses (X) |
|---|---|
| 158 | 1370 |
| 188 | 1505 |
| 192 | 2018 |
| 230 | 2568 |
| 234 | 3028 |
| 252 | 3706 |
| 285 | 3979 |
| 293 | 4591 |
| 315 | 4877 |
| 335 | 5618 |
| 353 | 6077 |
| 358 | 6620 |
| 375 | 7151 |

because she has a projected housing value for 1993 (7578). Substituting this value for $X$, Severe gets the following projection for 1993:

$$\hat{Y} = 125.5 + .035X = 125.5 + .035(7578) = 390.73$$

Using the standard error of the estimate, Severe can place 90% confidence limits on this estimate (df $= 11$).

$$390.73 \pm t \times S_{y|x}$$

$$390.73 \pm 1.796 \times 10.6$$

$$390.73 \pm 19.04$$

$$371.69 \text{ to } 409.77$$

How can Severe forecast sewage demand for 1994 through 1997? Severe needs the estimated number of houses in Stermerville. The estimated number of houses is the current number plus 90% of the building permits issued. If Severe could estimate the number of building permits for the next five years, then she could extrapolate the number of houses. Severe consults several local builders who tell her that they expect to reduce new starts to about 450 per year for the next four years. Severe makes the following estimates of housing:

| Projected Houses | = Last Year's Projection + | .9 × Permits | |
|---|---|---|---|
| Projected 1994 houses = | 7578 | + (.9 × 450) | = 7983 |
| Projected 1995 houses = | 7983 | + (.9 × 450) | = 8388 |
| Projected 1996 houses = | 8388 | + (.9 × 450) | = 8793 |
| Projected 1997 houses = | 8793 | + (.9 × 450) | = 9198 |

Severe then used these estimates to project future sewage demand.

| Year | $X \times b$ | $Xb + a = \hat{Y}$ |
|------|--------------|--------------------|
| 1994 | $7983 \times .035$ | $279.4 + 125.5 = 404.9$ |
| 1995 | $8388 \times .035$ | $293.6 + 125.5 = 419.1$ |
| 1996 | $8793 \times .035$ | $307.8 + 125.5 = 433.3$ |
| 1997 | $9198 \times .035$ | $321.9 + 125.5 = 447.5$ |

The projections show that Stermerville will not exceed its capacity of 500 tons per day in the next five years. Severe shows these data to Mr. Rhodes. Mr. Rhodes asks Severe how sure she is that demand in 1997 will not exceed 500 tons per day. Severe uses the standard error of the estimate to determine the probability that the 1997 estimate exceeds 500.

$$t = \frac{Y - \hat{Y}}{S_{y|x}} = \frac{500 - 447.5}{10.6} = 4.95$$

Looking up this value in the $t$ table (df $= 11$), Severe concludes that the probability is less than .0005. She reports this information to Mr. Rhodes. Rhodes then wants to know what year to expect the demand to exceed 500 so that he can plan. Severe substitutes a value of 500 for $\hat{Y}$ into the regression equation:

$$500 = 125.5 + .035X$$

$$374.5 = .035X$$

$$10,700 = X$$

Severe finds that when projected housing exceeds 10,700, then sewage will exceed 500 tons per day. When will this be? Severe consults her builder friends who tell her that 450 new starts will hold for the next ten years. Using this figure, Severe projects the following housing figures:

> 1998:  9,603
>
> 1999: 10,008
>
> 2000: 10,413
>
> 2001: 10,818

These figures indicate that the capacity of the sewage treatment plant will be adequate until the year 2001. Since forecasts involve greater risks the farther that they extend into the future, 2000 or even 1999 may well be a more appropriate year for plant expansion to be completed. Note that any changes in building permits should be monitored; any change in permits will require new forecasts.

## CHAPTER SUMMARY

Forecasting is an attempt to predict the future, usually through some reliance on statistical techniques. This chapter introduces some simple forecasting techniques based on linear regression.

The foundation on which data-based forecasting rests is time series analysis. A time series is a sequence of observations on some variable when the observations occur at equally spaced time intervals. Most time series will have some short-term fluctuations, which can be filtered out by using a moving average.

There are six basic steps in a time series analysis. First, plot the data. Second, examine the plot and determine if any short-term fluctuations exist. Third, if the data show a cyclical trend, determine the length of the short-term trend and filter the trend. Fourth, determine whether a relationship exists. Fifth, use linear regression to estimate the relationship between time and the variable being analyzed. Sixth, make a forecast by using the regression equation.

When the forecast involves an exponential trend—that is, the time series increases at a constant rate—the time series variable must be converted to logarithms. If the forecast involves short-term fluctuations, a moving average must be calculated.

When the independent variable in a set of observations is not time, the forecasting is called bivariate forecasting. The analysis process for this situation is somewhat similar to that for time series analysis; again, linear regression techniques are used.

## PROBLEMS

**18.1** John Johnson, warden of Ramsey Prison, believes that a relationship exists between the size of the state's population between the ages of 18 and 35 and the number of inmates assigned to Ramsey. John has his trusty analyst, J. R., go down to the Census Bureau's local office to get census estimates for the past 50 years. J. R. then regresses Ramsey's prison population on the size of the state's 18- to 35-year-old population. He finds the following:

$$\hat{Y} = -14 + .0005X \qquad \text{s.e.}_{\beta} = .0000003 \qquad S_{y|x} = 12.6 \qquad r^2 = .93$$

(a) The Census Bureau estimates that next year's population between the ages of 18 and 35 will be 934,000. What is the projected prison population? Place 99% confidence limits around this estimate.

(b) Ramsey's capacity is 500 persons. The old wing of the prison contains room for 100 persons. John would like to close this wing to save on maintenance. How small would the state's 18- to 35-year-old population need to be to do this?

**18.2** The Oklahoma State Department of Agriculture is concerned about the number of acres of farmland being withdrawn from farming. The department would like to propose new legislation to prevent this but would like to show the legislature what would happen if it does not act. Dewey Compost, the department's statistician, regresses the number of acres used for farming in the state on time (1939 = year 1). Dewey finds the following:

$$\hat{Y} = 2.743 - .027X \qquad \text{s.e.}_\beta = .0007 \qquad S_{y|x} = .013 \qquad r^2 = .89$$

(a) How strong is the relationship?
(b) If $\hat{Y}$ is in millions of acres, how many acres of farmland will be lost in the next ten years if the legislature does not act and if past practices continue?
(c) How many acres will be used for farming in 1992? Place a 90% confidence interval around this estimate.

**18.3** I. L. Iterate High School is the only high school in Milward, Iowa. The superintendent hires you to forecast future school enrollments so that the school can plan ahead. Using the accompanying data, what can you tell the superintendent?

| Year | Students |
| --- | --- |
| 1978 | 810 |
| 1979 | 1094 |
| 1980 | 1402 |
| 1981 | 1893 |
| 1982 | 2205 |
| 1983 | 2687 |
| 1984 | 3115 |
| 1985 | 3324 |
| 1986 | 3496 |
| 1987 | 3531 |
| 1988 | 3412 |
| 1989 | 3174 |
| 1990 | 2963 |
| 1991 | 2810 |
| 1992 | 2794 |

**18.4** The Chelsea City Police budget appears to be increasing at a rate of 10% per year. Could the city use linear regression to forecast this budget? What percentage will the budget increase in ten years?

**18.5** The Normal city economist, I. C. Recession, uses the previous year's growth in the money supply (in percent) to forecast the inflation rate (in percent) for Normal. Using data for 35 years, Recession has built the following regression model ($Y$ is inflation in percentage; $X$ is money supply growth in percentage):

$$\hat{Y} = -5.4 + 2.1X \qquad S_{y|x} = 2.0 \qquad \text{s.e.}_\beta = .007 \qquad r^2 = .99$$

Interpret this regression equation; then forecast next year's inflation rate if the money supply grows 8.2%. Place 90% confidence limits around this estimate. What is the probability that the rate of inflation will be over 15%?

**18.6** The Fifth Division of the U.S. Army wants to forecast personnel costs for the next five years. A search of the records reveals the accompanying data. Using these data, forecast personnel costs for 1993, 1994, 1995, 1996, and 1997. Place 90% confidence limits around these estimates.

| Year | Costs (thousands) |
| --- | --- |
| 1992 | 51,576 |
| 1991 | 49,015 |
| 1990 | 40,845 |
| 1989 | 34,497 |
| 1988 | 28,625 |
| 1987 | 25,376 |
| 1986 | 21,163 |
| 1985 | 18,468 |
| 1984 | 14,992 |
| 1983 | 13,633 |
| 1982 | 12,069 |
| 1981 | 11,452 |
| 1980 | 10,321 |
| 1979 | 9,329 |
| 1978 | 7,982 |
| 1977 | 7,877 |
| 1976 | 7,648 |
| 1975 | 7,071 |
| 1974 | 6,411 |
| 1973 | 5,409 |
| 1972 | 4,657 |
| 1971 | 4,017 |

**18.7** The number of patients at the Bluefield State Mental Hospital ($Y$) appears to be related to the state's population ($X$):

$$\hat{Y} = .07 + .0031X \qquad \text{s.e.}_\beta = .00013 \qquad S_{y|x} = 46 \qquad r^2 = .99 \qquad N = 35$$

Interpret the regression and forecast the number of patients if the state's population is predicted to be 876,451. How many additional patients would a population increase of 20,000 bring?

**18.8**   From the accompanying data on the White Hawk Indian Tribe, project the tribal population for 1993 and 1998. Place a 90% confidence limit around both projections.

| Year | Population |
|------|-----------|
| 1983 | 812 |
| 1984 | 831 |
| 1985 | 863 |
| 1986 | 901 |
| 1987 | 925 |
| 1988 | 963 |
| 1989 | 989 |
| 1990 | 1016 |
| 1991 | 1037 |
| 1992 | 1062 |

**18.9**   Metro City Police believe that the number of domestic disputes on any summer night is highly correlated with the temperature that night (the hotter the night, the more family fights there are). If the number of disputes can be forecast, the police department can use the results to allocate personnel. A research analyst regresses the number of domestic disputes ($Y$) on the Fahrenheit temperature at 4:00 in the afternoon ($X$). Interpret this regression for the Metro City Police.

$$\hat{Y} = 216 + 3.1X \qquad \text{s.e.}_\beta = 1.5 \qquad S_{y|x} = 18 \qquad r^2 = .81 \qquad \text{N} = 150$$

Forecast, with appropriate confidence limits, the number of disputes if the temperature is 95° at 4:00 P.M.

**18.10**   Using the number of traffic fatalities for the 30-year period beginning in 1962 (1962 = year 1), a western state wants to forecast traffic fatalities for 1992, 1993, and 1994. Using the following regression, make these forecasts, and place an 80% confidence limit around the forecasts.

$$\hat{Y} = 1246 + 36.4X \qquad \text{s.e.}_\beta = 1.9 \qquad S_{y|x} = 24 \qquad r^2 = .97$$

**18.11**   The city building permit agency is concerned about its future workloads. Initially, the agency thinks that it can predict the number of building permits that will be issued next year by simply using the year as the independent variable (1950 is year 1). This regression results in the following equation:

$$\hat{Y} = 2{,}256 + 234.6X$$

$$\text{s.e.}_\beta = 23.1 \qquad S_{y|x} = 154 \qquad r^2 = .65$$

The agency then uses the unemployment rate (percentage of unemployed), rather than the year, as the independent variable to predict building permits. This produces the following equation:

$$\hat{Y} = 13{,}413 - 678X$$

$$\text{s.e.}_\beta = 21.4 \qquad S_{y|x} = 108 \qquad r^2 = .78$$

Interpret each of these regressions. For each regression, predict the number of building permits that will be issued in 1993 if unemployment is 7.2 percent. Which of these equations is the better one from a managerial perspective?

**18.12**   The Mansfield school district wants to predict student enrollments for next year. They hire Daniel Mazmanian Educational Consultants to do this work. Using data from 1979 through 1992 (1979 = year 1), the consultants assume that all past trends will continue and use a time series regression to predict the total number of students enrolled ($Y$). They get the following equation:

$$\hat{Y} = 781 + 28.8X$$

$$\text{s.e.}_\beta = .68 \qquad S_{y|x} = 6.2 \qquad N = 14 \qquad r^2 = .9955$$

Interpret the slope, intercept, and $r^2$. Is there a relationship between time and enrollments? Predict the number of students for 1993, and place an 80% confidence limit around it. What is the probability that enrollments might be as high as 1300 next year?

**18.13**   The President needs to predict future expenditures on Medicaid. The Office of Management and Budget undertakes the task. With Medicaid expenditures expressed in millions of 1967 dollars and using data from 1961 (year 1) to 1992, the OMB gets the following regression:

$$\hat{Y} = -669.9 + 306X$$

$$\text{s.e.}_\beta = 10.77 \qquad S_{y|x} = 320 \qquad N = 22 \qquad r^2 = .98$$

Interpret this regression. What is your best guess as to Medicaid expenditures in 1993? In 1994? Place 90% confidence limits around these estimates.

**18.14**   The Department of Labor's division of workers compensation programs believes that it is unfair to charge that rising medical costs for workers compensation programs are the result of program expansion. The department believes that costs rise because medical costs in general rise. Using the total amount of money spent for workers compensation medical benefits in millions of dollars ($Y$), the department runs a regression using the Consumer Price Index for medical care as the independent variable (CPIMED = 100 in 1967). This produces the following regression:

$$\hat{Y} = -927.60 + 17.71X$$

$$\text{s.e.}_\beta = .22 \qquad S_{y|x} = 106.2 \qquad N = 45 \qquad r^2 = .9949$$

Interpret this regression. Present a hypothesis, a null hypothesis, and evaluate the hypothesis. State your conclusions in plain English.

**18.15** Expenditures for the WIC program in millions of 1967 dollars are regressed on time (year 1 = 1967):

$$\hat{Y} = 40.19 + 45.46X$$

$$\text{s.e.}_\beta = 3.87 \qquad S_{y|x} = 20.5 \qquad N = 26 \qquad r^2 = .97$$

Interpret this regression. Predict 1993 expenditures, and calculate 90% confidence limits.

## CHAPTER 19

# MULTIPLE

# REGRESSION

In the three preceding chapters, all regression problems were solved with simple regression (regression with only one independent variable). Unfortunately, in many management situations, a dependent variable will have more than one cause. Under such circumstances, simple regression is an inadequate technique. **Multiple regression** is a statistical procedure designed to incorporate more than one independent variable. In this chapter, we will discuss the techniques of multiple regression.

**multiple regression**

## AN EXAMPLE

The best way to illustrate the use of multiple regression is with an example. Charles Pyro, fire chief of Stermerville, has divided Stermerville into nine fire districts of approximately equal size. Pyro's problem is that Stermerville is planning to offer fire service to Boonsville, a neighboring town about the size of one of Stermerville's fire districts. Pyro would like to know how many fires a month he can expect to fight in Boonsville so that he can allocate his firefighters accordingly.

As an old hand at fire fighting, Chief Pyro knows that older houses are more likely to burn than are newer houses. He decides to see whether he can predict the number of monthly fires in a fire district by using the average age of district housing. Pyro has the data shown in Table 19.1.

After graphing these data, Pyro performs a regression on them to get the following results:

$$\hat{Y} = 28.6 + 1.12X \qquad \text{s.e.}_\beta = .414 \qquad r^2 = .51 \qquad S_{y|x} = 18.4$$

**TABLE 19.1**

Sternerville Fire Data

| District | Number of Fires ($Y$) | Average Housing Age ($X$) |
|----------|-----------------------|---------------------------|
| 1 | 44 | 23 |
| 2 | 94 | 35 |
| 3 | 38 | 4 |
| 4 | 65 | 49 |
| 5 | 95 | 48 |
| 6 | 57 | 12 |
| 7 | 20 | 14 |
| 8 | 52 | 33 |
| 9 | 64 | 25 |

Using this information to predict the number of fires in Boonsville, which has an average housing age of 42 years, Pyro finds

$$\hat{Y} = 28.6 + 1.12(42) = 28.6 + 47.02 = 75.6$$

Placing a 90% confidence limit around this prediction (df = 7), Pyro receives a shock.

$$75.6 \pm t \times S_{y|x}$$

$$75.6 \pm 1.895 \times 18.4$$

$$75.6 \pm 34.9$$

$$40.7 \text{ to } 110.5$$

The confidence interval on this estimate is so wide that it is of little value to Chief Pyro.

One way to interpret a regression with a low (in terms of need) $r^2$ is to conclude that some factors other than the independent variable explain the variation in $Y$. To identify these factors, one uses experience, intuition, theory, or even trial and error. In the present instance, Chief Pyro knows that there are fewer fires in homes that are owner-occupied than there are in homes that are rented. Pyro believes that he could accurately predict fires if he knew both the average age of housing in a fire district and the percentage of houses that are owner-occupied. In short, Pyro would like a prediction equation of the following form:

$$\hat{Y} = \alpha + \beta_1 X_1 + \beta_2 X_2$$

where $\hat{Y}$ is the number of fires, $X_1$ is the average age of housing, $X_2$ is the percentage of owner-occupied housing, and $\beta_1$ and $\beta_2$ are weights.

Obviously, Pyro could set up the prediction equation just stated; the key is the selection of the weights. Pyro would like to select weights so that his predictions of $Y$ are as accurate as possible. In short, Pyro would like to minimize the squared error, or $(\hat{Y}_i - Y_i)^2$. This is the familiar principle of least squares that we use in simple regression (see Chapter 16). In fact, multiple regression is nothing more than the assignment of weights so that $(\hat{Y}_i - Y_i)^2$ is minimized.

We will consider specifically how these regression coefficients are calculated shortly. But first we will discuss the interpretation of a multiple regression. Pyro's data analyst runs a multiple regression on the data in Table 19.2.

**TABLE 19.2**

Fire Data Including Owner-Occupied Homes

| Fire District | Fires per Month ($Y$) | Housing | |
|---|---|---|---|
| | | Age ($X_1$) | Percentage Owned ($X_2$) |
| 1 | 44 | 23 | 70 |
| 2 | 94 | 35 | 3 |
| 3 | 38 | 4 | 10 |
| 4 | 65 | 49 | 96 |
| 5 | 95 | 48 | 40 |
| 6 | 57 | 12 | 4 |
| 7 | 20 | 14 | 80 |
| 8 | 52 | 33 | 78 |
| 9 | 64 | 25 | 15 |

The regression program provides the following information:

$$\hat{Y} = 38.1 + 1.57X_1 - .49X_2 \qquad S_{y|x} = 3.55$$

$$\text{s.e.}_{\beta_1} = .087 \qquad \text{s.e.}_{\beta_2} = .036 \qquad R^2 = .98$$

The interpretation of this regression equation focuses on the estimated values of $\beta_1$ and $\beta_2$. These are the values of slopes, just as $\beta$ was in simple regression, only now the slopes are in three dimensions (and thus difficult to graph) rather than in two dimensions. The regression coefficient for age of housing ($b_1$) is equal to the increase in the number of fires in a district if the average age of all housing in the district increases by one year *and* the percentage of owner-occupied housing remains the same. In other words, $b_1$ is the increase in the number of fires resulting from increases in housing age, controlling for the percentage of owner-occupied housing. In the present case, a district will have 1.57 more fires for every year older its houses are if the percentage that are owner-occupied remains the same. Statisticians often refer to this slope as a **partial slope**.

**partial slope**

The regression coefficient for percentage of housing that is owner-occupied ($b_2$) has a similar interpretation. For every percentage increase in owner-occupied housing in a district, the district will have .49 fewer fires if the average age of houses remains the same.

Although the intercept remains the value of $\hat{Y}$ if both average age and percentage of owner-occupied houses are zero, $\hat{Y}$ can also have a value of 38.1 for numerous other values of $X_1$ and $X_2$. For example, if $X_1$ is equal to 10 and $X_2$ is equal to 32, $\hat{Y}$ is also equal to 38.1.

A variety of other factors must also be considered when interpreting a multiple regression. If all the assumptions of regression hold (see Chapter 17), sample estimates of the regression slopes are $t$-distributed. This means that each slope will have its own standard error. Note that two standard errors of the slope estimates have been presented. These standard errors can be used to determine the probability that the data came from a population with slopes equal to 0. When a partial slope equals 0, it means that the $X$ value in question is unrelated to $Y$ when the other $X$ values are controlled.

For $b_1$ the probability that the data came from a population with slope $= 0$ can be found as follows:

$$t = \frac{b_1 - 0}{\text{s.e.}_{b_1}} = \frac{1.57 - 0}{.087} = 18.0$$

To look up this $t$ value in Table 3 of the Appendix, you need to know the number of degrees of freedom. For a multiple regression, the degrees of freedom is equal to the number of cases (in this case, 9) minus the number of parameters estimated (in this case, 3; one intercept and two slopes). Using 6 degrees of freedom, this $t$ value has a probability of less than .0001. We can be fairly sure the slope in question is not zero. In the space provided, calculate the probability that $b_2$ came from a population with slope $= 0$.

If you found a probability of less than .0001 ($t = 13.6$), congratulations.

In the results just reported, you might have noticed this equality: $R^2 = .98$. $R^2$ is the symbol for the *multiple coefficient of determination*. $R^2$ is the percentage of variance in $Y$ that is explained by $X_1$ and $X_2$. Another interpretation of $R^2$ is that it is equal to the $r^2$ between $Y$ and $\hat{Y}$. Notice that $R^2$ is larger than $r^2$ in the simple regression of fires on age. This will always happen. When more variables are used to explain or predict the dependent variable, the coefficient of determination will increase.

Finally, notice that the value of the standard error of the estimate has dropped. If Boonsville has housing that is 42 years old on the average and is 80% owner-occupied, the number of fires per month can be predicted.

$$\hat{Y} = 38.1 + 1.57X_1 - .49X_2$$

For Boonsville, $X_1 = 42$ and $X_2 = 80$.

$$\hat{Y} = 38.1 + 1.57(42) - .49(80) = 38.1 + 65.9 - 39.2 = 64.8$$

Notice that this estimate is different from the simple regression estimate of 75.6.

Using the standard error of the estimate to place 90% confidence limits around this estimate (for multiple regressions the degrees of freedom is $n -$ the number of parameters estimated, or in this case, $9 - 3 = 6$), we find

$$64.8 \pm t \times S_{y|x}$$

$$64.8 \pm 1.943 \times 3.55$$

$$64.8 \pm 6.9$$

$$57.9 \text{ to } 71.7$$

This narrower range of confidence is one that Chief Pyro can use with some confidence.

# CALCULATING
# PARTIAL SLOPES

If we wish to calculate the slope values in a multiple regression, it is helpful to change the standard designation of a regression line to the following:

$$\hat{X}_1 = a + b_{12.3}X_2 + b_{13.2}X_3$$

where $b_{12.3}$ means the regression slope of $X_1$ on $X_2$ controlling for $X_3$ and $b_{13.2}$ means the regression slope of $X_1$ on $X_3$ controlling for $X_2$. Statisticians, using the principles of least squares, have found that

$$b_{12.3} = \frac{b_{12} - (b_{13})(b_{32})}{1 - (b_{23})(b_{32})}$$

If we performed all the simple regressions indicated on the right-hand side of the equation using the Stermerville fire data, we would find that

$$b_{12} = 1.12 \qquad b_{13} = -.24 \qquad b_{23} = .16 \qquad b_{32} = .93$$

If you do not believe that these are the correct slopes, feel free to calculate them yourself. Substituting these values into the equation for $b_{12.3}$, we find

$$b_{12.3} = \frac{1.12 - (-.24)(.93)}{1 - (.16)(.93)} = \frac{1.12 + .22}{1 - .15} = \frac{1.34}{.85} = 1.57$$

For $b_{13.2}$, the calculations are

$$b_{13.2} = \frac{b_{13} - (b_{12})(b_{23})}{1 - (b_{32})(b_{23})} = \frac{-.24 - (1.12)(.16)}{1 - (.16)(.93)} = \frac{-.41}{.85} = -.49$$

To calculate the value of the intercept, we use the following formula:

$$a = \overline{Y} - b_1\overline{X}_1 - b_2\overline{X}_2 = 58.8 - 1.57(27.0) - (-.49)44$$

$$= 58.8 - 42.4 + 21.6 = 38.1$$

$$\hat{Y} = 38.1 + 1.57X_1 - .49X_2$$

In the real world, very few analysts calculate the slopes and intercepts in multiple regression by hand. Several excellent computer programs can do this far more quickly and accurately than can any normal human being. The role of a manager, after all, is to make decisions based on the information available rather than to calculate regression coefficients.

# THE LOGIC OF CONTROLS

In Chapter 15, we introduced the logic of controls for nominal and ordinal data. The logic of control relationships applies equally well to interval-level data and multiple regression.

## A SPURIOUS RELATIONSHIP

The head statistician for the Normal City Police, Mr. A. Nalist, has discovered a startling new finding. When Mr. Nalist regresses the number of juvenile crimes in a precinct on ice cream consumption in that precinct, he finds the following:

$$\hat{Y} = 15.4 - .75X \qquad \text{s.e.}_\beta = .09 \qquad r^2 = .70$$

Ice cream consumption is a fairly good predictor of juvenile crimes. While Mr. Nalist was drafting a memo advocating the free distribution of ice cream to prevent crime, I. C. Fallacy (a research assistant) suggested that a multiple regression with both ice cream ($X_1$) and median income in the precinct ($X_2$) be used to predict juvenile crime ($Y$). A multiple regression reveals the following:

$$\hat{Y} = 6.5 - .03X_1 - .32X_2 \qquad \text{s.e.}_{\beta_1} = .47 \qquad \text{s.e.}_{\beta_2} = .006 \qquad R^2 = .85$$

Note that the regression slope for ice cream has fallen to 0 ($t$ score $= .06$), whereas income is strongly related to juvenile crime ($t = 53.3$). Whenever a relationship is spurious, the regression slope between these two variables will fall to zero if one includes a variable that causes both the other variables (in this case high income causes high ice cream consumption and low crime rates).

## A SPECIFICATION

A relationship is specified if two variables appear unrelated but become related in the presence of a third variable (see Chapter 15). For example, when absenteeism rates ($Y$) are regressed on the age of letter carriers ($X$) for the Ripple, North Dakota, Post Office, no relationsip exists:

$$\hat{Y} = 8.6 + .03X \qquad \text{s.e.}_{\beta} = .58 \qquad r^2 = .01$$

But when an analyst controls for the length of routes ($X_2$) by entering it into the regression equation, the following pattern emerges:

$$\hat{Y} = 4.7 + .18X_1 + 2.1X_2 \qquad \text{s.e.}_{\beta_1} = .021 \qquad \text{s.e.}_{\beta_2} = 1.1 \qquad R^2 = .50$$

When length of routes (in miles) is controlled, a relationship exists between absenteeism and age. Obviously, older letter carriers with longer routes have higher absenteeism rates. In the best of all possible worlds, the Ripple postmaster would reassign routes so that older letter carriers would have shorter routes. In theory, the result would be lower absenteeism and, thus, higher productivity.

## DUMMY VARIABLE
## REGRESSION

In Chapter 17, simple regression with a dichotomous independent variable was demonstrated. The results were identical to analysis of variance. Can regression be used with nominal independent variables when the independent variable has more than two categories? Yes, but only when the analyst constructs the regression carefully.

Suppose a police chief wants to see whether precinct crime rates are related to the different areas of the city. The chief is particularly concerned about the crime rates in the inner city, downtown, and the middle-class residential areas. One way to determine if the area of the city affects precinct crime rates is to regress crime rates in each precinct on area of the city. To do this, create a dummy variable $X_1$ that is coded 1 if the precinct in question is in the inner city, and is coded 0 if it is not. Another dummy variable, $X_2$, is created that is coded 1 if the precinct is downtown and coded 0 if it is not.

*Do not create a third dummy variable for middle-class areas.* Two dummy variables account for all three types of precincts, as illustrated below.

If $X_1 = 1$ and $X_2 = 0$, then precinct is *inner city.*

If $X_1 = 0$ and $X_2 = 1$, then precinct is *downtown.*

If $X_1 = 0$ and $X_2 = 0$, then precinct is *middle class.*

A regression of precinct crime rates on $X_1$ and $X_2$ might reveal the following:

$$\hat{Y} = 5463 + 2471X_1 - 1362X_2 \qquad \text{s.e.}_{\beta_1} = 236 \qquad \text{s.e.}_{\beta_2} = 147$$

This regression equation can be interpreted as follows. The intercept, 5463, is the mean crime rate of all middle-class precincts ($X_1 = 0$ and $X_2 = 0$). The mean crime rate for all inner-city precincts is $a + \beta_1$, or 7934. The mean crime rate for downtown precincts is $a + \beta_2$, or 4101. The standard errors of the regression slopes indicate that crime rates in the inner city and downtown are significantly different from those in the middle-class precincts. These results would match those for analysis of variance and are much easier to interpret.

## REGRESSION WITH THREE INDEPENDENT VARIABLES

Multiple regression can be used with an unlimited number of independent variables. Regression with three or more independent variables is nothing more than a straightforward extension of the two-variable case.

### AN EXAMPLE

Jack Sixgun, police chief of Metropolis, is concerned about the number of assaults made on police officers in Metropolis. Chief Sixgun asks his data analysts to study the assaults on Metropolis police over the past ten years. As the dependent variable, the analysts use a dummy variable coded 1 if a police officer was assaulted in a year and coded 0 if he or she was not.

Chief Sixgun suggests that the analysts use three independent variables. First, the height of the police officer—Chief Sixgun feels that taller officers command more authority and, therefore, are less likely to be assaulted. The analysts operationalize this variable as the number of inches in height a police officer is over the 5-foot-4-inch minimum. Second, Chief Sixgun believes that officers are less likely to be assaulted if they are operating in teams. This is a dummy variable coded 1 if the officer was teamed with another officer and coded 0 if the officer was not. Third, Chief Sixgun believes that rookies are more likely to make mistakes that will result in assaults. This variable was operationalized as the number of years the officer served on the force.

Using a multiple regression computer program, Sixgun's analysts find the following:

$$\hat{Y} = .11 + .05X_1 + .21X_2 - .03X_3 \qquad S_{y|x} = .08$$

$$\text{s.e.}_{\beta_1} = .016 \qquad \text{s.e.}_{\beta_2} = .062 \qquad \text{s.e.}_{\beta_3} = .008 \qquad R^2 = .73 \qquad N = 200$$

where $X_1$ is the police officer's height, $X_2$ is the team variable, and $X_3$ is the number of years on the force.

The regression equation is interpreted in the same way as was the equation for the two-variable case. The regression coefficient for height (.05) shows that the amount the probability of assault increases ($Y$ is a dummy variable; thus, $\hat{Y}$ becomes a probability) with each inch in height over 5 feet 4 inches if teams and time on the force are held constant. This finding shocks Chief Sixgun, because a 6-foot-6-inch police officer has a .7 greater probability of being assaulted than does a 5-foot-4-inch police officer.

The second regression coefficient is the increase in the probability of assault by being assigned to a team (.21) if height and time on the force remain constant. Again Chief Sixgun is surprised, because officers in teams are more likely to be assaulted than officers alone.

Finally, the third regression coefficient indicates that the probability of being assaulted drops .03 for every year the officer serves on the force (all other things being equal).

The intercept (.11) is the probability of being assaulted when $X_1$, $X_2$, and $X_3$ are all zero. In other words, our best estimate is that a 5-foot-4-inch police officer who is not teamed with another officer and is a rookie (0 years) has a .11 probability of being assaulted in the line of duty in a year's time.

Note that all three regression coefficients have standard errors. By determining the probability that each could be drawn from a population where $\beta = 0$, the strength of the relationships can be assessed. Do this in the space provided.

The preceding regression equation can be used in the same way that any other regression equation can be used. For example, we can predict the probability that a 6-foot-tall officer with three years on the force assigned to a team would be assaulted. We substitute the values of 8 (inches over 5 feet 4 inches), 1, and 3 for $X_1$, $X_2$, and $X_3$, respectively.

$$\hat{Y} = .11 + .05(8) + .21(1) - .03(3)$$
$$= .11 + .40 + .21 - .09 = .51 + .12 = .63$$

This officer has a .63 probability of being assaulted this year. Using the same standard error of the estimate (.08), we could place a 95% confidence limit around this estimate.

$$.63 \pm t \times S_{y|x}$$
$$.63 \pm 1.96 \times .08$$
$$.63 \pm .16$$
$$.47 \text{ to } .79$$

Chief Sixgun can also use the regression equation to make management decisions. Since teams increase the probability of assaults by .21, he may decide to eliminate team patrols. Because taller officers are more likely to be assaulted, he may decide to relax the height requirement for police officers.

## CALCULATING REGRESSION COEFFICIENTS

When you, as an analyst, must perform a regression with three or more independent variables, we strongly recommend that you use one of numerous computer programs to calculate the regression. Most programs will provide the values for all slopes, the intercept, all slope standard errors, the standard error of the estimate, and the coefficient of determination. For those who prefer to calculate regression slopes by hand, use the following formula:

$$b_{12.34} = \frac{b_{12.3} - (b_{14.3})(b_{42.3})}{1 - (b_{24.3})(b_{42.3})}$$

Note that this is only one slope needed for a regression with three independent variables. Other formulas for the intercept and the standard errors can be found in statistics texts (see Blalock 1972).

# TESTING A
# HYPOTHESIS

Several minority groups have charged that the Metro City civil service exam discriminates against minorities. In fact, whites are twice as likely to pass the exam as are minorities. Harlan Fitzgerald, the Metro civil service commissioner, counters these arguments with the argument that minorities taking the exam have less education, less job-related experience, and lower school grades and thus are more likely to fail for these reasons. Minority groups contend that even when these factors are considered, the exam still discriminates against minorities.

The dispute could be resolved if we could test Mr. Fitzgerald's hypothesis.

$H_0$: When education, job experience, and grades are controlled, race is unrelated to performance on the Metro City civil service exam.

Regression can be used to test this hypothesis. For each civil service applicant, the following information must be gathered:

$Y$ = score on the civil service exam

$X_1$ = number of years of formal education

$X_2$ = years of relevant job experience

$X_3$ = grade point average in college

$X_4$ = minority status (1 = minority, 0 = nonminority)

A regression line estimated for this information would be as follows:

$$\hat{Y} = \alpha + \beta_1 X_1 + \beta_2 X_2 + \beta_3 X_3 + \beta_4 X_4$$

Mr. Fitzgerald's hypothesis can be restated as follows:

$$H_0: \beta_4 \text{ is equal to zero}$$

$\beta_4$ is the relationship of race to civil service exam scores when education, experience, and grades are controlled. If $\beta_4$ equals zero, then race is unrelated to exam scores when the other factors are controlled. As Mr. Fitzgerald would say, the relationship between race and civil service exam scores is spurious. One can test whether $\beta_4$ is equal to zero by calculating a $t$ score and finding the probability of this $t$ score in Table 3 of the Appendix.

For the minority groups to prove their contention, not only would $\beta_4$ have to not be equal to zero, it would have to have a negative value. A negative slope demonstrates that minorities do worse on the exam than whites do when education, experience, and grades are controlled. If $\beta_4$ is positive, Mr. Fitzgerald still wins his argument (at least in regard to minority groups).

# POLYNOMIAL CURVE
# FITTING

Linear regression is only appropriate where the relationship between variables is linear. In Chapter 18, nonlinear regression with logarithms was demonstrated. Two other forms of nonlinear regression, also called *polynomial curve fitting*, are important to know: quadratic relationships and cubic relationships.

### QUADRATIC RELATIONSHIPS

Boomtown, Wyoming, a fast-growing new town in the western coal fields, has also experienced a phenomenal increase in its crime rate as the city's population has skyrocketed. The data of Table 19.3 show this increase.

**TABLE 19.3**
Crime Rate in Boomtown

| Year | Number of Crimes |
| --- | --- |
| 1985 | 1 |
| 1986 | 3 |
| 1987 | 10 |
| 1988 | 31 |
| 1989 | 69 |
| 1990 | 124 |
| 1991 | 183 |
| 1992 | 234 |

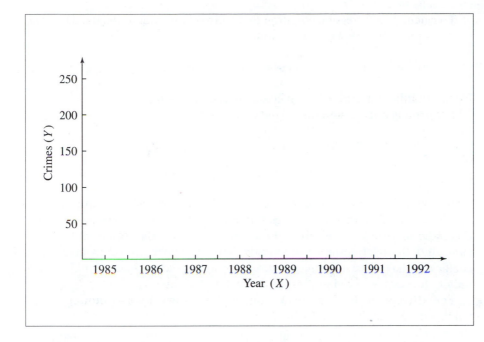

**FIGURE 19.1**
Graph Data Here

The county sheriff, Seymour "Tex" Critter, would like to forecast the number of crimes in Boomtown so that he can decide how may deputies to assign to Boomtown. Tex begins his analysis by graphing the data. Do this on the graph in Figure 19.1.

When Tex examines the graph of the data, he sees that the relationship is not linear; crime is increasing at an increasing rate. This is the general form of a quadratic relationship. To fit a curved line to these data, Tex must convert years to regular numbers for new $X$ values. Then these $X$ values must be squared. See Table 19.4.

**TABLE 19.4**

Calculations for Boomtown Data

| Year | $X$ | $X^2$ | $Y$ |
|------|-----|-------|-----|
| 1985 | 1 | 1 | 1 |
| 1986 | 2 | 4 | 3 |
| 1987 | 3 | 9 | 10 |
| 1988 | 4 | 16 | 31 |
| 1989 | 5 | 25 | 69 |
| 1990 | 6 | 36 | 124 |
| 1991 | 7 | 49 | 183 |
| 1992 | 8 | 64 | 234 |

To calculate a regression equation that will accurately describe the data, Tex must estimate the following regression:

$$\hat{Y} = \alpha + \beta_1 X + \beta_2 X^2$$

Notice that both $X$ and $X^2$ are included in the equation.

Performing a regression on the data, Tex finds

$$\hat{Y} = 8.9 - 15.1X + 5.5X^2 \qquad S_{y|x} = 7.04$$

$$\text{s.e.}_{\beta_1} = 5.0 \qquad \text{s.e.}_{\beta_2} = .54 \qquad R^2 = .996$$

From this information, Tex can determine whether the relationship is, in fact, quadratic. If the slope for $X^2$ does not equal zero, then the regression has a quadratic shape ($5.5 \div .54 = 10.2 = t$ score). In this case, the coefficient is significant, and the relationship is quadratic. To the novice, the individual slope coefficients have little meaning; do not worry about them. Since our objective is only to forecast, we need not interpret these coefficients.

Tex attempts to forecast 1993 crime in Boomtown by substituting in the value 9 for $X$ and the value 81 for $X^2$.

$$\hat{Y} = 8.9 - 15.1(9) + 5.5(81) = 8.9 - 135.9 + 445.5 = 318.5$$

Tex's forecast of 318.5 crimes appears reasonable given the pattern of the data. Using the standard error of the estimate, Tex could place a confidence limit around this estimate. Do this for Tex. Calculate the 90% confidence limits in the space provided.

To illustrate the utility of the quadratic forecast, Tex determined a straight linear forecast for crime in Boomtown.

$$\hat{Y} = -74.1 + 34.7X \qquad \text{s.e.}_{\beta} = 4.6 \qquad S_{y|x} = 30.0 \qquad r^2 = .90$$

Notice that, for the linear regression, $r^2$ is lower and the standard error of the estimate is higher. Forecasts with this model would be less accurate than would be those with the quadratic model. The forecast for 1993 would be as follows:

$$\hat{Y} = -74.1 + 34.7(9) = -74.1 + 312.3 = 238.2$$

The linear forecast for 1993 is only five crimes more than the 1992 figure. Clearly this forecast would not be accurate if past trends continued.

## CUBIC REGRESSION

The city of Xenith has been experimenting over the past year with the number of officers assigned to the vice squad. For the past eleven months, the city has gathered the information on prostitution arrests shown in Table 19.5.

**TABLE 19.5**
Xenith City Data on Prostitution Arrests

| Arrests | Number of Vice Squad Officers |
|---------|-------------------------------|
| 25 | 1 |
| 34 | 2 |
| 43 | 3 |
| 98 | 4 |
| 123 | 5 |
| 194 | 6 |
| 253 | 7 |
| 271 | 8 |
| 294 | 9 |
| 292 | 10 |
| 298 | 11 |

Currently, the city council wants the police department to double its vice squad to drive prostitution off the streets. The police chief would rather use these additional officers on homicide, because she believes that any increase in vice squad officers would have no impact on prostitution arrests.

The police chief begins her analysis by graphing the data. Do this for the police chief on the graph in Figure 19.2.

The police chief recognizes the pattern of a cubic relationship, as illustrated in Chapter 17. She then decides to run three regressions, one with $X$, one a quadratic, and one a cubic, as follows:

linear:     $\hat{Y} = a + \beta X$

quadratic:     $\hat{Y} = a + \beta_1 X + \beta_2 X^2$

cubic:     $\hat{Y} = a + \beta_1 X + \beta_2 X^2 + \beta_3 X^3$

To do this, the police chief squares and cubes the $X$ values, as shown in Table 19.6.

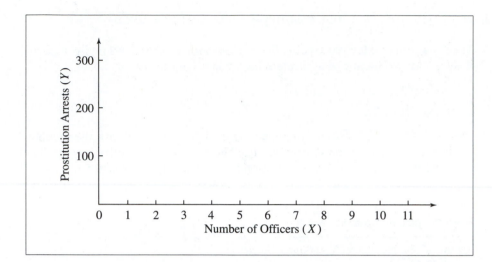

**FIGURE 19.2**

Graph Data Here

**TABLE 19.6**

Calculations for Xenith City Data

| Y | X | $X^2$ | $X^3$ |
|---|---|---|---|
| 25 | 1 | 1 | 1 |
| 34 | 2 | 4 | 8 |
| 43 | 3 | 9 | 27 |
| 98 | 4 | 16 | 64 |
| 123 | 5 | 25 | 125 |
| 194 | 6 | 36 | 216 |
| 253 | 7 | 49 | 343 |
| 271 | 8 | 64 | 512 |
| 294 | 9 | 81 | 729 |
| 292 | 10 | 100 | 1000 |
| 298 | 11 | 121 | 1331 |

The following regressions result:

Linear:

$$\hat{Y} = -23.4 + 32.8X \qquad \text{s.e.}_\beta = 2.5 \qquad S_{y|x} = 26.3 \qquad r^2 = .95$$

Quadratic:

$$\hat{Y} = -51.1 + 45.6X - 1.1X^2 \qquad R^2 = .96$$

$$\text{s.e.}_{\beta_1} = 10.8 \qquad \text{s.e.}_{\beta_2} = .9 \qquad S_{y|x} = 26.3$$

Cubic:

$$\hat{Y} = 42.8 - 32.0X + 14.4X^2 - .86X^3 \qquad R^2 = .995$$

$$\text{s.e.}_{\beta_1} = 12.1 \qquad \text{s.e.}_{\beta_2} = 2.3 \qquad \text{s.e.}_{\beta_3} = .13 \qquad S_{y|x} = 9.9$$

Notice the increase in the coefficient of determination for the cubic equation and the decrease in the standard error of the estimate. These results plus the standard errors of the slopes indicate that the relationship is cubic.

The real advantage of the cubic form is in forecasting. If the police chief forecasts the number of arrests with 11 officers by using the linear and cubic models, she finds

$$\text{linear:} \quad \hat{Y} = -23.4 + 32.8(11) = 337.4$$

$$\text{cubic:} \quad \hat{Y} = 42.8 - 32.0(11) + 14.4(121) - .86(1331)$$

$$= 42.8 - 352 + 1742 - 1145 = 288$$

Notice that not only is the cubic forecast more accurate, but the linear forecast is far too high. This result is important in decision making, since a linear forecast of 22 police officers would show a large increase in arrests, whereas the cubic forecast would not. (Note that forecasting arrests by 22 officers is extremely risky when data only contain information for 1 to 11 officers.)

## CHAPTER SUMMARY

Multiple regression is a technique used for interval-level data when the analyst has more than one independent variable. This chapter discusses the interpretation of multiple regression and the application of regression to two or more independent variables.

Two concepts involved in multiple regression are partial slopes and the multiple coefficient of determination; both are similar to their counterparts, the slope and the coefficient of determination, in simple linear regression. This chapter illustrated the interpretation of these terms.

The logic of control relationships, introduced in Chapter 15, applies equally well to multiple regression. Dummy variable regression can be used with nominal independent variables having more than two categories.

Multiple regression can be used to test hypotheses involving more than one independent variable. Multiple regression can also be used to estimate relationships that are not linear, a technique known as polynomial curve fitting.

## PROBLEMS

**19.1**  Forrest Tucker, head statistician for the National Parks Service, believes that park usage as measured by number of visitors ($Y$) is a function of the number of people who live within 200 miles of the park ($X_1$), the number of camping hookups available ($X_2$), and the mean annual temperature at the park ($X_3$). For a sample of 200 parks under Forrest's supervision, the following regression is calculated ($Y$ is number of visitors):

$$\hat{Y} = 147 + .0212X_1 + 15.4X_2 + 186X_3$$

$$\text{s.e.}_{\beta_1} = .0157 \qquad \text{s.e.}_{\beta_2} = 12.4 \qquad \text{s.e.}_{\beta_3} = 10.4 \qquad R^2 = .50$$

For this regression, what can you tell Forrest? Write a one-page memo with your assessment.

**19.2** If James Position-Classification, personnel officer for the Bureau of Forms, can forecast agency separations six months from now, he can plan recruitment efforts to replace these people. James believes that separations six months from now are determined by the number of agency people passed over for promotion ($X_1$), the number of agency people 64 years old or older ($X_2$), and the ratio of government salaries to private sector salaries ($X_3$). Using regression, James finds the following:

$$\hat{Y} = 27.4 + .35X_1 + .54X_2 - 271X_3 \qquad R^2 = .89$$

$$\text{s.e.}_{\beta_1} = .0031 \qquad \text{s.e.}_{\beta_2} = .0136 \qquad \text{s.e.}_{\beta_3} = 263 \qquad S_{y|x} = 54 \qquad N = 214$$

Write a one-page memo explaining the results, and then forecast the number of separations if 418 people are passed over for promotion, 327 people are 64 years old or older, and government salaries equal those in the private sector. Place a 90% confidence interval about this estimate.

**19.3** The Forest Service believes that it can predict the number of forest fires per month in a forest, knowing the amount of rainfall that fell the previous month ($X_1$) and the average daily temperature for that month ($X_2$), taken from historical records. A regression yields the following:

$$\hat{Y} = 2.0 - 1.1X_1 + .14X_2 \qquad R^2 = .96$$

$$\text{s.e.}_{\beta_1} = .021 \qquad \text{s.e.}_{\beta_2} = .003 \qquad S_{y|x} = 1.4 \qquad N = 136$$

(a) Write a brief memo interpreting the slopes, the intercept, and $R^2$.
(b) Barren National Forest has had 4 inches of rain in the last month and has a historical mean temperature of 84° for this month. What is the best estimate of the number of fires in Barren this month? Place an 80% confidence interval around this estimate. What is the probability that Barren will have 12 or more fires this month?

**19.4** McKeesport Fire Department wants to know how likely it is that a truck pump will fail. The fire chief, George Pyro (no relation), thinks pump failure is a function of age $(X_1)$ and water hardness $(X_2,$ measured on a scale of 1 to 10). The department statistician runs a regression on a dummy variable (coded 1 for failure and 0 for no failure) for 217 pumps. She finds the following:

$$\hat{Y} = .14 + .01X_1 + .05X_2 \qquad R^2 = .93$$

$$\text{s.e.}_{\beta_1} = .0002 \qquad \text{s.e.}_{\beta_2} = .025 \qquad S_{y|x} = .04$$

Write a memo explaining what the regression means. If the average water hardness is 3, and the chief would like to replace any pump with a probability of failing of .80 or more, at what age should pumps be replaced?

**19.5** Lieutenant Colonel Syl Verleaf is placed in charge of base security at all 240 military bases in Europe. Verleaf believes that the crime rate is positively correlated to the size of the base, the percentage of troops without high school degrees, and the number of women on base. Verleaf's statistician finds the following:

$$\hat{Y} = 47.3 + .031X_1 + 2.4X_2 - .065X_3 \qquad R^2 = .80$$

$$\text{s.e.}_{\beta_1} = .0021 \qquad \text{s.e.}_{\beta_2} = 3.0 \qquad \text{s.e.}_{\beta_3} = .0027 \qquad S_{y|x} = 17.1$$

where $X_1$ is the number of troops on the base, $X_2$ is the percentage of troops without high school degrees, $X_3$ is the number of women on the base, and $Y$ is the number of serious crimes in a month. Interpret all the regression coefficients, $R^2$, and the intercept. What is the most important independent variable? Ramstein Air Base has 15,000 troops, 42% of its troops have no high school degree, and there are 3,000 women on base. What is your best estimate of the number of crimes per month for this base? What is the probability that Ramstein will have more than 500 serious crimes in a month?

**19.6** Refer to Problem 19.5. The information for Rathesberg Base and Krasmic Kaserne appears in the accompanying table.

| Statistic | Rathesberg | Krasmic |
|---|---|---|
| $X_1$ (troops) | 12,000 | 14,000 |
| $X_2$ (% without high school degree) | 34 | 28 |
| $X_3$ (women) | 2,000 | 3,000 |
| $Y$ (no. of crimes) | 517 | 290 |

Calculate $\hat{Y}$ for each base. Why might it be interesting to study both bases in depth?

**19.7** The Missouri Department of Educaton has hired a program evaluation team to investigate why the average reading scores for all seniors vary from 9.4 to 13.1 for different high schools ($N = 326$). The program evaluation team believes that reading scores are affected by pupil-teacher ratios ($X_1$) and per student spending on education in a school district ($X_2$). Using regression analysis, the team finds

$$\hat{Y} = 10.6 - .091X_1 + .0031X_2 \qquad R^2 = .75$$

$$s.e._{\beta_1} = .017 \qquad s.e._{\beta_2} = .00061 \qquad S_{y|x} = .17$$

Interpret this equation for the department of education. The education department's budget has enough money to lower the pupil-teacher ratio by 5 or to increase the per student spending by $50. Which should it do?

**19.8** Several states have argued that the 65-mph speed limit has no justification and have refused to enforce it. The federal Department of Transportation (DOT) believes that the 65-mph limit saves lives. To illustrate its contention, the department regressed the number of traffic fatalities last year in a state ($Y$) on the state's population ($X_1$), the number of days of snow cover ($X_2$), and the average speed of all cars ($X_3$). It found

$$\hat{Y} = 1.4 + .00029X_1 + 2.4X_2 + 10.3X_3 \qquad R^2 = .78$$

$$s.e._{\beta_1} = .00003 \qquad s.e._{\beta_2} = .62 \qquad s.e._{\beta_3} = 1.1 \qquad S_{y|x} = 36.1 \qquad N = 50$$

Does reducing the average speed of cars have an impact? All other things being equal, how many lives would be saved in a state if the average speed were reduced from 75 to 65 mph?

**19.9** Stermerville Blue Cross wants to hold down hospital costs in the area hospitals. It regresses the average cost of a hospital stay ($Y$) on the number of days the person stayed in the hospital ($X_1$), the number of lab tests made ($X_2$), and the number of prescription drugs ordered ($X_3$). Interpret the following regression and decide whether any policy changes can be recommended.

$$\hat{Y} = 25.36 + 96.40X_1 + 24.90X_2 + 1.41X_3 \qquad R^2 = .96$$

$$s.e._{\beta_1} = 6.4 \qquad s.e._{\beta_2} = 3.2 \qquad s.e._{\beta_3} = 2.0 \qquad S_{y|x} = 12.50 \qquad N = 75$$

**19.10** The Buford State University chapter of the American Association of University Professors (AAUP) regressed the salaries of all BSU faculty ($Y$) on the number of articles each faculty member published ($X_1$) and the number of years the person has served on the faculty ($X_2$). Interpret the following regression:

$$\hat{Y} = 15,200 + 250X_1 + 750X_2 \qquad R^2 = .91$$

$$s.e._{\beta_1} = 180 \qquad s.e._{\beta_2} = 52 \qquad S_{y|x} = 524 \qquad N = 517$$

**19.11**  The state of Nevada is concerned about rising costs of health care for employees. Ten years ago, it shifted all employees to HMOs. Now it would like to evaluate the impact of the HMOs on the cost of health care to the state on a per person basis. Average health care costs are the dependent variable in a time series analysis that covers the years 1930 to 1985. The three independent variables are $X_1$ (a trend variable, a counter starting at 1 for 1930 and increasing by one per year), $X_2$ (a variable coded 0 before the introduction of the HMOs and coded 1 afterward), and $X_3$ (a variable coded 0 before the introduction of the HMOs and coded as a counter afterward, for example, 1, 2, 3, 4, ...). Costs are in dollars. Interpret the following regression and present a brief analysis of the impact of the HMOs on the cost of health care.

$$\hat{Y} = \$45.00 + \$51.45X_1 - \$123.69X_2 - \$7.25X_3$$

$$\text{s.e.}_\beta = \qquad\qquad 5.43 \qquad\qquad 49.67 \qquad\quad 1.14$$

$$S_{y|x} = 93.50 \qquad R^2 = .99$$

**19.12**  The state of Ohio has had an urban enterprise zone program in operation for the past 5 years. Local governments are free to set up three types of zones to attract new industry: zone A (businesses are exempt from taxes for 10 years), zone B (industries are exempt from taxes for 10 years, and they may use tax-free industrial development bonds), and zone C (the local government contributes to the capital investment of the industry). Local governments can set up one and only one type of urban enterprise zone. The state wants to know the impact of the zones on local unemployment rates ($Y$). To do this, it set up a dummy variable $X_1$ (coded 1 if the zone is a B-type zone and coded 0 otherwise), and another dummy variable $X_2$ (coded 1 if the zone is a C-type zone and 0 otherwise). It wants to control for the following variables: $X_3$, the percentage of unemployment in the counties surrounding the urban area with the zone; $X_4$, the median education level of the urban area in years; and $X_5$, the percentage of the urban area's employed population that is employed in services. $Y$ is measured in percentage unemployed. A regression for 136 cities reveals the following results:

$$\hat{Y} = 5.4 + 1.32X_1 - .64X_2 + .82X_3 - .07X_4 - .13X_5$$

$$\text{s.e.}_\beta = \qquad .31 \qquad .32 \qquad .03 \qquad .13 \qquad .031$$

$$S_{y|x} = .62 \qquad R^2 = .53$$

Interpret all slopes, the intercept, and the $R^2$. Analyze the slopes, including tests of significance, and express in clear English what this regression reveals. Youngstown has a zone C enterprise zone, with unemployment in the surrounding counties of 8.9%, median education of

10.8 years, and 31% of the city's employed working in services. What is your best guess of the percentage of unemployment in Youngstown? What is the probability that unemployment in Youngstown is more than 9%?

**19.13** The Strategic Air Command is concerned about the possibility that missiles will not launch successfully. Utilizing test data, they regress $X_1$ (the temperature at launch in degrees Fahrenheit), $X_2$ (the number of months since the last overhaul of the launch mechanism), and $X_3$ (the number of ICBMs sited within 800 meters). They get the following results with $Y$ (a dummy variable that is coded 1 if the launch fails):

$$\hat{Y} = .06 - .012X_1 + .006X_2 - .094X_3$$

$$\text{s.e.}_\beta = \qquad .0021 \quad .0015 \quad .087$$

$$S_{y|x} = .034 \qquad R^2 = .69 \qquad N = 214$$

Interpret the slopes, intercept, and $R^2$, and test the slopes for significance. SAC wants the probability of failure to be no more than 20%. If launches will proceed at $-10$ degrees with no other missiles within 800 meters, how often should launch mechanisms be serviced to be 90% sure that the failure rate will not be greater than 40%?

**19.14** At Eastern State University, a study of sex discrimination in salaries is undertaken. The analyst regresses the salary of each teaching professional on the number of years of experience ($X_1$), the number of publications ($X_2$), and the sex of the person ($X_3$, a dummy variable with male coded as 1). She gets the following results:

$$\hat{Y} = \$18,563 + \$2,235X_1 + \$65X_2 + \$1,150X_3$$

$$\text{s.e.}_\beta = \qquad 386 \qquad 39 \qquad 316$$

$$S_{y|x} = 2,690 \qquad R^2 = .68$$

Interpret the slopes, intercept, and $R^2$. Estimate with 80% confidence limits the salary of a male professor with 7 years' experience and 3 publications.

**19.15** The U.S. Department of Human Services research team has submitted a report to you on the infant mortality rate. The team uses a regression equation in which infant mortality (the number of infants who die per 1000 live births) is a function of the year ($X_1$, where 1951 = 1), Medicaid expenditures ($X_2$, in millions of dollars), and the expenditures on WIC supplemental food programs ($X_3$, also in millions of dollars). Interpret the following regression. Then predict the infant mortality rate for 1993 if $4536 million is spent on Medicaid and $774 million is spent on WIC.

Place a 90% confidence interval around this estimate. Which of the variables is the most important predictor? If you had $1 million to spend, what would be the most effective use of that money?

$$\hat{Y} = 28.32 - .239X_1 - .001476X_2 - .003266X_3$$

$$\text{s.e.}_\beta = \qquad\qquad .029 \qquad .000143 \qquad .00137$$

$$R^2 = .99 \qquad S_{y|x} = .32$$

**19.16** The state tax division is evaluating the money raised by state sales taxes. Using data from all states, division members regress the amount of money raised by the sales tax per capita on the average per capita income $(X_1)$ and a dummy variable coded 1 if the state taxed the sale of groceries $(X_2)$. They get the following results:

$$\hat{Y} = .03 + .0218X_1 + 147.18X_2$$

$$R^2 = .86 \qquad \text{s.e.}_{\beta_1} = .0043 \qquad \text{s.e.}_{\beta_2} = 36.3 \qquad S_{y|x} = 31.40$$

Interpret this regression. Present a hypothesis about placing a tax on the sale of groceries and evaluate this hypothesis. How much could a state with a per capita income of $11,947 and a tax on groceries raise per capita with a sales tax?

**19.17** The Oklahoma State Personnel Board wants to know whether merit system salaries are based on job responsibilities, education, or seniority. The board regresses the current annual salaries of employees $(Y)$ on the number of Hay Points $(X_1,$ a job responsibility scale that ranges from $0 =$ no responsibility to approximately $1500 =$ agency heads), the number of years in the agency $(X_2)$, and the number of years of formal education $(X_3)$. The board finds

$$\hat{Y} = \$4,195 + \$26.08X_1 + \$149X_2 + \$226X_3$$

$$\text{s.e.}_\beta = \qquad\qquad 1.19 \qquad 20.9 \qquad 58.0$$

$$S_{y|x} = \$2,755 \qquad R^2 = .70 \qquad N = 458$$

Interpret the slopes, intercept, and $R^2$. Test to determine whether each of the partial slopes is significant. What is your best guess as to the salary of a newly hired administrative assistant (270 Hay Points) with a two-year MPA who supervises three people? Place an 80% confidence limit around your estimate.

**19.18** The Department of Economic Development in Milwaukee County wants to evaluate the economic development program that it started in 1978. Its measure of success is the total number of persons employed in

Milwaukee County. Independent variables are $X_1$, a trend variable starting as 1 in the first year of the data, 1960; $X_2$, the percentage of persons unemployed at the national level; and $X_3$, a dummy variable coded as a counter variable after the start of the economic development program. A regression produces the following results:

$$\hat{Y} = 215,400 - 2,400X_1 - 4,235X_2 + 1,421X_3$$

$R^2 = .99$   $S_{y|x} = 4,300$   s.e.$_\beta =$        746        625        419

Interpret this regression. Predict the number of jobs in Milwaukee County in 1993 if unemployment is 5.1%. What is the probability that Milwaukee County will have as many as 140,000 jobs? What would you look at to see if that were true?

**19.19** You have been hired by the U.S. Supreme Court to find out if there is any racial bias against persons receiving the death penalty. Your data are 194 persons who were convicted of murder in six southern states. The dependent variable is a dummy variable coded 1 if the person received the death penalty and coded 0 otherwise. The independent variables are $X_1$, the number of persons killed by the convictee (ranges from 1 to 8); $X_2$, a dummy variable coded 1 if the person was able to pay for his/her own attorney (rather than having a court-assigned public defender); $X_3$, the number of years of formal education the person has; and $X_4$, a race variable coded 1 if the convictee was white and coded 0 otherwise. A regression analysis finds the following:

$$\hat{Y} = .54 + .05X_1 - .23X_2 - .02X_3 - .31X_4$$

$R^2 = .52$    $S_{y|x} = .14$    s.e.$_\beta =$        .042      .083      .006      .012

(a) Interpret this regression, including slopes, intercept, and $R^2$. Are the slopes significant? What does this regression say about the research question?

(b) How likely is it that a white man with a college degree, who paid for his own attorney, and who killed two people, will get the death penalty? Place 90% confidence limits around this estimate.

(c) How likely is it that a black man with an eighth-grade education, who had a public defender, and who killed one person, will receive the death penalty?

(d) How would you change this study to find out whether the victim's race mattered?

**19.20** Tax expert Bob Erikson is interested in the reliance of state governments on "sin taxes"—taxes on alcohol, tobacco, and gambling. The dependent variable is the percentage of state revenue that is raised from sin taxes. Three research hypotheses guide Bob's analysis. First, Bob believes that Catholics are generally "good-time" people who drink, smoke, and play bingo a lot; $X_1$ is the percentage of the state population who are Catholic. Second, Bob notes that Republicans seem less concerned than Democrats do that sin taxes might be regressive; $X_2$ is the percentage of the state legislature who are Republicans. Third, Bob suspects that sin taxes could be used to hold down the level of property taxes; $X_3$ is the per capita property tax in thousands of dollars. A regression program produces the following results:

$$\hat{Y} = 5.4 + .23X_1 + .11X_2 - 1.41X_3$$

$R^2 = .74 \qquad \text{s.e.}_\beta = \qquad .04 \qquad .087 \qquad .15 \qquad S_{y|x} = .74$

(a) Interpret the slopes, intercept, and $R^2$.
(b) What are the research hypotheses? Evaluate these hypotheses.
(c) Michigan has 20% Catholic constituents, 47% Republicans in the state legislature, and a property tax of \$2.5 per thousand. What is your best guess as to the sin tax rate in Michigan? Place a 90% confidence limit around this estimate.
(d) The actual sin tax rate in Michigan is 16.1%. What would you conclude about that?

## CHAPTER 20

# INTERRUPTED TIME  SERIES: PROGRAM AND POLICY ANALYSIS

In many cases, public managers or policymakers introduce a new program or policy to change a pattern of behavior. For example, the Whitefish Bay Sanitary Engineering Department believed that it costs too much to collect trash. The department introduced new trucks that could be operated by two people rather than by three, and the department provided incentives for the workers to collect trash faster. A program analyst might then want to know whether current trash collections cost less than they did before the changes. A variety of other examples of this kind of analysis exists. For instance, the state of Wisconsin adopted a "learnfare" program that denied welfare benefits to families whose school-age children were not attending school; the objective was to increase school attendance. As another example, proponents of a capital gains tax suggest that it will increase tax collections by providing an incentive to sell capital assets.

This chapter will provide an introduction to a set of techniques, called interrupted time series analysis, that are useful in evaluating changes in policies or programs. Interrupted time series analysis assumes that a person has a time series of observations such as the following:

$$O_1 \quad O_2 \quad O_3 \quad O_4 \quad O_5 \quad X \quad O_6 \quad O_7 \quad O_8 \quad O_9 \quad O_{10}$$

where each $O$ is an observation on an output variable of interest (garbage collected, class attendance, tax collections, and so on), and where $X$ is the implementation of a new program or policy.

In many cases, analysts simply compare observation 5 ($O_5$) with observation 6 ($O_6$) using a comparison of means or a proportions test (see Chapter 12). Such a comparison can be misleading, because the output measure might have been increasing or decreasing before the new program, and observation 6 might just be the continuation of a trend. Figure 20.1 illustrates this problem using the Whitefish Bay trash collection experiment.

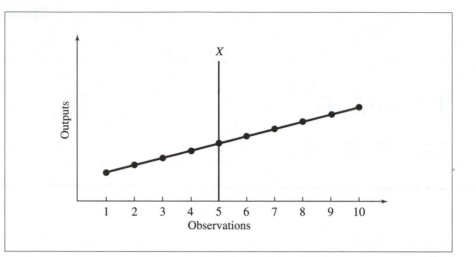

**FIGURE 20.1**

Observation 6 falls along a trend line that is simply the continuation of the line from observation 1 to observation 5. In this case, the new trucks made no difference that would not have occurred if past practices had simply continued. The pattern in Figure 20.1 represents the null hypothesis in interrupted time series. This is not the only "no impact" pattern, however; each of the trend lines in Figure 20.2 is also trend consistent with the null hypothesis of no impact.

## SHORT-TERM
## IMPACTS

Using interrupted time series analysis is a matter of recognizing a few basic patterns, and then knowing how to use multiple regression to provide a statistical test for the results. One common pattern is a short-term impact (or what analysts call a change in intercept). As Figure 20.3 shows, a short-term impact is one in which the output variable makes an immediate change (drop or rise), but the underlying trend of the data remains the same. Other patterns that reveal a short-term impact are shown in Figure 20.4.

Although the use of graphs to judge policy impact is both inexpensive and easy, at times it can be misleading when the graphs get complex. As a result, most analysts use multiple regression for their interrupted time series designs. We will illustrate this with an example. In 1974, as a result of the Arab oil embargo, the United States adopted a 55-mph speed limit. Although designed to save gasoline, a side benefit of the new speed was a decrease in traffic fatalities. Bob Savage, policy analyst for the state of Arkansas, gathered the data listed in Table 20.1 on traffic fatalities in Arkansas.

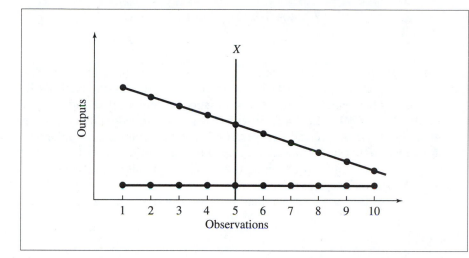

**FIGURE 20.2**
No Impact Patterns

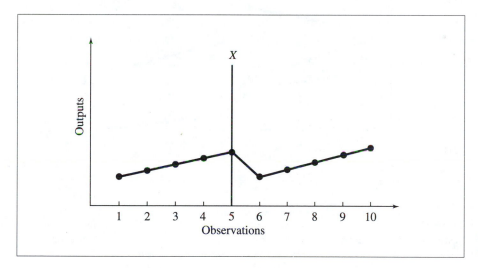

**FIGURE 20.3**
Short-Term Impacts

To determine whether a short-term impact occurred, two new variables are created. The first is a time variable similar to the time variables in Chapter 18. This variable $(X_1)$ is coded 1 in the first year of the study and is increased by 1 for every year thereafter. The second variable $(X_2)$, called the program variable, is a dummy variable coded 1 if the 55-mph speed limit is in effect (1974 and after) and coded 0 if it is not. Treating fatalities as the dependent variable and both time and program as independent variables, analyst Savage runs a regression to get the following results:

$$\hat{Y} = 409 + 8.9X_1 - 85.1X_2$$

$$S_{y|x} = 7.94 \qquad \text{s.e.}_{\beta_1} = 1.67 \qquad \text{s.e.}_{\beta_2} = 9.82 \qquad R^2 = .93$$

Examining this equation, Savage focuses on the regression coefficients. The first coefficient tells him that there is an annual increase in traffic fatalities in Arkansas of 8.9 per year. This increase is statistically significant as shown by a $t$-score of 5.33 ($t = 8.9 \div 1.67 = 5.33$) with 7 degrees of freedom. (If you have forgotten about $t$-scores, reread Chapter 16.) More important for Bob, the second slope reveals that traffic fatalities dropped by 85.1 in the year following the adoption of the 55-mph speed limit; this is a statistically significant drop ($t$-score = 8.67 with 7 degrees of freedom).

As an analyst, Bob can conclude that a statistically significant drop in traffic

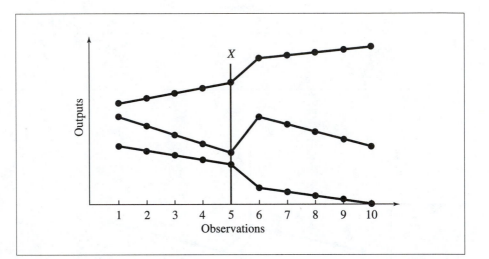

**FIGURE 20.4**

Additional
Short-Term Impacts

**TABLE 20.1**

Traffic Fatalities in Arkansas

| Year | Fatalities ($Y$) | Time ($X_1$) | Program ($X_2$) |
|------|------------------|--------------|-----------------|
| 1968 | 412 | 1 | 0 |
| 1969 | 437 | 2 | 0 |
| 1970 | 428 | 3 | 0 |
| 1971 | 453 | 4 | 0 |
| 1972 | 449 | 5 | 0 |
| 1973 | 463 | 6 | 0 |
| 1974 | 384 | 7 | 1 |
| 1975 | 395 | 8 | 1 |
| 1976 | 414 | 9 | 1 |
| 1977 | 406 | 10 | 1 |

fatalities occurred in Arkansas after the adoption of the 55-mph speed limit. Because he is a good analyst, Bob knows that he cannot conclude that the 55-mph speed limit caused this drop. A major threat to validity in an interrupted time series design (see Chapter 8) is history. Any event that occurred at the same time as the 55-mph speed limit (the gasoline shortage, the adoption of new license plates, and so on) might also have caused this drop. Bob's next task is to seek out these alterantive factors and to attempt to eliminate them as causes of the drop in fatalities.

# LONG-TERM
# IMPACTS

Short-term impacts are dramatic events. In most cases, we do not expect programs or policies to have such an immediate impact. Rather, when implementing a new management program, we often think that what will occur is some gradual improvement in efficiency over a relatively long period of time as employees get used to the program. Similarly, in designing policies, we often expect change to be slow and to occur over an extended period of time as the program is implemented. Let us use an example. The city of Stewartville is concerned about the rising insurance costs that the city has to pay for health insurance, life insurance (for employees), workers compensation insurance, and liability insurance (for auto accidents, accidents on city property, and other damages). Mayor Betty Sue Jaworski decides that the city needs a risk manager to oversee all insurance operations and to see if some cost savings can be made. Billy Joe Bob Zimmerman, the new risk manager, knows that it is unrealistic to expect a dramatic drop in insurance costs. What he hopes to achieve is a reduction in the long-term rate of growth in insurance costs. Figure 20.5 shows such an impact.

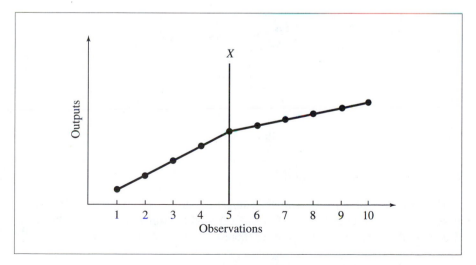

**FIGURE 20.5**
Long-Term Impacts

This pattern is called a long-term impact or a change in slope impact because the slope of the line changes after the program is implemented. Similar to short-term impacts, long-term impacts can have a variety of forms. Some of these forms are shown in Figures 20.6 and 20.7.

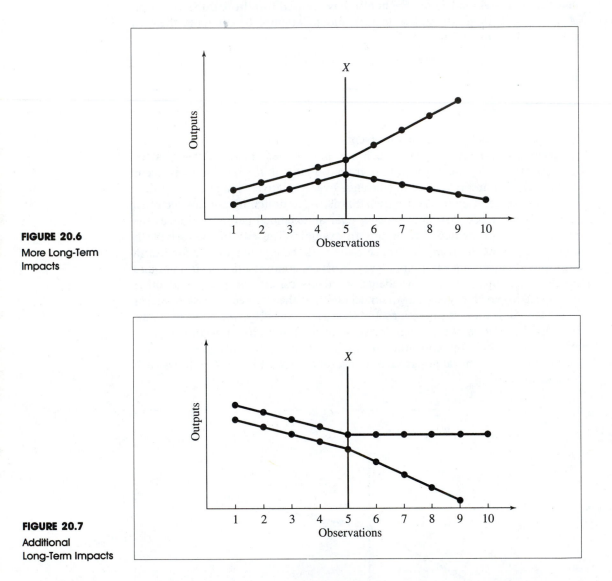

**FIGURE 20.6**
More Long-Term Impacts

**FIGURE 20.7**
Additional Long-Term Impacts

Determining a long-term impact using interrupted time series is similar to assessing a short-term impact, but with a slightly different twist. Table 20.2 shows the insurance costs data gathered by risk manager Billy Joe Bob

Zimmerman to evaluate the impact of consolidating the insurance programs and hiring the risk manager (in 1991).

**TABLE 20.2**

Insurance Costs in Stewartville

| Year | Insurance Costs ($Y$) | Time ($X_1$) | Program ($X_2$) |
|------|------|------|------|
| 1986 | 423,700 | 1 | 0 |
| 1987 | 516,900 | 2 | 0 |
| 1988 | 593,200 | 3 | 0 |
| 1989 | 684,300 | 4 | 0 |
| 1990 | 751,200 | 5 | 0 |
| 1991 | 814,300 | 6 | 1 |
| 1992 | 867,200 | 7 | 2 |
| 1993 | 941,300 | 8 | 3 |
| 1994 | 995,800 | 9 | 4 |
| 1995 | 1,056,700 | 10 | 5 |

The dependent variable in this analysis is insurance costs. The first independent variable is a time variable that accounts for any trend in the data, just as the time variable does in the short-term impact analysis. The second dependent variable is used to assess any long-term changes in the slope of the trend. This variable is coded 0 before the change in policy and is coded as a counter variable after the change $(1, 2, 3, 4, 5, \ldots)$.

Billy Joe Bob can then use these variables in a regression analysis to assess any long-term change in the growth of insurance costs. He gets the following results:

$$\hat{Y} = 348,857 + 81,381X_1 - 21,329X_2$$

$$S_{y|x} = 6,510 \qquad \text{s.e.}_{\beta_1} = 1,800 \qquad \text{s.e.}_{\beta_2} = 2,869 \qquad R^2 = .99$$

An examination of the two slopes tells Billy Joe Bob what he wants to know about the change in insurance programs. The first slope tells him that insurance costs were increasing at a rate of $81,381 ($t = 45.2$) per year before he was hired as risk manager. The second slope of $21,329 tells Billy Joe Bob that the trend in insurance costs was reduced by $21,329 per year ($t = 7.44$) after he was hired. This does not mean that insurance costs are actually declining, but rather, that they are increasing at a slower rate than they were before the change. By adding the two slopes together [$81,381 + (-$21,329)$], Billy Joe Bob can find the rate of increase after the change ($60,052). This means that insurance costs increased at a rate of $60,052 following the program changes. Although this still represents an increase, it is a statistically significant decrease from the trend that existed before Billy Joe Bob was hired.

Again, remember that what was found here was a statistical result. The analysis did not prove that hiring a risk manager and consolidating programs lowered insurance costs. The same threats to validity that were of concern for short-term effects remain a concern for long-term effects. To conclude that the changes made produced the insurance savings, Billy Joe Bob would have to examine all the other potential causes of this change and eliminate them as possibilities (see Chapter 8).

The reader should be aware that short- and long-term effects apply to the rate of change. A short-term effect should not be interpreted as a temporary effect. It is a permanent effect, but its impact is immediate (in the short term). A long-term effect is also permanent, but its impact takes place over a longer period of time.

## Both Short- and Long-Term Effects

In many cases, our theoretical understanding of how public policy affects individuals and outputs is only modest. For example, despite the fact that a great deal of effort is focused on understanding how the U.S. economy works, the impacts of various tax and spending policies are not completely understood. If an area such as macroeconomics is marred with theoretical uncertainty, so will most areas that a public manager deals with. As a result, the manager might not know whether he or she should expect a program change to have a short-term effect or a long-term effect. Or the program manager might expect that a program will have both a long- and a short-term impact.

Figure 20.8 illustrates one possible combination of short- and long-term effects. In this case, a short-term drop in the output occurs immediately; in addition, the long-term slope of the trend decreases. A variety of other short- and long-term impacts are shown in the graphs in Figures 20.9 and 20.10.

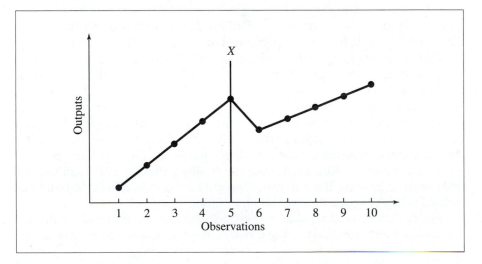

**FIGURE 20.8**
Short- and Long-Term Impacts

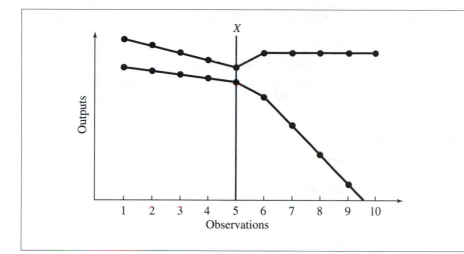

**FIGURE 20.9**

More Short- and Long-Term Impacts

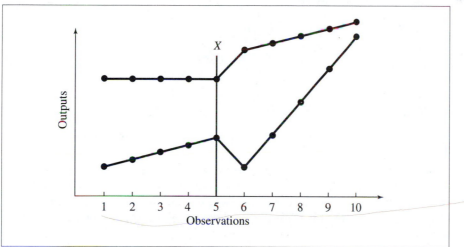

**FIGURE 20.10**

Additional Short- and Long-Term Impacts

To illustrate the technique for estimating both a short-term and a long-term impact, we present an example from Goose Pimple, Vermont. Police Chief Cynthia Weather has been receiving a lot of complaints from merchants about people who park illegally but do not get parking tickets. Chief Weather feels that this is a problem that can be solved. Rather than having regular officers take time away from law enforcement duties, she decides to hire and train a group of officers specifically for this task. She decides that these officers should wear cute uniforms and be called "meter boys." Chief Weather thinks that the new team will have an immediate impact on the number of parking tickets issued, and it will also have a long-term impact as the meter boys get used to their jobs.

After implementing the new approach, Chief Weather waits eight weeks to let the program have some impact. She then tells her trusty assistant, Cat Mandu, to determine whether the program has had an impact. Ms. Mandu collects data on parking tickets both before and after the new program started; the data are presented in Table 20.3.

**TABLE 20.3**

Parking Tickets Issued in Goose Pimple, Vermont

| Week ($X_1$) | Parking Tickets ($Y$) | Short-Term ($X_2$) | Long-Term ($X_3$) |
|:---:|:---:|:---:|:---:|
| 1 | 46 | 0 | 0 |
| 2 | 39 | 0 | 0 |
| 3 | 39 | 0 | 0 |
| 4 | 52 | 0 | 0 |
| 5 | 55 | 0 | 0 |
| 6 | 48 | 0 | 0 |
| 7 | 51 | 0 | 0 |
| 8 | 54 | 0 | 0 |
| 9 | 65 | 1 | 1 |
| 10 | 71 | 1 | 2 |
| 11 | 74 | 1 | 3 |
| 12 | 77 | 1 | 4 |
| 13 | 74 | 1 | 5 |
| 14 | 82 | 1 | 6 |
| 15 | 87 | 1 | 7 |
| 16 | 93 | 1 | 8 |

Since the weeks are already expressed as a number, Ms. Mandu uses this variable as a time trend variable. She then creates two more variables, as shown in Table 20.3: one for a short-term impact ($X_2$), and one for a long-term impact ($X_3$). These data are then used in a multiple regression to get the following results:

$$\hat{Y} = 40.18 + 1.74X_1 + 7.88X_2 + 1.80X_3$$

$$S_{y|x} = 4.05 \qquad \text{s.e.}_{\beta_1} = .63 \qquad \text{s.e.}_{\beta_2} = 4.10 \qquad \text{s.e.}_{\beta_3} = .88 \qquad R^2 = .87$$

Ms. Mandu makes the following interpretation based on the three slopes. First, the number of parking tickets was increasing by 1.74 per week even before the new program went into effect ($t = 2.78$). With the implementation of the new program, the number of parking tickets issued jumped immediately by 7.88 ($t = 1.92$). In addition, after implementation of the new program, the rate of increase in parking tickets increased by 1.80 per week ($t = 2.03$), for a total weekly increase after the new program of 3.54 (or $1.80 + 1.74$).

## PULSE EFFECTS

In some cases, policies will have only a short-term temporary effect on some policy output. Crackdowns on drunk driving, for example, appear to have a significant impact on traffic deaths (a 10% reduction or so) for approximately six months. Such a short-term temporary effect is known as a pulse effect. Illustrations of pulse effects are shown in Figure 20.11.

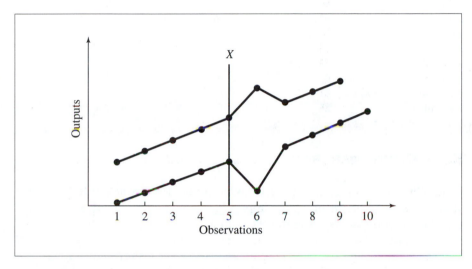

**FIGURE 20.11**
Pulse Effects

An illustration is in order. Bart Hawkins, chief administrator of Our Lady of Mercy Hospital, thinks that his city's month-long marijuana harvest festival affects the number of staff who are absent from work. The harvest festival begins October 1 and lasts for the entire month. Curious about this hypothesis, Bart uses his handy microcomputer to call up the number of absences for the past year. The data in Table 20.4 result.

Bart creates two independent variables. The first is a trend variable $(X_1)$ that will reflect any long-term gain or loss in absences. The second variable $(X_2)$ is a dummy variable, coded 1 for the month of interest and coded 0 otherwise. A multiple regression produces the following result:

$$\hat{Y} = 45.4 + 3.52X_1 + 24.4X_2$$

$$S_{y|x} = 2.2 \qquad \text{s.e.}_{\beta_1} = .19 \qquad \text{s.e.}_{\beta_2} = 2.4 \qquad R^2 = .99$$

Since Bart's only real concern is whether there is a pulse effect, he immediately examines the second regression coefficient. He finds that there are 24.4 more absences in October than would be predicted from a simple trend. This increase is statistically significant ($t = 10.2$).

**TABLE 20.4**

Absences at Our Lady of Mercy Hospital

| Month | Number Absent | Trend ($X_1$) | Pulse Effect ($X_2$) |
|---|---|---|---|
| January | 46 | 1 | 0 |
| February | 52 | 2 | 0 |
| March | 55 | 3 | 0 |
| April | 60 | 4 | 0 |
| May | 66 | 5 | 0 |
| June | 68 | 6 | 0 |
| July | 70 | 7 | 0 |
| August | 76 | 8 | 0 |
| September | 79 | 9 | 0 |
| October | 105 | 10 | 1 |
| November | 81 | 11 | 0 |
| December | 86 | 12 | 0 |

## SOME CONSIDERATIONS

Generally, when examining a program, you should decide whether to look for a short-term, a long-term, or a pulse impact based on theory—if any exists. Without theory, you can always graph the data and make a guess as to whether or not to estimate short-term, long-term, or pulse impacts. When you are not sure, you can estimate all three effects (although usually just a short- and a long-term effect are estimated). When proceeding in this manner, if you find that one of these impacts is not significant, then the regression should be rerun without the insignificant impact. This process will give you a more precise estimate of the impact that does exist.

A second consideration that you, as an analyst, should be aware of is autocorrelation. Recall that Chapter 17 stated that one of the assumptions of regression is that the errors are not correlated. Correlated errors or autocorrelation is usually a problem only in time series analysis. The problem created by autocorrelation is that the standard errors of the slopes are underestimated. In practical terms, autocorrelation can result in slopes that appear to be significant when in fact they are not. This means that a manager might conclude that a program has an impact when in fact it does not.

Dealing with autocorrelation is a fairly complex undertaking. Fortunately, there is a relatively simple test to see whether a regression equation has significant autocorrelation. This test is based on a statistic called the Durbin-Watson. Most regression programs will calculate a Durbin-Watson for you, if you ask it nicely. For the Goose Pimple, Vermont, parking regression (Table 20.3), the Durbin-Watson statistic is 1.85. Durbin-Watson statistics are close to 2.0 if there is no autocorrelation, equal to 0 if there is perfect positive autocorrelation, and equal to 4.0 if there is perfect negative autocorrelation.

Table 5 in the Appendix provides the Durbin-Watson table to test for autocorrelation at the .05 level of confidence. To use a Durbin-Watson table, you need to know the number of independent variables (in this example, 3) and the number of cases (in this example, 16). Using the table for $k = 3$ independent variables and $n = 16$ cases, we find two numbers, .857 and 1.728. The higher number, 1.728, is known as the upper limit (denoted $d_U$); the lower number is the lower limit ($d_L$). If the Durbin-Watson is greater than 1.728, you can reject the existence of autocorrelation with .05 confidence. If the number is less than .857, you can reject the hypothesis that there is no autocorrelation with .05 confidence. For numbers between .857 and 1.728, you cannot be certain whether or not autocorrelation exists. Since our Durbin-Watson is 1.85, we can be reasonably confident that autocorrelation is not a problem. If autocorrelation is a problem in any of your analyses, you should consult an advanced statistics text, such as Nelson (1973) or Ostrom (1983). Better yet, find a trained statistician to help you correct for this problem.

## USING DATA TO REPRESENT PROGRAM CHANGES

With all the interrupted time series models presented so far in this chapter, the independent variables have either been a trend variable, a dummy variable, or some type of counter variable. A dummy variable is a fairly crude indicator of a change in a policy or in a new program. Often the analyst will have a better measure of the policy change. For example, Michael Lewis-Beck and John Alford in the 1979 *American Political Science Review* analyzed the impact of government regulation on coal mine safety. Their dependent variable is coal mine safety deaths; their independent variable used to measure government regulation is federal expenditures for coal mine regulation. Although they could have used a dummy variable to measure when the federal government created a coal mine safety program, the use of budget figures was a more precise estimate of how much effort the federal government was putting into government regulation.

For example, let us suppose that the federal government wants to know whether the medicaid program (a health care program for poor people) has had any impact on infant mortality. The infant mortality rate (number of infant deaths per 1000 live births) is the dependent variable; the analysis will cover the years 1951 to 1988. The infant mortality rate in the United States was declining before the medicaid program was started (1965), as a result of general improvements in nutrition and medical care. To represent this general trend of improvement, a trend variable ($X_1$) is included that is coded as 1 for 1950 and increases by 1 each year after that. A traditional interrupted time series would create two new independent variables: one for a short-term effect, coded 1 after the medicaid program was started (1965) and coded 0 before it started ($X_2$); and one for a long-term effect, coded 0 before medicaid and coded as a counter variable afterward ($X_3$). This interrupted time series regression is shown as follows:

$$\hat{Y} = 28.3 - .250X_1 - .871X_2 - .409X_3$$

$$S_{y|x} = .76 \qquad \text{s.e.}_{\beta_1} = .05 \qquad \text{s.e.}_{\beta_2} = .50 \qquad \text{s.e.}_{\beta_3} = .05 \qquad R^2 = .96$$

According to this equation, the infant mortality rate was dropping at the rate of .25 per year ($t = 4.98$), a significant drop. The introduction of the medicaid program had an immediate short-term impact of a drop of .871 in the infant mortality rate ($t = 1.75$), and a long-term drop of .409 per year after the program's introduction ($t = 7.45$).

An alternative way to examine the impact of medicaid on infant mortality would be to use total medicaid expenditures (in millions of constant dollars). This interrupted time series is presented here:

$$\hat{Y} = 28.5 - .250X_1 - .0159X_2$$

$$S_{y|x} = .539 \qquad \text{s.e.}_{\beta_1} = .028 \qquad \text{s.e.}_{\beta_2} = .00013 \qquad R^2 = .99$$

This equation is more informative than the previous equation. The first slope still means that infant mortality rates dropped at a rate of .25 per year after 1951 ($t = 8.85$). The interpretation of the second coefficient, however, is the real difference. For every $1 million spent on medicaid, the U.S. infant mortality rate drops by .0159. This regression gives the analyst a more precise linkage between the medicaid program and infant mortality rates, suggesting that it is the total money spent on medicaid rather than just the existence of the medicaid program that affects infant mortality rates. In addition, this is a better prediction of infant mortality rates in the United States than was the previous equation, that is, the standard error of the estimate is smaller.

## CONTROLLING FOR OTHER VARIABLES

One advantage of interrupted time series analysis is that it allows the analyst to control for other factors that might influence the dependent variable by including these factors as additional independent variables. For example, in 1983, the federal government was very concerned about the rising level of health care costs being paid as part of medicare and medicaid. In that year, the federal government implemented something called Diagnostic Review Groups, which were designed to hold down the costs of health care. To determine whether this change had an impact on medicaid costs, you might use medicaid costs in millions of dollars as a dependent variable, and include a trend variable ($X_1$) that increases by 1 each year and a short-term impact variable ($X_2$) for the

Diagnostic Review Groups program. One problem with this estimation is that it does not take into account the rapid rise in health care costs as a result of inflation. Interrupted time series analysis can handle this problem simply by including a measure of inflation in the equation. In this case, a measure of medical prices (the medical price index, which equals 100 in 1967) is included as the third independent variable $(X_3)$. A regression yields the following results:

$$\hat{Y} = -5200 - 122X_1 - 4117X_2 + 8936X_3$$

$$S_{y|x} = 547 \qquad \text{s.e.}_{\beta_1} = 23 \qquad \text{s.e.}_{\beta_2} = 567 \qquad \text{s.e.}_{\beta_3} = 299 \qquad R^2 = .99$$

The large positive coefficient for medical prices reveals that a 1 point increase in the medical price index is associated with a \$8936 million increase in medicaid costs if you control for year and whether the Diagnostic Review Groups program was in effect $(t = 29.9)$. The second coefficient is the one that is of most concern. This coefficient reveals that the implementation of the Diagnostic Review Groups program resulted in a \$4117 million reduction in medicaid costs if you control for the year and rising medical care costs $(t = 7.25)$.

This example contains a single control variable. Additional control variables could be added if the analyst believes that these variables could affect medicaid costs. For example, total medicaid recipients or the national unemployment rate could be used as a measure of demand for this program.

## CHAPTER SUMMARY

This chapter examined a technique used to evaluate programs and policy when time series data are available. Interrupted time series analysis is an effort to estimate the impact of a policy or a program while controlling for any underlying trends in the data. This chapter showed how an analyst using multiple regression could estimate the short-term impact, the long-term impact, and a short-term temporary (pulse effect) impact of a policy or program. Because interrupted time series analysis uses multiple regression, the technique is very flexible. An analyst can use program expenditures as an independent variable and can control for a variety of variables that might also affect the dependent variable being analyzed.

## PROBLEMS

**20.1** The city of Madison, Wisconsin, needs to squeeze a bit more tax revenue out of its citizens. The city decides to charge \$200 for each ambulance call. It knows that health and automobile insurance companies will pay this fee for those individuals who carry insurance. One concern is that people will not use the ambulance after it arrives when they are informed of the charge; this is called a dry run. To assess the impact of the new fee on the percentage of dry runs, monthly data for 80 months is gathered. The dependent variable is the percentage of dry runs. The independent variables are $X_1$, a monthly fluctuation variable (ambulance calls are more frequent in the summer); $X_2$, a trend variable coded 1 in the first month and coded 80 in the last; and $X_3$, a long-term impact variable coded 0 before the $200 charge and coded as a counter variable (e.g., 1, 2, 3, 4, ...) after the charge. The following regression is produced:

$$\hat{Y} = 1.82 + 21.29X_1 + .026X_2 + .55X_3$$

$$R^2 = .57 \qquad \text{s.e.}_{\beta_1} = 3.14 \qquad \text{s.e.}_{\beta_2} = .0095 \qquad \text{s.e.}_{\beta_3} = .15 \qquad S_{y|x} = 1.74$$

Ignore the first independent variable. Interpret the remaining slopes and $R^2$.

**20.2** Jack "Crash" Craddock, chief analyst for the Federal Aviation Administration, wants to know whether airline deregulation had any impact on airline safety. As a measure of airline safety, he uses the number of near misses (a near miss is when planes come within a certain number of feet of each other) for each year. Using data from 1960 to 1992, Craddock collects the following independent variables: $X_1$, a counter variable coded 1 in 1960 and increasing by 1 each year; $X_2$, a long-term impact variable coded zero before deregulation (1978) and increasing by 1 each year thereafter; and $X_3$, a control for the state of the economy, percent growth in gross national product over the previous year (people fly more during good economic times). A regression shows the following:

$$\hat{Y} = 137.1 + 15.9X_1 + 12.3X_2 + 26.1X_3 \qquad N = 33$$

$$R^2 = .93 \qquad \text{s.e.}_{\beta_1} = 1.2 \qquad \text{s.e.}_{\beta_2} = 14.6 \qquad \text{s.e.}_{\beta_3} = 3.2 \qquad S_{y|x} = 20.1$$

Interpret the slopes, intercept, and coefficient of determination. Test each slope for significance. What can you say about airline deregulation?

**20.3** Sheriff S. Norton Koch wants to know if the number of drug arrests in Weed County has increased since the 1984 passage of a tough new state law on drug possession. His dependent variable is the number of drug arrests. He has three independent variables: $X_1$ is a trend variable coded 1 in the first year and increasing by 1 each year thereafter; $X_2$ is a short-term impact variable coded 0 before 1984 and coded 1 afterward; and $X_3$ is a long-term impact variable coded 0 before 1984 and increasing by 1 each year afterward. A regression produces the following results:

$$\hat{Y} = 546.5 - 5.1X_1 + 67.2X_2 + 4.3X_3 \qquad N = 32$$

$$R^2 = .99 \qquad \text{s.e.}_{\beta_1} = .92 \qquad \text{s.e.}_{\beta_2} = 17.3 \qquad \text{s.e.}_{\beta_3} = 1.3 \qquad S_{y|x} = 34.1$$

Interpret the slopes and coefficient of determination. Test the slopes for significance, and explain what this equation says about the drug law.

**20.4**  Roberta Refuse, head sanitation engineer for the metropolis of Stewartville, would like to assess the impact that a statewide recycling law on trash collection has in Stewartville. The law prohibits the disposal of yard waste in trash cans. If this law is having an impact, the amount of trash collected would drop. Weekly trash collection data are available. The dependent variable is total tons of trash collected. The independent variables are: $X_1$, the number of inches of rainfall the previous week (grass grows more when it rains); $X_2$, the mean Fahrenheit temperature for the previous week (grass grows better when it is warm); and $X_3$, a short-term impact variable coded 0 before the recycling law went into effect and coded 1 afterward. She gets the following results:

$$\hat{Y} = 12{,}405 + 140X_1 + 7.4X_2 - 575X_3 \qquad N = 75$$

$$R^2 = .63 \qquad \text{s.e.}_{\beta_1} = 31 \qquad \text{s.e.}_{\beta_2} = 2.0 \qquad \text{s.e.}_{\beta_3} = 45 \qquad S_{y|x} = 327$$

Interpret the slopes, intercept, and coefficient of determination. Test the slopes for significance, and explain what this equation says about the recycling law.

**20.5**  The infant mortality rate is considered a good indicator of overall health care in a country. The following regression uses the infant mortality rate in the United States from 1951 to 1989 (number of infant deaths per 1000 live births) as the dependent variable. The independent variables are: $X_1$, a trend variable coded 1 in the first year and increasing by 1 for each year thereafter; $X_2$, the amount of money spent in the federal medicaid program (a health care access program) in millions of dollars; and $X_3$, the amount of money spent in the federal supplemental program for women, infants, and children (WIC, a nutrition program).

$$\hat{Y} = 28.32 - .26017X_1 - .00138X_2 - .00211X_3 \qquad N = 39$$

$$R^2 = .99 \qquad \text{s.e.}_{\beta_1} = .00365 \qquad \text{s.e.}_{\beta_2} = .00017 \qquad \text{s.e.}_{\beta_3} = .00113 \qquad S_{y|x} = .12$$

Interpret the slopes, intercept, and coefficient of determination. Test the slopes for significance, and explain what this equation says about the impact of medicaid and WIC on the infant mortality rate.

**20.6**  The state of Florida has adopted a new sentencing law to increase the penalties for drug-related crimes. The state legislative research bureau is interested in knowing whether courts are upholding this law. The dependent variable that the bureau uses is the average number of months in prison that first-time drug offenders receive if convicted for sale of drugs. The independent variables are: $X_1$, a trend variable coded 1 in the first month of the study and increasing by 1 each month thereafter; $X_2$, a short-term impact variable coded 0 before the new law and coded 1 afterward; and $X_3$, a long-term impact variable coded 0 before the law and coded as a counter variable $(1, 2, 3, \ldots)$ afterward. A regression shows the following results:

$$\hat{Y} = 24.52 - .13X_1 + 27.4X_2 + 2.15X_3 \qquad N = 75$$

$$R^2 = .88 \qquad \text{s.e.}_{\beta_1} = 3.15 \qquad \text{s.e.}_{\beta_2} = 2.36 \qquad \text{s.e.}_{\beta_3} = 4.53 \qquad S_{y|x} = 5.4$$

Interpret the slopes and coefficient of determination. Test the slopes for significance, and explain what this equation says about the impact of the new sentencing law.

**PART VII**

# SPECIAL TOPICS IN
# QUANTITATIVE
# MANAGEMENT

## CHAPTER 21

# DECISION THEORY

According to Nobel prize–winning economist Herbert Simon, the essence of management is decision making. Managers must make decisions on how to organize an office, how to evaluate a program, the necessary skills needed in an agency position, how to motivate employees, and numerous other tasks in a public organization. A large body of literature has sprouted around the idea of management as decision making. This chapter will overview decision theory and its uses for public managers. Many of the approaches outlined in this chapter can be used to solve problems found in the other chapters.

## THE RATIONAL DECISION-MAKING MODEL

An ideal type of decision making has surfaced in a variety of management areas. Planning, program evaluation, performance appraisal, and budgeting are often structured to meet the ideal, *rational decision-making* goal. Many management theorists argue that good managers attempt to attain this ideal decision-making pattern. Although this position is not without challenge, rational decision making should be part of every manager's skills.

There are five steps in rational decision making.

**STEP 1**   Identify the problem. Although this first step appears simple, in many situations it is not. The U.S. Army, for example, has noted increased disciplinary problems, including drug usage, among its troops. The immediate problem is discipline, but the underlying problem may be something else. Inadequate training, lack of meaningful work assignments, absence of effective supervision, inadequate leadership, or re-cruitment problems generated by the volunteer army may be the real problem. Failure to identify the problem correctly may lead to a poor decision. If inadequate training is the problem and it results in less discipline, increasing punishments may have no impact on the disci-pline of troops. One secret of good management is to be able to diag-nose problems correctly.

**STEP 2**  Specify goals and objectives. Given a specific problem, exactly what does the organization wish to achieve? A state welfare office may have a problem if its payments are too high given the agency's resources. How the agency responds to this problem depends on its goals. If the goal is simply to lower costs, then word can be passed to deny more claims. If the goal is to restrict the amount of waste, control mechanisms to catch fraud could be implemented. If the goal is to make welfare recipients self-sufficient, then providing recipients with needed job skills might be an alternative. Without carefully specified goals, the rational decision-making model cannot function.

Specifying goals, although it seems a rational and commonsense thing to do, is not without its problems. First, whenever more than one person must accept a goal (normally the case in a public organization), agreement on goals becomes problematic. An individual's perception of agency goals will be a function of that person's role in the organization and that person's individual values and preferences. City planners, for example, may feel that the goal of an urban renewal project is to beau-tify the city. The chief fiscal officer may see the project as a way to increase the city's tax base. The community development director may see the project as a means of increasing employment opportunities through construction jobs. The public works head may see the project's goal as providing city goverment office space. These and numerous other goals can logically be offered as the goal of an urban renewal project. Without agreement on the goal of the project, decision making becomes difficult.

Second, as illustrated before, any one project or agency can have numerous goals. Even so simple a task as refuse collection can have several goals. Refuse is collected to avoid health problems that occur when garbage sits in alleys. Refuse collection also has cost goals; city managers would like to collect trash as cheaply as possible. Refuse collection has service goals; city residents may want garbage collected twice a week so that it does not pile up in yards. Multiple objectives mean several goals must be sought simultaneously, and this restriction creates problems for decision makers.

Third, where multiple goals exist, some are bound to conflict. In our example of urban renewal, maximizing employment opportunities may well conflict with the goal of holding down costs. Increasing the city's tax base conflicts with increasing the available city government office space. If conflicts between goals cannot be resolved, rational decision making is not possible.

Fourth, goal expression raises the specter of suboptimization. A single subunit of an agency maximizing its goals or a single agency of government maximizing its goals may produce results detrimental to the overall organization's goals. An audit division, for example, that is overzealous in its effort to prevent the waste of taxpayers' money may place such restrictions on operating agencies that the agencies spend more time responding to fiscal control than they spend delivering services. Although this situation may be rational for the audit agency, it is not rational from a governmentwide perspective.

**STEP 3**    Specify all alternatives available to attain the goals. Once goals have been established, the decision maker must then specify all the alternative options that he or she has to attain the goals. This does not mean the decision maker must list every alternative no matter how ridiculous; rather, some judgment is exercised to limit the alternatives considered to those that are politically and managerially feasible. The Florida State director of welfare, for example, when faced with the goal of reducing welfare costs, does not consider the alternative of simply lining up all welfare recipients and shooting them.

**STEP 4**    Evaluate the alternatives in light of the goals. Each alternative is examined to see whether it will attain the goals in question. All alternatives capable of attaining the ends in question are then compared to determine which alternative is the most likely to achieve the goals. At this stage of decision making, a variety of analytical tools can be used to contrast alternatives. Cost-benefit analysis, in which program costs are contrasted with program benefits, is the favorite of many program evaluators. Direct and indirect, as well as present and future, costs and benefits must be included. Creative analysis is needed to include the unanticipated second-order costs and benefits (a successful drug rehabilitation program, for example, will reduce the crime rate for robbery and burglary). Other offshoots of cost-benefit analysis, including system analysis, risk analysis, and feasibility analysis, are also used.

The evaluaton of alternatives need not be a sophisticated mathematical assessment. Alternatives may be judged on the basis of past experience, political information, and so on. In fact, these *extrarational* methods of analyzing options are often the only methods available to the decision maker. Even when sophisticated methods of analysis exist, the manager must determine how realistic the evaluation models are. As many Defense Department officials learned from the TFX project, a manager cannot defend a failure by blaming a cost-benefit model (at least not more than once).*

**STEP 5** Select the optimal alternative. From the alternatives considered in Step 4, the best alternative in terms of the goals established should be selected and then implemented. The last step is crucial; a brilliant decision that is not implemented is worse than no decision at all. At least if there is no decision, the agency personnel did not waste their time in a futile exercise.

## A Brief Critique

The rational decision model has been heavily criticized as an inaccurate description of how decisions are made. Herbert Simon, for example, argues that decision makers "satisfice" rather than maximize. When faced with a problem, decision makers do not specify goals or list all the alternatives. Rather they consider one or two alternatives that are not too different from current agency policy. If one alternative appears to satisfactorily solve the problem, it is implemented. If the alternative does not yield satisfactory utility, a few more alternatives are examined.

Simon's satisficing model and other incremental models probably do portray decision making as it actually occurs in many organizations. In many circumstances in which the benefits of two alternatives do not differ greatly, the decision costs of the rational model are not justified. In other situations, however, in which sufficient information is available to the decision maker, the rational model is a useful tool for the manager. The task of the manager is to determine whether a problem has the characteristics that permit the application of the rational model and to use this model where appropriate.

## Decision Making
## Under Certainty

**states of nature**

Any important variables that affect the outcome of a decision but are not under the control of the decision maker are **states of nature** (the conditions that exist when a decision is made). The major variation in decision theory concerns the

---

*A book as long as this one should have at least one lengthy footnote, and this is it. Some management theorists will be offended by our model of rational decision making because we have modified it to fit the real world. Such theorists would require the rational decision maker to analyze all possible costs and benefits for all possible alternatives. Management theorists who do this set up a straw man that is easily demolished as unrealistic. See Herbert Simon, *Administrative Behavior* (New York: The Free Press, 1947) or David Braybrooke and Charles Lindblom, *A Strategy of Decision* (New York: The Free Press, 1970). We believe that in many management decisions under certainty the rational model is appropriate. In many decisions under risk it is a useful model.

decision maker's knowledge about the various possible states of nature. When the states of nature are known before the decision is made, a state of **certainty** exists. When states of nature are unknown but can be assigned probabilities, decision making is under **risk**. When probabilities cannot be assigned, decision making under **uncertainty** is required.

**certainty**

**risk**

**uncertainty**

Decision making under certainty means that the decision maker's knowledge of the environment is complete, the problem is clearly identified, and goals are uniformly accepted and explicitly defined. Under such conditions, one best alternative exists that will attain the goals in question.

An example will illustrate the ideas. The Aberdeen Fire Department has two fire stations—one on the north side of town and one on the south side. When a fire call comes in, the dispatcher must decide whether to send a fire truck from the north side station or the south side station. The informal decision rule has been that any fire call north of the railroad tracks will be answered by the north side station. The south side station handles all other calls.

The goal of the Aberdeen Fire Department is to respond to fire calls as quickly as possible (this will help it attain a goal of minimum fire losses). For every point in the city, two alternatives exist: dispatch from the north side station or dispatch from the south side station. Because traffic congestion has increased around the south side station, trucks from the north side station may be able to reach some locations in the southwest part of town faster than could the south side trucks.

The fire chief authorizes a series of practice runs to determine which station can respond faster to various parts of the city. After numerous runs, the results are transferred to a map. A line is drawn that divides the city into two parts—a part from which the north side station can respond faster and a part from which the south side station can respond faster. The dispatcher's decision rules are changed so that any call north of the dividing line is assigned to the north side station, and vice versa. (In larger cities, dispatchers use an alphabetized Rolodex of street names. The Rolodex lists the station to be used plus all backup stations.)

Note the characteristics of the Aberdeen Fire Department problem. First, the goal was clear and unambiguous—to dispatch fire trucks so that they reach the scene of the fire as fast as possible. Second, only a limited number of alternatives were available (in this case, two). Third, each alternative could be directly evaluated in terms of the goal. Fourth, the states of nature were certain. Once a fire call is received, its location in the city can be pinpointed. Under such conditions of certainty, a rational decision model is appropriate. (An entire class of such problems, called linear programming problems, are discussed in Chapter 22.)

# DECISION MAKING
# UNDER RISK

A decision under risk exists when the decision maker cannot tell before a decision is made exactly what the state of nature is. The decision maker can, on the basis of logic or past experience, assign probabilities to the various states of nature. Decision making under risk is best illustrated with an example.

The city of Reginald, Ohio, must choose between one of three types of employment programs. The effectiveness of each program depends on the level of unemployment (the state of nature). What are the city's options?

**OPTION 1**    Do nothing. Reginald can simply ignore any unemployment problems and hope that the marketplace will correct any problems. Option 1 works best if unemployment is low, since the city will not spend any funds. If unemployment reaches moderate levels (5–9%), then costs to Reginald in terms of countercyclical aid and political unrest will be moderate. If unemployment is high (over 9%), option 1 becomes a disaster, with reduced demand for goods catapulting the Reginald area into a major recession.

**OPTION 2**    Operate a job placement center to locate jobs for persons currently out of work. Option 2 incurs minor fixed costs if unemployment is low, but returns major benefits where unemployment is moderate (5–9%). Under moderate unemployment the service still has sufficient jobs to place most temporarily out-of-work persons. If unemployment is high, however, the placement program will be inadequate.

**OPTION 3**    Implement a job training program. If unemployment is below 5%, this program's high fixed costs make it an unattractive alternative. Under moderate unemployment (5–9%), the program incurs some minor costs. The job training program works best under conditions of high unemployment, because it absorbs surplus labor and alters the work force's skills.

Reginald's choice of employment programs can be analyzed as a decision under risk. To do so, the following steps must be implemented.

**decision table**    **STEP 1**    Set up a **decision table**. Place each of the states of nature (in this case low, moderate, and high unemployment) across the top of the table. Note that the states of nature must cover all conceivable possibilities. Place each of the decision options down the left-hand side of the table. The decision table of Table 21.1 results.

**payoff**    **STEP 2**    Calculate the **payoff** to the city for each cell in the decision table. That is, what is the cost or benefit to Reginald if unemployment is low and the city does nothing? What is the cost to the city if unemployment is low and the city runs a placement service? Payoffs may be calculated in a variety of ways. The manager may assign payoffs based on past experience; cost-benefit calculations can be done for each option; and so

**TABLE 21.1**

Decision Table for Reginald, Ohio

| Decision Options | Unemployment | | |
|---|---|---|---|
| | *Low* | *Moderate* | *High* |
| Do nothing | | | |
| Placement | | | |
| Job training | | | |

on. The mayor of Reginald, Joyce Caruthers, asks Thomas Malthus, a labor economist at Reginald State University, to calculate the costs and benefits for each cell. Professor Malthus turns the project over to his graduate student, who produces the costs and benefits shown in Table 21.2 (where K = $1000).

**TABLE 21.2**

Costs and Benefits for Reginald

| Decision Options | Unemployment | | |
|---|---|---|---|
| | *Low* | *Moderate* | *High* |
| Do nothing | $20K | −$5K | −$120K |
| Placement | −$10K | $50K | −$30K |
| Job training | −$110K | $10K | $140K |

To interpret this table, one merely assigns the value listed to the decision option given a certain state of nature. For example, if unemployment is high and the city does nothing, the cost to the city will be $120,000.

**STEP 3** Determine the probability that each state of nature will occur; that is, for the period that the decision will cover, what is the probability of low unemployment (less than 5%), moderate unemployment (5–9%), or high unemployment (greater than 9%)? Mayor Caruthers asks Calvin Kent, a local economics consultant, to forecast the probability of low, moderate, or high unemployment. Kent predicts a .2 probability of low unemployment, a .3 probability of moderate unemployment, and a .5 probability of high unemployment. These figures are placed in the table next to the states of nature (see Table 21.3).

**STEP 4** Calculate the expected value for each decision option. The **expected value** of any choice (decision option) is the sum of all the values that can

**expected value**

**TABLE 21.3**

Probabilities for States of Nature

| Decision Options | Unemployment | | |
|---|---|---|---|
| | *Low (.2)* | *Moderate (.3)* | *High (.5)* |
| Do nothing | $20K | −$5K | −$120K |
| Placement | −$10K | $50K | −$30K |
| Job training | −$110K | $10K | $140K |

be attained times the probability that each of the values will be attained; that is,

$$EV = \Sigma P_i V_i$$

where EV is a choice's expected value, $V$ is the value that can be attained, and $P$ is the probability associated with each of the values.

To illustrate, the authors of this text are avid joggers who are known to consume a barley-based beverage (in fact, we were once charged with the crime of jogging only to make the beverage taste better). After jogging, both authors retire to a local establishment and drink two beverages each. One author proposes that each day they flip a coin. If it comes up heads, he will buy two drinks for both authors (a cost of $3.20); if it is tails, the other author will buy the refreshments. What is the expected value of this choice? It is the probability that a person will buy all the drinks (.5 if the coin is unbiased) times the cost of that option ($3.20) plus the probability that the same person will buy no drinks (.5) times the cost of that option ($0), or

$$EV = (\$3.20 \times .5) + (\$0 \times .5) = \$1.60 + \$0 = \$1.60$$

The expected value of this choice is $1.60.

Returning to our Reginald problem, we see that the expected value of doing nothing (option 1) is the sum of the products of each of the three payoffs associated with this option times their respective probabilities. In other words, the value of doing nothing is equal to $20,000 if unemployment is low, −$5000 if unemployment is moderate, and −$120,000 if unemployment is high. Since the respective probabilities of each of these states of nature are .2, .3, and .5, the expected value of doing nothing is

$$EV = (.2 \times \$20,000) + (.3 \times -\$5000) + (.5 \times -\$120,000)$$

$$= \$4000 + (-\$1500) + (-\$60,000) = -\$57,500$$

The expected value of doing nothing is a loss of $57,500.

The expected value for option 2, the placement option, is as follows:

$$EV = (.2 \times -\$10,000) + (.3 \times \$50,000) + (.5 \times -\$30,000)$$

$$= -\$2000 + (+\$15,000) + (-\$15,000) = -\$2000$$

Notice that the probabilities for the states of nature remain the same; only the values associated with each state change.

For the third option, the training program, the expected value is

$$EV = (.2 \times -\$110,000) + (.3 \times \$10,000) + (.5 \times \$140,000)$$

$$= -\$22,000 + \$3000 + \$70,000 = \$51,000$$

Mayor Caruthers's decision should be obvious. The expected value of doing nothing is a loss of $57,500. The expected value of placement is a loss of $2000, and the expected value of job training is a benefit of $51,000. The mayor selects the job training program.

### A CAVEAT

Decision making under risk makes some assumptions that may not be attractive to decision makers. First, it assumes that the decision maker has the same attitude toward risk regardless of the size of benefit involved. The expected value of a decision with a .25 probability of a $10,000 loss is the same as the expected value of a decision with a .0025 probability of a $1 million loss. A manager might well be willing to take the first risk yet find the second one unacceptable. Decision theory in the form presented above cannot incorporate this willingness to take risks. Second, the model assumes that expected value covers all the values the decision maker wants to maximize. A public sector decision maker may want to incorporate different values. If Milton Friedman were mayor of Reginald, he might wish to err on the side of less government and do nothing—or at most run only a placement program. Other public managers might echo Franklin Roosevelt's sentiments when he conceded that his policies might be wrong, but that it was better to try and fail than to not try at all. Both the amount of risk tolerated and the additional values considered are political criteria. These criteria, in addition to the results of the decision table, must be considered by public managers and policy analysts.

## THE VALUE OF PERFECT INFORMATION

Mayor Caruthers is visited by J. Barringford Tipton of Chaste Econometrics, a well-known economic forecasting firm. Tipton tells Caruthers that Chaste can

perfect
information

accurately forecast the unemployment rate in Reginald for the next year. Caruthers is enthused until Tipton tells her that the forecast will cost Reginald $25,000. Should Caruthers hire Chaste to forecast for her?

Another way of asking this question is to ask, What is the value of **perfect information**? (Perfect information means that you can specify the exact state of nature in advance.) Without any information concerning the states of nature (except their probabilities), Caruthers selected option 3, the job training program, with a value of $51,000. This figure needs to be compared with the expected value if the city had perfect information.

**TABLE 21.4**

Probabilities for States of Nature

| Decision Options | Unemployment | | |
|---|---|---|---|
| | *Low (.2)* | *Moderate (.3)* | *High (.5)* |
| Do nothing | $20K | −$5K | −$120K |
| Placement | −$10K | $50K | −$30K |
| Job training | −$110K | $10K | $140K |

Refer to the payoff table, Table 21.4. If the city knew that unemployment would be low, it would do nothing and reap a benefit of $20,000. Since low employment will occur 20% of the time, the expected value of this occurrence is $4000 ($20,000 × .2). If the city knows that unemployment will be moderate, the best decision would be a placement program with a payoff of $50,000. Since moderate unemployment will occur 30% of the time, the expected value of this occurrence is $15,000. Finally, if the city knew that unemployment would be high, it would run a job training program and receive $140,000 in benefits. Discounting this figure by its probability (.5) yields an expected value of $70,000. The expected value of decisions based on perfect information is the sum of all three payoffs:

$$(.2 \times \$20{,}000) + (.3 \times \$50{,}000) + (.5 \times \$140{,}000)$$

$$= \$4000 + \$15{,}000 + \$70{,}000 = \$89{,}000$$

With perfect information, the city could expect a long-run benefit of $89,000 every time this decision was made. Comparing this to the next best alternative (selecting option 3 without perfect information), the city's payoff is $89,000 versus $51,000. The difference ($38,000) is the value of perfect information. In other words, Reginald should purchase the forecast because its cost ($25,000) is less than its value ($38,000).

# Decision Making Under Risk: Decision Trees

Many times decision making under risk becomes far more complicated than indicated by the simple tables presented up to now. A decision maker will have several decisions to make in a variety of states of nature. In special circumstances, these states of nature are determined by other actors. Under complex conditions, decision analysts often represent decisions with **decision trees** rather than with a simple payoff table. One such tree is shown in Figure 21.1.

**decision tree**

The decision facing the analyst in the question represented in Figure 21.1 is whether to deploy the MX missile (a mobile U.S. strategic missile.) The initial decision point on the far left is the deployment decision. Any decision that the decision maker can resolve is referred to as a **decision node** and is designated with a box. Sometime after the United States decides whether to deploy the MX, the Soviets will decide whether to deploy their Backfire bomber (a tactical bomber with strategic capabilities). Because this decision cannot be controlled by the United States, it is designated as a **chance node** and is represented by a circle on the decision tree. For every chance event (or state of nature), a probability is listed. These probability estimates were made by national security analysts based on the information that they have at their disposal. Note that the probability that the Soviets will deploy the Backfire bomber is .7 if the United States deploys the MX missile and .4 if the United States does not deploy the MX.

**decision node**

**chance node**

After the Soviet decision has been made about deploying the Backfire bomber, the United States must decide whether to deploy the Cruise missile. This decision node is again denoted with a box. The final decision, which belongs to the Soviets, is whether to build up and modernize forces in Europe. These states of nature and the probabilities associated with them are represented to the right of the last column of circles.

The figures on the extreme right of the decision tree under the heading "Payoff" are the numbers of nuclear warheads that the United States will have available for a second strike if the events associated with limbs of the tree hold. For example, if the United States deploys both the MX and the Cruise and the Soviets deploy the Backfire and build up forces in Europe, then an estimated 5000 strategic nuclear warheads will survive a Soviet strike and be available for a U.S. second strike. The objective is to decide whether to deploy the MX and the Cruise missile so that the number of second-strike warheads is maximized.

Decision trees are solved by working backward from the branches of the tree to the trunk. Since each pair of branches representing the Soviet decision on building up forces in Europe has both probabilities and payoffs for both states of nature, an expected value can be calculated. For example, for the branch where the United States deploys the MX, the Soviets deploy the Backfire, and the United States deploys the Cruise, the expected value is as follows:

$$(.7 \times 5000) + (.3 \times 5500) = 3500 + 1650 = 5150$$

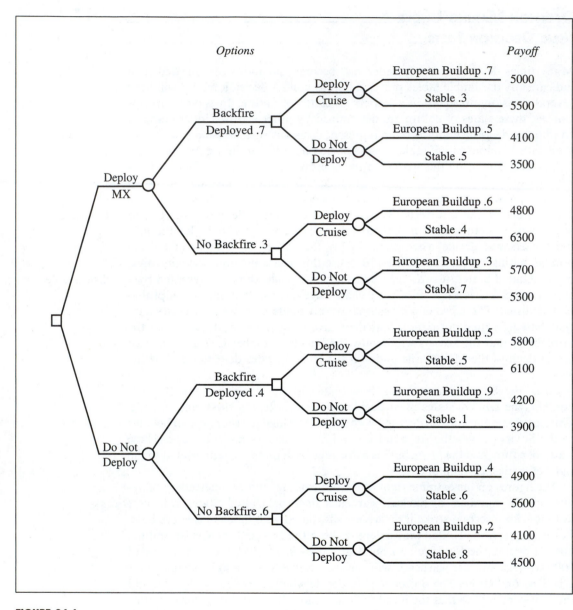

*Options*                                                                     *Payoff*

Deploy Cruise
— European Buildup .7 — 5000
— Stable .3 — 5500

Backfire Deployed .7

Do Not Deploy
— European Buildup .5 — 4100
— Stable .5 — 3500

Deploy MX

Deploy Cruise
— European Buildup .6 — 4800
— Stable .4 — 6300

No Backfire .3

Do Not Deploy
— European Buildup .3 — 5700
— Stable .7 — 5300

Deploy Cruise
— European Buildup .5 — 5800
— Stable .5 — 6100

Backfire Deployed .4

Do Not Deploy
— European Buildup .9 — 4200
— Stable .1 — 3900

Do Not Deploy

Deploy Cruise
— European Buildup .4 — 4900
— Stable .6 — 5600

No Backfire .6

Do Not Deploy
— European Buildup .2 — 4100
— Stable .8 — 4500

**FIGURE 21.1**
A Decision Tree

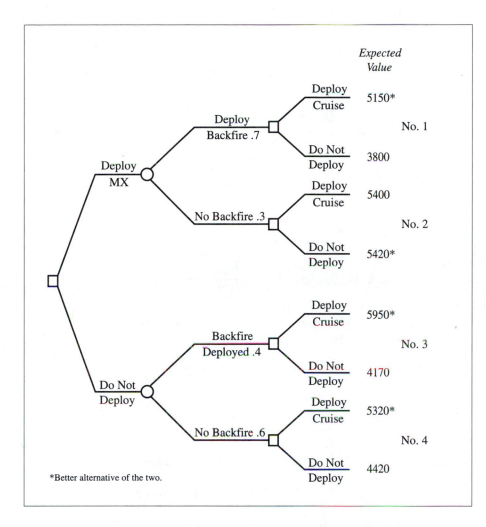

*Better alternative of the two.

**FIGURE 21.2**
Remaining
Decision Tree

The United States could expect to have 5150 remaining warheads if this option is pursued.

The remaining expected values are presented on the truncated tree in Figure 21.2. You may wish to calculate these expected values yourself to gain some practice with decision trees.

Once the expected values are calculated, the decision to deploy the Cruise missile is easy. Simply select the option that yields the greatest expected value. In Cases 1, 3, and 4, the Cruise should be deployed, because this option has the greatest expected value. Only in Case 2, in which the MX is deployed but the Backfire is not, should the United States not deploy the Cruise. These decisions reduce the decision tree to the tree shown in Figure 21.3.

For the expected value calculated previously and the assigned probabilities, the Soviet decision to deploy the Backfire can be reduced to expected values of

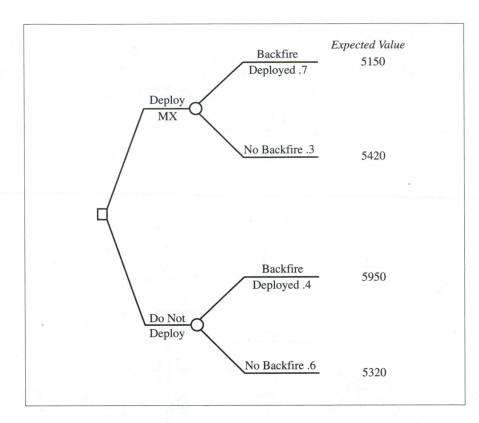

**FIGURE 21.3**
Decisions
Remaining

warheads remaining. For the Deploy MX option, the expected value is

$$(.7 \times 5150) + (.3 \times 5420) = 3605 + 1626 = 5231$$

For the Do Not Deploy option, the expected value is

$$(.4 \times 5950) + (.6 \times 5320) = 2380 + 3192 = 5572$$

According to the information presented, the United States should not deploy the MX missile. Then, no matter what the Soviets do regarding the Backfire bomber, the United States should deploy the Cruise missile. These two decisions maximize the expected number of warheads available for a second strike.

Decision trees often get more complex than the ones presented here. In many circumstances, so many options must be considered that only a computer can solve the resulting trees. Any manager or policy analyst who is basing a decision on a decision tree must remember that the key to using decision trees is to set up a tree that accurately reflects the real world. If all the probabilities and the payoffs are correct, the solution is easy. If they are not correct, the tree is less useful. Managers and analysts are paid to design acceptable decision trees where they are appropriate. Once this is done, the decision tree can be solved by a technician.

# DECISION MAKING
# UNDER UNCERTAINTY

In conditions of uncertainty, the decision maker has less information than is available under conditions of risk. Under uncertainty, the decision maker can specify the possible states of nature but cannot objectively assign probabilities to these states of nature. For example, R. E. Gressum, the head of research for Bayville, Iowa, must decide whether to write a federal grant to fund a halfway house for drug addicts. Gressum feels that it would cost the city about $5000 in time and materials to apply for the grant. If the application is successful, the city will receive $100,000. If Gressum does not apply for this grant, she is sure that the time could be used to write a Title I grant for training for $25,000 that would be funded. If the rehabilitation grants are funded, however, no money will be left for Title I grants, so Gressum could receive nothing if the first grant is funded. The decision table facing Gressum is as shown in Table 21.5.

**TABLE 21.5**
Decision Table for Gressum

| Gressum's Options | Federal Action | |
|---|---|---|
| | *Fund* | *Do Not Fund* |
| Write grant | $100K | −$5K |
| Do not write grant | $0K | $25K |

Notice that the optimal decision for Gressum depends on what the federal government does. If the federal government funds the grant, Gressum should apply for the funds. If the federal government will not fund the grant, Gressum would be better off not applying and trying to fund the Title I grant. Since the probability that the federal government will fund the grant is unknown, Gressum cannot unambiguously decide whether to submit the grant.

Decisions under uncertainty *can* be resolved through a variety of decision strategies. The five most common strategies are discussed next.

### STRATEGY I: THE BAYESIAN APPROACH

**Bayesian** statisticians believe that subjective judgments ought to be incorporated into any statistical analysis for which objective assessments are not available. In the present situation, if Gressum's analyst were a Bayesian, the analyst

**Bayesian**

would urge Gressum—on the basis of her experience, knowledge, and intuition—to assign a probability that the federal government will fund the halfway house grant. After some thought, Gressum believes that the probability that the federal government will fund the halfway house grant is .2; this means that the probability of not funding is .8. A Bayesian would then use these probabilities to calculate expected values for both of Gressum's options:

write grant:               $(.2 \times 100K) + (.8 \times -5K) = 20K - 4K = \$16K$

do not write grant:   $(.2 \times 0K) + (.8 \times 25K) = 0K + 20K = \$20K$

Using these expected values, Gressum should not write the grant, but rather, should concentrate her efforts on the Title I training grant.

### STRATEGY 2: THE INSUFFICIENT REASON APPROACH

**insufficient reason**

The principle of **insufficient reason** attempts to define order from uncertainty. If Gressum has no idea whether the federal government will fund the grant and has no idea whether the probability is large or small, the principle of insufficient reason holds the best estimate of the probability of one of two events is .5. In other words, if we have no way of establishing otherwise, we should assume that events are equally probable. (If three events were involved, the principle of insufficient reason would offer equal probabilities of .33.) With equal probabilities, expected values can be calculated for each option:

write grant:               $(.5 \times 100K) + (.5 \times -5K) = 50K - 2.5K = \$47.5K$

do not write grant:   $(.5 \times 0K) + (.5 \times 25K) = 0K + 12.5K = \$12.5K$

Under the principle of insufficient reason, Gressum should write the grant.

### STRATEGY 3: THE MAXIMIN PRINCIPLE

**maximin**

The **maximin** principle was discovered by a pessimist. Under maximin, Gressum should assume the worst that could happen. Examining the payoff table (Table 21.5) Gressum sees that the worst that could happen if she wrote the grant would be that the federal government would not fund it and that she would lose $5000 in expenses.

| Gressum's Options | Federal Action | |
|---|---|---|
| | *Fund* | *Do Not Fund* |
| Write grant | $100K | −$5K |
| Do not write grant | $0K | $25K |

If Gressum does not write the grant, the worst that could happen is that the federal government will fund the grant. In this case, Gressum would receive nothing. Maximin then requires that the worst cases be compared and the best of the worst cases be selected.

| Options | Worst Case |
|---|---|
| Write grant | −$5K |
| Do not write grant | $0K |

The best option, according to this criterion, is clearly to not write the grant and thus not lose any money. (Maximin gets its name from the logic it uses; the decision maker selects the *maxi*mum of the *mini*mum payoffs.)

### STRATEGY 4: MINIMAX REGRET

The **minimax regret** principle is based on opportunity costs. It asks the question, if we decide a certain way and make the wrong decision, what opportunity has been lost? For example, if Gressum does not write the grant and the grant would have been funded, Gressum would lose $100,000 in opportunity costs. If she writes the grant and it is funded, she loses nothing in opportunity or regret costs. If the grant is not funded, writing the grant is associated with an opportunity cost of $30,000; not writing the grant has no opportunity costs. Combining these opportunity costs into a single decision table, we get the results of Table 21.6.

**minimax regret**

**TABLE 21.6**
Opportunity Costs

| Gressum's Options | Federal Action | |
|---|---|---|
| | *Fund* | *Do Not Fund* |
| Write grant | $0K | $30K |
| Do not write grant | $100K | $0K |

Next, the maximum opportunity cost associated with each alternative is noted:

| Options | Maximum Opportunity Cost |
|---|---|
| Write grant | $30K |
| Do not write grant | $100K |

The minimax regret principle then designates the minimum opportunity cost as the best alternative. In this case, the best alternative is to write the grant, because the greatest opportunity cost is only $30,000 versus $100,000 for the other alternative. (Minimax regret gets its name because one selects the *mini*mum of the *maxi*mum regrets.)

### STRATEGY 5: MAXIMAX

**maximax**

**Maximax** is a decision principle supported by the same people who, in April, bet that the Chicago Cubs will win the World Series. Maximax is the principle of the optimist. The decision maker takes the position that the best will happen. In this situation, Gressum will assume that if she writes the grant, it will be funded (a gain of $100,000); and if she does not write the grant, the Title I project will be funded (a gain of $25,000). One simply compares the best that can happen with each option and selects the *maxi*mum *maxi*mum. In this case, Gressum would write the grant to get the $100,000 project funded.

### HOW TO DECIDE?

Decision rules are everywhere, but which to use? In a situation of uncertainty, should you select Bayesian, insufficient reason, maximin, minimax regret, or maximax? That decision should be based on two factors. First, how important is the decision? U.S. defense planners favor the maximin rule. They assume that the worst will happen and plan accordingly. That way, if less than the worst happens, the U.S. defenses are in better shape than necessary. In such a life-and-death situation, pessimism may be the best decision rule. If the decision has few consequences (such as, which of three grants we should apply for in our spare time), then maximax might be more appropriate. If the manager has confidence in his or her subjective probability estimates, then perhaps Bayesian decisions would work best. Second, the appropriate decision rule depends on the manager's attitude toward risk. Some of the decision rules require greater risks (maximax) in hopes for greater payoffs; other rules are conservative. A manager who thrives on risk may select one rule, whereas a risk avoider may select another. The appropriate decision rule, therefore, is a management decision.

## GAME THEORY

Often in a managerial or policy situation, states of nature are not naturally occurring; rather, they result from decisions made by others. When the other actor seeks to maximize his or her position and these actions affect us, a game situation exists. Game theory was developed to analyze competitive situations.

### ZERO-SUM GAMES

The simplest game is the two-person, zero-sum game. A two-person game obviously involves two people, and a zero-sum game is one in which one player's gains are the other person's losses, and vice versa. An illustration is in order.

Joe Atobelly, the personnel chief for the parks department, wants to increase his hiring level. Joe's opponent is Melvin Merit, the civil service commissioner, who wants to make sure that employee levels are kept as low as possible. Melvin has two options: he can insist that all applicants take and pass all civil service exams, or he can suspend tests and use a quicker temporary screening. Joe has three options: he can send over employees as regular employees, as special affirmative action employees, or as temporary employees. Joe sends over five employee names at a time.

If Joe sends over five names as regular employees, four will be hired if Melvin uses regular procedures, but only one will be hired if Melvin uses temporary procedures. If Joe uses the affirmative action option, two will be hired under regular procedures, but three will be hired if temporary procedures are used. If Joe uses the temporary strategy, only one will be hired if regular procedures are used, and two if the temporary procedures are. The payoff table for Joe is shown in Table 21.7. The values are the number of people hired.

**TABLE 21.7**

Joe's Payoff Table

| Melvin's Choice | Joe's Choice | | |
|---|---|---|---|
| | Regular | Affirmative Action | Temporary |
| Regular | 4 | 2 | 1 |
| Temporary | 1 | 3 | 2 |

Since Melvin wants to hold down employment, his payoff table looks like Table 21.8. Joe's gains are Melvin's losses.

**TABLE 21.8**

Melvin's Payoff Table

| Melvin's Choice | Joe's Choice | | |
|---|---|---|---|
| | Regular | Affirmative Action | Temporary |
| Regular | −4 | −2 | −1 |
| Temporary | −1 | −3 | −2 |

What strategy should Joe decide to use? At first glance, he notices that no matter what Melvin decides, Joe would always be better off stressing affirmative action rather than using the temporary strategy. When this situation exists, game theorists say that the affirmative action choice *dominates* the temporary choice. As a result, Joe need not consider the temporary help strategy. Joe then assumes that Melvin is out to hold down employment (which he is) and decides to act on a worst-case basis and use maximin. Under maximin, Joe would get one employee under regular procedures and two under affirmative action. He opts for affirmative action. Melvin also applies maximin since he distrusts Joe. Under maximin, Melvin could hold Joe to a maximum of four employees with regular procedures, or to a maximum of three if he uses temporary procedures. Melvin decides on temporary procedures.

The result of the two independent decisions means that Joe will get three employees of every five applicants sent to Melvin. Joe cannot improve this record, since he would only get one employee if he tried regular employees and if Melvin (rationally) stayed with temporary procedures. Melvin, however, notices that he could hold Joe to two employees if he invoked regular procedures. Melvin also sees that if he always had regular procedures, Joe would use regular employees and hire four of every five persons. So Melvin begins to act randomly, sometimes using regular procedures, sometimes temporary ones. Joe continues his affirmative action strategy and gets only an average of 2.5 employees every time. Melvin has finessed Joe out of one employee out of every ten. Melvin can do this because the present game does not have a *saddle point*—a single solution that yields the optimum for both actors.

Can Joe countract Melvin's randomness? No, because if Joe occasionally sent people over as regular employees, half of the time four would be hired and half of the time one would be hired, for an average of 2.5. In this situation, random action is a rational choice, but only for one of the actors.

## POSITIVE-SUM GAMES

A city police union must decide whether it should push for moderate demands or make strong demands on the city. The city manager must decide whether to settle quickly or to tolerate a strike. If the city settles quickly, the police will do better if they have high demands. If the city tolerates a strike, high demands reflect unfavorably on the union, and it will do less well. Although this situation looks much like the zero-sum game described before, the city has the option of turning it into a positive-sum game in which everyone benefits.

Let us say that the police union contract expires in an election year. As a result, the mayor does not want a strike and tells the city manager to avoid one. He also tells the city manager to hold down salary costs. The manager has an idea. He tells the union that if it will moderate wage demands, he will give the union more than it wants in pensions. This offer translates the game into a positive-sum game. The union is happy because it received everything it asked for, although not all of it in wages. The manager avoids a strike; and since the pensions will cost future managers rather than his administration, the manager is happy. Neither participant lost; hence the game is positive sum. (The only losers are future city managers and the taxpayers.)

### THE PRISONER'S DILEMMA

A special two-person game is called the prisoner's dilemma. The Equal Employment Opportunity Commission (EEOC) is investigating the Ajax Rubber Goods Company and its union for racial discrimination. The EEOC believes that the company and the union conspired to deny minorities employment. The EEOC tells the union and Ajax separately that if both admit guilt and provide all needed information, both will be fined $10,000. If one of the two admits guilt and provides the information that will implicate the other party, the admitting party will be fined $2000. The noncooperating party will then be prosecuted in court and in all probability will be fined $20,000. If neither party admits guilt, EEOC will begin court proceedings that will cost both parties $5000 each to defend the suits.

For Ajax Rubber Goods Company, their decision table appears as shown in Table 21.9. The Ajax manager reasons as follows: if the union does not plead guilty, the company would be better off if it pled guilty and implicated the union ($2000 versus $5000). If the union pleads guilty, the company would save $10,000 in fines if it also pled guilty ($10,000 versus $20,000). No matter what the union does, the company would always be better off by pleading guilty. Ajax notifies the EEOC it would like to plead guilty.

**TABLE 21.9**

Cost to Ajax

| Ajax Option | Union Action | |
| --- | --- | --- |
| | *No Plea* | *Pleads Guilty* |
| No plea | $5K | $20K |
| Guilty plea | $2K | $10K |

The union faces the decision table shown in Table 21.10. The union faces the same payoff table that Ajax faced. The union by similar reasoning decides to plead guilty and notifies the EEOC.

**TABLE 21.10**

Cost to Union

| Union Option | Ajax Action | |
| --- | --- | --- |
| | *No Plea* | *Pleads Guilty* |
| No plea | $5K | $20K |
| Guilty plea | $2K | $10K |

The EEOC then fines both the union and the company $10,000. Why is this a prisoner's dilemma? For a simple reason: had the union and the company talked to each other, they could have both said nothing. This action would cost each unit $5000 rather than $10,000. Therein lies the dilemma. Cooperation would make both the union and the company better off, but rationality leads to a less than optimal solution.

A manager faced with a prisoner's dilemma should seek to turn the game into a positive-sum game through collusion with the other players. If the players trust each other, then all parties will be better off than if they were caught on the horns of the dilemma.

**A FINAL COMMENT**

This section limits its discussion to two-person games. Game theory has developed beyond simple two-person games to three-, four-, and $n$-person games. Although these topics are too advanced for this introductory text, when gamelike situations exist in the real world that are not just two-person games, more complex models should be used. Consult any management science text for a treatment of more complex games (see Singleton and Tyndall 1974).

## CHAPTER SUMMARY _____

Decision theory is a set of decision approaches used to resolve managerial problems. For ideal conditions, five steps have been identified in the rational decision-making procedure. First, identify the problem. Second, specify goals and objectives. Third, specify all available alternatives. Fourth, evaluate the alternatives in light of the goals. Five, select the optimal alternative.

When all the crucial aspects (states of nature) of a decision are known, decision making takes place under certainty. When the environment of a decision can only be assigned probabilities, then decisions are made under risk. Decisions under risk involve decision tables, payoff tables, cost-benefit calculations, probability calculations for each state of nature, and expected value computations. In very complex situations, decision analysts often represent decisions under risk with decision trees rather than with a simple payoff table.

When nothing is known about the environment, decision making under uncertainty uses one of several strategies. Bayesian probabilities incorporate subjective judgments into the statistical analysis. The principle of insufficient reason attempts to define order from uncertainty. Under the maximin principle, the decision maker selects the maximum of the minimum payoffs (the best of the worst). Using minimax regret, one selects the minimum of the maximum regrets. Under the maximax principle, the decision maker selects the maximum of the maximum payoffs (the best of the best).

Often in a managerial situation, the states of nature result from decisions made by others. Game theory was developed to analyze these competitive situatons. In a zero-sum game, one player's gains are the other's losses, and vice versa. In a positive-sum game, everyone benefits.

## PROBLEMS

**21.1**  The department of social services is considering three programs to vocationally train the handicapped: a contract for teaching the unskilled labor skills, provided by a private vendor (program *A*); a proposal to train the handicapped as computer operators, provided by the state data processing center (program *B*); and a program to teach clerical skills, provided by a local business school (program *C*). Three states of nature affect the success of each program. State *A* is a pool of handicapped in which less than 20% are severely disabled; state *B* is 20–40% severely disabled; and state *C* is more than 40% severely disabled. The accompanying payoff table shows the number of handicapped who could be successfully rehabilitated in a year with the three programs and the three states of nature.

| Program | State of Nature | | |
|---|---|---|---|
| | *A* | *B* | *C* |
| *A* | 20 | 70 | 30 |
| *B* | 40 | 35 | 35 |
| *C* | 30 | 10 | 100 |

(a) Using the maximin criterion, what program would you select and why?

(b) Using the maximax criterion, what program would you select and why?

(c) Is maximin or maximax the more appropriate criterion in this case?

**21.2**  Refer to Problem 7.1.

(a) With minimax regret, what is the best decision?

(b) Using the principle of insufficient reason, what program would you select and why?

**21.3**  Refer to Problem 21.1. You are a Bayesian and your analyst tells you that she believes that the probability of each state of nature is .6 for *A*, .2 for *B*, and .2 for *C*.

(a) With this information, what is the best program?

(b) How much would the expected value of rehabilitated cases be affected by a survey that told you the exact number of severely disabled?

(c) Would you pay $30,000 for such a survey?

**21.4**   A. Rookie, assistant professor of human relations at the Jackson School of Public Affairs, wants to teach his class the value of cooperation. He divides the class into three teams. Each team must select a color, either red or green. If all three teams select green, Rookie will pay each team a dollar. If two teams select green, these two teams will pay the other team a dollar each. If one team selects green, it must pay $2 to each of the other teams. If all three teams select red, each team pays Rookie a dollar. After ten rounds of the game, Rookie discovers himself $24 richer. What has happened?

**21.5**   Ray Wiley decides that he wants to live a life of crime, since it is the only way he can support himself in the style to which he has become accustomed. Ray finds the figures shown in the accompanying table in the FBI crime statistics. What specialization should Ray select? Why?

| Crime | Average Taken | Probability of Not Being Caught |
|-------|---------------|-------------------------------|
| Bank robbery | $30,640 | .46 |
| Robbing convenience store | 850 | .75 |
| Corporate theft | 15,474 | .93 |
| Street robbery | 345 | .87 |
| Burglary | 1,247 | .98 |

**21.6**   Stanley E. Konomist, the chief financial officer for Breverham State University, must decide how to invest this year's private contributions. Stanley has four options. He can invest in corporate bonds, in the stock market, in treasury notes, or in land. The payoff is affected by the rate of inflation for the next year, as the accompanying table shows. Using maximin, maximax, minimax regret, and the principle of insufficient reason, what should Stanley do? Which is the most appropriate criterion?

| BSU Options | Inflation Rate | | |
|-------------|------|--------|-------|
|  | *0–4%* | *4–10%* | *10%+* |
| Corporate bonds | $75K | $70K | $70K |
| Stock market | $60K | $120K | $45K |
| Treasury notes | $100K | $80K | $60K |
| Land | $30K | $90K | $150K |

**21.7**   Refer to Problem 21.6. Pretend that you are a Bayesian. Assign subjective probabilities for each state of nature, and then select the best option. What would you pay for an accurate forecast of the inflation rate?

## CHAPTER 22

# LINEAR

# PROGRAMMING

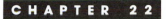

Linear programming is a quantitative technique that can optimally allocate an agency's resources under conditions of certainty. Before discussing the techniques for linear programming, some situations in which it could be used will be noted. A prison nutritionist needs to determine the proper mix of foods to buy so that a given level of nutrition is met at the least cost. An air force logistics officer needs to supply six bases in Europe from four supply depots at the minimum cost to the air force. A parks supervisor wants to assign her personnel to various parks so that she can maximize productivity given her budget constraints.

These are all linear programming problems. In each case, we want to find the optimal mix of resources. Variables that the manager can control—which foods to buy, which depots to use, where to assign personnel–are called **decision variables**, because the manager can decide how to allocate these variables. **Constraints** are variables that limit the choices of the manager: in the previous examples, a given nutrition level must be met; all six bases must be supplied; the park supervisor only has $X$ men. Some constraints are in the form of inequalities: for example, vitamin C intake level must be at least 5 milligrams; no more than 247 people can be used. Finally, **output variables** are those that the manager seeks to maximize or minimize—cost, productivity, and so on.

**Linear programming** seeks to optimize output variables by manipulating decision variables, subject to the restrictions of the constraints. Linear programming can only work under conditions of certainty. The manager must know the constraints and the exact relationship among all decision variables and the output variables. The air force officer must know, for example, the number of items each base needs, the number of items each depot has, the cost of transporting an item from every depot to every base, and so on. Unless such

**decision variables**

**constraints**

**output variables**

**linear programming**

certainty exists, linear programming can be used only as a way of thinking about problems.

Linear programming is a special form of programming in which all the relationships are linear. Other, more advanced forms of programming are available, but they are well beyond the scope of this text. Linear programming assumes, as we noted, that all relationships are linear (or proportional). If one apple and a sandwich contain 100 units of B-14, then two apples and two sandwiches contain 200 units of B-14. Linear programming also assumes that all inputs and outputs are infinitely divisible. Mowing the grass in one-half of a park or feeding every prisoner one-fourth of an apple are solutions that linear programming models find. Finally, linear programming assumes that the processes are interchangeable. If the parks department can either mow 1200 acres of grass or trim 4000 feet of hedges, it can also mow 600 acres of grass and trim 2000 feet of hedges.

In this chapter, we will introduce you to the techniques of linear programming.

## AN EXAMPLE

The Ware County Library maintains a book repair division in the basement of its central library. The repair unit has two functions; it puts hardcover bindings on paperback books, and it reconditions damaged hardcover books. The unit has more work than it can handle. Any excess work is farmed out to Orva's Bindery. Orva charges $12 to cover a paperback and $15 to repair a hardcover book.

The repair unit has four processes. Labeling is the process of writing the call numbers on the spine of the book. The labeling people can label 500 books a month; the distinction between hardcover and paperback does not affect them. The binding people can bind 400 paperback books a month or rebind (an easier process) 600 repaired hardbacks. The cover-cutting people can cut 350 covers a month; covers are only used on the paperback books. The repair people can process either 100 paperbacks or 450 hardback books a month.

**STEP 1** Decide what the agency wants to maximize or minimize. Since at Orva's, covering a paperback costs $12 and repairing a hardback costs $15, the value of the repair unit's activities is $12 for every paperback re-covered and $15 for every hardback repaired. So let

$$X_1 = \text{the number of paperbacks covered}$$

$$X_2 = \text{the number of hardbacks repaired}$$

The Ware County Library would like to maximize

$$\$12X_1 + \$15X_2$$

The decision will tell the library how many paperbacks to re-cover and how many hardbacks to repair to maximize the payoff.

**STEP 2**   Determine the constraints on each process. If the labeling people only label newly bound paperbacks, they can label 500 per month. Each paperback they label takes 1/500 of their total time. Similarly, each re-bound paperback requires 1/400 of the binding time, 1/350 of the cover-cutting time, and 1/1000 of the repair time. Each repaired hardcover requires 1/500 of the labeling time, 1/600 of the binding time, and 1/450 of the repair time. The labeling constraint on the repair unit can be expressed as

$$\left(\frac{1}{500}\right)X_1 + \left(\frac{1}{500}\right)X_2 \leq 1$$

That is, the number of paperbacks re-bound and the number of hardbacks repaired cannot exceed total labeling capacity. The other constraints are as follows:

$$\text{binding:} \quad \left(\frac{1}{400}\right)X_1 + \left(\frac{1}{600}\right)X_2 \leq 1$$

$$\text{cover cutting:} \quad \left(\frac{1}{350}\right)X_1 + 0X_2 \leq 1$$

$$\text{repair:} \quad \left(\frac{1}{1000}\right)X_1 + \left(\frac{1}{450}\right)X_2 \leq 1$$

Two other constraints must be noted, particularly if one uses computer routines to do linear programming. Both the number of paperbacks covered and the number of hardbacks repaired must be greater than or equal to zero (this may be logical to you, but it is not to the computer). Thus

$$X_1 \geq 0 \qquad X_2 \geq 0$$

**STEP 3**   Give the problem to your linear programmer to solve. In the present situation, with only two output variables (paperbacks and hardbacks), the problem can be solved by graphing. Draw a graph with one axis (say the horizontal) representing the number of paperbacks and the other axis representing the number of hardbacks (see Figure 22.1). This graph will be used to graph the constraints on the repair unit. To graph the labeling constraint, note that labeling can either process 500 paperbacks and 0 hardbacks or 0 paperbacks and 500 hard-

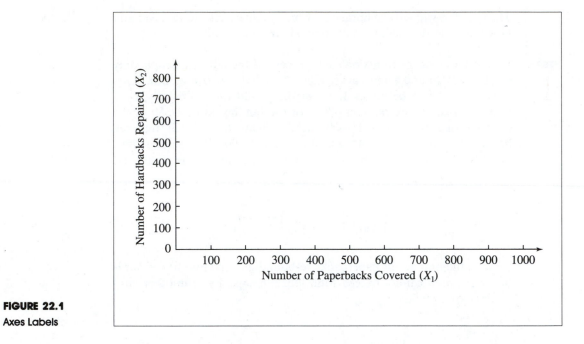

**FIGURE 22.1**
Axes Labels

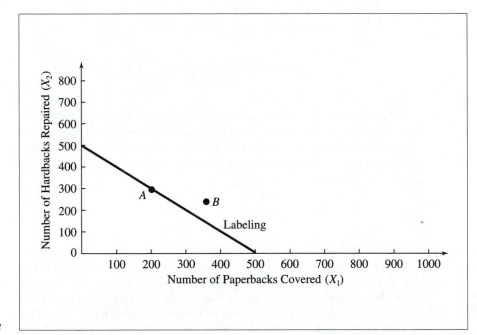

**FIGURE 22.2**
Line for the
Labeling Constraint

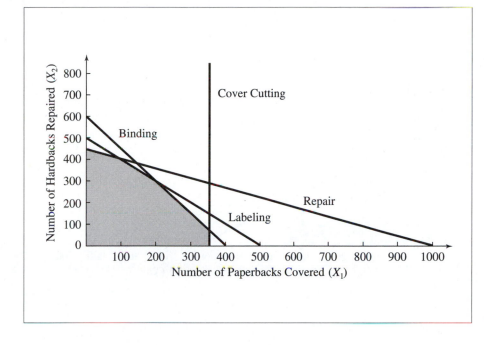

**FIGURE 22.3**

Constraints Graph

backs. Find these two points on the graph and connect them with a straight line. See Figure 22.2. This line represents the labeling constraints on the repair unit. Every point on the graph below and to the left of the line (including points on the line) is within the capacity of the repair unit. Point *A*, for example—300 hardbacks and 200 paperbacks—is within the capacity of the repair unit. Point *B*, however—250 hardbacks and 350 paperbacks—exceeds the repair unit's capacity.

The next step is to graph all the constraints on the same graph. This is done in Figure 22.3.

On the constraints graph, the only options that are open to management are those in the shaded area of the graph. One point within this area is the optimal ratio of hardbacks to paperbacks. The question is, which one? We will find the optimal point much as the computer does—by trial and error.

Start the trial-and-error process by setting the equation $12X_1 + 15X_2$ equal to some value, say $4200.

$$\$4200 = \$12X_1 + \$15X_2$$

The repair shop could produce $4200 worth of repairs by either covering 350 paperbacks (4200 ÷ 12) or 280 hardbacks. These values are plotted on the graph in Figure 22.4 and are connected with a line. Any value above and to the right of this line will yield a greater payoff

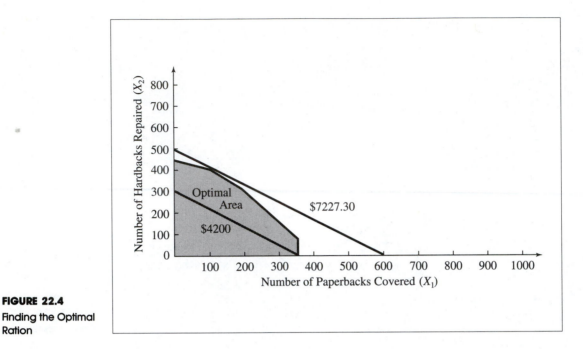

**FIGURE 22.4**

Finding the Optimal Ration

than any value on this line. Since many of the values above and to the right of this line are within the shaded area, a production value of more than \$4200 is possible. The computer tries several lines until it finds a line that has only one point within the shaded area. In this problem, the only line with only one point within the shaded area is

$$\$7227.30 = \$12X_1 + \$15X_2$$

This line touches the shaded area only where the labeling and the repair constraints intersect (see Figure 22.4). The optimal point will always be at the intersection of two or more constraints.

The next step is to determine the values of $X_1$ and $X_2$ at the optimal point. The labeling constraint is

$$\left(\frac{1}{500}\right)X_1 + \left(\frac{1}{500}\right)X_2 \le 1$$

The repair constraint is

$$\left(\frac{1}{1000}\right)X_1 + \left(\frac{1}{450}\right)X_2 \le 1$$

Multiply the repair constraint by 2 to get

$$\left(\frac{2}{1000}\right)X_1 + \left(\frac{2}{450}\right)X_2 \le 2$$

$$\left(\frac{1}{500}\right)X_1 + \left(\frac{2}{450}\right)X_2 \le 2$$

Subtract the labeling constraint from the new repair constraint.

$$\left(\frac{1}{500}\right)X_1 + \left(\frac{2}{450}\right)X_2 \le 2$$

$$-\left(\frac{1}{500}\right)X_1 - \left(\frac{1}{500}\right)X_2 \le -1$$

$$\overline{0X_1 + \left(\frac{2}{450}\right)X_2 - \left(\frac{1}{500}\right)X_2 \le 1}$$

$$\left(\frac{40}{9000}\right)X_2 - \left(\frac{18}{9000}\right)X_2 \le 1$$

$$\left(\frac{22}{9000}\right)X_2 \le 1$$

$$X_2 \le 409.1$$

To find the value for $X_1$, simply substitute 409 for $X_2$ in the labeling constraint.

$$\left(\frac{1}{500}\right)X_1 + \left(\frac{1}{500}\right)409 \le 1$$

$$\left(\frac{1}{500}\right)X_1 + \frac{409}{500} \le 1$$

$$\left(\frac{1}{500}\right)X_1 + .818 \le 1$$

$$\left(\frac{1}{500}\right)X_1 \le .182$$

$$X_1 \le 91$$

The optimal production point is to repair 409 hardcover books per month and to bind 91 paperbacks per month. This will return a value of $7227.

If the mathematics to solve this problem is intimidating, you can always use the graph to eyeball the answer. A linear programming problem solved by a computer program, however, would print out the optimal values.

## LINEAR PROGRAMMING WITH
## MORE THAN TWO VARIABLES

Rarely will a linear programming problem be so simple that a solution can be found graphically. But the public manager's function is not to solve linear programming problems. The manager's first function is to recognize problems that can be solved through linear programming. Any time a manager wants to maximize or minimize some value that is determined by some mix of inputs subject to constraints and the manager is operating under certainty (in regard to costs, relationships, and so on), then linear programming is a useful technique. The second managerial function in linear programming is to identify the constraints and relationships for the analyst. The third managerial function is to determine whether the optimal solution is feasible. Certain political constraints that could not be incorporated into the model, for example, might make the optimal solution impossible to obtain. In short, linear programming is a tool that provides valuable inputs into a manager's decision; it is not a decision-making device. After all, when was the last time a linear programming model was fired?

## CHAPTER SUMMARY

Linear programming is used to allocate inputs in order to maximize some outputs within constraints when conditions of certainty exist. This chapter illustrates only a very elementary version of linear programming that might be useful in public management.

Variables that the manager can control are called decision variables. Constraints are variables that limit the choices of the manager. Output variables are those that the manager wishes to maximize or minimize. Linear programming seeks to optimize output variables by manipulating decision variables, subject to the restrictions of the constraints.

Three basic steps are involved in linear programming. First, decide what it is you wish to maximize or minimize. Second, determine the constraints on each process. Third, if the problem is simple enough, solve it by graphing (otherwise a linear programmer must be brought in to solve the problem). Note that the manager's function is not to solve linear programming problems, but rather, to recognize that a problem can be solved by using these techniques and to identify the constraints and the relationships for the analyst.

# PROBLEMS

**22.1** An air force logistics officer has to transport 850 planes in the United States (500 at Minot Air Force Base and 350 at Offutt) to the Pacific. Of these 850 planes, 200 must go to Kadena, 150 to Guam, 400 to Osan, and 100 to Hickham. The costs of flying between each of these points are listed in the accompanying table. How can the officer transport these planes at the least cost? Set up the variables you want to minimize and the constraints on these variables.

| To | From | |
|---|---|---|
| | *Minot* | *Offutt* |
| Kadena | $600 | $ 900 |
| Guam | 700 | 600 |
| Osan | 800 | 1100 |
| Hickham | 400 | 300 |

**22.2** Beaver Falls City Hall has two incinerators to burn city hall trash. Together they burn 100 tons of trash per day, but the city hall produces 200 tons. The remaining trash is buried—a more expensive method. Incinerator $X$ can burn 40 tons of trash per day, but it releases 5 pounds of particles per ton and 12 units of hydrocarbons per ton. Incinerator $Y$ can burn 60 tons of trash per day, and it releases 3 pounds of particles and 16 units of hydrocarbons per ton. If the EPA will allow city hall to emit no more than 40 pounds of particles and 130 units of hydrocarbons, what is the most efficient use of the incinerators?

**22.3** The Conrad, North Carolina, Parks Department has been allocated 50 CETA employees for three months. These employees will be used to trim hedges and mow lawns. Normally these functions are contracted out to Greenthumb Lawn Care Company at a cost of $12 per acre of grass and $8 per 50 feet of hedges. One person can mow 6.5 acres of grass per day or trim 500 feet of hedges. The city has 38 lawn mowers and 35 hedge trimmers. How can the city use its CETA employees to its best advantage if there is more grass and there are more hedges than 50 workers can possibly service? Set up this problem and solve it graphically.

**22.4** Several years ago, an economist applied a linear programming model to a university. The output the university was to maximize was the earning power of its graduates, subject to constraints of money, faculty, buildings, and so on. Is this an appropriate use of linear programming? Why or why not?

**22.5** The General Services Administration's Office of Typewriters stores brand $X$ and brand $Y$ typewriters at four locations as follows:

| Location | Brand $X$ | Brand $Y$ |
| --- | --- | --- |
| Boston | 2400 | 1200 |
| Atlanta | 1200 | 3000 |
| Seattle | 6000 | 200 |
| Dallas | 3000 | 2000 |

Numerous typewriters must be shipped from these offices to the federal regional office centers. The centers' needs are as follows:

| Center | Brand $X$ | Brand $Y$ |
| --- | --- | --- |
| Kansas City | 3500 | 800 |
| Denver | 1500 | 700 |
| Chicago | 2700 | 2400 |
| Cincinnati | 4600 | 1100 |

The typewriters cost the same amount to ship, regardless of whether they are brand $X$ or brand $Y$, as follows:

| From | To | | | |
| --- | --- | --- | --- | --- |
| | K.C. | Denver | Chicago | Cincinnati |
| Boston | $18 | $24 | $13 | $ 9 |
| Atlanta | 21 | 32 | 17 | 11 |
| Seattle | 17 | 10 | 18 | 24 |
| Dallas | 4 | 14 | 12 | 15 |

Set up the linear programming problem to move the brand $X$ typewriters from the four warehouses to the four regional centers at the least cost.

**22.6**   Refer to Problem 22.5. Set up the problem to move the brand $Y$ typewriters from the four warehouses to the four regional centers at the least cost.

# ANNOTATED BIBLIOGRAPHY _____

Babbie, Earl R. *The Practice of Social Research,* Fourth Edition. Belmont, Calif.: Wadsworth, 1985. An excellent introductory guide to the design, conduct, and evaluation of research.

Babbie, Earl R. *Survey Research Methods*. Belmont, Calif.: Wadsworth, 1973. Focuses on the design of surveys and the analysis of results. Contains a chapter on survey ethics.

Bell, Colin E. *Quantitative Methods for Administration*. Homewood, Ill.: Irwin, 1977. A mathematically sophisticated business statistics text. An in-depth discussion of linear programming and its offshoots.

Benson, Oliver. *Political Science Laboratory*. Columbus, Ohio: Merrill, 1969. A simple workbook introduction to research questions and nonparametric statistics.

Bingham, Richard D., and Ethridge, Marcus E. (eds.). *Reaching Decisions in Public Policy and Administration: Methods and Applications*. New York: Longman, 1982. An interesting collection of readings illustrating various approaches to data collection and decision making in public administration.

Blalock, Hubert M. *Social Statistics*, Second Edition. New York: McGraw-Hill, 1972. The accepted intermediate-level statistics text for social scientists.

Buchanan, William. *Understanding Political Variables*. New York: Scribners, 1976. A well-written workbook in statistics in political research.

Campbell, Donald T., and Stanley, Julian C. *Experimental ad Quast-Experimental Designs for Research*. Boston, Mass.: Houghton Mifflin, 1966. Good introduction to the strengths and weaknesses of various research designs.

Cook, Thomas, and Campbell, Donald T. *Quasi-Experimentation*. Boston, Mass.: Houghton Mifflin, 1979. A thorough discussion of the analysis of public programs in field settings.

Cooley, William W., and Lohnes, Paul R. *Multivariate Data Analysis*. Melbourne, Fla.: Krieger, 1985. An advanced text with emphasis on factor analysis and similar techniques.

Garson, G. David. *Handbook of Political Science Methods*. Boston: Holbrook Press, 1971. A how-to-do-it handbook with political examples.

Hamburger, Henry. *Games as Models of Social Phenomena*. San Francisco: Freeman, 1979. This book applies game theory to many situations in everyday life. Illustrates the game nature of many situations.

Hanushek, Eric A., and Jackson, John E. *Statistical Methods for Social Scientists*. New York: Academic Press, 1977. An advanced book on regression techniques designed for social science researchers.

Hays, William L. *Statistics,* Third Edition. New York: Holt, Rinehart & Winston, 1981. A very complete, basic treatment of statistics.

Kerlinger, Fred N. *Foundations of Behavioral Research,* Third Edition. New York: Holt, Rinehart & Winston, 1986. A classic text in research methods for the social sciences.

Kerlinger, Fred N. *Behavioral Research: A Conceptual Approach.* New York: Holt, Rinehart & Winston, 1979. A good philosophical introduction to research methods.

Kleinbaum, David G., and Kupper, Lawrence L. *Applied Regression Analysis and Other Multivariate Methods.* N. Scituate, Mass.: Duxbury Press, 1978. For those advanced students who want a detailed discussion of regression and analysis of variance.

Labovitz, Sanford, and Hagedorn, Robert. *Introduction to Social Research,* Third Edition. New York: McGraw-Hill, 1981. A good introduction to research design and the philosophy of doing research.

Manheim, Jarol B., and Rich, Richard C. *Empirical Political Analysis: Research Methods in Political Science.* New York: Longman, 1986. A readable discussion of how to plan, conduct, and write up a data-based study.

McKenna, Christopher K. *Quantitative Methods for Public Decision-Making.* New York: McGraw-Hill, 1980. An intermediate-level presentation of useful managerial techniques, such as cost-benefit analysis, linear programming, and program evaluation review technique/critical path method (PERT/CPM). Good examples.

Mendenhall, William, and Reinmuth, James E. *Statistics for Management and Economics,* Fourth Edition. N. Scituate, Mass.: Duxbury Press, 1982. Focuses on parametric statistics. Good reference on probability and applied regression.

Miller, Delbert C. *Handbook of Research Design and Social Measurement,* Fourth Edition. New York: Longman, 1983. An excellent, comprehensive reference on the research process, especially study design, measurement, data collection, and reporting results.

Nachmias, David. *Public Policy Evaluation.* New York: St. Martin's Press, 1979. A program evaluation book with some statistics included. Excellent for public policy research design and measurement. Statistics concentrate on regression.

Nachmias, David, and Nachmias, Chava. *Research Methods for the Social Sciences,* Second Edition. New York: St. Martin's Press, 1981. A good introductory book on research design and statistics. Emphasizes social science problems.

Nelson, Charles R. *Applied Time Series Analysis for Managerial Forecasting.* San Francisco: Holden-Day, 1973. An excellent advanced text for students interested in time series analysis.

Neter, John, Wasserman, William, and Whitmore, G. A. *Applied Statistics.* Boston: Allyn & Bacon, 1978. A solid applied statistics text with business applications. Excellent on probability, inference, and introduction to time series.

Ott, Lyman. *An Introduction to Statistical Methods and Data Analysis.* N. Scituate, Mass.: Duxbury Press, 1977. Text contains a wide variety of problems from agriculture, politics, medicine, and so on. Fairly brief for the beginning student.

Palumbo, Dennis J. *Statistics in Political and Behavioral Science,* Second Edition. New York: Columbia University Press, 1977. A general, readable introductory text for social scientists. Good reference on decision analysis, sampling, and calculating statistics.

Poister, Theodore H. *Public Program Analysis.* Baltimore, Md.: University Park Press, 1978. Comprehensive statistics text with emphasis on public policy research problems. Good reference for public sector managers.

Singleton, Robert R., and Tyndall, William F. *Games and Programs.* San Francisco: Freeman, 1974. For students who want a more in-depth treatment of game theory and decision analysis.

Stokey, Edith, and Zeckhauser, Richard. *A Primer for Policy Analysis.* New York: Norton, 1978. Not a statistics text. Shows how some statistics can be used in policy analysis. One of the best introductions to linear programming.

Warwick, Donald P., and Lininger, Charles A. *The Sample Survey: Theory and Practice.* New York: McGraw-Hill, 1975. A handbook on sampling and survey techniques.

Webb, Eugene J., Campbell, Donald, Schwartz, Richard D., and Sechrest, Lee. *Unobtrusive Measures.* Skokie, Ill.: Rand McNally, 1973. A discussion of measurement under circumstances where good measures are difficult to find.

Welch, Susan, and Comer, John C. *Quantitative Methods for Public Administration: Techniques and Applications, Second Edition.* Pacific Grove, Calif: Brooks/Cole, 1988. A good introductory text for students intending to do research in policy and administration. Primarily uses policy examples.

White, Michael J., Clayton, Ross, Myrtle, Robert, Siegel, Gilbert, and Rose, Aaron. *Managing Public Systems: Analytic Techniques for Public Administration.* North Scituate, Mass.: Duxbury, 1980. An introductory treatment of selected managerial methods, including network analysis, flowcharting, and queueing theory.

# STATISTICAL TABLES

**TABLE 1**

The Normal Distribution

Each entry in the table indicates the proportion of the total area under the normal curve contained in the segment bounded by a perpendicular raised at the mean and a perpendicular raised at a distance of $z$ standard deviation units.

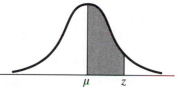

To illustrate: 43.57% of the area under a normal curve lies between the maximum ordinate and a point 1.52 standard deviation units away.

| z | 0.00 | 0.01 | 0.02 | 0.03 | 0.04 | 0.05 | 0.06 | 0.07 | 0.08 | 0.09 |
|---|------|------|------|------|------|------|------|------|------|------|
| 0.0 | 0.0000 | 0.0040 | 0.0080 | 0.0120 | 0.0160 | 0.0199 | 0.0239 | 0.0279 | 0.0319 | 0.0359 |
| 0.1 | 0.0398 | 0.0438 | 0.0478 | 0.0517 | 0.0557 | 0.0596 | 0.0636 | 0.0675 | 0.0714 | 0.0753 |
| 0.2 | 0.0793 | 0.0832 | 0.0871 | 0.0910 | 0.0948 | 0.0987 | 0.1026 | 0.1064 | 0.1103 | 0.1141 |
| 0.3 | 0.1179 | 0.1217 | 0.1255 | 0.1293 | 0.1331 | 0.1368 | 0.1406 | 0.1443 | 0.1480 | 0.1517 |
| 0.4 | 0.1554 | 0.1591 | 0.1628 | 0.1664 | 0.1700 | 0.1736 | 0.1772 | 0.1808 | 0.1844 | 0.1879 |
| 0.5 | 0.1915 | 0.1950 | 0.1985 | 0.2019 | 0.2054 | 0.2088 | 0.2123 | 0.2157 | 0.2190 | 0.2224 |
| 0.6 | 0.2257 | 0.2291 | 0.2324 | 0.2357 | 0.2389 | 0.2422 | 0.2454 | 0.2486 | 0.2518 | 0.2549 |
| 0.7 | 0.2580 | 0.2612 | 0.2642 | 0.2673 | 0.2704 | 0.2734 | 0.2764 | 0.2794 | 0.2823 | 0.2852 |
| 0.8 | 0.2881 | 0.2910 | 0.2939 | 0.2967 | 0.2995 | 0.3023 | 0.3051 | 0.3078 | 0.3106 | 0.3133 |
| 0.9 | 0.3159 | 0.3186 | 0.3212 | 0.3238 | 0.3264 | 0.3289 | 0.3315 | 0.3340 | 0.3365 | 0.3389 |
| 1.0 | 0.3413 | 0.3438 | 0.3461 | 0.3485 | 0.3508 | 0.3531 | 0.3554 | 0.3577 | 0.3599 | 0.3621 |
| 1.1 | 0.3643 | 0.3665 | 0.3686 | 0.3708 | 0.3729 | 0.3749 | 0.3770 | 0.3790 | 0.3810 | 0.3830 |
| 1.2 | 0.3849 | 0.3869 | 0.3888 | 0.3907 | 0.3925 | 0.3944 | 0.3962 | 0.3980 | 0.3997 | 0.4015 |
| 1.3 | 0.4032 | 0.4049 | 0.4066 | 0.4082 | 0.4099 | 0.4115 | 0.4131 | 0.4147 | 0.4162 | 0.4177 |
| 1.4 | 0.4192 | 0.4207 | 0.4222 | 0.4236 | 0.4251 | 0.4265 | 0.4279 | 0.4292 | 0.4306 | 0.4319 |

**TABLE 1**

(Continued)

| z | 0.00 | 0.01 | 0.02 | 0.03 | 0.04 | 0.05 | 0.06 | 0.07 | 0.08 | 0.09 |
|---|------|------|------|------|------|------|------|------|------|------|
| 1.5 | 0.4332 | 0.4345 | 0.4357 | 0.4370 | 0.4382 | 0.4394 | 0.4406 | 0.4418 | 0.4429 | 0.4441 |
| 1.6 | 0.4452 | 0.4463 | 0.4474 | 0.4484 | 0.4495 | 0.4505 | 0.4515 | 0.4525 | 0.4535 | 0.4545 |
| 1.7 | 0.4554 | 0.4564 | 0.4573 | 0.4582 | 0.4591 | 0.4599 | 0.4608 | 0.4616 | 0.4625 | 0.4633 |
| 1.8 | 0.4641 | 0.4649 | 0.4656 | 0.4664 | 0.4671 | 0.4678 | 0.4686 | 0.4693 | 0.4699 | 0.4706 |
| 1.9 | 0.4713 | 0.4719 | 0.4726 | 0.4732 | 0.4738 | 0.4744 | 0.4750 | 0.4756 | 0.4761 | 0.4767 |
| 2.0 | 0.4772 | 0.4778 | 0.4783 | 0.4788 | 0.4793 | 0.4798 | 0.4803 | 0.4808 | 0.4812 | 0.4817 |
| 2.1 | 0.4821 | 0.4826 | 0.4830 | 0.4834 | 0.4838 | 0.4842 | 0.4846 | 0.4850 | 0.4854 | 0.4857 |
| 2.2 | 0.4861 | 0.4864 | 0.4868 | 0.4871 | 0.4875 | 0.4878 | 0.4881 | 0.4884 | 0.4887 | 0.4890 |
| 2.3 | 0.4893 | 0.4896 | 0.4898 | 0.4901 | 0.4904 | 0.4906 | 0.4909 | 0.4911 | 0.4913 | 0.4916 |
| 2.4 | 0.4918 | 0.4920 | 0.4922 | 0.4925 | 0.4927 | 0.4929 | 0.4931 | 0.4932 | 0.4934 | 0.4936 |
| 2.5 | 0.4938 | 0.4940 | 0.4941 | 0.4943 | 0.4945 | 0.4946 | 0.4948 | 0.4949 | 0.4951 | 0.4952 |
| 2.6 | 0.4953 | 0.4955 | 0.4956 | 0.4957 | 0.4959 | 0.4960 | 0.4961 | 0.4962 | 0.4963 | 0.4964 |
| 2.7 | 0.4965 | 0.4966 | 0.4967 | 0.4968 | 0.4969 | 0.4970 | 0.4971 | 0.4972 | 0.4973 | 0.4974 |
| 2.8 | 0.4974 | 0.4975 | 0.4976 | 0.4977 | 0.4977 | 0.4978 | 0.4979 | 0.4979 | 0.4980 | 0.4981 |
| 2.9 | 0.4981 | 0.4982 | 0.4982 | 0.4983 | 0.4984 | 0.4984 | 0.4985 | 0.4985 | 0.4986 | 0.4986 |
| 3.0 | 0.4986 | 0.4987 | 0.4987 | 0.4988 | 0.4988 | 0.4989 | 0.4989 | 0.4989 | 0.4990 | 0.4990 |
| 3.1 | 0.4990 | 0.4991 | 0.4991 | 0.4991 | 0.4992 | 0.4992 | 0.4992 | 0.4992 | 0.4993 | 0.4993 |
| 3.2 | 0.4993 | 0.4993 | 0.4994 | 0.4994 | 0.4994 | 0.4994 | 0.4994 | 0.4995 | 0.4995 | 0.4995 |
| 3.3 | 0.4995 | 0.4995 | 0.4995 | 0.4996 | 0.4996 | 0.4996 | 0.4996 | 0.4996 | 0.4996 | 0.4997 |
| 3.4 | 0.4997 | 0.4997 | 0.4997 | 0.4997 | 0.4997 | 0.4997 | 0.4997 | 0.4997 | 0.4998 | 0.4998 |
| 3.5 | 0.4998 | 0.4998 | 0.4998 | 0.4998 | 0.4998 | 0.4998 | 0.4998 | 0.4998 | 0.4998 | 0.4998 |
| 3.6 | 0.4998 | 0.4998 | 0.4999 | 0.4999 | 0.4999 | 0.4999 | 0.4999 | 0.4999 | 0.4999 | 0.4999 |
| 3.7 | 0.4999 | 0.4999 | 0.4999 | 0.4999 | 0.4999 | 0.4999 | 0.4999 | 0.4999 | 0.4999 | 0.4999 |
| 3.8 | 0.4999 | 0.4999 | 0.4999 | 0.4999 | 0.4999 | 0.4999 | 0.4999 | 0.5000 | 0.5000 | 0.5000 |
| 3.9 | 0.5000 | 0.5000 | 0.5000 | 0.5000 | 0.5000 | 0.5000 | 0.5000 | 0.5000 | 0.5000 | 0.5000 |

**TABLE 2**

Poisson Probability Distributions

Entry is probability mass $f(x)$ corresponding to $X = x$, where $f(x) = \lambda^x \exp(-\lambda)/x!$.

| $x$ | $\lambda$ | | | | | | | | |
|---|---|---|---|---|---|---|---|---|---|
| | .1 | .2 | .3 | .4 | .5 | .6 | .7 | .8 | .9 |
| 0 | 0.9048 | 0.8187 | 0.7408 | 0.6703 | 0.6065 | 0.5488 | 0.4966 | 0.4493 | 0.4066 |
| 1 | 0.0905 | 0.1637 | 0.2222 | 0.2681 | 0.3033 | 0.3293 | 0.3476 | 0.3595 | 0.3659 |
| 2 | 0.0045 | 0.0164 | 0.0333 | 0.0536 | 0.0758 | 0.0988 | 0.1217 | 0.1438 | 0.1647 |
| 3 | 0.0002 | 0.0011 | 0.0033 | 0.0072 | 0.0126 | 0.0198 | 0.0284 | 0.0383 | 0.0494 |
| 4 | 0.0000 | 0.0001 | 0.0003 | 0.0007 | 0.0016 | 0.0030 | 0.0050 | 0.0077 | 0.0111 |
| 5 | 0.0000 | 0.0000 | 0.0000 | 0.0001 | 0.0002 | 0.0004 | 0.0007 | 0.0012 | 0.0020 |
| 6 | 0.0000 | 0.0000 | 0.0000 | 0.0000 | 0.0000 | 0.0000 | 0.0001 | 0.0002 | 0.0003 |

| $x$ | $\lambda$ | | | | | | | | |
|---|---|---|---|---|---|---|---|---|---|
| | 1.0 | 1.5 | 2.0 | 2.5 | 3.0 | 3.5 | 4.0 | 4.5 | 5.0 |
| 0 | 0.3679 | 0.2231 | 0.1353 | 0.0821 | 0.0498 | 0.0302 | 0.0183 | 0.0111 | 0.0067 |
| 1 | 0.3679 | 0.3347 | 0.2707 | 0.2052 | 0.1494 | 0.1057 | 0.0733 | 0.0500 | 0.0337 |
| 2 | 0.1839 | 0.2510 | 0.2707 | 0.2565 | 0.2240 | 0.1850 | 0.1465 | 0.1125 | 0.0842 |
| 3 | 0.0613 | 0.1255 | 0.1804 | 0.2138 | 0.2240 | 0.2158 | 0.1954 | 0.1687 | 0.1404 |
| 4 | 0.0153 | 0.0471 | 0.0902 | 0.1336 | 0.1680 | 0.1888 | 0.1954 | 0.1898 | 0.1755 |
| 5 | 0.0031 | 0.0141 | 0.0361 | 0.0668 | 0.1008 | 0.1322 | 0.1563 | 0.1708 | 0.1755 |
| 6 | 0.0005 | 0.0035 | 0.0120 | 0.0278 | 0.0504 | 0.0771 | 0.1042 | 0.1281 | 0.1462 |
| 7 | 0.0001 | 0.0008 | 0.0034 | 0.0099 | 0.0216 | 0.0385 | 0.0595 | 0.0824 | 0.1044 |
| 8 | 0.0000 | 0.0001 | 0.0009 | 0.0031 | 0.0081 | 0.0169 | 0.0298 | 0.0463 | 0.0653 |
| 9 | 0.0000 | 0.0000 | 0.0002 | 0.0009 | 0.0027 | 0.0066 | 0.0132 | 0.0232 | 0.0363 |
| 10 | 0.0000 | 0.0000 | 0.0000 | 0.0002 | 0.0008 | 0.0023 | 0.0053 | 0.0104 | 0.0181 |
| 11 | 0.0000 | 0.0000 | 0.0000 | 0.0000 | 0.0002 | 0.0007 | 0.0019 | 0.0043 | 0.0082 |
| 12 | 0.0000 | 0.0000 | 0.0000 | 0.0000 | 0.0001 | 0.0002 | 0.0006 | 0.0016 | 0.0034 |
| 13 | 0.0000 | 0.0000 | 0.0000 | 0.0000 | 0.0000 | 0.0001 | 0.0002 | 0.0006 | 0.0013 |
| 14 | 0.0000 | 0.0000 | 0.0000 | 0.0000 | 0.0000 | 0.0000 | 0.0001 | 0.0002 | 0.0005 |
| 15 | 0.0000 | 0.0000 | 0.0000 | 0.0000 | 0.0000 | 0.0000 | 0.0000 | 0.0001 | 0.0002 |

**TABLE 2**

(Continued)

| $x$ | $\lambda$ | | | | | | | | |
|---|---|---|---|---|---|---|---|---|---|
| | 5.5 | 6.0 | 6.5 | 7.0 | 7.5 | 8.0 | 9.0 | 10.0 | 11.0 |
| 0 | 0.0041 | 0.0025 | 0.0015 | 0.0009 | 0.0006 | 0.0003 | 0.0001 | 0.0000 | 0.0000 |
| 1 | 0.0225 | 0.0149 | 0.0098 | 0.0064 | 0.0041 | 0.0027 | 0.0011 | 0.0005 | 0.0002 |
| 2 | 0.0618 | 0.0446 | 0.0318 | 0.0223 | 0.0156 | 0.0107 | 0.0050 | 0.0023 | 0.0010 |
| 3 | 0.1133 | 0.0892 | 0.0688 | 0.0521 | 0.0389 | 0.0286 | 0.0150 | 0.0076 | 0.0037 |
| 4 | 0.1558 | 0.1339 | 0.1118 | 0.0912 | 0.0729 | 0.0573 | 0.0337 | 0.0189 | 0.0102 |
| 5 | 0.1714 | 0.1606 | 0.1454 | 0.1277 | 0.1094 | 0.0916 | 0.0607 | 0.0378 | 0.0224 |
| 6 | 0.1571 | 0.1606 | 0.1575 | 0.1490 | 0.1367 | 0.1221 | 0.0911 | 0.0631 | 0.0411 |
| 7 | 0.1234 | 0.1377 | 0.1462 | 0.1490 | 0.1465 | 0.1396 | 0.1171 | 0.0901 | 0.0646 |
| 8 | 0.0849 | 0.1033 | 0.1188 | 0.1304 | 0.1373 | 0.1396 | 0.1318 | 0.1126 | 0.0888 |
| 9 | 0.0519 | 0.0688 | 0.0858 | 0.1014 | 0.1144 | 0.1241 | 0.1318 | 0.1251 | 0.1085 |
| 10 | 0.0285 | 0.0413 | 0.0558 | 0.0710 | 0.0858 | 0.0993 | 0.1186 | 0.1251 | 0.1194 |
| 11 | 0.0143 | 0.0225 | 0.0330 | 0.0452 | 0.0585 | 0.0722 | 0.0970 | 0.1137 | 0.1194 |
| 12 | 0.0065 | 0.0113 | 0.0179 | 0.0263 | 0.0366 | 0.0481 | 0.0728 | 0.0948 | 0.1094 |
| 13 | 0.0028 | 0.0052 | 0.0089 | 0.0142 | 0.0211 | 0.0296 | 0.0504 | 0.0729 | 0.0926 |
| 14 | 0.0011 | 0.0022 | 0.0041 | 0.0071 | 0.0113 | 0.0169 | 0.0324 | 0.0521 | 0.0728 |
| 15 | 0.0004 | 0.0009 | 0.0018 | 0.0033 | 0.0057 | 0.0090 | 0.0194 | 0.0347 | 0.0534 |
| 16 | 0.0001 | 0.0003 | 0.0007 | 0.0014 | 0.0026 | 0.0045 | 0.0109 | 0.0217 | 0.0367 |
| 17 | 0.0000 | 0.0001 | 0.0003 | 0.0006 | 0.0012 | 0.0021 | 0.0058 | 0.0128 | 0.0237 |
| 18 | 0.0000 | 0.0000 | 0.0001 | 0.0002 | 0.0005 | 0.0009 | 0.0029 | 0.0071 | 0.0145 |
| 19 | 0.0000 | 0.0000 | 0.0000 | 0.0001 | 0.0002 | 0.0004 | 0.0014 | 0.0037 | 0.0084 |
| 20 | 0.0000 | 0.0000 | 0.0000 | 0.0000 | 0.0001 | 0.0002 | 0.0006 | 0.0019 | 0.0046 |
| 21 | 0.0000 | 0.0000 | 0.0000 | 0.0000 | 0.0000 | 0.0001 | 0.0003 | 0.0009 | 0.0024 |
| 22 | 0.0000 | 0.0000 | 0.0000 | 0.0000 | 0.0000 | 0.0000 | 0.0001 | 0.0004 | 0.0012 |
| 23 | 0.0000 | 0.0000 | 0.0000 | 0.0000 | 0.0000 | 0.0000 | 0.0000 | 0.0002 | 0.0006 |
| 24 | 0.0000 | 0.0000 | 0.0000 | 0.0000 | 0.0000 | 0.0000 | 0.0000 | 0.0001 | 0.0003 |
| 25 | 0.0000 | 0.0000 | 0.0000 | 0.0000 | 0.0000 | 0.0000 | 0.0000 | 0.0000 | 0.0001 |

**TABLE 2**
(Continued)

| x | λ 12 | 13 | 14 | 15 | 16 | 17 | 18 | 19 | 20 |
|---|---|---|---|---|---|---|---|---|---|
| 0 | 0.0000 | 0.0000 | 0.0000 | 0.0000 | 0.0000 | 0.0000 | 0.0000 | 0.0000 | 0.0000 |
| 1 | 0.0001 | 0.0000 | 0.0000 | 0.0000 | 0.0000 | 0.0000 | 0.0000 | 0.0000 | 0.0000 |
| 2 | 0.0004 | 0.0002 | 0.0001 | 0.0000 | 0.0000 | 0.0000 | 0.0000 | 0.0000 | 0.0000 |
| 3 | 0.0018 | 0.0008 | 0.0004 | 0.0002 | 0.0001 | 0.0000 | 0.0000 | 0.0000 | 0.0000 |
| 4 | 0.0053 | 0.0027 | 0.0013 | 0.0006 | 0.0003 | 0.0001 | 0.0001 | 0.0000 | 0.0000 |
| 5 | 0.0127 | 0.0070 | 0.0037 | 0.0019 | 0.0010 | 0.0005 | 0.0002 | 0.0001 | 0.0001 |
| 6 | 0.0255 | 0.0152 | 0.0087 | 0.0048 | 0.0026 | 0.0014 | 0.0007 | 0.0004 | 0.0002 |
| 7 | 0.0437 | 0.0281 | 0.0174 | 0.0104 | 0.0060 | 0.0034 | 0.0019 | 0.0010 | 0.0005 |
| 8 | 0.0655 | 0.0457 | 0.0304 | 0.0194 | 0.0120 | 0.0072 | 0.0042 | 0.0024 | 0.0013 |
| 9 | 0.0874 | 0.0661 | 0.0473 | 0.0324 | 0.0213 | 0.0135 | 0.0083 | 0.0050 | 0.0029 |
| 10 | 0.1048 | 0.0859 | 0.0663 | 0.0486 | 0.0341 | 0.0230 | 0.0150 | 0.0095 | 0.0058 |
| 11 | 0.1144 | 0.1015 | 0.0844 | 0.0663 | 0.0496 | 0.0355 | 0.0245 | 0.0164 | 0.0106 |
| 12 | 0.1144 | 0.1099 | 0.0984 | 0.0829 | 0.0661 | 0.0504 | 0.0368 | 0.0259 | 0.0176 |
| 13 | 0.1056 | 0.1099 | 0.1060 | 0.0956 | 0.0814 | 0.0658 | 0.0509 | 0.0378 | 0.0271 |
| 14 | 0.0905 | 0.1021 | 0.1060 | 0.1024 | 0.0930 | 0.0800 | 0.0655 | 0.0514 | 0.0387 |
| 15 | 0.0724 | 0.0885 | 0.0989 | 0.1024 | 0.0992 | 0.0906 | 0.0786 | 0.0650 | 0.0516 |
| 16 | 0.0543 | 0.0719 | 0.0866 | 0.0960 | 0.0992 | 0.0963 | 0.0884 | 0.0772 | 0.0646 |
| 17 | 0.0383 | 0.0550 | 0.0713 | 0.0847 | 0.0934 | 0.0963 | 0.0936 | 0.0863 | 0.0760 |
| 18 | 0.0255 | 0.0397 | 0.0554 | 0.0706 | 0.0830 | 0.0909 | 0.0936 | 0.0911 | 0.0844 |
| 19 | 0.0161 | 0.0272 | 0.0409 | 0.0557 | 0.0699 | 0.0814 | 0.0887 | 0.0911 | 0.0888 |
| 20 | 0.0097 | 0.0177 | 0.0286 | 0.0418 | 0.0559 | 0.0692 | 0.0798 | 0.0866 | 0.0888 |
| 21 | 0.0055 | 0.0109 | 0.0191 | 0.0299 | 0.0426 | 0.0560 | 0.0684 | 0.0783 | 0.0846 |
| 22 | 0.0030 | 0.0065 | 0.0121 | 0.0204 | 0.0310 | 0.0433 | 0.0560 | 0.0876 | 0.0769 |
| 23 | 0.0016 | 0.0037 | 0.0074 | 0.0133 | 0.0216 | 0.0320 | 0.0438 | 0.0559 | 0.0669 |
| 24 | 0.0008 | 0.0020 | 0.0043 | 0.0083 | 0.0144 | 0.0226 | 0.0328 | 0.0442 | 0.0557 |
| 25 | 0.0004 | 0.0010 | 0.0024 | 0.0050 | 0.0092 | 0.0154 | 0.0237 | 0.0336 | 0.0446 |
| 26 | 0.0002 | 0.0005 | 0.0013 | 0.0029 | 0.0057 | 0.0101 | 0.0164 | 0.0240 | 0.0343 |
| 27 | 0.0001 | 0.0002 | 0.0007 | 0.0016 | 0.0034 | 0.0063 | 0.0109 | 0.0173 | 0.0254 |
| 28 | 0.0000 | 0.0001 | 0.0003 | 0.0009 | 0.0019 | 0.0038 | 0.0070 | 0.0117 | 0.0181 |
| 29 | 0.0000 | 0.0001 | 0.0002 | 0.0004 | 0.0011 | 0.0023 | 0.0044 | 0.0077 | 0.0125 |
| 30 | 0.0000 | 0.0000 | 0.0001 | 0.0002 | 0.0006 | 0.0013 | 0.0026 | 0.0049 | 0.0083 |
| 31 | 0.0000 | 0.0000 | 0.0000 | 0.0001 | 0.0003 | 0.0007 | 0.0015 | 0.0030 | 0.0054 |
| 32 | 0.0000 | 0.0000 | 0.0000 | 0.0001 | 0.0001 | 0.0004 | 0.0009 | 0.0018 | 0.0034 |
| 33 | 0.0000 | 0.0000 | 0.0000 | 0.0000 | 0.0001 | 0.0002 | 0.0005 | 0.0010 | 0.0020 |
| 34 | 0.0000 | 0.0000 | 0.0000 | 0.0000 | 0.0000 | 0.0001 | 0.0002 | 0.0006 | 0.0012 |
| 35 | 0.0000 | 0.0000 | 0.0000 | 0.0000 | 0.0000 | 0.0000 | 0.0001 | 0.0003 | 0.0007 |
| 36 | 0.0000 | 0.0000 | 0.0000 | 0.0000 | 0.0000 | 0.0000 | 0.0001 | 0.0002 | 0.0004 |
| 37 | 0.0000 | 0.0000 | 0.0000 | 0.0000 | 0.0000 | 0.0000 | 0.0000 | 0.0001 | 0.0002 |
| 38 | 0.0000 | 0.0000 | 0.0000 | 0.0000 | 0.0000 | 0.0000 | 0.0000 | 0.0000 | 0.0001 |
| 39 | 0.0000 | 0.0000 | 0.0000 | 0.0000 | 0.0000 | 0.0000 | 0.0000 | 0.0000 | 0.0001 |

Source: From J. Neter, W. Wasserman, and G. A. Whitmore, *Applied Statistics*. Copyright © 1978 by Allyn and Bacon, Inc., Boston. Reprinted with permission.

**TABLE 3**

The *t* Distribution

| df | Level of Significance for One-Tailed Test | | | | |
|---|---|---|---|---|---|
|  | .10 | .05 | .01 | .005 | .0005 |
| 1 | 3.078 | 6.314 | 31.821 | 63.657 | 636.619 |
| 2 | 1.886 | 2.920 | 6.965 | 9.925 | 31.598 |
| 3 | 1.638 | 2.353 | 4.541 | 5.841 | 12.941 |
| 4 | 1.533 | 2.132 | 3.747 | 4.604 | 8.610 |
| 5 | 1.476 | 2.015 | 3.365 | 4.032 | 6.859 |
| 6 | 1.440 | 1.943 | 3.143 | 3.707 | 5.959 |
| 7 | 1.415 | 1.895 | 2.998 | 3.499 | 5.405 |
| 8 | 1.397 | 1.860 | 2.896 | 3.355 | 5.041 |
| 9 | 1.383 | 1.833 | 2.821 | 3.250 | 4.781 |
| 10 | 1.372 | 1.812 | 2.764 | 3.169 | 4.587 |
| 11 | 1.363 | 1.796 | 2.718 | 3.106 | 4.437 |
| 12 | 1.356 | 1.782 | 2.681 | 3.055 | 4.318 |
| 13 | 1.350 | 1.771 | 2.650 | 3.012 | 4.221 |
| 14 | 1.345 | 1.761 | 2.624 | 2.977 | 4.140 |
| 15 | 1.341 | 1.753 | 2.602 | 2.947 | 4.073 |
| 16 | 1.337 | 1.746 | 2.583 | 2.921 | 4.015 |
| 17 | 1.333 | 1.740 | 2.567 | 2.898 | 3.965 |
| 18 | 1.330 | 1.734 | 2.552 | 2.878 | 3.922 |
| 19 | 1.328 | 1.729 | 2.539 | 2.861 | 3.883 |
| 20 | 1.325 | 1.725 | 2.528 | 2.845 | 3.850 |
| 21 | 1.323 | 1.721 | 2.518 | 2.831 | 3.819 |
| 22 | 1.321 | 1.717 | 2.508 | 2.819 | 3.792 |
| 23 | 1.319 | 1.714 | 2.500 | 2.807 | 3.767 |
| 24 | 1.318 | 1.711 | 2.492 | 2.797 | 3.745 |
| 25 | 1.316 | 1.708 | 2.485 | 2.787 | 3.725 |
| 26 | 1.315 | 1.706 | 2.479 | 2.779 | 3.707 |
| 27 | 1.314 | 1.703 | 2.473 | 2.771 | 3.690 |
| 28 | 1.313 | 1.701 | 2.467 | 2.763 | 3.674 |
| 29 | 1.311 | 1.699 | 2.462 | 2.756 | 3.659 |
| 30 | 1.310 | 1.697 | 2.457 | 2.750 | 3.646 |
| ∞ | 1.282 | 1.645 | 2.326 | 2.576 | 3.291 |

Source: Adapted from *Applied Regression Analysis and Other Multivariable Methods* by David G. Kleinbaum and Lawrence L. Kupper, © 1978, Wadsworth, Inc., Belmont, Calif. 94002. Reprinted by permission of the publisher, Duxbury Press.

**TABLE 4**
The Chi-Square Distribution

| $p$ | 0.10 | 0.05 | 0.025 | 0.01 | 0.005 | $df$ |
|---|---|---|---|---|---|---|
| | 2.71 | 3.84 | 5.02 | 6.63 | 7.88 | 1 |
| | 4.61 | 5.99 | 7.38 | 9.21 | 10.60 | 2 |
| | 6.25 | 7.81 | 9.35 | 11.34 | 12.84 | 3 |
| | 7.78 | 9.49 | 11.14 | 13.28 | 14.86 | 4 |
| | 9.24 | 11.07 | 12.83 | 15.09 | 16.75 | 5 |
| | 10.64 | 12.59 | 14.45 | 16.81 | 18.55 | 6 |
| | 12.02 | 14.07 | 16.01 | 18.48 | 20.3 | 7 |
| | 13.36 | 15.51 | 17.53 | 20.1 | 22.0 | 8 |
| | 14.68 | 16.92 | 19.02 | 21.7 | 23.6 | 9 |
| | 15.99 | 18.31 | 20.5 | 23.2 | 25.2 | 10 |
| | 17.28 | 19.68 | 21.9 | 24.7 | 26.8 | 11 |
| | 18.55 | 21.0 | 23.3 | 26.2 | 28.3 | 12 |
| | 19.81 | 22.4 | 24.7 | 27.7 | 29.8 | 13 |
| | 21.1 | 23.7 | 26.1 | 29.1 | 31.3 | 14 |
| | 22.3 | 25.0 | 27.5 | 30.6 | 32.8 | 15 |
| | 23.5 | 26.3 | 28.8 | 32.0 | 34.3 | 16 |
| | 24.8 | 27.6 | 30.2 | 33.4 | 35.7 | 17 |
| | 26.0 | 28.9 | 31.5 | 34.8 | 37.2 | 18 |
| | 27.2 | 30.1 | 32.9 | 36.2 | 38.6 | 19 |
| | 28.4 | 31.4 | 34.2 | 37.6 | 40.0 | 20 |
| | 29.6 | 32.7 | 35.5 | 38.9 | 41.4 | 21 |
| | 30.8 | 33.9 | 36.8 | 40.3 | 42.8 | 22 |
| | 32.0 | 35.2 | 38.1 | 41.6 | 44.2 | 23 |
| | 33.2 | 36.4 | 39.4 | 43.0 | 45.6 | 24 |
| | 34.4 | 37.7 | 40.6 | 44.3 | 46.9 | 25 |
| | 35.6 | 38.9 | 41.9 | 45.6 | 48.3 | 26 |
| | 36.7 | 40.1 | 43.2 | 47.0 | 49.6 | 27 |
| | 37.9 | 41.3 | 44.5 | 48.3 | 51.0 | 28 |
| | 39.1 | 42.6 | 45.7 | 49.6 | 52.3 | 29 |
| | 40.3 | 43.8 | 47.0 | 50.9 | 53.7 | 30 |
| | 51.8 | 55.8 | 59.3 | 63.7 | 66.8 | 40 |
| | 63.2 | 67.5 | 71.4 | 76.2 | 79.5 | 50 |
| | 74.4 | 79.1 | 83.3 | 88.4 | 92.0 | 60 |
| | 85.5 | 90.5 | 95.0 | 100.4 | 104.2 | 70 |
| | 96.6 | 101.9 | 106.6 | 112.3 | 116.3 | 80 |
| | 107.6 | 113.1 | 118.1 | 124.1 | 128.3 | 90 |
| | 118.5 | 124.3 | 129.6 | 135.8 | 140.2 | 100 |

Source: Adapted from *Applied Regression Analysis and Other Multivariable Methods* by David G. Kleinbaum and Lawrence L. Kupper, © 1978, Wadsworth, Inc., Belmont, Calif. 94002. Reprinted by permission of the publisher, Duxbury Press.

**TABLE 5**
Durbin-Watson Statistic Test Bounds

Probability = .05

| n | k = 1 | | k = 2 | | k = 3 | | k = 4 | | k = 5 | | k = 6 | |
|---|---|---|---|---|---|---|---|---|---|---|---|---|
| | $d_L$ | $d_U$ | $d_L$ | $d_U$ | $d_L$ | $d_U$ | $d_L$ | $d_U$ | $d_L$ | $d_U$ | $d_L$ | $d_U$ |
| 6 | 0.610 | 1.400 | — | — | — | — | — | — | — | — | — | — |
| 7 | 0.700 | 1.356 | 0.467 | 1.896 | — | — | — | — | — | — | — | — |
| 8 | 0.763 | 1.332 | 0.559 | 1.777 | 0.368 | 2.287 | — | — | — | — | — | — |
| 9 | 0.824 | 1.320 | 0.629 | 1.699 | 0.455 | 2.128 | 0.296 | 2.588 | — | — | — | — |
| 10 | 0.879 | 1.320 | 0.697 | 1.641 | 0.525 | 2.016 | 0.376 | 2.414 | 0.243 | 2.822 | — | — |
| 11 | 0.927 | 1.324 | 0.758 | 1.604 | 0.595 | 1.928 | 0.444 | 2.283 | 0.316 | 2.645 | 0.203 | 3.005 |
| 12 | 0.971 | 1.331 | 0.812 | 1.579 | 0.658 | 1.864 | 0.512 | 2.177 | 0.379 | 2.506 | 0.268 | 2.832 |
| 13 | 1.010 | 1.340 | 0.861 | 1.562 | 0.715 | 1.816 | 0.574 | 2.094 | 0.445 | 2.390 | 0.328 | 2.692 |
| 14 | 1.045 | 1.350 | 0.905 | 1.551 | 0.767 | 1.779 | 0.632 | 2.030 | 0.505 | 2.296 | 0.389 | 2.572 |
| 15 | 1.077 | 1.361 | 0.946 | 1.543 | 0.814 | 1.750 | 0.685 | 1.977 | 0.562 | 2.220 | 0.447 | 2.472 |
| 16 | 1.106 | 1.371 | 0.982 | 1.539 | 0.857 | 1.728 | 0.734 | 1.935 | 0.615 | 2.157 | 0.502 | 2.388 |
| 17 | 1.133 | 1.381 | 1.015 | 1.536 | 0.897 | 1.710 | 0.779 | 1.900 | 0.664 | 2.104 | 0.554 | 2.318 |
| 18 | 1.158 | 1.391 | 1.046 | 1.535 | 0.933 | 1.696 | 0.820 | 1.872 | 0.710 | 2.060 | 0.603 | 2.257 |
| 19 | 1.180 | 1.401 | 1.074 | 1.536 | 0.967 | 1.685 | 0.859 | 1.848 | 0.752 | 2.023 | 0.649 | 2.206 |
| 20 | 1.201 | 1.411 | 1.100 | 1.537 | 0.998 | 1.676 | 0.894 | 1.828 | 0.792 | 1.991 | 0.692 | 2.162 |
| 21 | 1.221 | 1.420 | 1.125 | 1.538 | 1.026 | 1.669 | 0.927 | 1.812 | 0.829 | 1.964 | 0.732 | 2.124 |
| 22 | 1.239 | 1.429 | 1.147 | 1.541 | 1.053 | 1.664 | 0.958 | 1.797 | 0.863 | 1.940 | 0.769 | 2.090 |
| 23 | 1.257 | 1.437 | 1.168 | 1.543 | 1.078 | 1.660 | 0.986 | 1.785 | 0.895 | 1.920 | 0.804 | 2.061 |
| 24 | 1.273 | 1.446 | 1.188 | 1.546 | 1.101 | 1.656 | 1.013 | 1.775 | 0.925 | 1.902 | 0.837 | 2.035 |
| 25 | 1.288 | 1.454 | 1.206 | 1.550 | 1.123 | 1.654 | 1.038 | 1.767 | 0.953 | 1.886 | 0.868 | 2.012 |
| 26 | 1.302 | 1.461 | 1.224 | 1.553 | 1.143 | 1.652 | 1.062 | 1.759 | 0.979 | 1.873 | 0.897 | 1.992 |
| 27 | 1.316 | 1.469 | 1.240 | 1.556 | 1.162 | 1.651 | 1.084 | 1.753 | 1.004 | 1.861 | 0.925 | 1.974 |
| 28 | 1.328 | 1.476 | 1.255 | 1.560 | 1.181 | 1.650 | 1.104 | 1.747 | 1.028 | 1.850 | 0.951 | 1.958 |

| | | | | | | | | | | | |
|---|---|---|---|---|---|---|---|---|---|---|---|
| 29 | 1.341 | 1.483 | 1.270 | 1.563 | 1.198 | 1.650 | 1.124 | 1.743 | 1.050 | 1.841 | 0.975 | 1.944 |
| 30 | 1.352 | 1.489 | 1.284 | 1.567 | 1.214 | 1.650 | 1.143 | 1.739 | 1.071 | 1.833 | 0.998 | 1.931 |
| 31 | 1.363 | 1.496 | 1.297 | 1.570 | 1.229 | 1.650 | 1.160 | 1.735 | 1.090 | 1.825 | 1.020 | 1.920 |
| 32 | 1.373 | 1.502 | 1.309 | 1.574 | 1.244 | 1.650 | 1.177 | 1.732 | 1.109 | 1.819 | 1.041 | 1.909 |
| 33 | 1.383 | 1.508 | 1.321 | 1.577 | 1.258 | 1.651 | 1.193 | 1.730 | 1.127 | 1.813 | 1.061 | 1.900 |
| 34 | 1.393 | 1.514 | 1.333 | 1.580 | 1.271 | 1.652 | 1.208 | 1.728 | 1.144 | 1.808 | 1.080 | 1.891 |
| 35 | 1.402 | 1.519 | 1.343 | 1.584 | 1.283 | 1.653 | 1.222 | 1.726 | 1.160 | 1.803 | 1.097 | 1.884 |
| 36 | 1.411 | 1.525 | 1.354 | 1.587 | 1.295 | 1.654 | 1.236 | 1.724 | 1.175 | 1.799 | 1.114 | 1.877 |
| 37 | 1.419 | 1.530 | 1.364 | 1.590 | 1.307 | 1.655 | 1.249 | 1.723 | 1.190 | 1.795 | 1.131 | 1.870 |
| 38 | 1.427 | 1.535 | 1.373 | 1.594 | 1.318 | 1.656 | 1.261 | 1.722 | 1.204 | 1.792 | 1.146 | 1.864 |
| 39 | 1.435 | 1.540 | 1.382 | 1.597 | 1.328 | 1.658 | 1.273 | 1.722 | 1.218 | 1.789 | 1.161 | 1.859 |
| 40 | 1.442 | 1.544 | 1.391 | 1.600 | 1.338 | 1.659 | 1.285 | 1.721 | 1.230 | 1.786 | 1.175 | 1.854 |
| 45 | 1.475 | 1.566 | 1.430 | 1.615 | 1.383 | 1.666 | 1.336 | 1.720 | 1.287 | 1.776 | 1.238 | 1.835 |
| 50 | 1.503 | 1.585 | 1.462 | 1.628 | 1.421 | 1.674 | 1.378 | 1.721 | 1.335 | 1.771 | 1.291 | 1.822 |
| 55 | 1.528 | 1.601 | 1.490 | 1.641 | 1.452 | 1.681 | 1.414 | 1.724 | 1.374 | 1.768 | 1.334 | 1.814 |
| 60 | 1.549 | 1.616 | 1.514 | 1.652 | 1.480 | 1.689 | 1.444 | 1.727 | 1.408 | 1.767 | 1.372 | 1.808 |
| 65 | 1.567 | 1.629 | 1.536 | 1.662 | 1.503 | 1.696 | 1.471 | 1.731 | 1.438 | 1.767 | 1.404 | 1.805 |
| 70 | 1.583 | 1.641 | 1.554 | 1.672 | 1.525 | 1.703 | 1.494 | 1.735 | 1.464 | 1.768 | 1.433 | 1.802 |
| 75 | 1.598 | 1.652 | 1.571 | 1.680 | 1.543 | 1.709 | 1.515 | 1.739 | 1.487 | 1.770 | 1.458 | 1.801 |
| 80 | 1.611 | 1.662 | 1.586 | 1.688 | 1.560 | 1.715 | 1.534 | 1.743 | 1.507 | 1.772 | 1.480 | 1.801 |
| 85 | 1.624 | 1.671 | 1.600 | 1.696 | 1.575 | 1.721 | 1.550 | 1.747 | 1.525 | 1.774 | 1.500 | 1.801 |
| 90 | 1.635 | 1.679 | 1.612 | 1.703 | 1.589 | 1.726 | 1.566 | 1.751 | 1.542 | 1.776 | 1.518 | 1.801 |
| 95 | 1.645 | 1.687 | 1.623 | 1.709 | 1.602 | 1.732 | 1.579 | 1.755 | 1.557 | 1.778 | 1.535 | 1.802 |
| 100 | 1.654 | 1.694 | 1.634 | 1.715 | 1.613 | 1.736 | 1.592 | 1.758 | 1.571 | 1.780 | 1.550 | 1.803 |
| 150 | 1.720 | 1.746 | 1.706 | 1.760 | 1.693 | 1.774 | 1.679 | 1.788 | 1.665 | 1.802 | 1.651 | 1.817 |
| 200 | 1.758 | 1.778 | 1.748 | 1.789 | 1.738 | 1.799 | 1.728 | 1.810 | 1.718 | 1.820 | 1.707 | 1.831 |

Source: Reprinted with permission from *Biometrica*, Vol 38 (1951: 159–178).

# GLOSSARY

**addition, general rule of**  a probability rule that tells one how to calculate the probability of the union of two events.

**analysis of variance**  a statistical technique to determine whether two or more groups could be selected from the same population.

**assumptions**  untested propositions (usually within a theory).

**asymmetric distribution**  a frequency or percentage distribution that is not perfectly balanced about its midpoint.

**Bayesian**  an approach to statistics and decision making that relies on subjective probabilities.

**Bernoulli process**  a process in which the outcome of any trial can be classified into one of two mutually exclusive and jointly exhaustive outcomes and each trial is independent of all other trials.

**binomial probability distribution**  a discrete probability distribution for phenomena that can be described by a Bernoulli process.

**bivariate**  using two variables; contingency tables are bivariate presentations; simple regression is a bivariate technique.

**bivariate forecasting**  a time series in which the independent variable is a real variable rather than time.

**certainty**  a condition that exists when the state of nature is known before a decision is made.

**chi-square**  a measure of statistical significance for contingency tables.

**class**  one of the group categories used to cluster data in a frequency distribution.

**class frequency**  the number of items in any given class in a frequency distribution.

**class interval**  the distance between the upper class boundary and the lower class boundary in a frequency distribution.

**coefficient of determination**  a measure of goodness of fit for a regression line based on the ratio of explained variation to total variation.

**combination**  the number of ways a group of items can be clustered into subsets of similar size (such as a combination of five things taken three at a time).

**conditional probability**  the probability one event will occur given that another has occurred.

**confidence limits**  the upper and lower boundaries that one is $X$ percent sure the estimate falls within (as in 95% confidence limits).

**consensual validity**  an indicator has consensual validity when numerous researchers accept the indicator as valid.

**constraints**  in linear programming, the variables that restrict the options open to managers.

**contingency table**   a table that shows how two or more variables are related by cross-tabulating the variables.

**control variable**   a third variable introduced to determine if the relationship between two other variables is spurious.

**convergent validity**   if indicators of a concept produce similar results, the indicators have convergent validity.

**correlational validity**   validity established when an indicator correlates strongly with other accepted valid indicators.

**correlation coefficient**   the square root of the coefficient of determination with a plus or minus sign the same as that for the slope.

**Cramér's** $V$   a measure of association based on chi-square for cross-tabulations that include variables measured at the nominal or higher levels of measurement.

**cubic relationship**   a relationship between two variables that resembles an S-shaped curve.

**cumulative frequency distribution**   a frequency distribution in which one column contains the cumulative percentage of items and below in a given class.

**decision tree**   a method of analysis for analyzing a series of decisions.

**decision variables**   in linear programming, the variables that the manager can affect or change.

**degrees of freedom**   a measure needed to use many probability distributions, such as the chi-square or the $t$ distributions.

**dependent variable**   the variable that is caused or predicted by the independent variable (in regression the $Y$ variable).

**descriptive statistics**   statitics used to summarize a body of data; contrasted with inferential statistics.

**discriminant validity**   if an indicator distinguishes one concept from another similar but different concept, it has discriminant validity.

**dispersion (measures of)**   numerical designations of how closely data cluster about the mean or other measure of central tendency (see *standard deviation*).

**dummy variable**   a nominal-level variable coded with values of 1 and 0 and used in a regression.

**error, type 1**   rejecting the null hypothesis when it is true.

**error, type 2**   accepting the null hypothesis when it is false.

**expected value**   the sum of the products of all the values that can be attained and their respective probability of attainment.

**experimental designs**   research designs with rigid controls in a laboratory setting.

**exponential probability distribution**   a probability distribution used to estimate the length of time between events.

**external validity**   the degree to which research findings or results can be generalized to hold true in other populations, settings, or times.

**extrarational analysis**   analysis that goes beyond rational models and incorporates judgment, experience, and so on.

**face validity**   an indicator has face validity when the researcher accepts the indicator as valid.

**factorial**   the product of a number times every whole number smaller than itself but larger than 0.

**forecasting**   the use of statistical techniques—usually time series regression—to predict the future.

**frequency distribution**   a table that shows a body of data grouped according to numerical values.

**frequency polygon**   a graphic method of presenting a frequency distribution.

**functional relationship**   a relationship in which one variable is an exact weighted combination of one or more variables or constants (a relationship without statistical error).

**gamma**   an ordinal measure of association sensitive to curvilinear relationships.

**grouped data**   data that are grouped into classes, such as in a frequency distribution.

**histogram**   a bar graph representing a frequency distribution.

**homoscedasticity**   an assumption of linear regression that the size of the errors is not affected by the size of the independent variables.

**hypergeometric probability distribution**   a probability distribution used when trials are independent and the universe is finite.

**hypothesis**   a statement about the world that can be either true or false.

**independent, probability**   two events are independent if the occurrence of one event does not affect the probability of the second event.

**independent variable**   the variable that causes or predicts the dependent variable (in regression the $X$ variable).

**indicator**   a measurable aspect of a concept.

**inferential statistics**   using sample statistics to infer characteristics about the population.

**insufficient reason**   a principle that holds that events are equally probable unless one can establish otherwise.

**intercept**   the point at which the regression line crosses the $Y$-axis.

**internal validity**   the degree to which research findings or results satisfy all conditions for establishing causality.

**interval data**   the most precise level of data; values can be added and subtracted.

**jointly exhaustive**   a series of events are jointly exhaustive if they include all possible events under consideration (heads and tails jointly exhaust all outcomes of a coin flip).

**joint probability**   the probability of two events both occurring.

**Kendall's *tau-b* and *tau-c***   measures of association based on covariation for cross-tabulations that include variables measured at the ordinal level; *tau-b* is appropriate for square tables, and *tau-c* is appropriate for rectangular tables.

**lambda**   a nominal measure of association based on the principle of proportionate reduction in error.

**linear programming**   a management technique that allocates inputs to maximize outputs subject to constraints under conditions of certainty.

**linear regression**   regression in which the relationship between the variables is assumed to be linear.

**logarithmic relationship**   a relationship between two variables in which one increases at a constant rate.

**marginals**   the row or column frequency totals in a contingency table.

**maximax**   a criterion for decision making under uncertainty that assumes that the best situation will happen.

**maximin**   a criterion for decision making under uncertainty that is based on expecting the worst to happen.

**mean**   the arithmetic average for a group of data.

**measurement reliability**   an indicator is reliable if it consistently assigns the same numbers to similar phenomena.

**measurement validity** does the measure tap what the research analyst thinks it measures?

**median** the middle item in a group of data when the data are ranked in order of magnitude.

**minimax regret** a criterion for decision making under uncertainty that minimizes opportunity costs.

**mode** the most common value in any distribution.

**model** a simplified version of a theory that captures its key components and is amenable to empirical testing.

**multiple causation** the social science position that an event or phenomenon can have several causes.

**multiple regression** an interval level statistical technique that uses several independent variables to predict or explain one dependent variable based on minimizing squared error.

**multiplication, general rule of** a probability rule that tells one how to calculate the joint probability of two events.

**mutually exclusive** events are mutually exclusive if they both cannot happen at the same time.

**nominal data** data where items can only be classified into groups. The groups cannot be ranked.

**normal distribution** a bell-shaped curve that describes the distribution of many phenomena.

**null hypothesis** the hypothesis that there is no impact or change (nothing happened); the working hypothesis phrased negatively.

**objective indicators** indicators that are based on reports or documents and do not require any judgment on the researcher's part.

**ogive** a graphic presentation of a cumulative frequency distribution.

**one-tailed test** a significance test in which the hypothesis specifies a direction (and, therefore, uses only one tail of the normal curve or some other probability distribution).

**operational definition** a definition that specifies that a concept will be measured in a given way for purposes of the study in question.

**ordinal data** data for which only rank orders can be assigned.

**output variables** in linear programming, variables that the manager wants to maximize or minimize.

**parallel forms** the correlation between responses obtained on two sets of items measured for reliability.

**parameter** a measure used to summarize characteristics of a population based on all items in the population (such as a population mean).

**partial slopes** another name for regression coefficients in a multiple regression.

**percentage distribution** a frequency distribution that contains a column listing the percentage of items in each class.

**perfect information** information that allows one to specify in advance the state of nature that will occur.

**Poisson distribution** a probability distribution used when events occur at varying intervals of time, space, or distance.

**polynomial curve fitting** the use of regression to estimate nonlinear relationships.

**population** the total set of items that one wants to analyze (all bus users, all citizens of a city, and so on).

**positive-sum game**    a game that everyone can win.

**predictive validity**    validity established if an indicator correctly predicts outcomes that the indicator was designed to predict.

**prisoner's dilemma**    a game theory situation where rationality results in a suboptimal situation.

**probability, a priori**    probability based on reasoning rather than on a series of trials.

**probability, posterior**    probabilities generated by numerous trials; also called long-run probability.

**quasi-experimental designs**    research designs that lack the requirements of experimental designs but are structured in a similar fashion.

**rational decision making**    decision making following these steps: (1) identify the problem; (2) specify goals; (3) specify alternatives to reach goals; (4) evaluate alternatives in light of goals; (5) select the optimal alternative.

**regression**    a statistical technique used to describe the relationship between two variables based on the principle of minimizing errors in prediction.

**regression coefficient**    the weight assigned to independent variables in a regression (the beta or slope).

**residual variation**    the average squared error in prediction with a regression equation.

**risk**    a condition that exists when probabilities can be assigned to states of nature before a decision is made.

**sample**    a subset of the population usually selected randomly. Measures that summarize a sample are called sample statistics.

**satisficing**    selecting an alternative in decision making that will work rather than looking for the best alternative.

**short-term fluctuation**    a regular cyclical fluctuation in time series data.

**slope**    the degree that a regression line rises or falls as one moves along it from left to right (often called beta or the regression coefficient).

**Somers' $d_{yx}$ and $d_{xy}$**    measures of association based on covariation for cross-tabulations that include variables measured at the ordinal level.

**split-half reliability**    measure of reliability in which the set of items intended to measure a given concept is divided into two parts.

**spurious relationship**    a relationship between two variables that is caused by a third variable.

**standard deviation**    a measure of dispersion, the square root of the average squared deviation from the mean.

**standard error of the estimate**    an estimate of the error (equivalent to one standard deviation) in an estimate of $Y$ derived from a regression equation; a measure of goodness of fit.

**standard error of the mean**    an estimate of the amount of error in a sample estimate of a population mean.

**standard error of the slope**    a measure of goodness of fit in a regression; a measure of error in a slope estimated from sample data.

**subjective indicators**    indicators that are based on the judgment of one or more persons.

**suboptimization**    a subunit of an organization maximizing its goals in a manner detrimental to the goals of the entire organization.

**symmetric distribution**    a frequency or percentage distribution that is perfectly balanced about its midpoint.

**test-retest reliability**    method for assessing measurement reliability by measuring the same phenomenon or set of variables twice over a reasonably, short time period.

**theory**   an integrated set of propositions intended to explain or account for a given phenomenon.

**time series**   a variable measured at regular time intervals.

**$t$ test**   a statistical test based on the $t$ distribution used for slopes and for means when $n$ is less than 30 and the population is not normally distributed.

**two-tailed test**   a significance test in which the hypothesis does not specify direction (and, therefore, uses both tails of a probability distribution).

**uncertainty**   a condition in which the probability of any given state of nature is unknown.

**union of two probabilities**   the probability that either one of two events will occur.

**variance**   the average squared deviation from the mean; the square of the standard deviation.

**zero-sum game**   a game in which one person's winning means another person lost.

**$z$ score**   the number of standard deviations an item is from the mean; $z$ scores can be calculated for raw data, means, slopes, regression estimates, and so on.

# INDEX